296787

KU-677-137

Sport Tourism Destinations

*This book is dedicated to
Linda Buxton and George Higham*

Sport Tourism Destinations

Issues, opportunities and analysis

Edited by James Higham

Routledge
Taylor & Francis Group
LONDON AND NEW YORK

UCB

296787

First published 2005 by Butterworth-Heinemann

2 Park Square, Milton Park, Abingdon, Oxon OX14 4RN
711 Third Avenue, New York, NY 10017, USA

Routledge is an imprint of the Taylor & Francis Group, an informa business

First issued in hardback 2016

Copyright © 2005 Taylor & Francis.

All rights reserved. No part of this book may be reprinted or reproduced or utilised in any form or by any electronic, mechanical, or other means, now known or hereafter invented, including photocopying and recording, or in any information storage or retrieval system, without permission in writing from the publishers

Notice:
Product or corporate names may be trademarks or registered trademarks, and are used only for identification and explanation without intent to infringe.

British Library Cataloguing in Publication Data
A catalogue record for this book is available from the British Library

Library of Congress Cataloguing in Publication Data
A catalogue record for this book is available from the Library of Congress

ISBN 978-1-1381-5227-4 (hbk)
ISBN 978-0-7506-5937-6 (pbk)

Typeset by Charon Tec Pvt. Ltd, Chennai, India

Contents

Figures

Tables

Case studies

Contributors

Chris Bull, Canterbury Christ Church University College, UK
Dr Chris Bull is Head of the Department of Sport Science, Tourism and Leisure at Canterbury Christ Church University College. He has over 25 years' experience in teaching and researching leisure and tourism, and has published various articles, books and book chapters as well as undertaking a wide range of consultancy projects. His most recent publication is the Elsevier Butterworth-Heinemann text *Sport Tourism: Participants, Policy and Providers*, co-authored with Dr Mike Weed.

Richard Butler, University of Surrey, UK
Richard Butler is Professor of Tourism in the School of Management at the University of Surrey, having returned to England after 30 years in Canada at the University of Western Ontario. He trained as a geographer, with degrees from Nottingham (BA Hons) and Glasgow (PhD) Universities, and has served as President of the International Academy for the Study of Tourism, and of the Canadian Association for Leisure Studies. He has research interests in destination development, sustainability and tourism, tourism in small islands and remote locations, and the relationships between the media, popular culture and tourism. He is currently completing editing two volumes on the Tourism Area Life Cycle Model, and is the co-editor of the *Journal of Tourism and Hospitality Research*.

Laurence Chalip, University of Texas, Texas, USA
Laurence Chalip is Professor and Director of the Sport Management Program at the University of Texas at Austin. Prior to joining the faculty at Texas, he was on the faculty of the School of Marketing and Management at Griffith University in Australia. His research focuses on policy and marketing. He has published three books, three research monographs, and over 50 articles and book chapters. He is a Research Fellow of the North American Society for Sport Management, and has won two service awards from the Sport Management Association of Australia and New Zealand.

Richard Coleman, Sport Industry Research Centre, Sheffield Hallam University, UK
Richard Coleman is a Senior Researcher in the the major events team at the Sport Industry Research Centre. Since 1999 he has performed over 10 economic impact

studies for national agencies and local authorities. He was the project manager for the economic impact study of the London Marathon in 2000. He is also the author of UK Sport's major events review: *Measuring Success: The Economics* (2004).

Peter Cross, Glion Institute of Higher Education, Switzerland
Peter Cross is Program Leader for the Glion Sport Management School, based in Leysin, Switzerland. Peter has worked in the sport tourism industry for nearly 20 years, specializing in the French and European outdoor activity holiday market. In 1992 and 1994 he worked at the Albertville and Lillehammer Winter Olympics for CBS Television as their transportation manager and consultant. Prior to working for Glion Sport Management School, Peter was managing director of a company that managed several businesses in the sport tourism sector.

Suzanne de la Barre, Faculty of Physical Education and Recreation, University of Alberta, Canada
Suzanne de la Barre is a PhD student with the Faculty of Physical Education and Recreation at the University of Alberta. Her research interests include sustainable tourism in peripheral areas, and community sense of place.

Lisa Delpy Neirotti, The George Washington University, School of Business, Department of Tourism and Hospitality Management, USA
Lisa Delpy Neirotti, PhD, is the director of the graduate and undergraduate sport and event management degree programmes at The George Washington University. In addition to teaching, speaking at various conferences, conducting economic impact and market research, consulting with corporate sponsors, events and sport commissions, Dr Neirotti co-authored *The Ultimate Guide to Sport Marketing*, published by McGraw-Hill. Dr Neirotti also founded the TEAMS: Travel, Events, and Management in Sports conference in 1997; serves on the editorial board of *Sport Marketing Quarterly* and *SportsTravel* magazine; and is a member of the Women Sport Foundation (WSF) advisory board. Having travelled around the world studying the Olympic movement and conducting research at 11 consecutive Olympic Games, she is recognized as an Olympic scholar.

Sonia Francis, School of Hospitality, Tourism and Sport, La Trobe University, Australia
Sonia Francis is a lecturer in hospitality management and sport management at La Trobe University. During the 1990s, Sonia worked for Ernst & Young in New Zealand as a senior manager in the National Tourism and Leisure Consulting Group. She also worked with the Canterbury Rugby Football Union and the Crusaders Rugby Super 12 franchise in event management and media, communications, and the design and implementation of an elite athlete development model for the Crusaders that formed the basis for the programme that was adopted by the New Zealand Rugby Football Union. Sonia was involved in the destination selection process for the All Blacks team base during the 2003 Rugby World Cup. Sonia's current research focuses on sport tourism destinations from the active pro-sport tourist perspective, as well as the evaluation of elite athlete development programmes and the management of the relationship between the media and elite athletes.

Heather J. Gibson, Department of Recreation, Parks and Tourism, University of Florida, USA
Dr Gibson's research is focused on understanding sport, tourism and leisure behaviour. Her recent projects include investigating the meanings and motivations of college football (American) fans; examining the experiences associated with taking part in the Senior Games (Masters Games); and the perceptions of international ski/snowboard trip participants in terms of destination image, risk and expectations.

Chris Gratton, Sport Industry Research Centre, Sheffield Hallam University, UK
Chris Gratton is Professor of Sport Economics and Director of the Sport Industry Research Centre (SIRC) at Sheffield Hallam University. He is a specialist in the economic analysis of the sport market. He is author of eight books specifically on the sport and leisure industry, and has published over 100 articles in academic and professional journals.

C. Michael Hall, Department of Tourism, School of Business, University of Otago, New Zealand
Michael Hall is Professor in the Department of Tourism at the University of Otago, Dunedin, New Zealand and Honorary Professor, Department of Marketing, University of Stirling, Scotland. Co-editor of *Current Issues in Tourism*, he has written widely on various aspects of tourism, leisure, regional development and related policy issues.

James Higham, Department of Tourism, School of Business, University of Otago, New Zealand
James Higham holds the position of Senior Lecturer in the Department of Tourism, School of Business, University of Otago. He has been actively involved in researching sport and tourism for 10 years, focusing particularly on sports events, sport tourism development, sport and tourism seasonality and the spatial travel flows associated with different levels of sport competition. His published work appears in journals such as *Event Management*, *Current Issues in Tourism*, *Journal of Sports Management* and *Tourism Management*. He is on the editorial board of the *Journal of Sport Tourism* (Routledge). Most recently he has co-authored, with Tom Hinch, *Sport Tourism Development*, which was published in 2004.

Tom Hinch, Faculty of Physical Education and Recreation, University of Alberta, Canada
Tom is an Associate Professor with the Faculty of Physical Education and Recreation at the University of Alberta. He recently co-authored *Sport Tourism Development* with James Higham. In addition to a research programme in sport tourism, Tom has published in the area of tourism and indigenous people. A recurring theme in his research is the way that people relate to place, and the implications that this relationship has on sustainable development in tourist destinations.

Simon Hudson, Haskayne School of Business, University of Calgary, Canada
Simon Hudson is an Associate Professor in Tourism Management at the University of Calgary in Canada. He has held previous academic positions at universities in England, and has also worked as a visiting professor in Austria,

Switzerland, Fiji, New Zealand and Australia. Prior to working in academia Dr Hudson spent several years working in the tourism industry in Europe, and he now consults for the industry in Alberta and British Columbia. He has written three books; *Snow Business, Sports and Adventure Tourism*, and *Marketing for Tourism & Hospitality*. The marketing of tourism is the focus of his research, and he has published numerous journal articles and book chapters from his work. He has been invited to several international tourism conferences as a keynote speaker, including in China, New Zealand and the USA.

Peter Murphy, School of Hospitality, Tourism and Sport, La Trobe University, Australia

Professor Peter Murphy is the foundation professor and Head of the La Trobe School of Tourism and Hospitality. He is a recipient of the Roy Wolfe Award for research in tourism in North America, and is a member of the International Academy for the Study of Tourism. Professor Murphy has published or edited seven books and over 60 articles relating to tourism. In the area of sports events, he worked closely with the B.C. Games Society in analysing a series of their summer and winter games. He has written two articles on these assessments with Barbara Carmichael, which can be found in the *Journal of Travel Research* **29(3)**, 32–36 and *Festival Management and Event Tourism* **4**, 127–138.

Mark Orams, Massey University at Albany, New Zealand

Mark Orams is a New Zealander who has been involved in competitive sport (particularly yachting) for much of his life. He was part of the crew that won the 1989/1990 Whitbread Round the World Yacht Race, and was a member of Team New Zealand's successful defence of the America's Cup in 2000. He has continued his involvement in the sport at master's level, and won the World Laser Radial Master's Championships in 1999. Mark lectures at Massey University in New Zealand, and conducts research in the tourism and marine science areas.

Chris Ryan, Department of Tourism Management, University of Waikato Management School, New Zealand

Chris Ryan is Professor of Tourism at the University of Waikato, editor of *Tourism Management*, and a member of the International Academy for the Study of Tourism. He has written over 200 papers, including 71 refereed journal articles and a number of books.

Simon Shibli, Sport Industry Research Centre, Sheffield Hallam University, UK

Simon is a qualified management accountant who specializes in the economic and financial analysis of the sport and leisure industry. He is Deputy Director of the Sport Industry Research Centre. Since 1997, Simon has worked on a variety of economic impact studies of major sports events for national agencies (UK Sport, Sport England), governing bodies and local authorities. With Chris Gratton he is the author of *UK Sport's Guide to the Design and Implementation of Economic Impact Studies for Major Sports Events*.

Terry Stevens, Stevens & Associates, UK

Professor Terry Stevens is Managing Director of Stevens & Associates, international tourism consultants. He is Visiting Professor at Abertay Dundee and at

Bournemouth Universities, as well as being Vice Chair (Strategy) of the Wales Tourist Board. From 1992 to 1994 he was Director of the Stadium and Arena Management Unit in the UK, and he has published extensively on sport tourism.

Birgit Trauer, School of Tourism and Leisure Management, University of Queensland, Australia
Birgit Trauer is a tutor and doctoral candidate at the University of Queensland, having previously undertaken research and consultancy in the sphere of special interest tourism. Her current research agenda is focused on the emotional nature of involvement with specific reference to adventure tourism.

Steve Webb, Director of Strategy, Wales Tourist Board
Steve Webb joined the Wales Tourist Board in 1980 following six years of employment in local government. He has a geography degree from Exeter University and a Masters in Tourism Development from Cardiff University. He is a chartered town planner. In his present role he led the preparation of the national tourism strategy for Wales, 'Achieving our Potential', in 2000.

Mike Weed, Institute of Sport & Leisure Policy, School of Sport & Exercise Sciences, Loughborough University, UK
Mike Weed is with the Institute of Sport & Leisure Policy in the School of Sport & Exercise Sciences at Loughborough University. His research interests relate to all areas of the relationship between sport and tourism, but particularly to the motivations and behaviours of sports tourists and sports spectators. He is also interested in 'meso-level' and innovative qualitative approaches to research. He is author (with Chris Bull) of *Sport Tourism: Participants, Policy and Providers*, published by Elsevier.

Acknowledgements

Numerous people have contributed in various ways to the production of this book. This project was conceived in discussion with Sally North (Elsevier Butterworth-Heinemann) during the Tourism Research Conference 2002 in Cardiff, Wales. My gratitude is extended to her and to Holly Bennett, Claire Hutchins and Amanda Arthur (Elsevier Butterworth-Heinemann) for providing the personal interface with a supportive publisher. I am also grateful for the professionalism of the authors who contributed their original work to this book; Chris Bull, Richard Butler, Laurence Chalip, Richard Coleman, Peter Cross, Suzanne de la Barre, Lisa Deply Neirotti, Sonia Francis, Heather Gibson, Chris Gratton, Michael Hall, Tom Hinch, Simon Hudson, Peter Murphy, Mark Orams, Chris Ryan, Simon Shibli, Terry Stevens, Birgit Trauer, Steve Webb and Mike Weed. I am fortunate to work within the School of Business (University of Otago) and have benefited greatly from the support of David Buisson (Dean, School of Business), George Benwell (Associate Dean, Research), Alan MacGregor (Associate Dean, Academic) and Michael Hall (Head of Department, Department of Tourism). My academic and administrative colleagues at the Department of Tourism, University of Otago include Michael Hall, Hazel Tucker, Anna Carr, David Duval, Richard Mitchell, Brent Lovelock, Caroline Orchiston, Teresa Leopold, David Christiensen, Donna Keen, Andrea Valentine, Eric Shelton, Peter Treloar, Melinda Elliott, Frances Cadogan, Monica Gilmour and Diana Evans. They provide genuine collegiality and support, not to mention an enjoyable academic environment in which to work. The research assistance provided by Yusuf Riza (University of Otago) during the initial preparation of this book was of great value. I have also enjoyed the support of family and friends during this project, including Polly and Charles, Richard, Jane and Tom Higham, Emma Holt and Caroline Orchiston. Most particularly I am indebted to my immediate family, Linda, Alexandra, Kate and George, for their support.

1

Sport tourism destinations: issues, opportunities and analysis

James Higham

Introduction

Destinations are complex and multifaceted tourism systems (Ritchie and Crouch, 2001). While the reasons why people choose to travel to a particular destination may be many or few, one of the increasingly common reasons is to participate in or experience sports in one way or another. Few forces in contemporary society generate such significant and heterogeneous travel flows as sport. What is more, sports are motivated by and therefore associated with rich and diverse visitor experiences, and contribute to the profile and uniqueness of tourism destinations. Increasingly, examples exist of tourism destinations that have been developed or rejuvenated through the pursuit of sport-related tourism development initiatives (Weed and Bull, 2004). In recent years it has been noted that the extent and volume of sport-related travel has grown exponentially (Faulkner et al., 1998). Part of the reason for this lies in the diversity of ways in which sport may influence spatial travel flows and tourism destination development interests. Furthermore, sport (particularly domestic sports) offers the advantages of relatively reliable and resilient travel flows in times of crisis (Toohey *et al.*, 2004). Sports offer a broad range of development opportunities at national, regional and local tourism destinations.

Several prominent trends in western societies serve to explain the modern phenomenon of sport-related travel. These include increasing participation in sport, interest in health and fitness, and extended active and social participation in sports into middle age and beyond (Glyptis, 1989). These trends have been driven by changing social attitudes and values (Redmond, 1991; Kurtzman and Zauhar, 1995; Jackson *et al.*, 2001) and changing economic and political circumstances (Collins, 1991; Cooper *et al.*, 1993; Nauright, 1996; Gibson, 1998). They have also been facilitated by technological advances, such as satellite television broadcasting (Halberstam, 1999), that have influenced the 'sportification of society' (Standeven and De Knop, 1999). Glyptis (1989) highlights the manifestations of these trends in western European countries. These include strong growth in interest in recreational sport, increasing participation in sport across all social strata, and significant increases in youth holidays, short breaks and second holidays. The International Olympic Committee and World Tourism Organization (2001) report the continuation and acceleration of these trends in more recent years. These sources provide compelling evidence to suggest that sport-related travel will continue to grow and diversify.

Tourism destination managers have for some time been aware of a range of intangible and somewhat less measurable aspects of sport tourism development (Hinch and Higham, 2004). These relate to expanding global connectivity in the field of sports marketing, sports broadcasts that include images of recognizable destinations, expanding global sports media communications, and the association of historic sports events with specific places. It is evident that these may be utilized to serve the interests of sport tourism destinations. However, interests in sport tourism development at tourism destinations have prompted more specific consideration of these opportunities (Weed and Bull, 2004). It emerges that the ways in which sports may be harnessed to influence the fortunes of tourism destinations are manifold (Bull and Weed, 1999; Hinch and Higham, 2004) (Table 1.1). The relevance of sport to tourism destinations is amplified by the fact that the various avenues of sport tourism development apply in varying degrees at tourism destinations, whether they be national – local, urban – rural, and/or central – peripheral in location. Furthermore, many sports are regularly recurring on an annual or seasonal basis, and may therefore be developed with a long-term view in accordance with strategic tourism and economic development goals.

Table 1.1 Avenues of sport tourism development of relevance to destination managers

Avenue	Reference(s)
Tourist demand	Potential for sports at all levels to generate significant spectator and/or participant travel flows (Bale, 1989)
	Potential for sports-related travel to extend to experiences of tourist attractions and activities at a destination (Gibson, 1998)

(Continued)

Table 1.1 (*Continued*)

Avenue	Reference(s)
	Potential for sports events to stimulate conference, exhibitions, meetings, and incentive travel (Faulkner *et al.*, 1998)
Tourism development	Dynamics of recreational sports, including the developmentof new and hybrid sports that are often linked to specific resource requirements (Thomson, 2000; Keller, 2001) Potential for sports to be linked to wider service sector and tourism interests at a destination (Schaffer and Davidson, 1985) Role of sports in tourism destination regeneration and rejuvenation strategies (Hall, 1992a)
Service sector development	Economic impacts of sport-related travel (Shibli, 1998; Gratton and Taylor, 2000)
Event sport tourism	Use of one-off mega-sports events to reposition tourism destinations (Getz, 1991) Potential for sports events to generate travel flows that are concentrated in space and time (Hall, 1992a) Use of hallmark sports events to reflect the uniqueness of the destinations where they take place (Hinch and Higham, 2004)
Visitor experiences at tourism destinations	Authentic experiences of sports competitions and fandoms that may be consumed by casual sport tourists (Giulianotti, 1996; Stewart, 2001) Contribution of sports to heritage and the consumption of sports nostalgia by tourists (Gammon, 2001) Contribution of sport spectatorship to atmospheres of excitement and celebration (Giulianotti, 1995; Dauncey and Hare, 2000)
Destination profile	Opportunities to strengthen associations between specific sports and the specific locations which may serve as tourist destinations (Priestley, 1995) Contribution of live sport to destination profile (Higham and Hinch, 2002)
Destination media markets	Significance of sports and sports events to media markets (Burgan and Mules, 1992) Contribution of events to generating media coverage (Chalip, 2004) Role of hallmark sports teams in generating media attention (Bale, 1993; Stevens, 2001) Potential to attract media attention through the profile of sport celebrities (Andrews and Jackson, 2001)
Destination image	Use of sports events to enhance or change the imagery associated with tourism destinations (Whitson and Macintosh, 1996) Contribution of prominent sports venues to destination image (Chalip, 1992)

(Continued)

Table 1.1 (*Continued*)

Avenue	Reference(s)
	Contribution of cultural programmes and entertainment programmes to destination image (Hooper, 1998; Porteous, 2000)
	Role of sports, sports cultures and iconic sports people in ascribing unique meanings to the places with which they are associated (Andrews and Jackson, 2001)
	Contribution of sports histories and heritage to destination image (Gammon, 2002)
Uniqueness of tourism destinations	Links between specific sports and participants in those sports, which can be strategically used in product development and destination marketing campaigns (Heino, 2000)
	Harnessing the contribution of sports and sports teams to national/regional differentiation of tourism destinations (Higham and Hinch, 2003)
	Contribution of sport cultures to unique sense of place (Nauright, 1995)
	Use of sports to highlight and promote specific tourism attractions and resources at recognizable tourism destinations (Hinch and Higham, 2004)
Patterns of tourism seasonality	Strategic use of sports and sports events to ameliorate patterns of seasonality at tourism destinations (Higham and Hinch, 2002)
	Use of sports to transform destinations from single season, to multiple season or all year destinations (Hudson, 1999; Baum and Hagen, 1999)

The evolution of the sport and tourism industries

The modern development of sport and tourism over the last half a century offers striking parallels. During this time both sport and tourism have been democratized as restrictions on access and participation have eased or been removed (Standeven and De Knop, 1999). Both have evolved rapidly into global social phenomena and become powerful players in the global economy. During this time sport and tourism have also been subject to the forces of globalization, and both have confronted the negotiated processes of international partnership and control (Hinch and Higham, 2004).

The modern development of sport took place during the late nineteenth and early twentieth centuries (1880–1910). During this time sports were transformed through such developments as the codification of rules, bureaucratization (the development and regulation of competitions), specialization of player roles, quantification (measurement of performance) and the maintenance of records of achievement (Guttmann, 1974). Enhanced equality in access to competitive and recreational sport was one consequence of this dynamic (Standeven and De Knop 1999). Competitive sports were contested in local, regional and/or national leagues.

The professional development of sports codes was generally limited to such sports as rugby league (England), baseball and American football (USA). A rich heritage associated with many sports has emerged over time, most notably in association with the achievements of outstanding sports teams (e.g. the 1970 Brazilian soccer team) or the legendary feats of individual athletes (e.g. Sir Donald Bradman (cricket), Joe Di Maggio (baseball), Muhammed Ali (boxing) and Pele (soccer)).

A second period of dynamic change in the development of sport has taken place more recently. David Halberstam (1999) presents a critical examination of the trends in sport that emerged in the 1970s and 1980s. Halberstam (1999) examines the emergence of cable television and the broadcasting of live sport initiated by ESPN in 1978, the development of commercial and media interests in sport, and the emergence of new forms of sport celebrity. The transformation of modern sport is a by-product of Halberstam's (1999) biography of the basketball career of Michael Jordan (1978–1996). The professionalization of many sport codes during this time is a dominant feature of the period.

The repackaging of sports to compete in the entertainment industry has had wide ramifications. Sports have been modified by deliberate spatial and temporal rule changes aimed at increasing public appeal (Higham and Hinch 2003). In some cases sports have been reorganized in a temporal sense (e.g. scheduled start times, breaks in passages of play) to enhance media presentation and maximize commercial advertising revenue. The supporter, spectator, media and merchandise markets associated with some sports have expanded beyond the locations that individual athletes or teams actually represent in competition. Sports competitions have been augmented by rule changes aimed at spectacularization. As a consequence, 'its drama, its personalities and its worldwide appeal mean sport is the new Hollywood' (Bell and Campbell, 1999: 22). Standeven and De Knop (1999) describe this course of change as the 'sportification of society'. However, in critical social science terms such transformations have long been related to Debord's (1994; original 1967) notion of the 'society of the spectacle' (see Hall, 1992a).

A consequence for the tourism industry has been that sports, sports teams, sports events and sports facilities (e.g. stadiums, halls of fame and sports museums) have become transformed into tourism attractions in their own right (Rooney, 1988). Hinch and Higham (2004) explore the notion that individual sports stars may function as tourist attractions. The conceptualization of sport as a tourism attraction may offer sports managers new insights into expanding the market range of their sports or teams. Sports may perform varied functions of relevance to tourism destinations. In addition to being an attraction or activity that tourists seek to experience, sport may contribute to the uniqueness of destinations. The professionalization of sports has resulted in the expansion of existing and/or addition of new competition seasons, with implications for tourism seasonality (Butler, 1994; Higham and Hinch 2002). Sport may also be an important expression of culture at a tourism destination. This, and the deliberate branding of sports teams, may be harnessed to contribute to the regional differentiation of tourism products. This period has also witnessed the transformation of sporting celebrities from role models into powerful cultural, financial and media figures and image creators (Andrews and Jackson, 2002). The prominence of sports and sports people in the national and international media is such that sport has become a powerful tool in destination marketing (British Tourist Authority, 2000).

Conceptualizing sport, tourism and sport tourism

Attempts to conceptualize sport highlight that sport is 'a structured, goal-oriented, competitive, contest-based, ludic physical activity' (McPherson *et al.*, 1989: 15). Coakley (2004: 21) defines sport as 'institutionalised, competitive activities that involve rigorous physical exertion or the use of relatively complex physical skills by participants motivated by internal and external rewards'. This definition comprises four key parts. First, sports are physical activities. Although this is an arbitrary determination (e.g. figure skating is an Olympic sport whereas ballroom dancing was introduced to the Sydney 2000 Olympic Games only as a demonstration sport), it does allow for a distinction to be drawn between primarily physical activities and primarily cognitive activities, such as chess.

Second, sports are competitive. The goal orientation and contest-based nature of sports are manifest in the increasing specialization of player roles, standardized quantification and the keeping of records of performance (Guttmann, 1974). Sports competition ranges from elite competition to recreational or social sports. In its broadest sense, competition may be engaged with human opponents (e.g. opposing teams), judges (e.g. aesthetic sports such as diving and gymnastic routines), natural features (e.g. skiable terrain), forces of nature (e.g. waves, wind, white water) and timing devices (e.g. time trials). An essential element of sport is that competition should be evenly balanced to ensure that both participant and spectator interest is generated and maintained (Owen and Weatherston, 2002). It is uncertainty of outcome that generates and maintains suspense, which is important to both sport and tourism interests (Hinch and Higham, 2004).

Third, sports are activities that are institutionalized through such things as the imposition of rules (Loy *et al.*, 1978). Rules may be codified and enforced in the case of professional and competitive sports, and informal in the case of many recreational sports. It is not unusual for rules to be modified, reinterpreted and perhaps even rewritten over time, giving rise to hybrid sports or new sports in some instances (Hinch and Higham, 2001). A prominent trend in the last two decades has been growth in participation in 'less organized and less regulated' individual sports (Thomson, 2000: 34) which are (at least initially) free from the constraints of formal rule structures. Coakley (2004: 567) refers to these as sports based on the 'pleasure and participation model' as opposed to the 'power and performance model' of sport. Prominent examples include skateboarding, mountain boarding, kite surfing and ultimate frisbee.

Finally, sports are pursued by people for internal or external rewards (Coakley, 2004). Internal rewards associated with sports may include self-expression, spontaneity and challenge. Interestingly, these rewards parallel many of the push factors commonly associated with the study of tourism motivations (Clawson and Knetsch, 1966). External rewards that may be achieved through the pursuit of sports may include displaying physical skills, receiving the approval of peers, identification with a sport subculture, or the material rewards associated with sporting success.

Like sport, the conceptualization of tourism highlights several key parameters (Murphy, 1985). First, tourism involves the travel of non-residents to the destinations of their choice (Dietvorst and Ashworth, 1995). Thus, tourism involves the movement of travellers from their normal place of residence for an undisclosed time, prior to their return home. A second common dimension involves the temporal characteristics associated with tourism. Tourist trips are characterized by a 'temporary stay away from home of at least one night' (Leiper, 1981: 74). Definitions developed for statistical purposes often distinguish between tourists and excursionists. The distinction between the two is that the former visit a destination for at least one night, while the latter visit for less than 24 hours (World Tourism Organization, 1981). Third, tourism may be conceptualized based on the purpose of travel. It is the purpose of travel that has been widely (and perhaps inappropriately) used to define tourism and distinguish between different forms of it. For example, the focus of tourism on pleasure as the primary travel activity, at the exclusion of business-related travel, is clearly an academic point of debate that bears little relevance to the reality of tourism (Murphy, 1985). Thus, like sport, tourism must embrace both the leisure and recreational dimensions of the phenomenon, as well as business-related travel. So while the World Tourism Organization (1981) lists sport as a subset of leisure-related travel activities, the study of professional sport and sports-related business travel is now an important aspect of the study of sport tourism.

These definitions imply a significant convergence of interests in tourism and sport. Economic development through the medium of sports events has been, and remains, a prominent avenue of sport tourism development (Hall, 1992a,b). Sport and tourism development opportunities associated with large-scale hallmark and mega-sports events have been expanded with the professionalization of the events industry (Allen et al., 2000). In recent years, however, the links between sport and tourism have diversified far beyond tourism, economic development and urban regeneration interests associated with sports events (Weed and Bull, 2004).

It is important to highlight the heterogeneity of sports-related tourism (Weed and Bull, 2004). Given this heterogeneity, it is evident that many different types of sports and forms of involvement in sport may be incorporated into the study of sport tourism (Hinch and Higham, 2001). These include elite sport competition and spectatorship, social and recreational sports, active sport tourism, sport tours, and heritage/nostalgia sport tourism (Redmond, 1990; Gammon and Robinson, 1997; Gibson, 1998; Weed and Bull, 2004). It is also evident that manifestations of sport differ significantly between places on a national and regional basis (Rooney and Pillsbury, 1992). Sport therefore offers unique tourism development opportunities that vary markedly between the motivations of different participants (both active and passive), and between the local/regional contexts within which sport takes place.

Attempts to articulate the domain of sport tourism have resulted in a proliferation of definitions (Ruskin, 1987; Hall, 1992b; Gammon and Robinson, 1997; Standeven, 1997; Weed and Bull, 1997; Gibson, 1998). Most definitions tend to parallel the spatial, temporal and activity dimensions of key definitions for tourism (Gibson, 1998), generally at the neglect of the defining parameters of sport (Hinch and Higham, 2004). Several definitions of sport tourism place emphasis on leisure-based travel (e.g. Weed and Bull, 1997) or exclude professional sports and business travel associated with sport (Hall, 1992a; Standeven, 1997). Sport is often only mentioned as the primary travel activity although Gammon and Robinson (1997) make the important distinction between sport tourists and tourism sports. The latter recognizes sport as a secondary and sometimes even an incidental travel activity. Perhaps the broadest definition of sport tourism is provided by Standeven and De Knop (1999: 12), who define sport tourism as 'all forms of active and passive involvement in sporting activity, participated in

7

casually or in an organized way for non-commercial or business/commercial reasons, that necessitate travel away from the home and work locality'. While this definition does not accurately articulate the key defining parameters of either sport or tourism, its value lies in the fact that, practically speaking, it captures the broad range of interests that exist in the study of sport tourism destinations.

Sport tourism destinations

Tourism destinations are places that attract and provide for the needs of visitors. Such places exist when the resources, infrastructures and services required to facilitate travel to the destination, and the attainment of satisfactory visitor experiences at the destination, are in place. As with sport and tourism, a general lack of consensus is associated with the definition of destinations (Laws, 1995). The terms 'destination' and 'resort' are often used interchangeably, although the latter is more commonly used in reference to individual complexes, such as hotels, which position themselves as self-contained resorts (Gunn, 1988). Destinations, then, can range from purpose-built resorts through to entire countries. In between these extremes, historic towns, capital cities, provinces and macro-regions within a country or entire nation states may be referred to as destinations.

While conceptually simple, in practice the definition of destinations may be an exercise in futility. Destinations are commonly defined and resourced on the basis of existing administrative boundaries (Laws, 1995). The use of political boundaries to define destinations is an obvious consequence of public decision-making structures. Thus local, regional and/or national government decisions will be made relating to the development, positioning, branding and marketing of tourism destinations. Yet tourists are generally not limited in their spatial travel flows by local, regional or national administrative boundaries. This situation can give rise to conflicts of interest between local/regional/national interests and action relating to the development and management of tourism destinations.

Historically tourism destinations have developed at locations favoured by resources such as iconic cultural attractions, outstanding natural landscapes and/or favourable natural resources for leisure tourism (e.g. climate, beaches). More recently, the development potential of tourism destinations has been based on a capacity to serve specific business, leisure and recreation interests (Hall and Weiler, 1992). One particularly dynamic and powerful domain of tourism, which offers tourist destinations opportunities of scope, scale and diversity, is that relating to sport. This fact has been increasingly recognized in the academic community. A groundswell of academic attention has been paid to sport tourism in recent years. These efforts have centred on sports events (e.g. Burgan and Mules, 1992; Chalip, 1992), sport tourism and destination management (e.g. Chernushenko, 1996; Bull and Weed, 1999), travel flows relating to specific sports (e.g. Priestley, 1995; Higham and Hinch, 2003), niche sport travel markets (e.g. Giulianotti, 1995; Gibson et al., 2002) and sport tourism resources such as heritage sport tourism (Gammon, 2002). Interestingly, government and tourism industry responses to sport tourism have emerged relatively belatedly. For instance, a draft Federal Sport Tourism policy in Australia, considered a leader in sport tourism development (Hinch and Higham, 2004), took place as recently as 2001.

Conclusion

Both sport and tourism have diversified rapidly into a range of distinct forms. During this course of parallel evolution, mutual interests in sport management and tourism management have expanded considerably (Hinch and Higham, 2004; Weed and Bull, 2004). The constant evolution of new or hybrid sports with specific natural or built resource requirements represents emerging opportunities for tourism destinations where these requirements are, or could be, best satisfied. The convergence of interests in sport and tourism combine, in the study of sport tourism, into a powerful avenue of development and consequently an important field of study. Sport tourism represents an avenue of development at tourism destinations that is, through its continuing growth and increasing diversity, rich in opportunity. This raises important questions for tourism destination managers, including:

- How can existing sports resources be utilized and/or further developed to enhance the tourism product at a destination?
- How can the potential for sports to generate significant temporary flows of travellers be captured by tourism destinations in order to increase visitor numbers or counter existing patterns of seasonality?
- How can sports cultures, sports heritage and subculture associated with specific sports best be utilized to generate destination image?
- How can sports be used in tourism promotions to enhance destination brands?
- What niche markets associated with sports offer the greatest opportunities for specific tourism destinations?
- What are the economic expenditure profiles of specific sport tourism markets?
- What visitor experiences are sought at sport tourism destinations, and to what extent do they complement or conflict with experiences sought by existing visitor markets?
- How can sports and sports events contribute to business and sports media travel flows to a destination?
- How might coordinated sport and tourism planning interests contribute to the development or periodic under-utilization of facilities and infrastructure at a tourism destination?

This book builds upon an expanding literature in the field of sport tourism. Authored books by Standeven and De Knop (1999) and Turco et al. (2001) have provided general introductions to the impacts of sport tourism and the marketing and operational perspectives in sport tourism respectively. More advanced, theoretically informed and research-based contributions have been published in recent times (Hinch and Higham, 2004; Weed and Bull, 2004). Conferences resulting in edited contributions have provided disparate collections of papers on the subject of sport tourism (e.g. Garmise, 1987; Gammon and Kurtzman, 2002). This book is distinguished from these contributions in so far as it brings together the works of internationally prominent researchers in a range of fields of expertise relating to sport tourism destinations in a coordinated and planned edited text (Figure 1.1).

To recognize and achieve the potential of sport tourism it is first necessary to understand the common development interests in the fields of sport and tourism

Sport tourism destinations

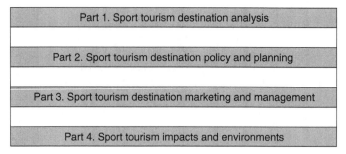

Figure 1.1 Schema representing the sustainable development of sport tourism destinations

resource analysis, policy, planning, development and management. This book explores and assimilates the rapidly expanding and dynamic inter-relationships between the fields of sport management, sport and tourism policy and planning, and the sustainable development and management of tourism destinations. It seeks to explore fundamental aspects of sport tourism of relevance to tourism destinations. These fundamentals include a critical analysis of destination resources, the policy and planning frameworks for sport and tourism, destination marketing and management, and the analysis and management of tourism impacts and environments. These fields have received the attention of increasing scholarship in recent years. They provide the subject of, and structure for, the chapters in this book.

References

Allen, J., O'Toole, W., McDonnell, I. and Harris, R. (2000). *Festival & Special Event Management*. Sydney: John Wiley & Sons Australia Ltd.

Andrews, D. L. and Jackson, S. J. (eds) (2001). *Sports Stars: The Cultural Politics of Sporting Celebrity*. New York: Routledge.

Bale, J. (1989). *Sports Geography*. London: E & FN Spon.

Bale, J. (1993). *Sport, Space and the City*. London: Routledge.

Baum, T. and Hagen, L. (1999). Responses to seasonality: the experiences of peripheral destinations. *International Journal of Tourism Research*, 1, 299–312.

Bell, E. and Campbell, D. (1999). For the love of money. *The Observer*, 23 May, p. 22.

British Tourist Authority (2000). *Sporting Britain: Play it, Love it, Watch it, Live it, Visit*. London: Haymarket Magazines Ltd.

Bull, C. and Weed, M. (1999). Niche markets and small island tourism: the development of sports tourism in Malta. *Managing Leisure*, 4(3), 142–155.

Burgan, B. and Mules, T. (1992). Economic impact of sporting events. *Annals of Tourism Research*, 19(4), 700–710.

Butler, R. W. (1994). Seasonality in tourism: issues and problems. In A. V. Seaton (ed.), *Tourism: The State of the Art*. Chichester: John Wiley & Sons, pp. 332–339.

Chalip, L. (1993). The construction and use of polysemic structures: Olympic lessons for sport marketers. *Journal of Sport Management*, 6, 87–98.

Chalip, L. (2004). Case study: Olympic teams as market segments. In T. D. Hinch and J. E. S. Higham (eds), *Sport Tourism Destinations*. Clevedon, OH: Channel View, pp. 52–54.

Chernushenko, D. (1996). Sports tourism goes sustainable – the Lillehammer experience. *Visions in Leisure and Business*, 15(1), 65–73.

Clawson, M. and Knetsch, J. (1966). *The Economics of Outdoor Recreation*. Baltimore, MD: Johns Hopkins Press.

Coakley, J. (2004). *Sports in Society: Issues and Controversies* (8th edn). Boston, MA: McGraw Hill Higher Education.

Collins, M. F. (1991). The economics of sport and sports in the economy: some international comparisons. In C. P. Cooper (ed.), *Progress in Tourism, Recreation and Hospitality Management*. London: Belhaven Press, pp. 184–214.

Cooper, C., Fletcher, J., Gilbert, D. and Wanhill, S. (1993). *Tourism: Principles and Practice*. Harlow: Longman Group Limited.

Dauncey, H. and Hare, G. (2000). World Cup France '98: metaphors, meanings and values. *International Review for the Sociology of Sport*, 35(3), 331–347.

Debord, G. (1994). *The Society of the Spectacle* (trans. Donald Nicholson-Smith). New York: Zone Books.

Dietvorst, A. G. J. and Ashworth, G. J. (1995). Tourism transformations: an introduction. In G. J. Ashworth and A. G. J. Dietvorst (eds), *Tourism and Spatial Transformations: Implications for Policy and Planning*. Wallingford: CAB International, pp. 1–13.

Faulkner, B., Tideswell, C. and Weston, A. M. (1998). *Leveraging Tourism Benefits from the Sydney 2000 Olympics*. Paper presented at the Sport Management Association of Australia and New Zealand, Gold Coast, Australia, 26–28 November.

Gammon, S. (2002). Fantasy, nostalgia and the pursuit of what never was. In S. Gammon and J. Kurtzman (eds), *Sport Tourism: Principles and Practice*. Eastbourne: Leisure Studies Association, pp. 61–72.

Gammon, S. and Kurzmann, J. (eds) (2002). *Sport Tourism: Principles and Practice*. Eastbourne: Leisure Studies Association.

Gammon, S. and Robinson, T. (1997). Sport and tourism: a conceptual framework. *Journal of Sport Tourism*, 4(3), 8–24.

Garmise, M. (1987). *Proceedings of the International Seminar and Workshop on Outdoor Education, Recreation and Sport Tourism*. Israel: Emmanuel Gill Publishing.

Getz, D. (1991). *Festivals, Special Events and Tourism*. New York: Van Nostrand Reinhold.

Gibson, H. J. (1998). Sport tourism: A critical analysis of research. *Sport Management Review*, 1(1), 45–76.

Gibson, J. J., Willming, C. and Holdnak, A. (2002). Small-scale event tourism: college sport as a tourist attraction. In S. Gammon and J. Kurtzman (eds), *Sport Tourism: Principles and Practice*. Eastbourne: Leisure Studies Association.

Giulianotti, R. (1995). Football and the politics of carnival: an ethnographic study of Scottish fans in Sweden. *International Review for the Sociology of Sport*, 30(2), 191–223.

Giulianotti, R. (1996). Back to the future: an ethnography of Ireland's football fans at the 1994 World Cup finals in the USA. *International Review for the Sociology of Sport*, 31(3), 323–347.

Glyptis, S. A. (1989). *Leisure and Patterns of Time Use.* Paper presented at the Leisure Studies Association Annual Conference, Bournemouth, England, 24–26 April 1987. Eastbourne: Leisure Studies Association.

Gratton, C. and Taylor, P. (2000). *Economics of Sport and Recreation.* London: E & FN Spon.

Gunn, C. A. (1988). *Tourism Planning.* New York: Taylor and Francis.

Guttmann, A. (1974). *From Ritual to Record: The Nature of Modern Sports.* New York: Columbia University Press.

Halberstam, D. (1999). *Playing for Keeps: Michael Jordan and The World He Made.* New York: Random House.

Hall, C. M. (1992a). *Hallmark Tourist Events: Impacts, Management and Planning.* London: Belhaven Press.

Hall, C. M. (1992b). Review: adventure, sport and health tourism. In B. Weiler and C. M. Hall (eds), *Special Interest Tourism.* London: Belhaven Press, pp. 186–210.

Hall, C. M. and Weiler, B. (eds) (1992). *Special Interest Tourism.* London: Belhaven Press.

Heino, R. (2001). What is so punk about snowboarding? *Journal of Sport and Social Issues,* 24(1), 176–191.

Higham, J. E. S. and Hinch, T. D. (2002). Sport, tourism and seasons: the challenges and potential of overcoming seasonality in the sport and tourism sectors. *Tourism Management,* 23, 175–185.

Higham, J. E. S. and Hinch, T. D. (2003). Sport, space and time: effects of the Otago Highlanders franchise on tourism. *Journal of Sports Management,* 17(3), 235–257.

Hinch, T. D. and Higham, J. E. S. (2001). Sport tourism: a framework for research. *The International Journal of Tourism Research,* 3(1), 45–58.

Hinch, T. D. and Higham, J. E. S. (2004). *Sport Tourism Development.* Clevedon: Channel View.

Hooper, I. (1998). *The Value of Sport in Urban Regeneration – a Case Study of Glasgow.* Paper presented at the Sport in the City Conference, Sheffield, 2–4 July.

Hudson, S. (1999). *Snow Business: A Study of the International Ski Industry.* London: Cassell.

International Olympic Committee and World Tourism Organization (2001). *Conclusions of the World Conference on Sport and Tourism.* Barcelona: International Olympic Committee and World Tourism Organization. Lausanne: International Olympic Committee.

Jackson, S. J., Batty, R. and Scherer, J. (2001). Transnational sport marketing at the global/local nexus: The Adidasification of the New Zealand All Blacks. *International Journal of Sports Marketing & Sponsorship,* 3(2), 185–201.

Keller, P. (2001). *Sport and Tourism: Introductory Report.* Paper presented at the World Conference on Sport and Tourism, Barcelona, Spain, 22–23 February. Madrid: World Tourism Organization.

Kurtzman, J. and Zauhar, J. (1995). Tourism Sport International Council. *Annals of Tourism Research,* 22(3), 707–708.

Laws, E. (1995). *Tourist Destination Management: Issues, Analysis and Policies.* London: Routledge.

Leiper, N. (1981). Towards a cohesive curriculum for tourism: the case for a distinct discipline. *Annals of Tourism Research,* 8(1), 69–74.

Loy, J. W., McPherson, B. D. and Kenyon, G. (1978). *Sport and Social Systems: A Guide to the Analysis of Problems and Literature*. Reading: Addison Wesley.

McPherson, B. D., Curtis, J. E. and Loy, J. W. (1989). *The Social Significance of Sport: An Introduction to the Sociology of Sport*. Champaign, IL: Human Kinetics Books.

Murphy, P. E. (1985). *Tourism: A Community Approach*. New York: Methuen.

Nauright, J. (1995). Introduction. In J. Nauright (ed.), *Sport, Power and Society in New Zealand: Historical Contemporary Perspectives*. Sydney: University of New South Wales Printery.

Nauright, J. (1996). 'A besieged tribe?': nostalgia, white cultural identity and the role of rugby in a changing South Africa. *International Review for the Sociology of Sport*, 31(1), 69–89.

Owen, P. D. and Weatherston, C. R. (2002). Uncertainty of outcome and Super 12 rugby union attendance: application of a general-to-specific modelling strategy. *Economics Discussion Papers*, No. 0211. Dunedin: University of Otago.

Porteous, B. (2000). Sports development: Glasgow. *Leisure Manager*, 18(11), 18–21.

Priestley, G. K. (1995). Sports tourism: the case of golf. In G. J. Ashworth and A. G. J. Dietvorst (eds), *Tourism and Spatial Transformations: Implications for Policy and Planning*. Wallingford: CAB International, pp. 205–223.

Redmond, G. (1990). Points of increasing contact: sport and tourism in the modern world. In A. Tomlinson (ed.), *Sport in Society: Policy, Politics and Culture*. Eastbourne: Leisure Studies Association, pp. 158–167.

Redmond, G. (1991). Changing styles of sports tourism: industry/consumer interactions in Canada, the USA and Europe. In M. T. Sinclair and M. J. Stabler (eds), *The Tourism Industry: An International Analysis*. Wallingford: CAB International, pp. 107–120.

Ritchie, J. R. B. and Crouch, G. I. (2003). *The Competitive Destination: A Sustainable Tourism Perspective*. Wallingford: CAB International.

Rooney, J. F. (1988). *Mega Sports Events as Tourist Attractions: A Geographical Analysis*. Paper presented at the Tourism Research: Expanding the Boundaries. Travel and Tourism Research Association, Nineteenth Annual Conference. Montreal, Quebec.

Rooney, J. F. and Pillsbury, R. (1992). Sports regions of America. *American Demographics*, 14(10), 1–10.

Ruskin, H. (1987). Selected views of socio-economic aspects of outdoor recreation, outdoor education and sport tourism. In M. Garmise (ed.), *Proceedings of the International Seminar and Workshop on Outdoor Education, Recreation and Sport Tourism*. Israel: Emmanuel Gill Publishing.

Schaffer, W. and Davidson, L. (1985). Economic impact of the Falcons on Atlanta: 1984. Suwanee, GA: The Atlanta Falcons.

Shibli, S. (1998). *The Economic Impact of Two Major Sporting Events in Two of the United Kingdom's 'National Cities of Sport'*. Paper presented at the Sport in the City Conference, Sheffield, 2–4 July.

Standeven, J. (1997). Sport tourism: joint marketing – a starting point for beneficial synergies. *Journal of Vacation Marketing*, 4(1), 39–51.

Standeven, J. and De Knop, P. (1999). *Sport Tourism*. Champaign, IL: Human Kinetics.

Stevens (2001). Stadia and tourism related facilities. *Travel and Tourism Analyst*, 2, 59–73.

Stewart, G. (2001). Fab Club. *Australian Leisure Management*, Oct/Nov, 16–19.

Thomson, R. (2000). Physical activity through sport and leisure: traditional versus non-competitive activities. *Journal of Physical Education New Zealand*, 33(1), 34–39.

Toohey, K., Taylor, T. and Choong-Ki Lee (2004). The FIFA World Cup 2002: the effects of terrorism on sport tourists. *Journal of Sport Tourism*, 8(4), in press.

Turco, C. M., Riley, R. and Swart, K. (2001). *Sport Tourism*. Morgantown, WV: Fitness Information Technology.

Weed, M. E. and Bull, C. J. (1997). Influences on sport tourism relations in Britain: the effects of government policy. *Tourism Recreation Research*, 22(2), 5–12.

Weed, M. E. and Bull, C. J. (2004). *Sports Tourism: Participants, Policy and Providers*. Oxford: Elsevier Butterworth-Heinemann.

Whitson, D. and Macintosh, D. (1996). The global circus: international sport, tourism and the marketing of cities. *Journal of Sport and Social Issues*, 23, 278–295.

World Tourism Organization (1981). *Technical Handbook on the Collection and Presentation of Domestic and International Tourism Statistics*. Madrid: World Tourism Organization.

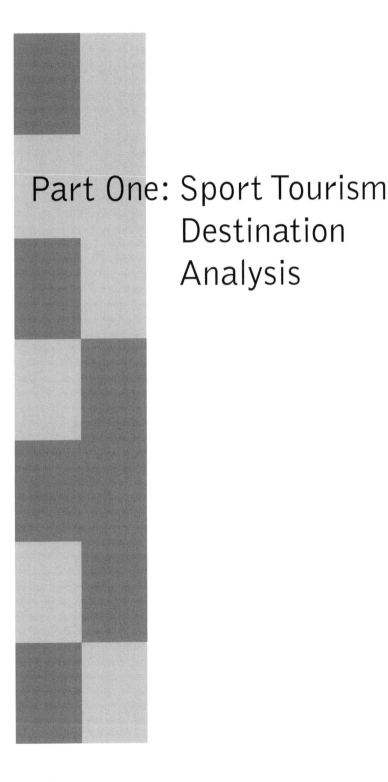

Part One: Sport Tourism Destination Analysis

2

Introduction to sport tourism destination analysis

James Higham

Resource analysis represents an important first step in the development and management of sport tourism destinations. Different destinations offer specific sport tourism experiences because they are characterized by distinct sport and tourism resources. These resources may, within the tourism sphere, relate to tourism infrastructure, levels of service development, tourist attractions and information services. The sports resource may include sports venues such as stadia and arenas, training facilities, sport science resources, and sports medicine facilities (Maier and Weber, 1993). Standeven and De Knop (1999) recognize the considerable common interests that link the resources utilized by the sport and tourism industries.

An important point of differentiation exists between sport tourism resources that are built and those that are primarily nature-based. The resource base for sport tourism at many urban sport tourism destinations increasingly centres upon major stadium facilities that have in recent years been planned and developed in tourism precincts alongside other entertainment venues, attractions and tourist services (Stevens and Wootton, 1997; Stevens, 2001). At local or regional destinations, the scale of tourism development is quite different. The resource base for sport tourism at a regional community level commonly includes local club-based sports facilities, and such things as community-funded walkways, riverside cycle tracks, and municipal recreation facilities such as swimming pools and public racquet sports venues (Weed and Bull, 2004). However, the potential benefits of sport tourism at the community level are no different when they take place in smaller geographical areas (Getz, 1991). The specific challenges that such destinations face often relate to accessibility, distance from tourist generating regions, and lack of tourism infrastructure and service development. Herein lie significant challenges for sport tourism destinations located in regional or peripheral areas.

Established sport tourism resources exist within a hierarchy that is dynamic (Bale, 1989). This applies to both natural and built sport tourism resources. Nature-based sports offer great opportunities to destinations that may be positioned favourably within the sports location hierarchy. Sports such as ski-jumping (e.g. at Holmenkollen, Norway), surfing (e.g. at Bali and Hawaii), hang gliding (e.g. at Omarama, New Zealand) and surf lifesaving (e.g. the Gold Coast, Australia) are closely associated with prominent destinations because of the natural phenomena and/or climatic conditions that exist at those places. The emergence of new or growth in existing nature-based sports such as kite-surfing and base-jumping offer considerable opportunities for tourist destinations that (a) recognize the natural resources that may serve new forms of tourist demand, and (b) respond efficiently and appropriately to emerging sport tourism opportunities (see Case study 2.1).

The location hierarchy theory applies equally to built sports facilities. Baseball facilities in the USA range from local parks throughout the country at the base, to venues such as Yankee Stadium (New York) and Camden Yards Stadium (Baltimore) at the apex of the hierarchy. In the sport of cricket, the location hierarchy in England ranges from local village cricket grounds to internationally prominent venues such as Lords (London) and Edgbaston (Birmingham). Each obviously caters for quite different participant and spectator markets, with the distinction between professional and amateur sports facilities most clear, and provides equally distinct visitor experiences. Sport tourism resources and facilities that exist throughout the local hierarchy contribute, albeit in very different ways, to the resource base for sport tourism.

Case study 2.1 Hosting the XXXII defence of the America's Cup

In 2003 the Swiss Alinghi syndicate defeated Team New Zealand in Auckland (New Zealand) to win the America's Cup. This victory saw the return of the America's Cup to Europe for the first time in 152 years of international competition. As a landlocked nation, it was impossible for the Swiss to defend the America's Cup in Switzerland, so competition began between destinations seeking to host the Louis Vuitton Challenger series (April 2007) and XXXII defence of the America's Cup scheduled to begin in June 2007. The search for a destination to host the America's Cup in Mediterranean Europe was contested between the Atlantic city of Lisbon (Portugal) and the Mediterranean cities of Valencia

(Spain), Marseille (France) and Naples (Italy), after the cities of Palma de Majorca, Barcelona (Spain), Porto Cervo and Elba (Italy) were excluded from further consideration. The right to host the XXXII defence of the America's Cup was awarded to Valencia (Spain). In addition to the Louis Vuitton and America's Cup regattas, Valencia will host a series of preliminary regattas from September 2004 as part of the build-up to the 2007 event. Interestingly, the host city decision was based primarily on superior meteorological conditions relating to the optimal wind conditions for the sport of America's Cup-class yacht racing. Clearly, it is necessary that destination managers are cognizant of the resources that exist at a specific destination, the relevance of these resources to different sports, and the immediate or long-term tourism development opportunities that they may offer. The case of the America's Cup yachting regatta, which is associated with demonstrated and significant economic and tourism development opportunities (Orams and Brons, 1999), demonstrates these points.

(Source: http://news.bbc.co.uk/sport1/hi/other_sports/3239636.stm)

Various approaches to understanding sport tourism resources exist. These include the classification of resources that are nature-based (albeit usually with some form of cultural development) or built specifically for the purposes of sport (Hinch and Higham, 2004). The quality of sport tourism resources, be they natural or built, will bear upon the local/regional, national and/or international tourist catchments that they may influence. Thus the analysis of sport tourism resources is incomplete without consideration being given to the quality, uniqueness and status of those resources and their tourism market range.

Issues of resource quality and market demand are of great relevance to sport tourism destinations. The resource requirements of a given sport differ significantly based on types of sporting pursuit, with the distinctions between amateur/professional, novice/elite and recreational/competitive participants particularly evident. This point is well illustrated by the sport of skiing. The physical resource requirements for this sport are, essentially, skiable terrain and adequate seasonal snow cover. However, the specific resource requirement of skiers vary between the following groups:

- Competing professional athletes (e.g. event management resources)
- Elite training athletes (e.g. sports science and sports medicine facilities)
- Extreme skiers (e.g. appropriate terrain)
- Recreational skiers (e.g. visitor facility development and terrain that offers appropriate levels of challenge)
- Novice skiers (e.g. ski hire and ski school services)
- Family holiday skiers (e.g. accommodation and leisure facilities).

Thus, again, the link between a physical resource inventory and the market demands for a specific resource is evident.

Standeven and De Knop (1999) articulate the importance of understanding tourism infrastructure and superstructure as part of the destination resource analysis process. Levels of appropriate accommodation, transport infrastructure, tourist information services, ancillary attractions and tourist activities are important elements of the destination resource base. Proximity to visitor markets and accessibility are important factors in the analysis of sport tourism destinations, particularly in the case of regular season sport competitions, and one-off or recurring sports events. However, it is also noteworthy that, for some, the experience of exotic and unique destinations, and perhaps even travel to the destination itself, is an important part of the overall visitor experience (Clawson and Knetch, 1966).

Sport tourism resource analysis must also consider matters that lie beyond the 'bricks and mortar' of sports facilities and tourism infrastructure. Institutional arrangements form a critical element of resource analysis (Mitchell, 1989). The extent to which policy and planning agencies at a destination are willing and able to collaborate is an important political dimension of the sport tourism resource analysis (Weed and Bull, 2004). So, too, are coordinated public and private sector interests, and the availability of capital investment. These human and financial resources are instrumental in fields of sport tourism, determining such things as the timely and appropriate development of sports facilities, and the success of national and international sports events at a destination.

Human resources of relevance to sport tourism destinations include cultural capital. Sport tourism has been described as an experience of physical activity, active or passive, that takes place within the context of the experience of a specific place (Standeven and De Knop, 1999). Thus, the cultural text with which sports are associated at a given destination is an important element of sport tourism. Masters golf courses and grand slam tennis venues are set apart from other venues because of the prominence and significance of the events that they host. Wimbledon has a status elevated above all other tennis venues, with implications for visitor market catchments, because of its heritage and aura of tradition. The status of sport tourism destinations, and the value of imagery associated with sports that take place at specific and recognizable tourism destinations, is promoted by elements of uniqueness.

An understanding of sport and tourism resources at a destination is incomplete without an appreciation of sport tourism participants (Weed and Bull, 2004). Sport tourism is widely viewed as a niche sector for the tourism industry (Commonwealth Department of Industry, Science and Resources, 2000) that may be targeted to broaden the suite of visitor markets that is attracted to a destination (Bull and Weed, 1999). Sport tourism participants are often viewed as a collective market that may be approached generically, as demonstrated in the promotion of major sports events to mass audiences. The reality, however, is that sport tourism is comprised of a diverse range of niche markets (Maier and Weber, 1993; Delpy, 1997; Collins and Jackson, 2001). For instance, many Australian cities targeted specific market segments during the lead-up to the 2000 Olympic Games (Chalip, 2001). Thus, while Bull and Weed (1999: 143) identify that 'sport tourism (represents) a collection of separate niches', the extent to which sport generates a broad range of niche tourism markets is not fully recognized. Understanding sport tourist markets is an important step in understanding the development potential of sport tourism at a destination.

It is important that destination analyses extend to a consideration of sport tourism market demand. At the most fundamental level, sport tourism markets may be divided into leisure and business travel markets. Both are characterized by a diversity of specialized markets that can be profiled for destination marketing and development purposes. The former include visitors who attend, as participants or spectators, non-elite sports events, activity holiday centres, fantasy camps, and outdoor adventure pursuits, among many others (Delpy, 1998). The latter include professional sports teams, elite athletes, team management, sports marketing agencies, media, and professional sports administrators. Within these general classifications exist a vast range of specific niche markets that can be identified and, if strategically worthwhile, targeted by sport tourism destinations.

It is then important for destination managers to understand what motivates sport tourists, and the experiences that members of specific market segments seek. Research into tourist motivations is concerned with why people travel, the benefits they seek and the experiences they pursue to satisfy their needs and desires (Cooper *et al.*, 1993). Tourist motivation is a function of the self-perceived needs of the traveller, which drive the decision-making process, and the purchase of tourism products (Collier, 1999). The motivational profile of the traveller is a combination of intrinsic and extrinsic factors. These factors have been described in terms of push (psychological) and pull (cultural) factors (Dann, 1981). The former are intrinsic and unique to each tourist, as they are determined by the personality and attitude of the individual. Pull factors include price, destination image, marketing and promotion. Destination image, which is a function of physical and abstract attributes (Echtner and Ritchie, 1993), plays an important part in the formulation of expectations. Physical attributes include attractions, activities, sporting facilities and physical landscapes. Abstract attributes are less readily measured, and include atmosphere, crowding, safety and ambience. These attributes may be utilized by tourism organizations to foster a distinct destination brand and advantageous destination imagery.

Sport tourism, like other forms of travel, entails a set of motivations that are established in anticipation of the fulfilment of desired needs. According to Stewart (2001), sport tourists may, to some degree, be motivated by push factors – including escape from everyday life, the search for camaraderie, and to develop friendships and a sense of belonging. Sport tourists may, additionally or alternatively, be motivated by pull factors that include the atmosphere and excitement of competitive sports. Tourist motivations are critical to understanding why people do or do not travel, their choice of destination and various aspects of tourist behaviour.

An appreciation of the motivations and desired experiences of leisure travellers is central to the success of sport tourism destinations (Gibson, 1998). The relative significance of motivations such as competition, mastery of specific skills or disciplines, participation, camaraderie, and experiencing the tourism product at a tourism destination, all of which may vary between specific travel markets, needs to be understood if satisfactory visitor experiences are to be achieved. The analysis of sport tourist motivations and experiences in a way that is theoretically informed represents an important contribution to the study of sport tourism.

Conversely, the needs of business travellers centre primarily on the fulfilment of professional business objectives. The infrastructural and service requirements of sport tourism-related business is an obvious point of difference between leisure and business sports travel markets. However, it is noteworthy that business travel markets, be they professional athletes, team management or representatives of sports organizations, are no less likely to have leisure and recreational interests that need to be satisfied at the tourist destination. This aspect of sport tourism represents an important avenue of investigation, given the growing significance of professional sports as a travel market and the specific motivations and needs of professional sports people. The team sports travel market in the United States alone is estimated to be over $US 6.1 billion per annum (see Chapter 4). The dynamic and changeable nature of professional sports competitions ensures that opportunities for tourist destinations to function as a base for a professional sports franchise (or seasonal base for touring sports teams during periods of competition), or occasionally to host elite level sports competitions, are constantly being renegotiated.

In understanding sport tourism destinations it is necessary to appreciate why people are (or may in the future be) attracted to different destinations. Any such understanding requires insights into both supply (destination resources) and demand (visitor demands) for sport tourism. In terms of supply, it is necessary to understand what resources for sport tourism exist at a destination, and precisely what visitor experiences those resources offer. Equally, on the demand side, an appreciation of the values, interests and motivations of defined market groups, and the characteristics of members of specific sport-related tourism markets, is required. Such insights offer sport tourism practitioners and destination managers the opportunity to recognize in full the development potential of sport tourism. They may also allow emerging sports-related development opportunities to be identified and assessed in a timely and competitive manner.

Part One of this book comprises of five chapters (Chapters 2–6) that critically examine issues relating to sport tourism destination analyses. In Chapter 3, Chris Bull explores what constitutes sport tourism destination resource analyses. This chapter highlights the fact that creating an inventory of sport and tourism resources at a destination is only a first step in the resource analysis process. Of equal importance, it is necessary to understand how such resources are perceived, appraised and valued by stakeholder groups including sport tourists, but extending beyond visitors to sports clubs, sports administrators, private sector interests, policy-makers, planners and local community residents. He also highlights the need to critically understand human resources, such as the willingness of stakeholders to share visions, and collaborate in pursuing strategic goals, as an important part of the resource analysis.

In Chapter 4, Lisa Delpy Neirotti presents a descriptive analysis of the scope and scale of sport tourism markets. This chapter illustrates the diversity of specific market segments of relevance to the sport tourism sector. It gives separate consideration to leisure and business sport tourism markets, and provides insights into the close links that can be developed between specific sport tourism markets and specific tourism destinations. Chapter 5 then provides theoretically informed insights into sport tourist visitor experiences. Heather Gibson highlights the relevance of such insights by demonstrating that understanding the desired experiences of sport tourists should direct targeted sport tourism destination promotions if they are to be successful.

It has been noted that the travel demands of professional athletes, elite sports teams and professional team management are not well understood. Professional and elite sports offer potentially lucrative opportunities for destinations that are able to meet the increasingly specific needs of this market. The first part of Chapter 6, by Sonia Francis and Peter Murphy, addresses this subject. It highlights the rapidly changing field of professional sport and the heightened attention being paid by professional sports organizations to creating the desired environment for professional athletes competing 'away from home'. This is a direct response to the recognized correlation between 'away games' and the likelihood of defeat (Bale, 1989). This situation has drawn a direct and proactive response from professional sports organizations in order to enhance sports performances in unfamiliar 'away' locations. Familiarity with living environments, training facilities and playing conditions of international competition is an important part of this response. The demands of elite athletes and professional sports teams have become increasingly specific in pursuit of the highest probability of victory in away competition. In addition, Chapter 6 offers the contrasts of insights into the demands and resource requirements of non-elite competitive sport tourists.

References

Bale, J. (1989). *Sports Geography*. London: E & FN Spon.

Bull, C. and Weed, M. (1999). Niche markets and small island tourism: the development of sports tourism in Malta. *Managing Leisure*, 4(3), 142–155.

Chalip, L. (2001). Sport and tourism: conceptualising the link. In D. Kluka and G. Shilling (eds), *The Business of Sport*. Oxford: Meyer and Meyer, pp. 78–89.

Clawson, M. and Knetsch, J. (1966). *The Economics of Outdoor Recreation*. Baltimore, MD: Johns Hopkins Press.

Collier, A. (1999). *Principles of Tourism: A New Zealand Perspective* (5th edn). Auckland: Longman.

Collins, M. F. and Jackson, G. (1999). The economics of sport tourism. In J. Standeven and P. De Knop (eds), *Sport Tourism*. Champaign, IL: Human Kinetics, pp. 170–201.

Collins, M. F. and Jackson, G. (2001). *Evidence for a Sports Tourism Continuum*. Paper presented at the Journeys in Leisure: Current and Future Alliances Conference, Luton, UK.

Commonwealth Department of Industry, Science and Resources (2000). *Towards a National Sport Tourism Strategy* (draft report). Canberra: Commonwealth Department of Industry, Science and Resources.

Cooper, C., Fletcher, J., Gilbert, D. and Wanhill, S. (1993). *Tourism: Principles and Practice*. Harlow: Longman Group Limited.

Dann, G. M. S. (1981). Tourist motivation: an appraisal. *Annals of Tourism Research*, 8(2), 187.

Delpy, L. (1997). An overview of sport tourism: building towards a dimensional framework. *Journal of Vacation Marketing*, 4(1), 23–38.

Delpy, L. (1998). Editorial. *Journal of Vacation Marketing*, 4(1), 4–5.

Echtner, C. M. and Ritchie, J. B. R. (1993). The measurement of destination image: an empirical assessment. *Journal of Travel Research*, Spring, pp. 3–13.

Getz, D. (1991). *Festivals, Special Events and Tourism*. New York: Van Nostrand Reinhold.

Gibson, H. J. (1998). Sport tourism: a critical analysis of research. *Sport Management Review*, 1(1), 45–76.

Hinch, T. D. and Higham, J. E. S. (2004). *Sport Tourism Development*. Clevedon: Channel View.

Maier, J. and Weber, W. (1993). Sport tourism in local and regional planning. *Tourism Recreation Research*, 18(2), 33–43.

Mitchell, B. (1989). *Geography and Resource Analysis* (2nd edn). Harlow: Longman Scientific and Technical.

Orams, M. B. and Brons, A. (1999). Planning for a major sport/tourism event: the America's Cup 2000, Auckland, New Zealand. *Visions in Leisure and Business*, 18(1), 14–28.

Standeven, J. and De Knop, P. (1999). *Sport Tourism*. Champaign, IL: Human Kinetics.

Stevens, T. (2001). Stadia and tourism related facilities. *Travel and Tourism Analyst*, 2, 59–73.

Stevens, T. and Wooton, G. (1997). Sports stadia and arena: realizing their full potential. *Tourism Recreation Research*, 22(2), 49–56.

Stewart, B. (2001). Fab Club. *Australian Leisure Management*, Oct/Nov, pp. 16–19.

Weed, M. E. and Bull, C. J. (2004). *Sports Tourism: Participants, Policy and Providers*. Oxford: Elsevier Butterworth-Heinemann.

3

Sport tourism destination resource analysis

Chris Bull

Introduction

According to Standeven and De Knop (1999: 60), 'the experience of place is a key component of the sport tourism experience'. Not only does the separate sphere of tourism involve people being attracted to destinations with distinctive characteristics and qualities, but sport also requires specific spatially located resources. These resources may involve particular environments or facilities, but the essential point is that generally they are not ubiquitous; they are found at specific locations. While some resources may be more widespread than others, such as routeways along which people may run or cycle, facilities for activities such as skiing or rock climbing are less widespread. However, even where resources are more readily available the quality may be variable, with high-quality resources only to be found in a few locations. Football, played and observed at a premier league stadium, is a very different experience to that encountered in the local park, and cycling through the scenically attractive landscapes of national parks contrasts markedly with cycling along the busy streets of towns and cities. Thus engagement with sport (whether as participant or spectator) will often require travel, some of which will clearly be to destinations away from the home environment, and this will inevitably constitute sport tourism. In seeking greater understanding of the sport tourism phenomenon it is important to establish why people are attracted to different destinations, and thus an understanding of the places involved is essential. In analysing the resources of such destinations various factors need to be considered, such as inherent physical characteristics and qualities, accessibility, associated infrastructural arrangements and level of development. The analysis is far from simple, however, as not only does sport tourism involve a wide variety of different activities, each with its own resource requirements, but also the respective participants and spectators may vary in terms of their interests, motives and values. Consequently, a further set of factors that needs to be part of the analysis is the way in which resources are perceived and culturally appraised.

Physical characteristics and qualities

Various attempts have been made to classify physical resources associated with recreation, leisure and tourism (Clawson et al., 1960; ORRRC, 1962; DREE, 1972; Coppock and Duffield, 1975; Chubb and Chubb, 1981; Smith, 1983), and summaries of such classifications, as well as others, can be found in a variety of recent tourism geographies (e.g. Pearce, 1995; Williams, 1998; Hall and Page, 2002; Shaw and Williams, 2002). While there have been few attempts at classifying sports resources per se – the work of Bale (e.g. 1994 and 2003) in relation to sports spaces and landscapes being an important exception – much of the general literature relating to recreation is also relevant to sport. Implicit in much of the discussion underpinning such classifications is the idea of some form of 'continuum ranging from biophysical resources to man-made facilities' (Kreutzwiser, 1989: 22), a concept with considerable relevance for sports resources as it accommodates outdoor pursuits at one end of the spectrum, with those facilities, often urban-based, that have been specifically designed for sport at the other.

One of the earliest examples of such a classification, and possibly 'one of the most useful', according to Boniface and Cooper (1994: 20), is that suggested by Clawson et al. (1960) and based on location and other characteristics such as size, major use and degree of artificial development. Under this system, areas were arranged on a continuum of recreational opportunities from user-oriented through intermediate to resource-based. User-oriented areas were those located close to users, with small space demands and often artificial features; they included such resources as urban parks, swimming pools, golf courses and playgrounds, where the landscape elements are less important. Resource-based areas, at the other end of the continuum, involved an emphasis on the quality of the physical resource, with large land units involved and remoteness being a basic ingredient. National parks, forests, upland and wilderness areas catering for such activities as orienteering, canoeing, skiing and rock climbing were typical of this group. Intermediate areas were located between the two extremes, both spatially and in terms of activity. Accessibility was relatively important, with most sites within one or two hours' drive from potential users. Facilities for camping, picnicking, hiking, swimming, hunting and fishing were included in this category. This system was subsequently applied to England and Wales (Law, 1967) and, according to Hall and Page (2002: 86), it confirms the importance of distance and the 'zones of influence' of recreational resources together with their national, regional, sub-regional, intermediate or local zone' significance (see also the discussion on accessibility in the following section).

Another useful classification of tourism resources is that by Burton (1995), who identified five separate resource characteristics: climatic; coastal; landscape and wildlife; historic; and cultural, entertainment and man-made. Standeven and De Knop (1999) acknowledge this refinement of Clawson's categories as being particularly relevant to sport tourism, especially the climatic resource aspect. While the historic one may not appear immediately relevant it does accommodate the growth of nostalgia sport tourism (see, for example, Gibson, 1998, 2002; Gammon, 2002), and the inclusion of the climatic element embraces both the need for ambient climate for many activities as well as very precise (even extreme) climates for certain others, such as snow skiing, surfing and various extreme sports. Skiing, for example, requires a particular type of upland environment with appropriate physical conditions, namely snow cover and slopes. Snow cover is the main determinant of the length of season, and related aspects such as duration, earliness of first snow, quality of snow cover and reliability of snow cover from year to year are all key factors in establishing the quality, and hence success, of a particular location.

The Clawson system has been criticized for its somewhat confusing terminology in that it involves a rather narrow interpretation of the term 'resources' and seemingly ignores the fact that all recreation areas must be user-oriented to some extent (Pigram, 1983). Nevertheless, it still has some contemporary relevance, for it can be modified to cover certain forms of sport and it also begins to provide a solution to the distance problem relating to sport tourism. Under this system user-oriented resources would not be included within sport tourism, as they are specifically local, often being used after school or work, with no significant travel involved, although of course some may be used by tourists who are visiting the destination primarily for other purposes. Conversely, the other two areas would be involved in sport tourism as the resource-based areas are associated with vacations and the intermediate areas with day outings and weekend visits. Unfortunately, however, not all forms of sporting activity can be accommodated by such a scheme.

The essential problem with the Clawson model is that it does not accommodate certain quality issues. A central tenet of sport is challenge. This challenge may be interpersonal, but more often than not some form of natural or man-made resource is part of that challenge (Haywood et al., 1995). It is also pursued at different levels – recreational, competitive and elite. As a result, a number of different environmental/resource requirements are associated with sport. One relates to the necessary resource required to enable even the most basic activity to be undertaken. Local parks, for example, provide open space for various types of recreational sport – 'jumpers for goalposts' being the epitome of this level of resource provision. However, where sport is pursued at a competitive or elite level, higher-quality resources may be preferred, even required, and such resources are only found in certain locations. They may be specific natural or semi-natural resources, such as mountains, rivers, lakes, waves and forests, and thus located where they are as a result of physical geography. These resources, catering for such sports as skiing, climbing, canoeing, surfing and orienteering, would clearly be accommodated in the Clawson model in terms of both their environmental and their locational characteristics. Other high-quality sports resources, however, may be found in very different places, located in key urban centres. These resources are characterized by their purpose-built features designed specifically for sport, and their spatial distribution is conditioned by economic factors such as market thresholds (Bale, 2003), social and political considerations linked to social policy (Henry, 2001), or urban regeneration linked to tourism (Page, 1990; Law, 1992). For the people who live in such centres these sports places have a user-oriented location, but from the perspective of those who lack such facilities in their home town and who choose to travel to such centres to participate the pattern is clearly very different.

Accessibility and infrastructural arrangements

One key attribute in determining the value of particular resources is the ease with which potential users can travel to access them and the extent to which they can be accommodated in the destination. In classical spatial analysis, accessibility is related to concepts of distance and the efficiency of transport networks. Those resources most accessible to the greatest number of users are generally regarded as more valuable than those that are less so, and simple ideas of distance decay and market accessibility help explain the locational value of most spatial phenomena. In the case of sports facilities, for example, Veal (1987) has shown that distance, travel time and travel costs all constrain access, and it is certainly the case that much competitive sport is organized through local and regional leagues, ensuring that both teams and supporters do not have to travel far in relation to 'away' matches. In addition, Bale (2003: 85) has demonstrated the importance of central place concepts in the distribution of sports places such that those which are 'able to draw on a regional catchment are located further apart than those catering for a district catchment which, in turn, are sited at more distant intervals than those only able to draw on a local sphere of influence'. While these concepts are also relevant in explaining the distribution of many tourist resources and related patterns of travel, the overall situation has to be qualified, however, by the simple fact that, with tourism, not only is travel a requirement but it may also be a key motive. Ease of accessibility through minimizing distance travelled may not always be the over-riding concern. This is not to say that people necessarily wish to travel enormous distances, as travel statistics highlight the importance of tourist flows between neighbouring regions and countries (Pearce, 1995; Williams, 1998; Shaw and Williams, 2002). However, escaping from the home environment is certainly important, and for some the journey itself may be part of the attraction. Various studies have suggested the importance of escapism as a key motive for tourism (Leiper, 1984; Mannell and Iso-Ahola, 1987; Iso-Ahola, 1989; Reeves, 2000; Urry, 2002), and Weed and Bull (2004) have suggested that this would also be true of sports tourists, who are likely to enjoy enhanced experiences by pursuing their sport in a range of interesting and unusual places away from their home environment. Furthermore this is not a new phenomenon for, as Holt (1988) points out in relation to English football, 'for Northern fans who made up the great majority of spectators at professional football before 1914, the chance to go to London for a big game was the experience of a lifetime'.

Nevertheless, despite the importance of the travel element, most studies of sport tourism do highlight the significance of accessibility. The various case studies recently discussed by Weed and Bull (2004) all demonstrate the importance of accessibility: the location of sports training camps in the Mediterranean is clearly influenced by the relatively short flight times from the cities of northern Europe; the transport hub advantages of large towns and cities, where motorway networks and intercity train services converge and where international and regional airports are located, make them convenient locations for a variety of sporting events; the proximity of rural Wales to key population centres such as the West Midlands, Merseyside and Greater Manchester, the Bristol area and urban areas of South Wales provides substantial potential for short break activity holidays; and the fact that the European Alps provides the most developed area for skiing in the world is due to its proximity to substantial affluent populations. In relation to this last example, the proximity of the Alps has meant that a variety of travel options – road, rail and air – is available, and also the short travel times provide opportunities for weekend trips as well as longer stays. The influence of accessibility is illustrated in relation to the travel characteristics of United Kingdom skiers, with France, the most accessible location, dominating the market. France accounts for 36 per cent of all UK skiing holidays, followed by Austria (19 per cent) and Italy (14 per cent). While other factors have played a key role, such as purpose-built resorts with substantial accommodation geared to the mass market and the establishment of a large number of tour operators specializing in these resorts, the ease of access to the French resorts does attract independent holidaymakers who can travel by train or car, or fly cheaply with the low-cost carriers (Mintel, 2002). Accessibility is particularly important in relation to day and weekend skiers, and this is also the case for many North American resorts (Hudson, 2000).

A further important aspect in determining the quality and importance of sport tourism places is that of the presence of various facilities that allow visitors to stay in the destination and provide for their needs, such as accommodation, catering and entertainment facilities. The importance of cities as sport tourist destinations is partly due to their established importance for other forms of tourism, such that they can also provide accommodation, restaurants, bars, clubs and various forms of entertainment for the sports person beyond the immediate attractions of sport. Not only are cities able to accommodate travelling spectators, but part of the attraction of travelling away to watch sport may also include experiencing the nightlife and other facilities available to the mainstream tourist.

The unique environment of the modern ski resort provides a further example of a sport tourist destination that embraces more than simply the basic resource required for the sport itself. In addition to there being sufficient natural environment, ski resorts also require a collection of built features, such as ski lifts, ski schools, equipment shops, accommodation, restaurants, car parking and various leisure facilities to provide for après ski entertainment. Nevertheless, these facilities can vary in terms of both their levels of development and the quality of the accommodation offered. For example, Barker (1982, cited in Shaw and Williams, 2002) identified differences between the eastern and western Alpine resorts, with the former (having been developed at lower altitudes) being more integrated with the economic and cultural lives of the indigenous communities than the high altitude resorts of the western Alps, where more external capital and labour were involved. Some resorts have also developed a significant summer season based on warm-weather pursuits or developing means to transport tourists to high altitude skiing areas, and Shaw and Williams (2002: 236) have produced a continuum of skiing resorts based on these differences, ranging from those at the low-altitude end of the continuum with varied functions to those at high altitudes constituting distinct sport tourism places. The French resorts in particular have been developed for the mass market and, as Mintel (2002) points out, they have been mostly purpose-built and designed to provide a high level of convenience for the skier. However, convenience has been provided at the expense of ambience, and the French resorts tend to lack the Alpine charm of the more traditional resorts found in Austria and Switzerland (Mintel, 2002). French resorts also offer a wide range of accommodation, although much of it is provided in apartments rather than hotels, and the apartment blocks, built during the early development of the mass-market ski industry, are cramped and fall short of the expectations of today's tourists (Mintel, 2002) – a feature reminiscent of much apartment development in many coastal Mediterranean mass tourist resorts.

The provision of a complementary infrastructure has also been shown to be important for 'activity tourism', which includes a range of outdoor pursuits undertaken for physical pleasure (Mintel, 1999). Various different forms of facility and accommodation are involved, ranging from specialized centres run by local authorities, schools, and voluntary organizations, as well as the private sector, to small private concerns involving guest houses, farm-based accommodation, and caravan and camping sites. The unique characteristic of activity tourism is the specialist activity centre which, although specializing in particular activities, also offers opportunities for a much greater range of pursuits. According to Clark et al. (1994), such multi-activity centres provide a wide range of activities, the average number being eleven, with the four most common being rock climbing, orienteering, skiing and canoeing. Plas-Y-Brenin in North Wales, for example, which is run by the Mountain Training Trust on behalf of the Sports Council, boasts a training wall, an artificial ski slope and a canoe pool, and offers courses in rock climbing, summer mountaineering and hill walking, winter climbing and mountaineering, alpine skiing and mountaineering, mountaineering qualifications and awards, kayaking and canoeing, paddlesport qualifications, alpine paddling, and various courses relating to personal and professional development. In addition to providing courses, it also offers accommodation for those who wish to visit the area and make their own activity arrangements (Weed and Bull, 2004).

Multiple sport activity holiday centres, which have expanded in recent years, are not confined to upland environments. The club formula camps such as Club Med are situated in a variety of beautiful locations, many in coastal Mediterranean or sub-tropical areas. Club Med has 98 villages in 40 countries on five continents (Standeven and De Knop, 1999), and there are other similar club organizations. For example, 'Club La Santa in the Canary Islands markets itself as "The World's No 1 Sports Resort", offering what it describes as world-class facilities for over 20 sports' (Standeven and De Knop, 1999: 102). A further variant of this type of club centre that has been developed throughout Europe involves those that provide sport opportunities in year-round, weather-independent facilities (such as Center Parcs, Gran Dorado and Sun Clubs) (Standeven and De Knop, 1999: 102). Center Parcs was established in the Netherlands in 1967 for high-income customers who wanted a short-stay active holiday (Standeven and De Knop, 1999). It provides very comfortable, well-designed accommodation in villas set in wooded environments, and its signature feature is a large domed building that houses a landscaped tropical pool, plus play zones, restaurants, shops and spa, together with outdoor recreational activities ranging from archery to zip wires, rafting, raft-building, pony riding, inline skating and ice-skating. There are over a dozen such facilities in Western Europe, including four in Britain.

Political and economic resources

As is clear from the previous discussion, the built environment constitutes an important part of the sport tourism destination, even in so-called 'resource-based' environments. The development of both sports facilities and related infra-structure requires the investment of capital, and thus the quality of destinations will depend on the extent to which the private and/or public sector is willing to invest in such places. Traditionally, the state has been more willing to invest in sports facilities but less inclined to provide for tourism. However, given the importance of both sport and tourism in modern societies this position has been changing, and in recent times governments have been equally interested in develop-ing tourism – often in partnership with private enterprise – and sport tourism has been especially important. One of the principal locations for such investment has been the city. Cities exhibit a number of attractions for the development of sport tourism, especially in relation to spectator sports. Given their size and market influence, they inevitably possess high-quality facilities and stadia, established initially for their own residents and sports teams. However, domestic and subse-quent international competitions have encouraged substantial numbers of people to travel to cities either to support their teams or to experience the sporting spec-tacle. In addition, cities are increasingly hosting mega-sporting events, utilizing their existing facilities as well as creating new ones specifically for such purposes.

As Weed and Bull (2004) have highlighted, it is the larger cities that are particu-larly prominent, with their sports teams attracting greater potential support and subsequent income, which itself attracts financial investment from both local and external businesses, thus helping to maintain future success and support. This clear advantage of larger cities is further reinforced through the infrastructural and other peripheral facilities mentioned in the previous section that such urban centres possess. The large local catchments, transport foci and general tourist infrastructure also mean that large cities, and especially capital cities, are the logical locations for national stadia. Various sports have their respective national stadia in London, with Wembley (currently being rebuilt), Twickenham, Lords and Wimbledon being obvious examples, although other UK cities are also cap-able of hosting national and international events (e.g. the Millennium Stadium in Cardiff, Meadowbank in Edinburgh, and the Don Valley Stadium in Sheffield). More recently, however, cities have become even more important sport tourism destinations owing to two overlapping influences. The first involves a recognition of the importance of mega-events (including major sporting events) in the shap-ing of both the national tourism product and the long-term city product (Ritchie, 1984; Getz, 1991; Hall, 1992; Tyler et al., 1998), and the second is the way that sport in general has been utilized as part of tourism's role in urban regeneration.

Special sporting events have emerged as major tourism policy instruments for governments keen to boost local business as a result of visitor spending (Mules,

1998). Not only do they provide considerable revenue – according to Collins and Jackson (1999), the 1996 Atlanta Olympics generated £645 million – they are also seen as a means of changing the image of both the city and the state as a whole (Robertson and Guerrier, 1998). In fact, Weiler and Hall (1992: 1) argue that 'hallmark events are the image builders of modern tourism', while Waitt (1999) suggests that the Olympic Games as spectacle is the ultimate tourist attraction. Such events can enhance the status of smaller states, as in the Seoul Summer Olympic Games, and also non-capital cities, as in the Barcelona and Los Angeles Olympics, the Adelaide Grand Prix, the Calgary Winter Olympic Games or the Victoria (British Columbia) Commonwealth Games (Collins and Jackson, 1999). The Barcelona Olympic Games also helped Spain demonstrate an alternative tourism product to the mass tourism of the 'costas' (Robertson and Guerrier, 1998), and the city has subsequently become one of the top European tourism destinations, being ranked fifth in terms of visitor numbers in the late 1990s after London, Paris, Rome and Dublin (Wöber, 1997). More recent work by Waitt (2003: 112), who examined the social impacts of the Sydney Olympic Games, has also suggested that such impacts are positive and can 'generate patriotism and a sense of community or belonging, particularly among the young and ethnic minorities'. He believes that such 'global sporting events provide the opportunity for government and city authorities to (re)establish or increase the attachment and identification of people to place'. Whatever the overall benefits, there is intense competition amongst nations to host such prestigious events, and governments are willing to help finance bids and fund the building of stadia and related infrastructure, as well as sending delegations on 'charm offensives' in order to help secure them. Sport England invested £3.4 million in the bid for the 2006 FIFA World Cup, a decision that the government fully endorsed (DCMS, 2001).

Hallmark events are also part of sport tourism's wider role in helping urban regeneration. The idea of using tourism as a spur to urban economic and environmental regeneration originally came from North America, but has now been adopted in many towns and cities throughout the developed world (Law, 1992, 1993; Swarbrooke, 2000). Various dockland areas such as Liverpool and London are classic examples of this, influenced to a large extent by the success of similar developments in the city of Baltimore (Shaw and Williams, 2002). As in Baltimore, where Oriole Park Stadium was sited to anchor the south side of the city's waterfront regeneration scheme (Stevens and Wootton, 1997), sport has often played a prominent role in the regeneration of other cities. London Docklands now contains the Docklands Sailing Centre, Surrey Docks Water Sports Centre, and the London Wetbike Club, and has become an important tourist destination (see also Hall and Page, 2002). The 1992 Barcelona Olympic Games led to US$ 8300 million of public and private sector investment in the area, including a new airport, a ring road, and clearance of a derelict waterfront area for the construction of an Olympic village (Chalkley et al., 1992; Stevens, 1992). Furthermore, the Camp Nou Stadium, home of FC Barcelona, 'is one of the city's architectural marvels and the largest stadium in Europe with a capacity of 120,000' and provides 'a range of other facilities for the community, including a multi-purpose arena and ice rink' (Stevens and Wootton, 1997: 53).

Some cities have specifically marketed sport tourism as a central feature of their tourism-led regeneration. Manchester's failed bid for the 2000 Olympic Games acted as a catalyst for a 'vision' for change and expansion (Shaw and

Williams, 2002), creating investment and development opportunities and allowing linkages and partnerships to flourish. Sport has subsequently become a crucial part of a central marketing initiative involving its football teams, cricket, the new swimming and diving complex at the University, the Velodrome, and the Commonwealth Stadium, which hosted the Commonwealth Games in 2002. Birmingham also failed in bids for previous Olympics but, like Manchester, gained in civic reputation and sports facilities, which included an indoor arena with 20 000 seats, a 50-metre pool and a refurbished stadium (Collins and Jackson, 1999). Likewise, Glasgow and Sheffield have used sport as part of their regeneration attempts. Sheffield's city council invested £147 million in sport venues for the 1991 World Student Games (Bramwell, 1998), a project which was designed, amongst other things, to reorient the image of Sheffield from 'City of Steel' to 'City of Sport' (Dobson and Gratton, 1995; Dulac and Henry, 2001), a title subsequently awarded by the Sports Council (see Weed and Bull, 2004 for a summary of sport tourism in Sheffield).

Cultural and perceptual aspects

As various writers have pointed out, sport is a cultural form (e.g. Bourdieu, 1978; Hargreaves, 1982) and so too is tourism (e.g. MacCannell, 1976). As Standeven and De Knop (1999) argue, sport is a cultural experience of physical activity and tourism is a cultural experience of place. However, as well as defining these two different cultural experiences as separate spheres it must also be the case that the two are combined when the resources that people feel they need are not readily available in their immediate neighbourhood. This combining of different cultural experiences adds further complexity to the assessment of resource quality as it is linked to the way people evaluate and perceive resources generally. It can be argued that all resources are in one way or another cultural appraisals (Short, 1991; Everden, 1992; Simmons, 1994), and nowhere is this more true than with various environments used for sport (Bale, 1994, 2003). While many people can quite easily pursue their sport close to home, they often choose to travel elsewhere to participate in what might be regarded as a preferred environment. This is not because the standard of the facility itself is necessarily better elsewhere, but rather because of the ambience of the place – the climate may be better, the environment less polluted, less crowded or more peaceful, or the general landscape more scenically attractive – although for some spectators being part of a vociferous crowd may also be part of the attraction. An additional point is also provided by Urry (2002: 12) concerning the carrying out of familiar activities in unusual visual environments. He cites swimming and other sports which 'all have particular significance if they take place against a distinctive visual backcloth. The visual gaze renders extraordinary activities that otherwise would be mundane'. The example of cyclists preferring to cycle through rural rather than urban areas has already been mentioned, but another example is British golfers who might prefer to play golf in Southern Spain or the Algarve instead of, or in addition to, using courses at home. Of course the distinctive backdrop does not have to be rural; it could equally be an urban setting with a different cultural significance, examples being the various sporting 'Meccas' such as Lords Cricket Ground and Wimbledon in London, or the Yankee baseball stadium in New York, which attract visitors from far afield. An important aspect of this last point is that of fashion. In most sports there are particular places that are more fashionable than others. In certain instances their elevated status is due to their inherent qualities (the fastest slopes, the biggest waves, the longest footpaths, the largest stadia); in others it may be due to their historical legacy (e.g. the place where the sport first developed or where the organization which controls the sport is based) or to associations with fashion icons, style-setters or other celebrities who in some way have links with the destination.

In addition to the way people's own particular cultural experiences shape their perceptions of such destinations, they may also be influenced by marketers and those who wish to promote particular places. For example, Alpine ski resorts have clearly been socially constructed as mass tourist destinations – as recognizable places for the tourist gaze through various markers and signposts (Urry, 2002). According to Shaw and Williams (2002: 218), in the latter half of the twentieth century the tourist image creators promoted ski resorts along with seaside resorts and, to a lesser extent, rural idylls such as national parks, as the rightful objects of the tourist gaze. Although the Alps had originally been an area of summer tourism, related to the romantic tourist gaze through the attractions of climbing, walking and viewing the scenery, writers and other image creators subsequently re-imaged the Alps as a highly desirable winter tourist destination. The transformation of Newquay in Cornwall from a small fishing village into Britain's premier surfing destination has also involved the introduction of key markers and signposts, with its surf shops, surf schools and symbols from Australia's surfing environments, such as backpackers' accommodation and a 'Walkabout Inn Australasian Bar'.

The above discussion, as well as that in previous sections, has placed significant emphasis on the idea that places are special and unique. Nevertheless, while this uniqueness may be valid in many respects, some places that provide facilities for modern sport are very similar, with the sports landscape displaying 'increasing sameness' (Bale, 2003: 148). Two processes in particular seem to be influencing this trend. One is that of globalization and the ease with which international capital can be invested worldwide to produce indentikit stadia and other facilities. The second involves the increasing application of science and technology to sport and the need to reduce any influences from the natural environment that might have adverse effects on performance. Some sports, in fact, take place in such environments in order to coerce the athlete into 'continued repetition of the same precisely fixed and isolated narrow tasks' (Rigauer, 1981, quoted in Bale, 2003: 151). Thus, according to Bale (2003: 153), 'sport is reduced to theatrical spectacle' as a result of 'glassed-in suites, closed-circuit television, domed stadia and synthetic pitches which eliminate the chance elements of nature'.

The way in which sport tourists perceive and experience such environments is clearly contentious. For some, especially elite athletes, playing sport in environments that enhance performance will no doubt be attractive, whereas for others pitting their skills against the elements may be part of the attraction. Similarly with spectators, the 'safer', instantly recognizable environments may be preferable, and just as people travel to experience spectacle in other spheres, then it may be that this is the principal attraction for many sport tourists. Nevertheless, some have argued that the blandness of stadia, the more standardized experience of the crowd and the more divorced spectators become from the action of the sport in ever larger stadia may make it less attractive for some (Bale, 2003).

Conclusion

In attempting to analyse the resources of sport tourism destinations, this chapter has sought to focus on the various factors that influence the supply and quality of such places as well as the ways in which they are perceived. The great variety of sports activity together with the many different resource requirements means that it is difficult to provide simple resource classifications, although, as outlined in the initial section, some attempts based on relative location can provide a useful starting point to discuss such issues. Some sports clearly require (or at least prefer) the use of natural or semi-natural environments, but the presence of such resources is no guarantee that sport tourism will occur – the destination also needs to be accessible, developed, and perceived as suitable and attractive. As a result, those destinations that are most accessible to affluent markets and have attracted investment and suitable promotion are generally the most successful in attracting substantial numbers of sport tourists. While natural environments are clearly important for certain types of sport tourism, other sports are better catered for by the built environment, with cities being especially important. Large cities have particular advantages in terms of their accessibility and general tourist infrastructure, and the recent growth of mega-sports events and the importance of sport tourism for urban regeneration have further reinforced the importance of such destinations. While it is possible to identify a variety of places and resources that cater for sport tourism, this chapter has also highlighted the fact that certain destinations are particularly prominent, either because their tourism significance is primarily concerned with sport (such as skiing resorts or sports holiday camps) or because sport tourism forms a major part of the overall tourism product (as in certain upland areas or cities). Such places are not simply tourist destinations that provide opportunities for sporting activity, but can rightly be regarded as distinct sport tourism destinations.

Acknowledgement

Much of this chapter is derived from material previously published in Weed and Bull (2004).

References

Bale, J. (1994). *Landscapes of Modern Sport*. Leicester: Leicester University Press.

Bale, J. (2003). *Sports Geography* (2nd edn). London: Routledge.

Barker, M. L. (1982). Traditional landscape and mass tourism in the Alps. *Geographical Review*, 72, 395–415.

Boniface, B. and Cooper, C. (1994). *The Geography of Travel and Tourism*. Oxford: Butterworth-Heinemann.

Bourdieu, P. (1978). Sport and social class. *Social Science Information*, 18(6), 820–833.

Bramwell, B. (1998). Strategic planning before and after a mega-event. *Tourism Management*, 18(3), 167–176.

Burton, R. (1995). *Travel Geography*. London: Pitman Publishing.

Chalkley, B., Jones, A., Kent, M. and Sims, P. (1992). Barcelona: Olympic city. *Geography Review*, 6(1), 2–4.

Chubb, M. and Chubb, H. (1981). *One Third of our Time? An Introduction to Recreation Behaviour and Resources*. New York: Wiley.

Clark, G., Darrall, J., Grove-White, R., Macnaghten, P. and Urry, J. (1994). *Leisure Landscapes, Leisure Culture and the English Countryside: Challenges and Conflicts*. Lancaster: Centre for Environmental Change, Lancaster University/CPRE.

Clawson, M., Held, R. and Stoddard, C. (1960). *Land for the Future*. Baltimore, MD: Johns Hopkins Press.

Collins, M. F. and Jackson, G. A. M. (1999). The economic impact of sport and tourism. In J. Standeven and P. De Knop (eds), *Sport Tourism*. Champaign, IL: Human Kinetics, pp. 169–201.

Coppock, J. T. and Duffield, B. (1975). *Outdoor Recreation in the Countryside: A Spatial Analysis*. London: Macmillan.

Department of Culture, Media and Sport (2001). *Staging International Sporting Events*. Government Response to the Third Report from the Culture, Media and Sport Committee Session 2000–2001, presented to Parliament by the Secretary of Culture, Media and Sport By Command of Her Majesty, October 2001. London: DCMS.

Department of Regional Economic Expansion (1972). *The Canada Land Inventory: Land Capability Classification for Outdoor Recreation*, Report No 6. Ottawa: Queens Printer for Canada.

Dobson, N. and Gratton, C. (1995). From 'City of Steel' to 'City of Sport': An Evaluation of Sheffield's Attempts to Use Sport as a Vehicle for Urban Regeneration. Paper presented at the Recreation in the City conference, Staffordshire University, Stoke on Trent, Great Britain.

Dulac, C. and Henry, I. (2001). Sport and social regulation in the city: the cases of Grenoble and Sheffield. *Society and Leisure*, 24(1), 47–78.

Everden, N. (1992). *The Social Creation of Nature*. Baltimore, MD: Johns Hopkins Press.

Gammon, S. (2002). Fantasy, nostalgia and the pursuit of what never was. In S. Gammon and J. Kurtzman (eds), *Sport Tourism: Principles and Practice*. Eastbourne: LSA, pp. 61–71.

Getz, D. (1991). *Festivals, Special Events and Tourism*. New York: Van Nostrand Rheinhold.

Gibson, H. J. (1998). Sport tourism: a critical analysis of research. *Sport Management Review*, 1(1), 45–76.

Gibson, H. J. (2002). Sport tourism at a crossroad? Considerations for the future. In S. Gammon and J. Kurtzman (eds), *Sport Tourism: Principles and Practice*. Eastbourne: LSA, pp. 111–128.

Hall, C. M. (1992). *Hallmark Tourist Events: Impacts, Management and Planning*. London: Belhaven.

Hall, C. M. and Page, S. J. (2002). *The Geography of Tourism and Recreation: Environment, Place and Space* (2nd edn). London: Routledge.

Hargreaves, J. (1982). Sport, culture and ideology. In J. Hargreaves (ed.), *Sport, Culture and Ideology*. London: Routledge and Kegan Paul, pp. 32–61.

Haywood, L., Kew, F. C., Bramham, P., Spink, J., Capenerhurst, J. and Henry, I. P. (1995). *Understanding Leisure* (2nd edn). Cheltenham: Stanley Thornes.

Henry, I. P. (2001). *The Politics of Leisure Policy* (2nd edn). London: Palgrave.

Holt, R. (1989). *Sport and the British: A Modern History*. Oxford: Oxford University Press.

Hudson, S. (2000). *Snow Business*. London: Cassell.

Iso-Ahola, S. E. (1989). Motivation for leisure. In E. L. Jackson and T. L. Burton (eds), *Understanding Leisure and Recreation: Shaping the Past, Charting the Future*. State College, PA: Venture Publishing, pp. 247–279.

Kreutzwiser, R. (1989). Supply (outdoor recreation). In G. Wall (ed.), *Outdoor Recreation in Canada*. Toronto: J. Wiley and Sons, pp. 21–41.

Law, C. M. (1992). Urban tourism and its contribution to economic regeneration. *Urban Studies*, 29, 599–618.

Law, C. M. (1993). *Urban Tourism, Attracting Visitors to Large Cities*. London: Mansell.

Law, S. (1967). Planning for outdoor recreation. *Journal of the Town Planning Institute*, 53, 383–386.

Leiper, N. (1984). Tourism and leisure: the significance of tourism in the leisure spectrum. *Proceedings of the 12th New Zealand Geography Conference*. Christchurch: New Zealand Geography Society.

MacCannell, D. (1976). *The Tourist*. London: Macmillan.

Mannell, R. and Iso-Ahola, S. E. (1987). Psychological nature of leisure and tourism experience. *Annals of Tourism Research*, 14(3), 314–331.

Mintel (1999) *Leisure Intelligence: Activity Holidays*. London: Mintel

Mintel (2002). *Leisure Intelligence: Snowsports*. London: Mintel.

Mules, T. (1998). Events tourism and economic development in Australia. In D. Tyler, Y. Guerrier and M. Robertson (eds). *Managing Tourism in Cities: Policy, Process and Practice*. Chichester: John Wiley & Sons, pp. 195–214.

Outdoor Recreation Resources Review Commission (1962). *Outdoor Recreation for America*, Washington DC: Government Printing Office.

Page, S. (1990). The role of sport tourism: arena development and urban regeneration in the London Docklands. *The Geographer*, 8(4), 18–25.

Pearce, D. G. (1995). *Tourism Today: A Geographical Analysis* (2nd edn). Harlow: Longman.

Pigram, J. (1983). *Outdoor Recreation and Resource Management*. Beckenham: Croom Helm.

Reeves, M. R. (2000). *Evidencing the Sport – Tourism Interrelationship*. Loughborough University: Unpublished PhD Thesis.

Rigauer, B. (1981). *Sport and Work*. New York: Columbia University Press.

Ritchie, J. R. B. (1984). Assessing the impact of hallmark events: conceptual and research issues. *Journal of Travel Research*, 23(1), 2–11.

Robertson, M. and Guerrier, Y. (1998). Events as entrepreneurial displays: Seville, Barcelona and Madrid. In D. Tyler, Y. Guerrier and M. Robertson (eds), *Managing Tourism in Cities: Policy, Process and Practice*. Chichester: John Wiley & Sons, pp. 215–228.

Shaw, G. and Williams, A. M. (2002). *Critical Issues in Tourism: A Geographical Perspective*, 2nd edn. Oxford: Blackwell.

Short, J. R. (1991). *Imagined Country: Society, Culture and Environment*. London: Routledge.

Simmons, I. G. (1994). *Interpreting Nature: Cultural Constructions of the Environment*. London: Routledge.

Smith, S. L. J. (1983). *Recreation Geography*. Harlow: Longman.

Standeven, J. and De Knop, P. (1999). *Sport Tourism*. Champaign, IL: Human Kinetics.

Stevens, T. (1992). Barcelona: the Olympic city. *Leisure Management*, 12(6), 26–30.

Stevens, T. and Wootton, G. (1997). Sports stadia and arena: realizing their full potential. *Tourism Recreation Research*, 22(2), 49–56.

Swarbrooke, J. (2000). Tourism, economic development and urban regeneration: a critical evaluation. In M. Robinson *et al.* (eds), *Reflections on International Tourism: Developments in Urban and Rural Tourism*. Sunderland: Centre for Travel and Tourism, pp. 269–285.

Tyler, D., Guerrier, Y. and Robertson, M. (eds) (1998). *Managing Tourism in Cities: Policy, Process and Practice*. Chichester: John Wiley & Sons.

Urry, J. (2002). *The Tourist Gaze* (2nd edn). London: Sage.

Veal, A. J. (1987). *Using Sports Centres*. London: Sports Council.

Waitt, G. (1999). Playing games with Sydney: marketing Sydney for the 2000 Olympics. *Urban Studies*, 36, 1055–1077.

Waitt, G. (2003). Social impacts of the Sydney Olympics. *Annals of Tourism Research*, 30(1), 194–215.

Weed, M. and Bull, C. (2004). *Sports Tourism: Participants, Policy and Providers*. Oxford: Elsevier Butterworth-Heinemann.

Weiler, B. and Hall, C. M. (eds) (1992). *Special Interest Tourism*. London: Belhaven.

Williams, S. (1998). *Tourism Geography*. London: Routledge.

Wöber, K. (1997). International city tourism flows. In J. A. Mazanec (ed.), *International City Tourism*. London: Pinter, pp. 39–53.

4

Sport tourism markets

Lisa Delpy Neirotti

Introduction

The study of sport tourism destinations reveals a
vast number of specialized markets to explore. A
frequently used definition of sport tourism is travel
to play sports (active sport tourism), travel to watch
sports (event sport tourism), and travel to visit or
venerate famous sports-related attractions (nostalgia sport tourism) (Delpy, 1998; Gibson, 1999). The
Sports Tourism International Council segments
sport tourism into resorts, participation activities,
cruising, events and tours. The most common market
researched in the literature is event sport tourism.
Various sport tourism markets, including event
sport tourism, outdoor and adventure travel, health
spa tourism, educational travel, cultural heritage and
competitive sport travel, exist as sub-sets of the two
major fields of tourism demand; leisure travel and
business travel. This chapter gives consideration to
these distinct sport tourism markets.

Leisure travel

Leisure travel is defined as any discretionary travel
undertaken with the intent of satisfying one or more
leisure-related need(s) (Harris and Howard, 1996).
The Travel Industry of America Association (TIA)
further defines leisure travel as 'any trip where the

primary purpose of the trip is given as visit friends or relatives, outdoor recreation, entertainment, or personal' (TIA, 2003). For some sport tourism markets, specifically youth and adult sport travel and incentive travel, it is debatable which tourism category, leisure or business, it should be located in. Incentive travel, for example, is a way to reward employees or customers through a leisure travel experience. This demonstrates the merging of interests in business and leisure travel.

Event sport tourism

Whether on a tour or travelling independently, fans will find a way to attend a sport event to support and affiliate with their team (Case study 4.1). For the 2003 World Cricket competition in South Africa the total number of visitors was approximately 30 000; Indian cricket fans accounted for approximately 10 000 of these, Australians for 3000 and Pakistanis for 1000 (*Economic Times*, 2003). Another type of affinity travel is where travellers visit a destination to feel as though they are a part of the sport. Over 50 000 people tour Madison Square Garden (New York) per year.

There are sport tour operators in the USA that specialize in a specific sport such as football, soccer, tennis, motor racing or baseball, others that offer packages to major sports events such as the Olympic Games, Super Bowl and the Masters golf tournament, and a few larger companies that offer packages for almost every sport and event. A total of 166 companies, or 26.9 per cent of the National Tour Association's tour operator membership, provides spectator sports tours. The larger sport tour operators in the USA gross $US 6–10 million per year, while the single sport operators generally gross $US 500 000–$US 1 million per year. Packages range from tickets and hospitality only, for $US 500, to charter air transportation, housing, tickets, hospitality, transfers and a special VIP event such as a visit to the team locker room, crew pit, or drinks with a coach or player, for $US 7500.

Case study 4.1 Motor sport destinations in the USA

With over 75 million NASCAR fans, there is an opportunity for specialized tour operators such as 'Choice Racing' and 'There and Back Again'. Although the majority of fans who attend races camp on-site, there is a significant number of older fans (late 30s to mid-40s) with more disposable income (over $US 50 000 per year) who are looking for a more comfortable alternative. Corporations are also looking at these packages for incentive programmes and bonuses. Two examples of corporate clients for Choice Racing include Dairy Queen in Kentucky, and the Bank of North Dakota.

Choice Racing was actually purchased by a Carlson Wagonlit Travel Agency in Pittsburgh, Pennsylvania, to help counter the decline of corporate and leisure travel after 11 September 2001. Thus far the strategy has worked, with earnings of $US 300 000 per year just on race business (D. Underwood, President of Choice Racing: personal communication, 15 December 2003). There and Back Again is one of the more established companies in the motor sports tours area. It has been in business since 1988 and runs tours to 28 races, whereas many others only offer tours to some of the larger races. The two most popular races for Choice Racing are the Las Vegas race and the Bristol, Tennessee race. Interestingly, each of these races attracts a different type of clientele. For the Las Vegas race, the majority of travellers are new NASCAR fans looking to experience a NASCAR event but also to enjoy Las Vegas. Those who travel to Bristol, however, are the more traditional race-car fans, not looking for anything more than good racing. The demographics skew higher with the new race fans versus traditional race fans. The average price of a basic package of two nights in a hotel, race tickets and transfer is $US 550. Thirty per cent of Choice's clients select the upgraded package, adding pit passes, an opportunity to mingle with racers in a hospitality tent and other amenities, increasing the cost to $US 1000 per package. Hospitality-only packages run from $US 195–250, excluding hotel. Of those fans who travel to races, most attend at least two races per year. Since North Carolina is considered the hub of NASCAR, with 50 teams, it sees an influx of visitors who not only travel to attend events held at Lowe's Motor Speedway or one of the other 32 ovals and 18 drag strips located in North Carolina, but also to visit the cluster of team race shops, the 13 race-related museums and the souvenir stores (E. McClain, Executive Director North Carolina Motor Sports Association: personal communication, 10 December 2003). Based on a study conducted by University of North Carolina–Charlotte economist John Connaughton (Spanberg, 2003), out-of-town NASCAR fans generate approximately $US 200 million a year. More than 90 per cent of the fans attending the two Winston Cup (now Nextel Cup) races held at the Lowe's Motor Speedway come from at least 75 miles away. The two races are scheduled 1 week apart, which encourages fans to spend more than a weekend in town. Many stay a week or longer.

In North Carolina, NASCAR-related business is one of the largest contributors to the state's economy. As legendary driver Richard Petty frames the discussion, 'the state's traditional economic engines of tobacco and textiles are gone or going. Racing is here and is still growing' (Spanberg, 2003). A study is currently being conducted to determine the exact impact of motor sports on the state's economy.

Indianapolis is the third area that is impacted by motor sports, specifically open-wheel racing, with Champion Auto Racing Teams (CART) and Indy Racing League (IRL) located in Indianapolis along with the Indianapolis Speedway and a number of auto-related businesses. The three races held at the Indianapolis Speedway (Indianapolis 500, Brickyard 400 and the F1 race) add $US 727 million of economic activity to the Central Indiana economy each year (Rosentraub, 2000). The Speedway events have more impact than three National Football League Super Bowls, and this impact occurs every year in Indianapolis. Some of the assumptions made in calculating just the impact of the F1 event ($US 170.8 million) are that 200 000 people attend the event; approximately 63 per cent of spectators will be out of town visitors, and these visitors will spend $US 35 per day on food and beverages; $US 50 on all retail purchases (including souvenirs, local transport and gasoline), and $US 101.97 per night for lodging plus the cost of tickets at $US 85 each. These figures are based on data from previous events.

Motor racing teams such as NASCAR also have an extensive travel budget. Typically each team has two crews, the race-track crew or pit crew, and the road crew. Each crew consists of approximately eight people. In addition, there is the driver, owner, marketing manager and others that attend races. Based on figures received from Dale Earnhardt's racing team and other motor sports teams, approximately $US 4000–5000 is spent on hotels per race weekend, another $US 900 is spent on car rental, and if teams do not own their own plane they charter one at a cost of $US 650 per seat for 20 passengers – equating to another $US 13 000. In order to move the car from race to race most professional teams own their own million-dollar trailer/bus, often referred to as a 'totter home', but they must pay for a driver and fuel. Costs related to food and entertainment differ per team. Some have gourmet chefs cooking food for the team and catering expenses of $US 7000 per weekend (L. Miller: personal communication, 13 August 2003).

In total, one race team might spend $US 20 000 on travel expenses per race weekend – and this does not include the cost of purchasing the million-dollar trailer or bus and the aircraft that the team may own. If 43 teams compete in each of the 40 Nextel 2004 cup events and spend $US 20 000 per race weekend, this equates to $US 34 400 000 per season on NASCAR race-team travel spending. In addition, there are 34 races in the Busch Series and 25 races in the Craftsman Truck Series.

Cultural heritage tourism

Sport is a universal language, and athletes are revered worldwide. This is why sport halls of fame and museums are such popular tourist attractions. In 2002, 348 906 people visited the Baseball Hall of Fame and Museum in Cooperstown, New York. The Basketball Hall of Fame is expected to have 300 000 visitors in 2003, its first year in a new facility. The old museum received approximately 100 000 visitors annually. In one decade, the International Olympic Museum in Lausanne, Switzerland celebrated its two-millionth visitor. This represents an average of 200 000 visitors per year from throughout the world. Although the majority of visitors in 2002 came from Europe (81.9 per cent, of which two-thirds were from Switzerland), 5.5 per cent visited from Asia and 5.3 per cent from the USA.

Fantasy camps

Fantasy sport camps provide an opportunity for adults to train with their favourite sport stars, with the coach of a popular team and/or at a famous sport venue. Based on an Internet search, over 200 fantasy sport camps were identified. Most limit the number of participants to 50 or less, except for some baseball camps. Almost every major league baseball (MLB) team offers a fantasy camp. The price per person ranges from $US 250 for a minor league baseball fantasy camp to $US 15 000 for the Michael Jordan Flight School, which is sold out a year in advance (Feinstein, 2003). Using a conservative mean of $US 1500 per fantasy camper, the economic impact of fantasy camps in the USA is approximately $US 15 million. Most participants are Caucasian males between their early 30s and mid-60s with high incomes of over $US 75 000 (Feinstein, 2003). Honorary coaching positions are available for those who may have the physical capacity to play.

Sport cruising

In the past a cruise has commonly been associated with pure leisure and relaxation, but this is increasingly not the case. Most ships have designated decks for jogging and power walking, and many ships have created fitness programmes that let passengers put some fun into their exercise regimens by earning rewards. Holland America Line's Passport to Fitness programme, for example, designates various daily activities – both individual and staff led – and stamps the passenger's booklet for each accomplishment. Even the health club facilities are designed in an ingenious way to keep workouts from being boring by providing spectacular views both above and below the water. Also, more and more cruise lines are installing virtual bikes and stairmasters that give the illusion of negotiating a mountain path, travelling along a snowy landscape or the like. A number of ships now have water sports platforms with a stock of banana boats, water skiing equipment, sailboards and similar aquatic toys. Princess Cruises is the first to offer passengers an opportunity to become certified scuba divers during a cruise. Some cruises offer a golf academy at sea, with a PGA instructor on board who runs clinics and seminars and then accompanies groups while they play on shore. Others market special sport celebrity cruises where a professional athlete, coach or sport journalist is on board to offer entertaining discussions.

The roster of sport-related shipboard activities keeps expanding on the latest generation of cruise ships. Some of the sport activities include a nine-hole, par 36 golf course, an 18-hole miniature golf course, a lifesize golf simulator where players can tee off on some of the great courses of the world, skating (both ice and in-line), rock-climbing walls, and regulation-size sports courts for basketball, volleyball and tennis. These sports activities cater for a specific market. Cruise passengers tend to be mature (median age of 52 years), have higher household incomes ($US 57 000+) and have higher levels of educational attainment (56 per cent college graduates and 24 per cent postgraduates). Cruisers are also more likely to be married (78 per cent) and retired (37 per cent) (Cruise Lines International Association, 2003).

Outdoor and adventure travel

Adventure travel is becoming big business as more and more people find a better balance between work and recreation, and learn to appreciate a healthy environment and the great outdoors. Over $US 115 billion is spent on adventure travel annually in the USA, with another $US 125 billion spent on outdoor recreational equipment. There are currently 8500 tour operators in the USA offering various adventure trips, with women booking 65 per cent of all adventure travel. A growing trend is for grandparents to take grandchildren on adventure trips (Mallet, 2002). Women-only adventure sport travel groups are growing in popularity, especially for skiing, sailing, mountain and rock climbing, and white water rapids. Woodswomen Adventure trips has seen a triple-digit increase in participants.

Other adventure trips, such as cattle drives, Alaskan fishing trips and hang gliding are more appealing to men. The Specialty Travel Index is an excellent resource for affinity sport and adventure trips (www.specialtytravel.com). According to the Association of British Travel Agents, active holidays (those that include cycling, skiing and water sports) now make up 8 per cent of package holidays (Browne, 2004). During 2002, nearly one-quarter (22 per cent) of Americans aged 16 years and older took a vacation for the primary purpose of experiencing an outdoor adventure or adventurous activity (Leisure Trends Group, 2003). This was up 22.2 per cent from 2001 levels, possibly reflecting a renewed interest in and willingness to travel following the events of 2001. The top five activities that motivated Americans to take an adventure/outdoor vacation were hiking (12.8 per cent, or 6.1 million Americans), golf (12.8 per cent, 6.1 million), fishing (11.1 per cent, 5.3 million), camping (10.9 per cent, 5.2 million) and swimming (10.6 per cent, 5.1 million). Other activities that encouraged travel included walking, skiing/snowboarding, hunting, biking, rafting, scuba diving, kayaking, running/jogging, rock climbing and mountain climbing. According to the Adventure Travel Society, adventure travellers are evenly split between male and females, earn over $US 30 000 annually, and range from 25 to 80 years old.

Scuba diving is one example of a sport that motivates significant domestic and outbound international travel flows from the USA (Figure 4.1). Within the USA, where 63.4 per cent of all dives by Americans take place, Florida (43.9 per cent) and California (26.8 per cent) are the areas that are most visited, but other states – including New York (10.7 per cent) and Texas (8.8 per cent) – are also visited by divers. International dive trips by Americans take place in the Caribbean/Atlantic regions (53.5 per cent), Western/South Pacific (27.4 per cent), Eastern Pacific (11.7 per cent), Red Sea/Mediterranean (4.3 per cent) and Indian Ocean (1.5 per cent). Among the one-quarter of divers who have been to the Western/South Pacific region for diving, Hawaii (54.5 per cent), Australia (26.1 per cent), Guam (15.9 per cent), and the Philippines (14.8 per cent) are the most favoured destinations (Leisure Trends, 2002).

Health spa tourism

Throughout history people have travelled great distances in search of rejuvenation and curative powers of certain waters and treatments (Spivack, 1998). According to a 2002 report conducted by Pricewaterhouse Coopers for the International Spa Association (ISPA), the United States spa industry had larger revenues, $US 10.7 billion, than amusement/theme parks and box office gross receipts in 2001. This represents a 114 per cent growth between 1999 and 2001.

There were nearly 156 million spa visits in the USA in 2001, with day spas accounting for 68 per cent (106.2 million) of these visits. Resort/hotel and club spas received the next largest numbers of spa visits. One reason stated for the

Hiking	12.8%	6.1 million Americans 16 and older
Golf	12.8%	6.1 million
Fishing	11.1%	5.3 million
Camping	10.9%	5.2 million
Swimming	10.6%	5.1 million
Walking	6.0%	2.9 million
Skiing/snowboarding	5.5%	2.6 million
Hunting	4.9%	2.3 million
Biking	3.1%	1.5 million
Rafting	2.1%	1.0 million
Scuba diving	2.0%	957 thousand
Kayaking	1.9%	909 thousand
Running/jogging	1.8%	861 thousand
Rock climbing	1.8%	861 thousand
Mountain climbing	0.7%	335 thousand

Figure 4.1 Activities that motivated Americans to travel (LeisureTRAK®; Leisure Trends Group, 2002)

dramatic increase is that people are no longer seeing spas as 'pampering', but as a necessity in order to stay healthy. The study further states that consumers have limited free time to spend at the spa and are looking for simplicity in their spa experience, thus there is a refocus on the basics (Pricewaterhouse Coopers, 2002). Furthermore, an increasing number of corporations now embrace the spa industry and promote health and fitness programmes to their employees as incentives. Meetings and incentives planners are also booking board meetings and entire conferences around the spa experience (Sabene, 2001). The ISPA 2001 Spa User Study identifies that the majority of spa users are married with no children under the age of 18 living in the household; college graduates or higher; and employed full-time.

The average age of day spa users is 41 years, of resort/hotel spa users is 44 years and of destination spa users is 45 years. The average annual household income of day spa users is $US 96 000, of resort/hotel spa users is $US 122 000 and of destination spa users is $US 125 000. Over 75 per cent of all spa users expect to return to a spa the following year, and when selecting a spa consider the type of spa treatments and atmosphere of the spa more than personal growth classes and activities (Cox Consulting, 2002).

Resort destinations contesting sport tourism markets

The use of sports to attract specific tourist markets has expanded considerably in recent years. The Tourism Authority of Thailand (TAT) actively promotes both diving and golf as part of the tourism product. Thailand attracts approximately 40 000 international diving tourists per year, and golf tourism accounts for about 5 per cent of Thailand's overall tourist arrivals. According to TAT, in 1999 the average golf tourist spent $US 162 per day, and visitors from Asia stayed 1 week while visitors from the West spent 2 weeks (Xinhua News Agency, 1999). Specific resort destinations around the world are also using sport not only to develop a niche but also to market themselves (Case study 4.2). Resorts have become increasingly aware of the need to provide top-of-the-line facilities for the active sport tourist, and thus have become Meccas for the active sport tourist (Gibson, 1998). The popular New Zealand resort of Queenstown uses the combination of adventure sports and skiing to position itself for success all year round. The resort's infrastructure is in place and positioned to support these activities. This focus builds on itself, marketing the resort through its sports.

Club La Santa, located in the Canary Islands, is marketed as the world's leading sport and leisure resort. This all-year resort attracts a wide range of visitors, from elite athletes and teams from a mix of sports to the casual guest seeking leisurely sport and recreational activity. The resort uses special sports promotions like Sport Week to market itself. 'During periods of low demand, leading figures, often World or Olympic champions in particular events, are encouraged to hold training weeks. These events attract large numbers of participants and are deliberately scheduled at times when demand is normally low' (Thwaites, 1999: 500). In exchange for free accommodation the star athletes coach and advise guests, resulting in a win–win situation for all parties involved. Club La Santa also hosts a number of internationally recognized sport events, such as the Volcano Triathlon, to boost attendance during off-peak times. These events provide Club La Santa with important publicity opportunities, as journalists attend the events and then provide coverage of the events in sports-related media that reach the resort's targeted audience.

Case study 4.2 The Bitter End Yacht Club, Virgin Gorda, British Virgin Islands

The Bitter End Yacht Club (BEYC) sails full sheets to the wind with its sport marketing tack. The resort is located on the island of Virgin Gorda in the British Virgin Islands, and attracts sailors, adventure travellers, divers, honeymooners and families alike. This 85-room family-owned and operated resort boasts the largest complimentary club fleet in the world (Donlan, 1998). In addition to the sailing and motor-boating opportunities, the water sports programme includes windsurfing, snorkelling, scuba diving and sea kayaking. There are hiking trails on the property with breathtaking views, as well as tennis or shuffleboard courts. According to John Glynn, the Director of Special Events and Public Relations, the resort has used water sports to develop its niche and position itself through sports and sport events with water sports enthusiasts. Glynn commented that 'Bitter End Yacht Club is a boating and sailing resort combined with other water sports. It's our raison d'etre'.

When planning resort activities, BEYC has taken into consideration the:

> ... three types of active sport vacations: the pure sport holiday, where
> the primary purpose is to take part in sports such as skiing or golf;
> the vacation in which sport is not the primary purpose but individuals
> make use of the sports facilities in their vacation locale; and the private
> sporting holiday, where people take part in informal 'pick-up' games
> such as beach volleyball. (Gibson, 1999: 36)

The water sports programme is designed with competition elements (regattas), instructional elements (sailing school) and social and leisure elements (evening sails on a 48-foot catamaran). BEYC's sailing school is world-renowned, and 'graduates more than 3000 eager novice sailors a year' (Bishop, 2002: 35).

The primary marketing of the resort is accomplished through its sports events. The resort hosts more than five major regattas a year, along with other sport events. These special events generate considerable public relations for the resort. Journalists attend these events and provide BEYC with publicity in a number of magazines and other publications, such as Condé Nast Traveler and Travel and Leisure. With this amount of publicity directed at BEYC's targeted audience, it is not surprising that the resort uses very little paid advertising. This public relations creates a spin-off effect where a potential guest hears about the event and maybe can't attend that week but is impressed with the information on the event and books a later week at the resort.

With 2000 resorts of 10 rooms or more in the Caribbean there is a lot of competition, and these sport events set BEYC apart from its competition. The events have different purposes and are aimed at different targeted audiences for the resort. The annual Pro Am Regatta provides sailing enthusiasts with the chance to sail with and compete against America's Cup winners, Olympic gold medallists and other world-renowned champions of the sailing world. This regatta is the only event of its type in the world, and combines racing with information sessions, an awards party and other social events.

An event of a more instructional nature is the 12th Annual Dry Creek Vineyard Women's Sailing Week. 'The annual event, designed to teach determined beginners how to sail and help experienced sailors hone their skills, is the ultimate women's getaway' (Matte, 2003: 71). Two of the world's top sailors instruct and run the activities. Daily activities include fitness programmes; lectures, slide presentations and of course sailing instruction; cocktail receptions; and food and fun that takes a girls' night out to a new level. The Flotilla Sailing Week is yet another sport instruction-based promotion where big boat cruising and navigation is taught by cruising expert Doug Logan. The flotilla mixes learning with fun as guests sail and visit legendary sites around the British Virgin Islands.

BEYC is careful to include family events in its sports mix with Thanksgiving Sail Caribbean Week. During the week, Sail Caribbean, the famous sailing programme for children and young adults, offers instruction on a number of sail boat, motorboat and safety topics. The instruction ends with families competing together in the Turkey Day Regatta, followed by the BEYC Thanksgiving Day Feast. The emphasis here is:

> ...the family that plays together stays together. Additionally, there are events that appeal to other water sports enthusiasts like the 2nd Annual Thanksgiving Game Fish Challenge and windsurfing competitions and scuba diving photo contests. Other regattas include Nation's Cup Challenge, Spring Regatta and Sailing Festival and the Bucket Regatta for mega yachts of over 100.

BEYC has events all year round to attract guests and build relationships with them so they will return to BEYC and market the resort through word-of-mouth.

Business travel

The definition of business travel is trips and visits made by employees and others in the course of their work, including attending meetings, conferences and exhibitions (Medik, 2003). Others add that business travel is required or obligated travel as part of employment or position (V. Lucian, Owner/Chairman of Worldtek Travel: personal communication, 2003). Sport marketing agencies such as SFX and IMG spend approximately 8–10 per cent of business expenses on travel, or approximately $US 25 000 per year per non-clerical employee. There is a number of different sport tourism markets that may be examined under the category of business travel. These include professional sport team travel, educational travel, sport management and marketing agency travel, and sport organizations. Also included is adult and youth travel, considering that athletes who are part of a team sign up knowing that they will be expected to participate in both local and away competitions. Other areas that could be included, but are not studied in this chapter, are sport sponsor travel and sport media travel.

Sport organizations

In each country there is a number of National Sport Federations (NSF) that are responsible for preparing and sending athletes to compete at regional, national and world competitions. In the USA there is a total of 47 NSFs or National Governing Bodies (NGB), such as US Swimming, USA Track and Field and US Soccer, recognized by the United States Olympic Committee. Based on the responses of 10 NGBs in the USA, the average travel expenditure per NGB is $US 856 047, with a range from $US 45 000 to $US 2 million and a median of $US 272 680. Travel expenditures include travel for competition as well as for business. Utilizing the mean average, the total travel expenditures for all United States NGBs is approximately $US 40 234 209.

For International Federations recognized by the General Association of International Sports Federations (GAISF), the mean travel expenditure is approximately $US 350 000. This is primarily for business purposes, as IFs do not necessarily send teams to compete. With 99 IFs, the total estimated travel impact is approximately $US 34 650 000. The annual travel expenditures of the United States Olympic Committee, averaged over the three years 2000–2002 inclusive, is $US 8 904 909 – or approximately 7 per cent of functional expenses. This includes travel for competition (sending athletes to international competitions), management and fundraising. Olympic Solidarity, a programme under the International Olympic Committee, has a budget of $US 209 484 000. Since the majority of the programmes sponsored by Olympic Solidarity involve sending athletics, coaches and administrators to training camps, courses and competitions, a good portion of this budget is spent on travel.

The National Collegiate Athletic Association (NCAA) spent $US 34.1 million on travel for the fiscal year 2002–2003 season (approx. $US 28 million on championships and $US 6.1 million on staff/committee travel). This is up from $US 33.4 million in 1999. Travel expenditure per university will be discussed later in this chapter.

Sport team and individual travel

Professional market
The *Sports Business Journal* (Broughton, 2002) reports that the teams in the big four professional leagues in the USA (National Football League, Major League Baseball, National Basketball Association and National Hockey League) spend $US 335.4 million per annum on travel. There are 30 MLB teams, 32 NFL teams, 29 NBA teams and 30 NHL teams (121 teams in total). The majority of NBA teams own or charter their own planes. For other sports, depending on the proximity of their opponent, some teams will travel by bus or train. Each team hires a travelling secretary or manager to handle the travel negotiations and arrangements. The minor league teams account for $US 113.4 million worth of travel, and most of their travel is via bus. PGA tour players spend approximately $US 3 million on travel to tournaments, and LPGA players approximately $US 1.5 million. Each professional tennis tournament spends over $US 500 000 on hotel expenses for players, coaches and officials (Delpy Neirotti, 2004). A popular trend now is for top tier athletes to lease private jets for travel to events.

Collegiate market
There are currently 607 universities competing in the National Association of Collegiate Athletics (NCAA) Divisions I and II in the USA. Based on a 2001 NCAA financial report, the total amounts spent on travel were as follows: Division 1-A $US 213 525 000; Division 1-AA $US 77 077 000; Division 1-AAA

$US 44 528 000; Division II with a football programme $US 30 955 000; and Division II without football $US 19 456 000. These collectively total $US 385 541 000. For Division I-A, the average travel budget was $US 1 825 000. Approximately $US 500 000–750 000 of this was spent on accommodation, $US 1 million on air transportation (including charter flights for football teams) and the rest for meals. When broken down by sport programmes, the average for all divisions was 56 per cent for men's sports, 41 per cent for women's sports and 3 per cent for administrative and non-gender sports.

In addition, there are 427 universities competing in NCAA Division III plus 300 universities competing under the National Association of Intercollegiate Athletics (NAIA), an alternative governing body for collegiate athletics, and 530 Junior Colleges competing under the National Junior College Athletic Association (NJCAA). Teams competing at these levels also travel, although not to the same extent as NCAA Division I and II teams. They may stay in less expensive accommodation, and travel for shorter distances and less frequently. These schools spend approximately $US 100 million on sports competitions.

Youth market

There are over 38 million youths that participate in some type of competitive sports programme in the USA. If only 10 per cent of these travel to just one sport event per year at an average expenditure of $US 100 per athlete, this equates to $US 380 000 000. The Amateur Sports Travel Group estimates that, on average, travelling teams spend six weekends per year on the road, booking 15 rooms per weekend at $US 50–70 each (G. Henderson, President, Custom Business Solutions: personal communication, 15 December 2003). Although the United States Youth Soccer Association says it keeps no official records on 'travel' teams, it estimates that there are 50 000 travel teams nationwide. They also estimate that the average number of trips is two to three per year (US Youth Soccer Association: personal communication, 12 November 2003). The Maryland Soccer Federation does keep statistics, and states that travel teams represent 40 per cent of all teams, with each taking four to six trips per year and spending between $100 and $300 per person per trip (T. Heffelfinger: personal communication, 10 November 2003).

One example of a youth sport event is the Disney Soccer Showcase. This event is a three-night tournament attracting 300 teams. Each team typically books approximately 12–15 rooms, resulting in a total of about 10 000 room nights. The youth sport event that generates the most economic return is a 10-year-old girls' event. Parents are more likely to accompany young female athletes on sport trips and bring their siblings as well. The older the athlete, the less likely that guests will join them. Overall, the travel party that accompanies male athletes is consistently smaller (J. Anthony, CEO Anthony Travel: personal communication, 10 December 2003).

From an event standpoint, it is not always the high-profile events that provide the greatest opportunity for local communities. In the USA, industry representatives concur that youth soccer and baseball and adult softball tournaments generate more real economic impact than professional sports events. Higham (1999) explains that small-scale sports events usually operate within existing infrastructure constraints, require minimal investments of public funds, and are more manageable in terms of crowding and congestion compared to many hallmark events.

Adult market

Based on the Travel Industry Association of America (TIA) *Profile of Travelers Who Attend Sports Events* (TIA, 1999), 11.9 million adults in the USA participated in a sport event that they travelled over 50 miles (80 km) to attend. This represents 16 per cent of all those who travel to sport events. The other 84 per cent travel to watch sport events.

Ironman triathlons are a perfect example of sport events with the majority of participants in their mid-30s to 40s. There are seven Ironman races within the mainland USA, twelve internationally, plus the world championship in Hawaii. Each race attracts 1500–1700 participants, each of whom brings an average of two supporters. Women's professional bowling is a sport that involves middle-aged women and generates a large economic impact. The Women's International Bowling Congress (WIBC) Championship Tournament is the premier event for amateur women bowlers. The 2004 Championship in Wichita, Kansas will attract approximately 42 500 women, with an estimated economic impact of more than $US 22 million on the local economy (WIBC, 2003).

Senior market

The National Senior Summer Games held biennially in the USA attracts 11 000 athletes plus 2.1 visitors per participant. Between 30 000 and 50 000 hotel room nights are booked for this event, with a typical stay being 4.5 nights. In addition, each state holds qualifying competitions and some Winter Games. Although senior athletes tend to be budget conscious, they will spend a fair amount if they see the value and it is marketed effectively. In 2002, Anthony Travel sold 5000 packages to the Senior Games held at Disney's Wide World of Sport for $US 500 each. Another example of an event focused on the older generation is The Golden Oldies World Rugby Festival. This tournament, which attracts between 3500 and 4000 people, was held in Brisbane, Australia in May 2002, and will be held in San Diego in 2005.

Disabled sports

The disabled sports market is a rapidly growing domain of domestic and international sport. Remarkably little is known about this form of sport tourism. The Society for the Advancement of Travel for the Disabled, an advocacy group in New York, estimates that the disabled travel market equates to approximately 36 million travellers per annum (Murphy, 1997).

Educational travel

Although difficult to quantify, each sport organization conducts numerous educational clinics, certification courses and development camps for players, coaches and referees that require participants to spend at least 1 night away from home. In addition, there are typically two governing board meetings per year plus a national conference for various stakeholders. The NCAA, for example, holds a conference each year that attracts approximately 1600–1700 attendees for an average of 3 nights. The General Association of International Sport Federations (GAISF), along with the Association of Summer Olympic International Federations (ASOIF), the Association of the International Olympic Winter Sport

Federations (AIOWF) and the International Olympic Committee (IOC), organizes the annual Sport Accord International Sport Convention, which gathers between 800 and 1000 participants for 5 nights. The football coaches' association meeting brings 6000 football coaches together for 3 days. Another large sport-related conference is the Golf Course Superintendent convention, with 30 000 delegates.

Overall impact of sport tourism markets

In recent years there have been a few organizations that have tried to estimate the economic impact of the sports travel industry. According to Hudson (2003), 'In industrialized countries, sport tourism contributes between 1 and 2 per cent to the gross domestic product (GDP), and the contribution of tourism as a whole is between 4 and 6 per cent'. Furthermore, the growth rate for the sport tourism industry is estimated at about 10 per cent per annum.

The Travel Industry Association of America (TIA) released a report in 1999 on the *Profile of Travelers Who Attend Sports Events*. This report has been widely quoted, but unfortunately the study focuses only on adult sport-related travel. The data relevant to youth in this study show that 24 per cent of all adults who travel to sport events do so to watch their children or grandchildren compete. The TIA estimates that $US 27 billion per year is generated from adults travelling to sport events, either to watch or to participate.

Sport Travel Magazine released figures in 2000 based on its readership organizations, stating that the sports travel industry generates $US 118 billion. Included in this estimate is:

- Team and participant travel $US 6.1 billion
- Family and spectators $US 47.3 billion
- Corporate incentive travel $US 2.1 billion
- Adventure and fantasy travel $US 62.8 billion.

In 2002, the *Sports Business Journal* released figures on money spent by groups for travel to and from organized sporting events. These included:

- Collegiate sports $US 1.11 billion
- Four pro leagues $US 335.4 million
- Minor leagues $US 113.4 million
- Spectators $US 12.40 billion
- Other $US 2.10 billion.

It is evident that sports play an important role in many facets of the tourism industry and, as evidenced by the difficult times in 2001, sports travel remains more resilient compared to traditional sources of business and leisure travel – particularly family trips associated with children/youth sports competitions. There are factors that routinely impact the size of the sports travel market. At the collegiate level, realignment of conference leagues may reduce travel distances and costs, along with a tightening of athletic department budgets. With the increase in sports commissions there are more cities capable of holding events, giving amateur teams a closer and less expensive alternative for competing in a tournament in their sport (SBJ, 2002: 39). At the professional level, the addition of new leagues and the expansion of these leagues such as the WNBA and AFL expands travel opportunities, whereas realignment of divisional opponents decreases travel.

There is also a number of other factors that influence the economic impact of sport travel, especially sport event travel (see also Case study 4.3). These include:

1 *Type of sport*. Sports such as polo, lacrosse, and equestrian and sailing events typically involve participants and spectators with higher demographics and more disposable income than other sports.
2 *Format and length of the event*. Events that are short in duration and schedule participants to be at the sport venue the majority of time do not allow visitors an opportunity to explore the area and spend money beyond the sport event.
3 *Team qualification and elimination process*. The further out a team qualifies to participate the more visitors travel with the participant, as there is time to plan and secure travel discounts. Similarly, if the event is single elimination, those participants eliminated early may elect to return home rather than stay for the entire competition.
4 *Level of competition*. Foreign participants in international events tend to stay longer and spend more money on shopping and other activities during their visit, whereas for regional and local events participants may be able to travel to and from their home, minimizing the economic impact.
5 *Novelty and interest in destination*. Events that are held in the same location year in and year out may not generate the same economic spending as those that move from place to place. Destinations such as Orlando and San Diego, however, have a strong appeal as a family resort; thus the number of visitors per participant is higher than for other cities.
6 *Location of sport event in relation to business district*. If an event is held on a college campus that is isolated from the downtown business district, participants may not spend as much money as if the event were convenient to local shops and restaurants.
7 *Supporting infrastructure*. Often participants will visit more local attractions if the city and local organizing committee provides convenient access to such attractions. Participants attending an event at Disney's Wide World of Sport have the opportunity of purchasing theme park tickets in a package with hotel and event registration, and have bus transportation to the attractions from the hotel.

Case study 4.3 Destinations targeting sport tourism markets

Worldwide there are a number of countries that have incorporated sport tourism into their national marketing plans, including the USA, Malaysia, China, Ireland, Thailand, Korea, Nepal, Barbados, Brunei, Portugal and Australia. In the USA there are over 2570 cities or regions that are actively engaged in pursuing and attracting sport events to their region (NASC: personal communication, 2003). Most of these cities or regions have formed a sports commission or sports authority that bid to host new events and support existing events. These groups are organized as part of a convention and visitors' bureau, a chamber of commerce or as a private entity. The number of staff ranges from 1 to 25, with annual operating budgets from $US 100 000 to over $US 1 000 000 per year. In Ireland the national tourism marketing body, Bord Failte, was granted Euro 55.3 million by the government to attract big sporting events (Hancock, 2003). The international sport tourism initiative was launched at the start of 2000, and has resulted in hosting of the Special Olympics World Summer Games, Rugby's Heineken European Cup Final, the European Eventing Championship and the Smurfit European Open Golf. Bord Failte's aim is to stimulate the economy and increase tourism.

The China National Tourism Administration (CNTA) declared China Sports Tours as the theme of its annual tourism campaign for 2001. In addition to developing tour packages for domestic and overseas markets around big sport events in the country, Chinese inbound operators were encouraged to develop sports-related tour packages in the western region of China to speed up economic development in that area, and these included rock climbing, desert exploration, rafting, skiing, golfing and martial arts elements. The China International Travel Service (CITS) is also cooperating with the China National Athletics Association to market the Beijing International Marathon (Jiannu, 2000). China has scheduled a number of sport events, such as Real Madrid exhibition matches, as part of the government's post-Sars revival efforts (Hong, 2003).

A new Formula One race will be held in Shanghai in September 2004. This event is aimed to stimulate China's tourism as well as the automobile economy. Major car manufacturers such as Renault, Toyota, Ferrari and Honda use F1 as an advertising showcase. The economic impact is estimated to be $US 80–100 million, and the cost of the facility is $US 310 million. The International Circuit of Shanghai (ICSH) holds Formula One rights from 2004 to 2010. In 2008 Beijing will host the Olympic Games, and a strategy to maximize opportunities to increase tourism before, during and after the Games is currently being developed.

Conclusion

Sport tourism is big business, and has become an important economic and marketing strategy for destinations, hoteliers, resorts, events and corporations. The opportunities associated with event and active sport travel packages are still in their infancy as more and more people look for life-enhancing experiences and to increase their physical fitness. It is important for professionals in various industries, sports, tourism and events to work together to meet the needs of consumers and maximize the potential that sport offers tourism destinations. This requires that research be conducted into profiling and understanding existing and emerging sport tourism markets.

References

Bishop, B. (2002). Come sail away: British Virgin Islands offer the perfect Caribbean sailing vacation. *Medical Post*, 38, 35.

Broughton, D. (2002). Dollars in sports. *Sports Business Journal*, 4(47), 39.

Browne, D. (2004). Confidence grows in adventure travel despite global terrorism threat (available at http://www.eturbonews.com, accessed 22 January 2004).

Cox Consulting (2001). *ISPA 2001 Spa User Studies*. International Spa Association.

Cruise Lines International Association (2003). *Cruise Industry Overview Marketing Edition*, Spring. CLIA.

Delpy, L. (1998). An overview of sport tourism: building towards a dimensional framework. *Journal of Vacation Marketing*, 4(1), 23–38.

Delpy Neirotti, L. (2004). Economic Impact of Professional Tennis Tournaments. Unpublished report. George Washington University.

Donlan, T. G. (1998). Family vacation. *Barron's*, 78(42), T8.

Economic Times (2003). Forget the Cup, Indians still flock to South Africa. 5 April.

Feinstein, J. (2003). The Sport Fantasy Camp Market. Unpublished research.

Gibson, H. J. (1998). The wide world of sport tourism. *Parks & Recreation*, 33(9), 108–115.

Gibson, H. J. (1999). Sport tourism: the rules of the game. *Parks & Recreation*, 34(6), 36.

Hancock, C. (2003). Sports puts tourism back on the map. *The Sunday Times*, 12 January.

Harris, R. and Howard, J. (1996). *Dictionary of Travel, Tourism, and Hospitality Terms*. Melbourne: Hospitality Press.

Higham, J. E. S. (1999). Commentary – sport as an avenue of tourism development: an analysis of the positive and negative impacts of sport tourism. *Current Issues in Tourism*, 2(1), 82–90.

Hong, S. (2003). Yao Ming faces tall order of reviving our post-Sars fortunes. *South China Morning Post*, 5 August.

Hudson, S. (2003). *Sport and Adventure Tourism*. New York: The Haworth Hospitality Press.

Jiannu, B. (2000). China to focus on sports tourism. *Travel Trade Gazette Asia*, 10 November.

Leisure Trends Group (2002). *Most Active Americans Panel*. LTG.

Leisure Trends Group (2003). *National Skier/Boarder Opinion Survey (NSOS): Historical Perspectives Report*. LTG.

Mallet, J. (2002). The evolution of adventure travel. Salida, CO: Adventure Travel Society.

Matte, L. (2003). Getaways expand on idea of girls' night out. *The Boston Herald*, 10 June, p. 71.

Medik, S. (2003). *Dictionary of Travel, Tourism, and Hospitality*, 3rd edn. Oxford: Butterworth-Heinemann.

Murphy, K. (1997). Barriers drop for the disabled. *Business Week*, 31 March, p. 99.

Pricewaterhouse Coopers (2002) *ISPA 2002 Spa Industry Study*. Lexington, KT: International Spa Association.

Rosentraub, M. (2000). The Economic Value of IMS' Three Races. Indianapolis Speedway Corporation.

Sabene, K. (2001). Capitalizing on current trends – selling spas. *Network Newsletter, International Airline Travel Agent Network*, Jan/Feb.

Spanberg, E. (2003). Collection of NASCAR shops turns May races into tourist season for Charlotte. *Sports Business Journal*, 26 May.

Spivack, S. (1998). Health spa development in the US: a burgeoning component of sport tourism. *Journal of Vacation Marketing*, 4(1), 78–90.

Thwaites, D. (1999). Closing the gaps: service quality in sport tourism. *The Journal of Services Marketing*, 13(6), 500.

Travel Industry Association of America (1999). *Profile of Travelers Who Attend Sports Events*. Washington, DC: TIA.

Travel Industry Association of America (2003). *Domestic Travel Market Report*. Washington, DC: TIA.

Women's International Bowling Congress (2003). WIBC announces city options for 2008 Championship Tournament. Annual Meeting, 10 October.

Xinhua News Agency (1999). Thailand to promote diving as sport-tourism market. 3 May.

5

Understanding sport tourism experiences

Heather J. Gibson

Introduction

Cohen (1972) was one of the first to postulate that there is not one type of tourist but many. In his classic 1972 article he proposed a typology of tourist roles whereby different tourists could be distinguished by their preference for varying degrees of novelty or familiarity in their travel experiences. Since then various scholars have developed tourist role typologies, some building upon Cohen's work (e.g. Pearce, 1985; Yiannis and Gibson, 1992; Mo et al., 1993) and others distinguishing tourist types on a range of characteristics (e.g. Plog, 1974; Redfoot, 1984; Smith, 1989; Ryan, 1995; Wickens, 2002). Taken in aggregate, these studies suggest that to understand tourist behaviour and experiences we must realize that tourists not only differ in the types of activities they take part in on vacation, but also that these choices need to be placed in the context of a number of factors including motivation (e.g. Crompton, 1979), age or life stage (e.g. Gibson and Yiannakis, 2002), family lifecycle stage (e.g. Lawson, 1991), gender (e.g. Squire, 1994), degree of risk adversion/adventuresomeness (stimulation seeking) (e.g. Cohen, 1972; Lepp and Gibson, 2003), social class (e.g. Gottlieb, 1982; Graburn, 1983), race (Phillipp, 1993), and even degree of authenticity sought in a vacation experience (Redfoot, 1984). Moreover, there is agreement in the literature that the different tourist types also seek varying degrees of institutionalization in tourism facilities in a destination, and as a result have differing impacts on the host communities, or residents, of the tourist destination (e.g. Cohen, 1972; Plog, 1974; Smith, 1989).

In examining the experiences of sport tourists, many of these same concepts are relevant to understanding behavioural choices and patterns. Indeed, the proposition that different types of sport tourists can be identified is well established in the growing body of scholarship devoted to the topic. At the very least there is a distinction between active sport tourists who take part in sport on vacation and passive sport tourists who watch others participating in sport (e.g. Hall, 1992; Standeven and De Knop, 1999; Hinch and Higham, 2001). Taking a lead from Redmond (1991), Gibson (1998a, 1998b) proposed that there are three major forms of sport tourism: active, event and nostalgia. (Nostalgia sport tourism involves travelling to visit such sport attractions as famous stadia or halls of fame, or going on sports-themed cruises.) This chapter examines the experiences of different sport tourists and offers some models of explanation that might be used to understand these experiences.

Motivation: why sport tourists choose to do what they do

Underlying all behaviour are needs and motivations rooted in the basic physiological and socio-psychological wants of all humans. The classic theories of motivation commonly applied to understanding leisure, sport and tourism behaviour are Murray's (1938) Needs Theory of Personality, Maslow's (1943) Hierarchical Theory of Needs and Berlyne's (1960) concept of optimal level of stimulation.

Murray (1938: 123) explained that 'A need is a stimulus – a force pushing an individual in a certain direction or to behave in a certain way'. He identified 12 physiological or viserogenic needs and 28 psychological or psychogenic needs. The viserogenic needs are viewed as primary needs, and include air, water, food and security. The pyschogenic needs are viewed as secondary needs, and are related to mental or emotional satisfaction – including achievement, autonomy and affiliation. Needs are dynamic in that they rise and fall in importance as they are satisfied. Indeed, Murray suggested the idea of a need cycle whereby needs are dormant during the refractory period, are susceptible to inducement from relevant stimuli during the ready period, and determine an individual's behaviour during the active period. Furthermore, he suggested that it is likely that needs work in combination with each other.

Maslow's (1943) Hierarchical Theory of Needs is probably the most well known theory of motivation. Like Murray, Maslow proposed that people's behaviour is driven by both physiological and socio-psychological needs; however, he postulated a more structured hierarchical order to the activation and satisfaction of needs. Physiological needs form the base of the hierarchy, followed by safety needs. Maslow suggested that these lower-order needs must be satisfied before an individual can work on the higher-order needs of love, belongingness and self-esteem. The top of the hierarchy is the need for self-actualization, which is an opportunity for individuals 'to become everything that one is capable of becoming' (Maslow, 1943: 382). This peak experience cannot be experienced until the other four needs have been satisfied. Like Murray, Maslow (1970) postulated that behaviour may be motivated by more than one need and, as such, he suggested that the hierarchy of needs may not be as rigid as it first implies – for example, some people may be motivated by the need for self-esteem without playing heed to affiliation needs, which are the stage below in the hierarchy.

Findings from a range of studies in leisure, sport and tourism that have used either Murray's or Maslow's theories, or a combination of both, have concluded that the relationship between needs and activity choice is quite complex (e.g. Driver and Knopf, 1977; Tinsley *et al.*, 1977; Allen, 1982; Iso-Ahola and Allen, 1982; Pearce, 1982; Beard and Ragheb, 1983; Pearce and Caltabiano, 1983; Mills, 1985). As such it is not sufficient to pair a set of needs with an activity for, as Maslow and Murray suggested, behaviour is multidimensional. In fact, the same activity may be motivated by different needs at different times for one individual, or one activity may represent different meanings to another individual at the same time (Crandall, 1980). Nonetheless, despite the complexity of the relationship, motivation theory still provides insights into why people choose to take part in certain activities. Moreover, perhaps, as Hebb and Thompson (1954) suggested, the key to understanding people's behavioural choices may lie in the fact that individuals differ in their levels of optimal stimulation. Some individuals prefer highly stimulating situations and will seek activities that match their high thresholds of stimulation, whereas others may prefer less stimulating contexts and avoid situations they feel are above their optimal level of arousal (Berlyne, 1960). Iso-Ahola (1984) proposed that the optimal level of stimulation is a balance between the need for stability and the need for variety. He suggested that leisure, sport and tourism behaviour are motivated by two dialectical forces; seeking and escaping – in terms of either personal and/or interpersonal contexts. While the escape motive is likely to be predominant in tourism behaviour because of the very nature of travel away from the everyday environment, travel may also provide opportunities for seeking opportunities that may not be available at home (Iso-Ahola, 1983). Thus, because most people *choose* to take part in tourism and sport, they can select activities that match their optimal levels of stimulation. As such, this may partially explain why different people choose different activities on vacation and in their leisure. Certainly Wahlers and Etzel (1985) found that people with higher optimal levels of stimulation sought vacations that were adventurous, invigorating and novel, whereas stimulus avoiders tended to choose vacations that were enriching and to some extent structured, such as organized tours with planned itineraries. Similarly, Lepp and Gibson (2003) found that some tourists tended to avoid situations they perceived as risky whereas others sought out environments with inherent risks.

In tourism research, the idea of matching an individual's optimal level of stimulation to an activity or environment has been conceptualized as the need to match an individual's motivations (push factors) and expectations regarding a vacation with the attributes of a particular destination (pull factors). Crompton (1979) identified seven push factors or socio-psychological motives associated with vacations – escape, self-exploration, relaxation, prestige, regression, enhancement of kinship relations, and social interaction. He also identified two cultural motives – novelty and education – which he suggested are related to the characteristics of a destination and as such can be regarded as pull factors. The congruence between push factors and pull factors has been called the destination–motivation fit (Goeldner and Ritchie, 2003), and is an important factor contributing to vacation satisfaction. Lounsbury and Polik (1992) found a strong relationship between vacation satisfaction and motivation, with the need for stimulus avoidance (i.e. Iso-Ahola's escaping) and social interaction (Iso-Ahola's seeking) being particularly important in understanding why people travel and their subsequent experiences while on vacation.

In sport tourism research, motivations, activities and destination selection have featured in various studies. Gammon and Robinson (1997) addressed the idea of the degree to which sport is the primary purpose or secondary purpose of a trip. While the authors did not investigate the underlying motivations behind selecting a trip where sport is either the primary purpose (sport tourism) or the secondary activity (tourism sport) *per se*, this is an important dimension in understanding the experiences of sport tourists. Conceivably, individuals who are motivated to take a vacation where sport predominates will engage in different activities on their trip than will individuals who regard sport as only one of a number of vacation activities. A consistent finding in sport tourism research has been that sport tourists, particularly event sport tourists, tend to be what Faulkner *et al.* (1998) called 'sport junkies', interested in little else other than attending the sports event they came to see. In a study of rugby fans, Garnham (1996) found that they spent most of their money on food, drink and other game-related expenditures rather than patronizing the shops in the city hosting the event – much to the dismay of the shop owners. Similarly, Ritchie *et al.* (2000), in a study of Super 12 rugby fans in Canberra, Australia, identified three types of fan: the avid spectator/fan, the frequent spectator/fan, and the casual spectator/fan. Avid spectator/fans were motivated to watch the game and were interested in little else that was not associated with sport. Thus their trip tended to be dominated by game-related activities, and they were more likely to be day-trippers than the casual spectator/fan. For the casuals, attending the game was part of their overall trip to Canberra and as such was regarded as another tourism attraction. Not surprisingly, the casual spectator/fan tended to stay longer in Canberra and spend more money on other attractions and entertainment opportunities. These casual spectator/fans were also more likely to be staying with friends or family. The frequent spectator/fans tended to have mixed motivations. They were similar to the avid fans in that they were interested in the game and had come to Canberra to watch their team. However, if they found something that interested them they were also susceptible to taking part in other activities while in town.

Both Garnham and Ritchie *et al.*'s studies provide insights on the multi-motivational nature of attending rugby matches. There seems to be a continuum of motivation and behaviour that describes these fans/spectators, from uni-motivational behaviour that is solely centred on sport to spectators who, as Gammon and Robinson described, view sport as secondary or as just another activity take part in while away from home. Both studies provide some discussion as to the variable tourism impacts that these types of fans have on the host communities. When bidding to host sporting events, the economic potential for businesses in the community is often touted as a benefit of holding the event (Danylchuk, 2003). However, findings from these studies seem to indicate that not all fans will take advantage of attractions and amenities in the community other than those directly related to sport.

In our work on event sport tourists who follow University of Florida (Gators) sports, notably college football (American football), we conducted an in-depth study of fan behaviours in terms of both the rituals that surround game-day behaviour and travel patterns (Gibson *et al.*, 2002a, 2003a). Our findings mirror those described above in that the Gator fans ranged from avid fans whose activities were sport-related, to those fans that viewed Gator football as a chance to socialize. For home games at the University of Florida, during the day or weekend (as many drove long distances to attend the game arriving Friday night and leaving Sunday morning) the activities were centred on tailgating (picnicking and/ or barbecuing and socializing before the game) and visiting the bars and restaurants in town to further socialize with their friends and family. Many of these fans had developed quite elaborate rituals over the years, and many of the tailgates were multi-generational family groups through which the children were socialized into being a Gator fan from an early age. The community tourism agency has been trying to entice these Gator fans to take advantage of the other activities and attractions on offer in the area, with little success. It appears that when in Gainesville (home of the Gators), the fans are motivated to socialize and enjoy the game rather than anything else besides a little shopping. However, when these fans visit other university towns for away games then they often use the opportunity to explore the local sights. Thus, for away games the Gator fans seem to be multi-motivated by the chance to take part in both sport and other tourism activities. This change in motivation from one context to another is illustrative of Maslow's and Murray's proposition that needs are dynamic, and in order to understand behaviour (and in our case sport tourism behaviour) we need to take this into consideration.

What makes a good sport tourism experience? Keeping sport tourists happy

The idea of matching the sport tourist's motivations with the characteristics of a destination and the type of vacation is a key concept in understanding the experiences and satisfactions of particular tourists (see Case study 5.1). In the Gators study, most of the event sport tourists were interested in watching the game and socializing with their family and friends. Thus, if we were to measure their motivations, we might find that affiliation needs, esteem (through identifying with a winning team) and a quest for excitement and/or peak experience might underlie the behaviours of many of these fans. Most of these fans are regular visitors to Gainesville, hence they know that, contingent on the team winning (which is based on the uncertainty of outcome that is characteristic of sport), their trip experiences will satisfy most of their motivations. Thus the destination–motivation fit of these fans is quite high. However, many sport tourism experiences do not enjoy such regularity of repeat visitation and therefore have higher uncertainty in matching motivations with experiences. In this situation, research findings and knowledge of such concepts as motivation and destination image theories might be of use.

Green and Chalip (1998), in their study of a women's flag football tournament, found that participants were not only motivated by competency and mastery which underlies much sport participation, but also by affiliation needs. The participants expressed dissatisfaction over the lack of opportunities to socialize as the tournament organizers had over-scheduled the experience. Moreover, the authors suggested that understanding the norms and values associated with the subculture of women's flag football was also necessary in meeting their needs and expectations. Likewise Fairley (2003), in a study of a group of fans who take an annual bus trip to watch an Australian rules football team play, not only invoked ideas related to subculture but also Turner's (1969) theory of ritual process to understand the role of nostalgia in the experiences of these fans. In the liminoid space formed on the trip, the fans socialized newcomers into the norms, values and rituals associated with being a member of the group. (Liminoid is a concept borrowed from anthropology. It is the secular form of liminality, and describes the situation whereby individuals are separated from their everyday environments and as a result find themselves free from the norms and values governing their behaviour. Free from these constrictions, they frequently behave in different ways and are more likely to form bonds with people they may not socialize with at home.) Moreover, nostalgia figured prominently in the experience, in terms of both a motivation and shaping the behaviours of the group members throughout the duration of the trip. Indeed, nostalgia and its associated rituals were an integral part of the group's experiences, and opportunities to relive past memories contributed to their overall satisfaction with the trip and motivated the fans to embark on the arduous trip the next year.

Another related concept in understanding the experiences of sport tourists is their level of involvement or specialization in their chosen sport. The degree to which sport tourists are engaged in their sports has been examined using a number of different paradigms, including skilled consumption (Richards, 1996), involvement (Gibson et al., 2003b; McGehee et al., 2003) and serious leisure (Gibson et al., 2002a). Richards, in a study of British skiers, found that, based on skill level and involvement in the sport, the skiers searched for different attributes in a vacation – including terrain, cost, and opportunities for different activities. McGehee et al. (2003) used a similar concept, that of involvement, to investigate the experiences of another group of active sport tourists, roadrunners. The construct of involvement comes from the consumer behaviour and marketing literature (e.g. Bloch et al., 1986; Assael, 1987; Broderick and Mueller, 1999), and has been applied to the leisure, sport and tourism literature (e.g. Havitz and Dimanche, 1990; 1997). In consumer behaviour and marketing, an individual's degree of involvement with a product has been linked to information search behaviour and decision-making, brand loyalty and the salience of different advertising strategies. High levels of involvement in a product are related to higher brand loyalty and more active product evaluation behaviours, while individuals with lower levels of involvement are more passive in their information search and tend not to exhibit high levels of brand recognition (e.g. Assael, 1987; Beatty and Smith, 1987; Maheswaren and Meyers-Levy, 1990). In leisure, tourism and sport the involvement construct has been used to study, among other activities, fitness participation (Dimanche et al., 1991), white water recreationists (Bricker and Kerstetter, 2000), anglers (Perdue, 1993) and vacation behaviour (Norman, 1991). McGehee et al. (2003), in their study of individuals who travel to take part in running competitions, found that runners with higher levels of involvement in their sport were more likely to take part in competitions that involved an overnight stay at a destination. Moreover, these runners reported that they would like to take part in more of these competitions;

however, they felt constrained by a number of facets in their lives. While McGehee *et al.* (2003) did not specifically measure constraints and so the specific barriers to participation were not identified, there is a body of literature that has investigated the reasons why people may not participate in recreation and leisure activities.

Early constraints research in leisure studies started as a concern over non-participation in recreation activities and an attempt at identifying barriers to participation so that practitioners might alleviate them (Jackson and Scott, 1999). As this line of research progressed there was a growing understanding that as well as external barriers or constraints (such as lack of money or time), social and psychological constraints might be as influential as if not more so than external factors in explaining people's participation and non-participation patterns in recreation activities (e.g. Crawford and Godbey, 1987; Jackson, 1990). In an extension of this line of thinking, Crawford *et al.* (1991) proposed a hierarchical model of leisure constraints that suggests that there are three distinct categories of constraints: intrapersonal, interpersonal and structural. Intrapersonal constraints (individual preferences, psychological feelings about an activity) and motivation combine to shape preferences for an activity or experience. Whether an individual chooses to participate in activity or not may be further influenced first by interpersonal constraints (e.g. having a companion to participate with) and then by structural constraints (such as time, money or availability of an activity). Crawford *et al.* (1991) suggested that these constraints are encountered in sequence and, if they are present (constraints may not always be present when choosing to participate in an activity), they must be negotiated if a person is to participate. This hierarchical model of constraints has guided work both in tourism (e.g. Blazey, 1987) and in sport tourism research, with a particular focus on skiing (e.g. Williams and Lattey, 1994; Gilbert and Hudson, 2000; Hudson, 2000; Williams and Fidgeon, 2000).

Case study 5.1 The use of image in active sport tourism: the case of skiing

Throughout the 1990s most forms of sport tourism experienced growth; indeed, the Travel Industry Association of America found that between 1994 and 1999 75.3 million US adults travelled to take part in some kind of organized sport either as a spectator or a participant (www.tia.org press release dated 25 August 1999). However, contrary to this general growth pattern, alpine skiing in North America and much of the world has plateaued. While participation levels in snowboarding have increased, the number of skier days in 1992 was 10.8 million and this had dropped to 7.7 million in 1998 (National Sporting Goods Association, 2000). This pattern has led to concern in the ski industry about the long-term viability of their product. Thus a number of studies have been commissioned that have used Crawford et al.'s (1991) hierarchical model of leisure constraints to guide their investigations into why people drop out or have never participated in skiing. The consistent finding from these studies is that the sport is perceived as being too expensive, dangerous and crowded, and needing too much athleticism to participate (Williams and Lattey, 1994; Gilbert and Hudson, 2000; Hudson, 2000; Williams and Fidgeon, 2000). These studies also found that among non-skiers images of pain, cold and injury were pervasive and were reinforced by advertising for the sport, which tends to depict a lone skier flying off a cliff or skiing down a very steep incline. Instead of encouraging non-skiers to participate, these images discouraged them and served to reinforce their negative perceptions. On the contrary, as people who ski know, the sport caters to people of all skill levels, it is a social experience, and is a great way to spend time outside during the winter. Technology has done much to improve clothing and therefore the ability to stay dry and warm, and the developments in shaped skis have improved the skill level of all types of skiers. Thus the mismatch between the images put forth by the industry and reality is a major barrier to participation among non-skiers.

Williams and Fidgeon (2000) also suggested that the ski industry needed to pay more attention to the tourism associated with the sport. Many people who ski travel long distances to participate, and constitute a major form of active sport tourism. However, among academics in both sport and tourism studies, and ski and tourism practitioners, the tourism component has largely been ignored until recently. Richards (1996), in a study of UK skiers, found that skill level and involvement in the sport (or what he termed 'skilled consumption') was influential in the type of vacation experience a skier was likely to choose. Beginner skiers were likely to be more price conscious, and advanced skiers paid more attention to sport-related attributes in a destination – such as extensiveness of terrain and pitch of ski runs. Combining the ideas of involvement in the sport and destination image (pull factors) (Fakeye and Crompton, 1991) with benefits sought (which ties into the underlying motivations or push factors related to the trip), Gibson, Williams and Pennington-Gray (2003b) investigated the experiences of participants on a university-sponsored international ski trip.

In 2000, Gibson and Pennington-Gray used a case study approach to examine the destination images and benefits sought among members of a community ski club sponsored trip to Italy (Gibson and Pennington-Gray, 2001). The researchers used a pre-post test design whereby participants were surveyed before and after their trip about their experiences. The study was grounded in Fakeye and Crompton's (1991) Tourist's Image Formation Process Model. The tenets of this model are that initially the potential tourist holds an organic image of a particular destination that is largely formed by exposure to the media. As individuals become motivated to take a vacation they seek out various sources of information about potential destinations; thus the original organic images individuals hold of a destination become largely shaped by tourism brochures and travel information on the Internet, and now constitute an induced image of a particular destination. Fakeye and Crompton (1991) proposed that there is a relationship between benefits sought (shaped by underlying motivations), destination image, and subsequent satisfaction with a vacation. Moreover, satisfaction level with a vacation will influence repurchase – that is, the likelihood that the tourist will return to the destination for another visit. The complex image formed by tourists is based on actual experience of a destination, and will ultimately influence their overall evaluation of a particular location. Thus the idea of the destination–motivation fit that was discussed earlier is relevant in understanding this relationship. Conceivably, if tourists experience a mismatch between the benefits they were seeking on vacation, their induced images of the destination and their actual experience, this will be reflected in their overall satisfaction with their vacation.

Gibson and Pennington-Gray found that for the skiers on their trip to Italy, 10 items pertaining to destination image were better than expected, including those related to scenery, great skiing opportunities and the variety of terrain. For these trip participants, Italy proved to be a better ski destination than they had been expecting. In terms of benefits sought, expectations were high at the start of the trip and the trip experience largely met these expectations, with opportunities for meeting interesting people, feeling good after being physically active, taking part in skilful activities, and plenty of chances to socialize cited as benefits that increased significantly over the course of the trip. Thus, a mixture of ski-related destination attributes and social opportunities appeared to be related to overall satisfaction with the trip for these US adults. In a follow-up study, Gibson et al. (2003b) conducted a similar study of a ski trip to Switzerland; this time the construct of involvement was added to the questionnaire.

For the participants on this second trip, Switzerland proved to have stronger organic and induced images as a ski destination that were largely confirmed by actually visiting it. Before the trip, respondents viewed Switzerland as being beautiful with attractive scenery, with numerous cultural and historical attractions. As Switzerland has a worldwide reputation for snow sports, while the ski-related destination attributes were confirmed for this group of Americans, other destination attributes (such as the nature of historical attractions and the friendliness of the local people) proved to be mediated by actual experience. Level of involvement in skiing appeared to have little influence on these complex images; however, in terms of benefits sought, those with higher levels of involvement in skiing or snowboarding were more motivated by opportunities to take part in these sports and meeting interesting people than were those with less involvement. In fact, there was a mismatch in benefits sought and actual experience regarding the degree to which the trip would be relaxing and a chance to take it easy among those with less involvement in the sports (of these a high proportion were beginner skiers and/or snowboarders). Anybody that takes part in snow sports knows that such a vacation is quite physically demanding and often requires early morning starts to experience the best snow or to catch buses or trains that take you to the mountains. It appears that some among those who had very little experience with snow sports were expecting a relaxing, laid-back vacation, and it did not live up to their expectations; in fact, over the course of the week only a hard-core group of skiers and snowboarders continued to take the buses to the resorts each morning. The less involved skiers and snowboarders spent their days taking part in more traditional tourist activities such as shopping and sightseeing. Contentment with these activities probably accounts for the high overall levels of satisfaction with their trip, as potentially the mismatch between their expectations and the actual reality of a ski/snowboard trip could have resulted in much dissatisfaction.

Thus, these studies suggest that the match between destination image and motivation is important in explaining and predicting sport tourism experiences. With particular relevance to the ski industry, all of these studies suggest that while the images of thrill and excitement may entice some to ski or snowboard, these are likely to be those who are already quite involved in the sports. Perhaps alternative images might focus on the social nature of the sports and the chance to enjoy spectacular scenery, rather than the steepness of the slopes. Furthermore, in terms of choosing ski destinations for a vacation, attention should be given to opportunities for other non-ski-related activities in a resort for those with less involvement in the sport. These conclusions take us back again to the idea of an optimal level of stimulation (Berlyne, 1960). Conceivably, thrill seekers will be enticed by the lone skier flying off a cliff, although this is likely to be moderated by not only skill level but also such factors as gender and age (Gibson, 1996). In fact, Berlyne suggested that an individual's optimal level of stimulation is shaped by personality, culture, education and present psychological state. Perhaps, therefore, as Crompton (1979) postulated, motivation may be only one variable in the equation explaining tourist behaviour.

Who is likely to be a sport tourist? The influence of age, gender, class, race and disability

In a critical analysis of the 'average sport tourist', Gibson (1998b) suggested that participants are overwhelmingly white, middle class, and more likely to be men than women. Subsequent studies of sport tourists of various different types support this finding (e.g. Ritchie et al., 2000; Gibson et al., 2002a; McGehee et al., 2003). While implications for broadening the profile of participants in sport tourism still remain, this chapter is limited to an examination of the influence of various socio-structural characteristics on participation patterns and experiences.

There has been a growing body of work that has investigated the influence of life stage or family lifecycle stage on sport, leisure and tourism preferences. The difference between life stage and family lifecycle stage lies in the choice of a particular theoretical model to guide a study. Wells and Guber (1966) suggested that family life can be viewed as a sequence of nine stages, from bachelorhood to newly married, through three full nest stages, two empty nest stages and two stages of widowhood. During each of these stages individuals are preoccupied with various different socio-psychological tasks associated with separating from families of origin (bachelorhood), raising children (full nest), adjusting to life without children in the home (empty nest) and life without a spouse (widowhood). Rapoport and Rapoport (1975) suggested that leisure provides a context in which many of these tasks can be completed; for example, finding a potential mate is often facilitated in leisure contexts for those in the bachelorhood stage. At the same time, family life stage responsibilities may also shape and/or constrain leisure choices. Lawson (1991) examined tourists visiting New Zealand using the family lifecycle as a guide for his analysis. He found that during the full nest stages, particularly when children were very young, vacations were largely spent visiting extended family members, and that later, as children matured, vacation activities were chosen with them in mind. He also suggested that discretionary income was related to family life stage, with the childrearing stages and retirement tending to be more constrained financially than the empty nest stages, and so income also influenced vacation experiences.

Life course, lifespan or lifecycle theories tend to focus on the individual's journey through life rather than that of the family *per se*. This is not to say that the influence of family and friends is not considered as part of these theories, as Levinson *et al.* (1978) suggested that an individual's lifecycle is a product of psychological needs, sociological influences such as gender and class, and the individuals' roles and responsibilities in his or her own community. Gibson (1989, 1994), in work with Yiannakis (e.g. Gibson and Yiannakis, 2002), framed an analysis of tourist role preference using Levinson's model of the adult lifecycle. They found that preference for some tourist roles (such as the active sport tourist, thrill seeker and action seeker) declined with age, whereas preference for other tourist roles increased with age. The latter types of vacations tended to be cultural, educational or of the organized mass tourist varieties. With particular reference to active sport tourism, even though these vacations tended to be more popular among individuals under the age of 40, certainly for men during their 60s there was a slight rekindling of interest in active sport tourism as a vacation choice. The authors speculated that this was probably fuelled by golf vacations during retirement. While their data showed that women participated in active sport tourism, throughout the life course fewer women took sport-oriented vacations. In related studies, Gibson *et al.* (2002a) found that some women were actively engaged in event sport tourism in their support of Gator football. These women regarded tailgating as a chance to socialize with friends and family. Tailgating was also regarded as a lifelong activity where different generations could participate, from the new grandchild to the newly married couple and those who were grandparents. The social aspect of sport tourism is a recurring theme throughout many of the studies we have reviewed in this chapter. In fact, in a study of individuals aged between 50 and 86 years who participate in senior games competitions (Masters games), Gibson *et al.* (2002b) found that many of the athletes they interviewed spent weekends and sometimes even weeks travelling overseas to compete in senior games competitions, and that part of the appeal was meeting up with other competitors with whom they had developed friendships at previous events.

As noted above, studies in sport tourism consistently show that women participate less than men in this type of travel. In leisure, sport and tourism studies there are many studies that document the influence of gender on participation patterns and show inequity in access to some activities, particularly sport (e.g. Deem, 1986, 1996; Henderson and Bialeschki, 1991; Shaw, 1994; Wearing, 1998). While it may be more socially acceptable for girls and women to take part in sport and physical activity today, there still remain constraints on their participation in terms of the type of sporting activities that are deemed as acceptable. Team sports such as American football, football (soccer), ice hockey and rugby still embody masculine ideals (Theberge, 1987; Hargreaves, 1994), and women are largely excluded from participating in these sports either as players or spectators. Indeed Tripp (2003), in an ethnographic study of fans attending University of Florida football games, found that while women were in attendance at the games, their presence was tolerated rather than embraced by many male fans. In fact, the language used by the crowd at the games was often misogynistic. Tripp also found that the crowd could be quite racist. While they venerated black players on the field (as long as they were playing well), there were few black fans in attendance. In focus groups with black students she found that they felt uncomfortable attending games because of the language and attitudes they encountered among some members of the crowd.

Thus, in studies of sport tourism we need to be aware and examine further the ways gender, age, class and race influence experiences. As yet such studies are lacking, and constitute work that needs to be done. Nonetheless, while socio-structure may constrain behaviour there is also evidence to suggest that sport and sport tourism experiences provide opportunities to resist oppressive social forces. In our study with senior athletes, much of what they told us centred on how privileged they feel to be competing in sport in their 60s, 70s or 80s. They enjoy the look on people's faces when they talk about their athletic accomplishments, as there is still an ageist attitude in the belief that competitive sport is the realm of younger people. In our study of elite female wheelchair athletes, sport afforded them a way to resist negative societal attitudes about being disabled and they found that being part of a team of strong athletic women was an empowering experience (Ashton-Shaeffer *et al.*, 2001). Moreover, the international travel that they did as members of a national team enabled them to be ambassadors for their sport and to share their message about the empowering nature of sport for people with disabilities around the world.

In bringing this chapter to a close, we can see that in our quest to understand the experiences of sport tourists a multi-dimensional approach that addresses both motivation and socio-structural characteristics will provide the best understanding. From a practical point of view, these theoretical constructs are also very relevant. The manager who understands the underpinnings of social behaviour is somebody who can better predict and cater to the needs and wants of his or her clients. In tourism, a satisfied guest is one who is more likely to return and will speak positively to friends and family about the experiences that they achieved at the sport tourism destination.

References

Allen, L. (1982). The relationship between Murray's Personality Needs and leisure interests. *Journal of Leisure Research*, 14, 63–76.

Ashton-Shaeffer, C., Gibson, H., Holt, M. and Willming, C. (2001). Women's resistance and empowerment through wheelchair sport. *World Leisure*, 43(4), 11–21.

Assael, H. (1987). *Consumer Behavior and Marketing Action* (3rd edn). Boston, MA: Kent Publishing Company.

Beard, J. and Ragheb, M. (1983). Measuring leisure motivation. *Journal of Leisure Research*, 15, 219–228.

Beatty, J. and Smith, S. (1987). External search efforts: an investigation across several product categories. *Journal of Consumer Research*, 14, 411–423.

Berlyne, D. (1960). *Conflict, Arousal and Curiosity*. New York: McGraw-Hill.

Blazey, M. (1987). The differences between participants and non-participants in a senior travel program. *Journal of Travel Research*, 26, 7–12.

Bloch, P., Sherrell, D. and Ridgeway, N. (1986). Consumer search: an extended framework. *Journal of Consumer Research*, 13, 119–126.

Bricker, K. and Kerstetter, D. (2000). Level of specialization and place attachment: an exploratory study of whitewater recreation. *Leisure Sciences*, 22, 233–257.

Broderick, A. and Mueller, R. (1999). A theoretical and empirical exegesis of the consumer involvement construct: the psychology of the food shopper. *Journal of Marketing Theory and Practice*, 7(4), 97–108.

Cohen, E. (1972). Towards a sociology of international tourism. *Sociological Research*, 39, 164–182.

Crandall, R. (1980). Motivations for leisure. *Journal of Leisure Research*, 12, 45–54.

Crawford, D. and Godbey, G. (1987). Reconceptualizing barriers to family leisure. *Leisure Sciences*, 9, 119–127.

Crawford, D., Jackson, E. and Godbey, G. (1991). A hierarchical model of leisure constraints. *Leisure Sciences*, 13, 309–320.

Crompton, J. (1979). Motivations for pleasure vacation. *Annals of Tourism Research*, 6, 408–424.

Danylchuk, K. (2003). Bidding for major events: implications for sport managers. In E. Fors (ed.), *Proceedings of the European Association for Sport Management Congress, College of Physical Education, Stockholm, Sweden, September 10–13*. Stockholm: College of Physical Education (available on CD), pp. 97–99.

Deem, R. (1986). *All Work and No Play? The Sociology of Women and Leisure*. Milton Keynes: Open University Press.

Deem, R. (1996). Women in the city and holidays. *Leisure Studies*, 15, 105–119.

Dimanche, F., Havitz, M. and Howard, D. (1991). Testing the Involvement Profile (IP) Scale in the context of selected recreational and touristic activities. *Journal of Leisure Research*, 23, 51–66.

Driver, B. and Knopf, R. (1977). Personality, outdoor recreation, and expected consequences. *Environment and Behavior*, 9, 169–193.

Fakeye, P. and Crompton, J. (1991). Image differences between prospective, first-time, and repeat visitors to the Lower Rio Grande Valley. *Journal of Travel Research*, 30(2), 10–16.

Fairley, S. (2003). In search of relived social experience: group-based nostalgia sport tourism. *Journal of Sport Management*, 17, 284–304.

Faulkner, B., Tisdell, C. and Weston, A. (1998). Leveraging tourism benefits from the Sydney 2000 Olympics. Keynote presentation, Sport Management: Opportunities and Change, Fourth Annual Conference of the Sport Management Association of Australia and New Zealand, Gold Coast, Australia, November 26–28.

Gammon, S. and Robinson, T. (1997). Sport and tourism: a conceptual framework. *Journal of Sports Tourism*, 4(3), 8–24.

Garnham, B. (1996). Ranfurly Shield Rugby: an investigation into the impacts of a sporting event on a provincial city, the case of New Plymouth, Taranaki, New Zealand. *Festival Management and Event Tourism*, 4, 145–149.

Gibson, H. (1989). Tourist roles: stability and change over the life cycle. Unpublished Master's thesis, University of Connecticut, Storrs.

Gibson, H. (1994). Some predictors of tourist role preference for men and women over the adult life course. Unpublished doctoral dissertation, University of Connecticut, Storrs.

Gibson, H. (1996). Thrill seeking vacations: a lifespan perspective. *Loisir et Societe/Society and Leisure*, 19(2), 439–458.

Gibson, H. (1998a). Sport tourism: a critical analysis of research. *Sport Management Review*, 1, 45–76.

Gibson, H. (1998b). Active sport tourism: who participates? *Leisure Studies*, 17, 155–170.

Gibson, H. and Pennington-Gray, L. (2001). Destination Images and Benefits sought from an International Ski Trip: A Case Study in Active Sport Tourism. Paper presented at the North American Society for Sport Management Conference, Virginia Beach, Norfolk, VA, May 30–June 3.

Gibson, H. and Yiannakis, A. (2002). Tourist roles: needs and the adult life course. *Annals of Tourism Research*, 29, 358–383.

Gibson, H., Willming, C. and Holdnak, A. (2002a). 'We're Gators not just a Gator fan:' serious leisure, social identity and University of Florida football. *Journal of Leisure Research*, 14, 397–425.

Gibson, H., Ashton-Shaeffer, C. and Kensinger, K. (2002b). It Wouldn't Be Long Before I'd be Friends with an Undertaker: What it Means to be a Senior Athlete. Paper presented at the Leisure Research Symposium, National Recreation and Park Association Congress, Tampa, FL, October 16–19.

Gibson, H., Willming, C. and Holdnak, A. (2003a). Small-scale event sport tourism: college sport as a tourist attraction. *Tourism Management*, 24, 181–190.

Gibson, H., Williams, S. and Pennington-Gray, L. (2003b). Destination images and benefits sought from an international ski and snowboard trip: a follow-up study. In E. Fors (ed.), *Proceedings of the European Association for Sport Management Congress, College of Physical Education, Stockholm, Sweden, September 10–13*, pp. 167–169. Stockholm: College of Physical Education (available on CD).

Gilbert, D. and Hudson (2000). Tourism demand constraints on skiing participation. *Annals of Tourism Research*, 27(4), 906–925.

Gottlieb, A. (1982). American's vacations. *Annals of Tourism Research*, 9, 164–187.

Graburn, N. (1983). The anthropology of tourism. *Annals of Tourism Research*, 10, 9–33.

Green, B. and Chalip, L. (1998). Sport tourism as the celebration of subculture. *Annals of Tourism Research*, 25, 275–292.

Goeldner, C. and Ritchie, J. R. B. (2003). *Tourism: Principles, Practices and Philosophies*. New York: John Wiley & Sons.

Hall, C. (1992). Adventure, sport and health tourism. In B. Weiler and C. M. Hall (eds), *Special Interest Tourism*. London: Belhaven Press, pp. 141–158.

Hargreaves, J. (1994). *Sporting Females: Critical Issues in the History and Sociology of Women's Sports*. London: Routledge.

Havitz, M. and Dimanche, F. (1990). Proposition for testing the involvement construct in recreation. *Leisure Sciences*, 12, 179–195.

Havitz, M. and Dimanche, F. (1997). Leisure involvement revisited: conceptual conundrums and measurement advances. *Journal of Leisure Research*, 29, 245–278.

Hebb, D. and Thompson, W. (1954). The social significance of animal studies. In G. Lindzey (ed.), *Handbook of Social Psychology*. Reading, MA: Addison-Wesley, pp. 551–552.

Henderson, K. and Bialeschki, M. D. (1991). A sense of entitlement to leisure as constraint and empowerment for women. *Leisure Sciences*, 12, 228–243.

Hinch, T. and Higham, J. (2001). Sport tourism: a framework for research. *International Journal of Tourism Research*, 3, 45–58.

Hudson, S. (2000). The segmentation of potential tourists: constraint differences between men and women. *Journal of Travel Research*, 38(4), 363–369.

Iso-Ahola, S. (1983). Toward a social psychology of recreational travel. *Leisure Studies*, 2, 45–56.

Iso-Ahola, S. (1984). Social psychological foundations of leisure and resultant implications for leisure counseling. In E. Dowd (ed.), *Leisure Counseling, Concepts and Applications*. Springfield, IL: Charles C Thomas, pp. 97–125.

Iso-Ahola, S. and Allen, J. (1982). The dynamics of leisure motivation: the effects of outcome on leisure needs. *Research Quarterly for Exercise and Sport*, 53, 141–149.

Jackson, E. (1990). Trends in leisure preferences: alternative constraints-related explanations. *Journal of Applied Recreation Research*, 15(3), 129–145.

Jackson, E. and Scott, D. (1999). Constraints to leisure. In E. Jackson and T. Burton (eds), *Leisure Studies: Prospects for the Twenty-first Century*. State College, PA: Venture Publishing, pp. 299–334.

Lawson, R. (1991). Patterns of tourist expenditures and types of vacation across the family lifecycle. *Journal of Travel Research*, 21, 12–18.

Lepp, A. and Gibson, H. (2003). Tourist roles, perceived risk and international tourism. *Annals of Tourism Research*, 30(3), 606–624.

Levinson, D., Darrow, C., Klein, E., Levinson, N. and McKee, B. (1978). *The Seasons of a Man's Life*. New York: Knopf.

Lounsbury, J. and Polik, J. (1992). Leisure needs and vacation satisfaction. *Leisure Sciences*, 14, 105–119.

Maheswaren, D. and Meyer-Levy, J. (1990). The influence of message framing and involvement. *Journal of Marketing Research*, 27, 361–367.

Maslow, A. (1943). A theory of human motivation. *Psychological Review*, 50, 370–396.

Maslow, A. (1970). *Motivation and Personality* (2nd edn). New York: Harper and Row.

McGehee, N. G., Yoon, Y. and Cárdenas, D. (2003). Involvement and travel for recreational runners in North Carolina. *Journal of Sport Management*, 17, 305–324.

Mills, A. (1985). Participation motivations for outdoor recreation: a test of Maslow's theory. *Journal of Leisure Research*, 17, 184–199.

Mo, C. D., Howard, D. and Havitz, M. (1993). Testing an international tourist role typology. *Annals of Tourism Research*, 20, 319–335.

Murray, H. (1938). *Exploration and Personality*. New York: Oxford University Press.

National Sporting Goods Association. (2000). Ten year history of sports participation (available at www.nsga.org, accessed 1 February 2002).

Norman, W. (1992). An investigation of the relationship between leisure constraints and the recreation specialization of current participants. In L. Caldwell and C. Riddicks (eds), *Abstracts from the 1992 Symposium on Leisure Research*. Arlington, VA: National Recreation and Park Association, p. 43.

Pearce, P. (1982). *The Social Psychology of Tourist Behaviour*. Oxford: Pergamon.

Pearce, P. (1985). A systematic comparison of travel-related roles. *Human Relations*, 38, 1001–1011.

Pearce, P. and Caltabiano, M. (1983). Inferring travel motivation from traveler's experience. *Journal of Travel Research*, 21, 16–20.

Perdue, R. (1993). External information search in marine recreational fishing. *Leisure Sciences*, 15, 169–187.

Plog, S. (1974). Why destination areas rise and fall in popularity. *The Cornell Hotel and Restaurant Administration Quarterly*, 14, 55–58.

Philipp, S. (1993). Racial differences in the perceived attractiveness of tourism destinations, interests, and cultural resources. *Journal of Leisure Research*, 25, 290–304.

Rapoport, R. and Rapoport, R. N. (1975). *Leisure and the Family Lifecycle*. London: Routledge and Kegan Paul.

Redfoot, D. (1984). Tourist authenticity, tourist angst and modern reality. *Qualitative Sociology*, 7, 291–309.

Redmond, G. (1991). Changing styles of sports tourism: industry/consumer interactions in Canada, the USA and Europe. In M. Sinclair and M. Stabler (eds), *The Tourism Industry: An International Analysis*. Wallingford: CAB International, pp. 107–120.

Richards, G. (1996). Skilled consumption and UK ski holidays. *Tourism Management*, 17, 25–34.

Ritchie, B., Mosedale, L. and King, J. (2000). Profiling sport tourists: the case of Super 12 Rugby Union in the Australian capital territory. *Current Issues in Tourism*, 5(1), 33–44.

Ryan, C. (1995). Islands, beaches and life-stage marketing. In M. Collins and T. Baum (eds), *Island Tourism: Management Principles and Practice*. New York: Wiley & Sons, pp. 79–93.

Shaw, S. (1994). Gender, leisure, and constraint: towards a framework for the analysis of women's leisure. *Journal of Leisure Research*, 26, 8–22.

Smith, V. (ed.) (1989). *Hosts and Guests: The Anthropology of Tourism* (2nd edn). Philadelphia, PA: University of Pennsylvania Press.

Squire, S. (1994). Gender and tourist experiences: assessing women's shared meanings for Beatrix Potter. *Leisure Studies*, 13, 195–209.

Standeven, J. and De Knop, P. (1999). *Sport Tourism*. Champaign, IL: Human Kinetics.

Theberge, N. (1987). Sport and women's empowerment. *Women Studies International Forum*, 10, 387–393.

Tinsley, H., Barrett, T. and Kass, R. (1977). Leisure activities and need satisfaction. *Journal of Leisure Research*, 9, 111–120.

Travel Industry Association of America (1999). *Profile of Travelers who Attend Sports Events* (available at www.tia.org.com, accessed 3 February 2001).

Tripp, L. (2003). It's great to be a Florida Gator: fans negotiating ideologies of race, gender, and power. Unpublished doctoral dissertation, University of Florida, Gainesville.

Turner, V. (1969). *The Ritual Process*. Chicago, IL: Aldine.

Wahlers, R. and Etzel, M. (1985). Vacation preference as a manifestation of optimal stimulation and lifestyle experience. *Journal of Leisure Research*, 17, 283–295.

Wearing, B. (1998). *Leisure and Feminist Theory*. London: Sage Publications.

Wells, W. and Guber, G. (1966). The lifecycle concept in marketing research. *Journal of Marketing Research*, 3, 355–363.

Wickens, E. (2002). The sacred and the profane: a tourist typology. *Annals of Tourism Research*, 29(3), 834–851.

Williams, P. and Fidgeon, P. (2000). Addressing participation constraint: a case study of potential skiers. *Tourism Management*, 21, 379–393.

Williams, P. and Lattey, C. (1994). Skiing constraints for women. *Journal of Travel Research*, 32, 21–25.

Yiannakis, A. and Gibson, H. (1992). Roles tourists play. *Annals of Tourism Research*, 19, 287–303.

6

Sport tourism destinations: the active sport tourist perspective

Sonia Francis and Peter Murphy

Introduction

Sport tourism is increasingly being utilized by established tourism destinations to gain a competitive edge in the marketplace. McDonnell *et al.* (1999: 29) discuss the advantages of major sporting events such as the 2000 Sydney Olympics in providing 'newness, freshness and change in a destination to enhance its appeal to visitors'. Sport tourism is a new growth industry now recognized by government agencies, which are committing increased resources to its development. The Australian Government's Department of Industry, Tourism and Resources stated on its website (www.industry. gov.au) in November 2003 that there is further scope to develop this industry sector (with the collaboration of tourism and sporting organizations) by developing sport tourism niche products. Such development can have positive economic consequences.

The exact revenue generated by the sport tourism industry is unknown because of the difficulty of separating it from the generic tourism industry and the sport industry. However, both of these are large markets. Shanks (2002) estimates the global sports industry to currently be worth $US 213–350 billion annually. The World Travel and Tourism Council (2002, 2003) indicates the tourism industry to be worth $US 3.4 trillion worldwide, and to be responsible for 200 million jobs and over 10 per cent of global GDP.

Athletes, sporting teams and their support management are classified as active sport tourists when they participate in sporting activities that take them away from their home base. Professional athletes and their professional sporting bodies (team and support management) are one sub-set of this classification, and are referred to in this chapter as 'active pro-sport tourists'. The other sub-set of the classification is amateur athletes and their respective sporting body, team and support management. They are referred to as 'active amateur-sport tourists'.

The first part of this chapter considers the advancements in professional sport, and their implications for sport tourism destination planning. It focuses on visionary thinking by professional sports administrators in creating an environment for optimal performance, the importance of understanding team culture, how the active pro-sport tourist perceives the service quality of sport tourism destinations, and the elements that need to be present for a strategic fit between a sport tourism destination and the active pro-sport tourist.

In this part of the chapter, Melbourne, Australia is used to illustrate a sport tourism destination. Melbourne is recognized as the sporting capital of Australia because of its ability to attract major sporting events such as Formula One Grand Prix, the Australian Tennis Open and national and international football code fixtures. This is mainly attributable to the city's sporting, accommodation and hospitality facilities, and associated internal and external transportation infrastructure. The recent sporting event of the International Rugby Board Rugby World Cup 2003 (RWC 2003) is examined in Case study 6.1, to illustrate the perceived service quality gaps in Melbourne's support structure when professional sporting bodies (PSBs) were attempting to find a suitable environment to prepare for the RWC 2003. Key criteria for service quality in a sport tourism destination from the active pro-sport tourists' perspective are outlined. In addition, a framework for the proactive sport tourist to assess the strategic fit of sport tourism destinations is provided.

Not all tourist destinations can afford or justify such a commitment to sport tourism as can Melbourne or other major cities. However, many of the considerations presented here apply equally to smaller and amateur sports events and festivals. Thus the second part of this chapter examines amateur sport and the considerations required for sport tourism destination planning. B.C. Games in Canada is used as an example of this scale of facility planning and destination development. The B.C. Games is an agency jointly funded by provincial government and corporate sources tasked with the responsibility of holding amateur tournaments that encourage young athletes to develop their skills and others to maintain their interest in various sporting activities. As such it has developed a similar set of objectives and operational criteria to the larger sport event organizers when staging events such as the B.C. Games.

The professionalization of sport has increased over the past decade, driven by national and international sporting competitions securing lucrative media rights sponsorship. This has placed demands on sporting organizations that seek to participate in such competitions to move beyond an amateur structure managed by volunteers to a formal business structure with qualified administrative and coaching staff. Massey (1996: 75–78), in a review of Australian business and sport, noted that: 'today sport managers are challenged to upgrade their knowledge and skills to ensure that organizations within the sport industry remain competitive and financially viable'. These two factors have changed the dynamics of how sporting organizations approach and plan their involvement in sporting competitions at destinations away from their 'home venue'.

Sport tourism is a client-based service industry that Lovelock *et al.* (2001) distinguish from a goods-based industry by the generic characteristics of variability, intangibility, inseparability and perishability. Sport tourism destination planners need to consider that active pro-sport tourists are seeking a greater involvement in the service offerings of sport tourism destinations, and they are becoming more sophisticated in analysing the pre-match risk and uncertainty of such a destination. These two factors are becoming relevant for active pro-sport tourists when making a sport tourism destination decision.

Sports facilities require large sums of money to construct and significant sums to maintain and operate over their lifespan. As a consequence, all jurisdictions with expensive sport and recreational facilities to maintain are keen to find ways to increase their patronage. Most studies of facilities approach this issue from a consumer and marketing perspective. A good example is the work of Shilbury *et al.* (1999), who discuss 'the place of facility' in terms of its role in the marketing mix, noting that 'with production and consumption of the sport products taking place in the facility, not only current provision but also future provision needs to be taken into consideration' (Shilbury *et al.*, 1999: 266).

With the business perspective of modern sport, an emphasis on the marketing side is natural. There has also been some examination of the supply side. Cities contemplating the building of expensive sport and recreation facilities need to gauge long-term demand for their planned facilities, especially in the case of facilities designed for large-scale hallmark events. The difficulties experienced in Montreal in utilizing the Olympic Stadium after the 1976 Olympics provided a salutary lesson. Consequently, the literature in tourism and sport cites the growing need to tailor stadiums for multiple functions and smaller crowds after the main event in order to obtain the best return from the initial investment (Hall, 1992; Getz, 1997; Standeven and De Knop, 1999).

Sydney's Olympic Park (Stadium Precinct) provides a good example of this trend. This is now a sports complex in the suburb of Homebush, which is attempting to turn the Olympic facilities into an ongoing sport and recreational centre for the city. One of the first actions to achieve this goal was to reduce the seating capacity of the main stadium. Another was to encourage several professional teams either to make Sydney Olympic Park their home ground or to include it in some of their fixtures. Other actions were to encourage schools to use the facility for special tournaments or finals, and to draw visitors for a day or half-day of sightseeing and recreational pursuits.

A notable gap in the literature pertaining to optimization of existing or planned sports facilities and associated support environments is the perspective of sports teams and athletes. They are neither the major consumer interest (traditionally, the spectators) nor a supply consideration (because when teams or franchises have been discussed it has been in respect to ownership or management concerns).

Yet the case can be made that it is the team's and the individuals' performances that are the key attraction. These performances can be influenced by how they view the facilities and associated support environments.

The active sport tourist

Historically, key drivers of sport tourism destination development have been city developers, government agencies, facility owners and event organizers. Today, however, active sport tourists (including amateur athletes, professional athletes and professional sporting bodies) are emerging drivers of sport tourism. Contemporary professional sporting bodies (PSBs) have distinct characteristics. PSBs with a well-developed organizational culture (where the team and administration sides of the business work well together) are recognized as 'communal organizations' by Goffee and Jones (1996). This type of organization has the ability to adapt quickly to changing environmental conditions in order to stay competitive both on and off the field (Amis and O'Brien, 2001). A shift in thinking by PSBs as to how to achieve optimal performance has led to a new planning approach when considering the preparation phase for matches held away from the 'home venue'. This shift has implications for the development of sport tourism destinations, especially those competing to host major sporting competitions.

Sporting cultures that traditionally revolved around a specific 'playing venue' are no longer the norm. Instead, sporting organizations construct their 'away game' planning around the creation of an environment that assists optimal performance. The types of destinations these sporting organizations seek are those that have a strategic fit with the team culture. For example, destination choice is not necessarily determined by geographical proximity to the 'playing venue'; however, transportation links are a key consideration.

In professional sporting competitions, the sporting team has little say over the facilities selected as playing venues except where there are safety issues. Competition owners and media rights holders hold the decision-making power for facilities. While team management does not determine the choice of venue, it does have a direct influence on the destination selected and revenue spent for 'away match' preparation. This fact needs to be considered during the feasibility stage of sport tourism destination development. Developers must be aware that teams now view playing venue destinations from a service quality perspective for competition preparation. For example, the 'ripple' effect arising from a professional team's choice to stay at a destination other than the playing venue is that the team's supporters (passive sport tourists) who normally have a strong attachment to the team's itinerary will also wish to locate themselves close to the team.

Active pro-sport tourists and the passive sport tourists (spectators) have differing perspectives when considering a destination. Each type will consider the basic needs of accommodation facilities, transportation, food and beverage services, retail businesses and attractions. Both, however, have a higher level of needs they wish to satisfy, and these higher needs differ. One concept that can be used to explain the difference in motivations is US marketing expert Abraham Maslow's 'Hierarchy of Needs' theory (1943). Once the active pro-sport tourist and the passive sport tourist have satisfied the basic needs for food and shelter, they move on to higher needs, which Maslow refers to as the 'self-actualization' area (where one attempts to gain fulfilment of creative and intellectual potential). The active pro-sport tourist seeks an environment that not only fulfils basic needs but also is conducive to achieving on-field optimal performance.

During the amateur era of sport, the active sport tourist had limited involvement or influence over the 'away' destination used for preparation for a competition. This was partly because of limited offerings, but also because of the reluctance of lodging and facility operators to accommodate sporting teams. Often, lodging operators viewed sporting teams as a business liability because of costs associated with physical damage and the loss of goodwill by other guests. The professional era of sport has changed this view. The main reason for this change is that a PSB's success is now closely aligned with its public image, positive media attention and sponsorship deals. An integral part of the PSB's success formula is the employment of professional athletes and administrators who abide by a code of conduct, and hence unacceptable behaviours that prevailed and were accepted or ignored during the amateur era are no longer condoned and sanctions are imposed. This now makes the active pro-sport tourist a lucrative proposition for lodging establishments, because of the revenue spent and the leverage the lodging establishment can use in its marketing campaigns as the preferred establishment for a particular sporting team. Lodging establishments are also now more receptive to assisting active pro-sport tourists to customize their environment. This is described later in this chapter.

Service quality is now a key consideration in the destination selection process for away matches. The challenge for destination developers is to close the gap in service quality perceptions by the active pro-sport tourist. Parasuraman et al. (1985) developed a service quality model that identifies how customers' quality perceptions are influenced by five different gaps of expectations and perceptions. McDonald et al. (1995) adapted the model to measure the service quality of professional team sports using the following five dimensions:

1 Tangibles
2 Reliability
3 Responsiveness
4 Assurance
5 Empathy.

The active pro-sport tourist considers these five dimensions in destination selection, with the tangibles, reliability and responsiveness being the most important dimensions.

Sport tourism destination and active pro-sport tourist strategic fit

The process used to achieve a strategic fit between the pro-sport tourist and the sport tourism destination uses the three core principles of the sport management process described by Smith and Stewart (1999), namely:

1 Strategic planning
2 Total quality management
3 Culture and change management.

Achieving a strategic fit between the sport tourism destination and the active pro-sport tourist therefore requires careful planning and the ability to apply visionary thinking (think outside the square), a range of quality accommodation and sporting facilities, and an understanding of the pro-sport team's culture and specific needs.

Strategic considerations occur in a changing operational environment. In the sporting environment, there is a need to adjust quickly to change if an organization is to remain successful and viable. These points are well recognized in the literature. Consider, for example, the following propositions:

- Viljoen and Dann (2000) state that an important analytical component of strategic thinking is to take the 'fuzzy' or unclear notions of mission, environment and resources and combine them into a cohesive plan
- Amis and O'Brien (2001) describe change in a sporting organization as an important factor in staying competitive
- Carlopio *et al.* (1997) go further to suggest that strategic change in organizations is inevitable and organizations need to keep re-orientating themselves to accommodate change.

These propositions provide us with key reasons why the active pro-sport tourist has become an emerging driver of sport tourism destinations.

Team culture

A sporting team's culture is unique – only rarely can it be blueprinted and replicated elsewhere. A sporting team that develops a culture for success looks at all aspects of its environment to create one that allows for optimal performance. Home-ground advantage is believed to play a factor in competitive sport. Statistical evidence in professional football leagues supports this theory. It is perceived that this advantage is achieved because of the athletes' familiarity with the ground and prevailing conditions; home crowd support; the athlete's ability to have as normal daily routine as possible leading up to the competition; and the absence of long haul travel, time zone differences, the need for acclimatization and variances in altitude.

To counter the perceived disadvantages of away games, professional sporting teams have invested heavily in addressing these factors in their quest to win such games.

The sport tourism destination

Cities around the globe are often recognized by unique physical icons – for example, Paris has the Eiffel Tower, New York has the Statue of Liberty and Sydney has the Opera House. The city of Melbourne, Australia, does not have a unique physical icon; however, its great sporting events have themselves become the city's recognizable icon. For example, the headline on the front page of the Melbourne edition of the *Herald Sun* (2003) read: 'Sport City'. Its by-line read

'A sensational Melbourne feast of sport is expected to attract more than 200 000 fans this weekend'. The story that accompanied this headline described three international sporting events (International Rules Test between Ireland and Australia, RWC 2003 quarterfinal playoffs between France and Ireland and between New Zealand and South Africa, and the Melbourne Cup) that had attracted 200 000 fans to the city and millions more in global TV viewers. Melbourne gained immense exposure as a sport tourism destination during these sporting events. Melbourne's vibrancy and ability to cater for the transportation, lodging, food and beverage, entertainment, and sporting interests of the passive sport tourist has made Melbourne an attractive destination for the active pro-sport tourist.

The ability to showcase Melbourne's unique characteristics and sell the image of the destination as a 'Sport City' is described by Hall (1989) as one of the advantages of sport events working with tourism. Melbourne has achieved its 'Sport City' status over a period of time by developing quality sporting facilities (such as the Telstra Dome, Australian Tennis Centre, Melbourne Cricket Ground, Flemington Racecourse and the Melbourne Swimming and Aquatic Centre), hospitality and entertainment precincts (such as the Crown Casino and Southbank), transportation links, and the visionary thinking of government agencies that have strategically developed and marketed Melbourne's sporting events to local, domestic and international sport tourists.

McDonnell *et al.* (1999: 25) discuss the significance of city infrastructure improvements in accommodation, transport and communications (for a destination such as Sydney) that can be achieved through the staging of major sporting events such as the 2000 Olympics Games. Melbourne has been able to achieve its infrastructure improvements through the staging of recurring annual major sporting events such as the Australian Tennis Open, Formula One Grand Prix, Australian Football League Grand Final and the Spring Racing Carnival (including the Melbourne Cup). These recurring events have placed Melbourne in a position of strength when bidding for the rights to host one-off major sporting events such as international cricket test matches, rugby union test matches, rugby league test matches and the 2006 Commonwealth Games. The advantages of recurring annual major sport events versus one-off major sporting events for sport tourism destination planning is an area that warrants further research for developers of destinations.

Sport tourism destination service quality

Destination service quality needs vary between active pro-sport tourists. Variations occur due to the nature of the sport, personal preferences and the level of quality desired. The active pro-sport tourist's perception of the actual service quality of a destination will also be determined by the level of importance placed on each need. In addition, Zeithaml *et al.* (1990) state that word of mouth, external communications and past experience build up a level of expected service quality. Shilbury *et al.* (1999) recommend that in order to optimize service quality before production and consumption in the service marketing function, you need to know where differences in perceptions occur. The following service quality model for sport tourism destinations has been adapted from the 10 dimensions of service quality identified by the Zeithaml *et al.* (1990) and Parasuraman *et al.* (1985)

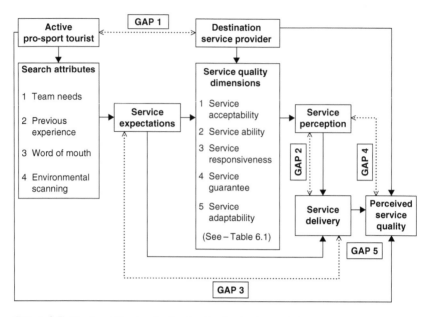

Figure 6.1 The Sport Tourism Destination Service Quality Model

conceptual models of service quality, and the service quality dimensions used by McDonald *et al.* (1995) in their 'TEAMQUAL: measuring service quality in professional team sports'.

The Sport Tourism Destination Service Quality Model described in Figure 6.1 identifies four 'search attributes' and five dimensions for service quality that the active pro-sport tourist is expected to use in their destination selection process. Each dimension has a set of variables considered essential in the selection process (see Table 6.1). These variables need to be controlled by destination planners when attempting to deliver service quality for the active pro-sport tourist. One distinct application difference of the modified Service Quality Model is its use for business-to-business transactions (as between the destination service provider and the active pro-sport tourist).

In this modified model (Figure 6.1), there are five gaps that can occur between service expectations and service perception:

- *Gap 1* is the difference between the active pro-sport tourist's expectations and the destination service provider's perception of the active pro-sport tourist's expectations
- *Gap 2* is the difference between the destination service provider's perception of the service expected by the active pro-sport tourist and the service delivered by the destination service provider
- *Gap 3* is the difference between the actual service delivered and the advertising and promotional material relied upon by the active pro-sport tourist to form service expectations

...ourism destination service quality variables

	Service ability	Service responsiveness	Service guarantee	Service adap...
...ity	*Physical facilities* A. Past experience B. Ability to adapt physical facilities	A. Efficiency in service B. Willingness to meet team	A. Commitment to deliver as promised B. Professional delivery C. Ability to deliver a secure environment	A. Ability t... and its d and prof
...pects				
...on				
...ations				
...ons				
...e				
...facilities				
...ndards	*Management/staff* A. Professionalism B. Willingness to customize an environment			
...t				
...clusive use				
...e conditions				
...vacy				

- *Gap 4* is the difference between the active pro-sport tourist's perception of the service to be delivered and what the destination service provider actually delivers
- *Gap 5* is the difference between the active pro-sport tourist's perception of the service quality and the destination service provider's perception of service quality.

Case Study 6.1 The IRB Rugby World Cup 2003, Australia

The following case study focuses on professional rugby union as a sport and on the IRB Rugby World Cup 2003 held in Australia to illustrate how professional sporting teams set about ensuring the sport tourism destination has a strategic fit with their team culture. The lessons from this case study are applicable to any sporting code or team, but the order of priority may vary.

Rugby union was an amateur sport until 27 August 1995, when the IRB, in a meeting in Paris, 'abolished amateurism' (Dabscheck, 2003). In 1996, southern hemisphere rugby commenced its first professional rugby competition with the inception of the South Africa, New Zealand and Australian Rugby (SANZAR) Super 12 competition. The professionalization of the sporting bodies involved in the competition has been rapid, with proper businesslike structures being put in place to replace pre-existing amateur frameworks. Sponsorship of the competition via media rights enabled these PSBs to employ full-time professional administrators, coaching staff and athletes. The Super 12 competition is the primary feeder for athletes and coaching staff selected for the national teams of New Zealand (All Blacks), Australia (Wallabies) and South Africa (Springboks).

In the formative years of the Super 12 competition, most teams invested heavily in techniques and methods for improving the fitness and skill levels of their athletes as well as in technology that improved game analysis techniques. Some teams achieved success very quickly by applying these new concepts, while other teams were slower to adapt. Super 12 teams that had achieved superior levels of fitness in their athletes and applied sophisticated technical analysis of the game started to pay much closer attention to the environment in which the team prepared for competition. Measures were put in place to achieve a home base for optimal performance, whilst carefully thought-out strategies were adopted in planning for away games.

One of the PSBs in the Super 12 competition is the Crusaders' franchise, based in Christchurch, New Zealand. It is seen as a leader in professional development on and off the field. For example, in recent years the Crusaders' franchise has paid particular attention to creating the right environment to win 'away' games. The Crusaders' franchise was able to improve its away game record in 2002 by winning all of its away games (Table 6.2). The Crusaders' coach, Robbie Deans, said this improvement was in part due to the creation of the right environment for pre-match preparation for away games (R. Deans: personal communications: 2002–2003). Other Super 12 teams have adopted a similar strategy as active pro-sport tourists. For example, in 2003 the NSW Waratahs established

---

a relationship with the Clearwater Resort (on the outskirts of Christchurch, New Zealand) as its base for all its away games played in New Zealand during the Super 12 competition.

Table 6.2 Crusaders' home and away success rate

Year	Home game success	Away game success
2001	3/5	1/6
2002	8/8	5/5

National rugby teams such as the Wallabies and the All Blacks have dedicated training bases in their own countries, such as Camp Wallaby in the Novotel Resort, Coff's Harbour, New South Wales, Australia, and the All Blacks' dedicated training facility at the Massey Institute of Sport, Palmerston North, New Zealand. The Wallabies were fortunate in being able to base themselves at Camp Wallaby in Coff's Harbour for the RWC 2003. The All Blacks needed to find a suitable environment in Australia as a base for match preparation. They started the search for the required environment 16 months prior to the commencement of the RWC 2003. A major consideration for the All Blacks was that their scheduled matches were on the eastern seaboard of Australia, with matches in Melbourne, Brisbane and Sydney. The management team ranked these three destinations in an order of preference and then set out to match desired environment criteria with the destination. The All Blacks management ranked Melbourne as its first choice for climatic and transportation accessibility reasons, and then attempted to find a base that could provide suitable extended-stay lodging and training facilities at the same location or within close proximity to one another. Melbourne's training facilities were easy to assess, but lodging proved more difficult as most establishments did not meet the All Blacks' specifications. After an extended environmental scanning exercise an establishment was identified that was able to meet team specifications with some modification. Table 6.3 identifies the key considerations by the All Blacks management in establishing its base for the RWC 2003.

The All Blacks finished third in the RWC 2003 and were placed under heavy scrutiny regarding why they fell short of winning the World Cup. The Wallabies finished second in the RWC 2003. Both the Wallabies and the All Blacks were provided with a carefully customized environment in which to prepare their campaigns. Professional athletes such as veteran All Black Justin Marshall publicly stated that the team environment created for the RWC 2003 campaign was the most enjoyable of all the test matches and two RWC campaigns he had been involved in as an active pro-sport tourist. The All Blacks' base in Melbourne was the Somerset Suites (an all suites hotel) in the St Kilda road precinct (an area adjacent to Melbourne city's central business district and close to parklands and training and major sporting facilities). The team's environment within the hotel was tailored to foster the team's culture. The team used the Melbourne Swimming and Aquatic Centre and nearby sports grounds for its training needs.

Table 6.3 All Blacks scoping exercise for the team base for RWC 2003

Priority One	To find a destination with regular air links to 'playing venue' destinations
Priority Two	To create a suitable extended stay environment that allowed athletes and management to have as normal a daily routine for training and day-to-day living as possible
Priority Three	To find lodging and training facilities that were at one location or in close proximity to one another
Action One	Consult with Australian contacts and Australian Tourism Board representatives
Action Two	Review destinations and airlinks
Action Three	Undertake a destination scoping exercise
Decision One	Melbourne became the destination of first choice because of the RWC 2003 match itinerary, Melbourne's sporting facilities, transportation links and climatic conditions
Decision Two	Melbourne provided limited lodging facilities that met All Blacks' service quality needs and were located at the same place or within easy access to training facilities and transport links, and provided an environment suited to an extended stay
Decision Three	Management defined a further set of criteria and developed a strategy for modification of lodging facilities to meet their needs; if a suitable lodging establishment could not be found then other destinations would be reviewed again
Criteria One	Training facilities such as the Melbourne Swimming and Aquatic Centre became the focal point for finding a suitable lodging establishment
Criteria Two	A defined radius excluding the central business district was created
Criteria Three	Apartment-style accommodation was preferred in a residential and business mixed-use precinct
Criteria Four	Key management personnel and senior players were asked to assess the lodging and training facility suitability as well
Final Decision	Melbourne did not have a location that provided both the lodging and training facility needs in one place, so it was decided to secure a lodging establishment that met All Blacks' criteria and was close to training facilities. Somerset Suites, St Kilda Rd, Melbourne provided apartment-style living with hotel amenities. There were some private meeting areas, but limited informal areas for the team to relax. The All Blacks management addressed these limitations by seeking an arrangement with the Somerset Suites to modify an area for relaxation and provide a secure area for team analysis activities. Somerset Suites became the preferred establishment because of its proximity to MSAC and training facilities

These facilities were able to accommodate the training requirements and requests for exclusive use of certain areas at certain times.

Robbie Deans, the All Blacks coaching coordinator and Crusaders coach, was involved in the All Blacks' destination exercise from the initial scoping phase. Although the All Blacks did not fulfil their World Cup dream, Deans believes that the customization of the environment provided the athletes with the best possible environment to prepare for the competition.

Closing service quality gaps

The active pro-sport tourist

Case study 6.1 highlights a gap in the Melbourne accommodation sector for extended stay active pro-sport tourists. Melbourne will partly address this gap in its construction of an athlete's village for the Commonwealth Games in 2006; however, this village is earmarked for residential apartment-style living after the Commonwealth Games. This will still leave a gap in the marketplace for an extended stay resort-style complex for active pro-sport tourists.

The proactive approach of the All Blacks management towards their team's RWC 2003 base meant that only minor modifications to lodging arrangements were required during the tournament. These modifications related to the physical-setting needs of food and beverage services and relaxation areas. The All Blacks were able to close the potential service quality gaps using a sport management process of strategic planning, total quality management and the nurturing of the culture. Gaps 1 and 2 were closed by an in-person meeting with the Somerset Suites management and formal documentation of specific needs. Gaps 3 and 4 were closed by key All Blacks management undertaking early site visits (at different times) to Somerset Suites. These personnel stayed (sometimes not identified as All Blacks personnel) and utilized facilities to ensure that expectations and delivery could be matched. Gap 5 was monitored and minor service issues were managed by close interaction between the All Blacks and Somerset Suites management during the All Blacks' stay.

Another way by which the active pro-sport tourist can ensure that service quality gaps are minimized prior to contracting to use a specific destination service provider is to engage a 'location scout' (similar to those used in the TV and film industry) to source service providers at a sport tourism destination that meet the active pro-sport tourist's specific needs. Location scouts are experienced in assessing facilities, atmospheric and aesthetic aspects of destinations from the client's point of view.

Based on the experience of Case study 6.1, the Service Acceptability Matrix (Table 6.4) provides a useful framework for the proactive sport tourist or location scout to assess the strategic fit of a sport tourism destination. The service criteria framework identifies six key areas for lodging facilities. The areas are:

1 Public area aspects
2 Accommodation room specifications
3 Communications
4 Accessibility
5 Meeting room facilities
6 Destination service provider management and staff.

The five key areas for the service criteria framework for training facilities are:

1 Gymnasium
2 Aquatic facilities
3 Athletic track facilities
4 Training ground/medical facilities
5 Destination service provider management and staff.

Table 6.4 Sport tourism destination service acceptability matrix for the active pro-sport tourist

Service criteria	Not required	Meets requirements	Doesn't meet requirements	Acceptable with modification	Not able to be modified

Lodging
Public area aspects
24-hour reception
Privacy aspects
Aesthetics
Road noise levels
Public area noise
   levels
Security
On-site parking/valet
   parking
Porter service
Information desk
Informal food and
   beverage outlet
On-site facilities
Door/room heights
Lifts
Goods lift

Accommodation room
specifications
Bedding style/
   configuration
In-room facilities
Door/room heights
Suite availability
Suite availability
   for medical team
   set-up
Lodging floor layout
Floor security system
Room key security

Communications
In-room Internet/
   phone ports
Business centre
In-room cable/pay TV

Accessibility
Bus access
Airport
Training facilities
Playing venue
Medical facilities
Business precinct
Parks precincts

(Continued)

Table 6.4 (*Continued*)

Service criteria	Not required	Meets requirements	Doesn't meet requirements	Acceptable with modification	Not able to be modified
Entertainment precinct					
Public transport					
Meeting room facilities					
Private meeting room					
Private food and beverage facilities					
Management/staff					
Professionalism					
Willingness to customize environment					
Training facilities					
Gymnasium					
Equipment and layout					
Ability for exclusive use					
Aquatic facilities					
Layout					
Ability for exclusive use					
Athletic track facilities					
Surface condition					
Ability for exclusive use					
Training ground/ medical facilities					
Changing room/physio/ medical facilities					
Ability for exclusive use					
Surface condition					
Ability for privacy					
Management/staff					
Professionalism					
Willingness to customize environment					

The active amateur sport tourist

At the other end of the continuum are amateur sports, with their tournament appeal to destinations. Sport tourism via amateur tournaments is a growing feature of destination marketing because such tourists can make use of existing facilities and each participating team often has its own 'supporters' club', which means extensive local spending on accommodation, meals and shopping. However, if destinations are to capitalize on their tournament potential they need to make themselves attractive to the organizers who make the decision to select from a growing number of alternative locations, or the participants that choose whether to participate.

Amateur tournaments require destination features that differ from professional sports organizations. They need facilities, but these do not have to be the best or the most central. Rather they need to be adequate and able to handle several games at the same time. They need to be convenient to a wide range of accommodation and support facilities. In some instances the accommodation is provided free of charge to participants and linked to some form of public institution such as schools. In all instances the sport facilities and accommodation need to be conveniently accessible to motor transport, as most visitors will have driven to the destination. A significant difference from professional sport involves the need for volunteers, and the presence of a pool of goodwill and volunteer labour to assist in the delivery of the tournament.

An example of this type of tournament tourism can be found in the B.C. Games programme in the large western province of British Columbia, Canada. The purpose of the B.C. Games is:

> To provide an opportunity for the development of athletes, coaches and officials in preparation for higher levels of competition in a multi-sport event that promotes interest and participation in sport and sporting activities, individual achievement and community development.
> (B.C. Games, undated)

Within these broad goals are some specific objectives. Among those that relate specifically to this chapter are the following:

- To provide each hosting community with a legacy of experienced volunteers and facility improvements
- To celebrate the community. (B.C. Games, undated)

As indicated by these goals and objectives, there are both political and sport agendas behind these Games. They are designed to bring these events to as many cities and towns throughout B.C. as possible. If it is necessary to upgrade some of the local sport and recreational facilities, that encourages local authorities to link their capital spending with these events. The Games are designed not only for sport development purposes but also for general community development, raising the awareness of the local location's tourism potential and awakening the community spirit.

A key feature of team culture at tournaments is to have fun, and that is mainly limited to post-game celebrations and recreation opportunities with family and friends who have accompanied the participants to the destination. In short, tournaments provide a strong motivation for short family vacation breaks. In addition to the increased hotel patronage there will be extensive use of local restaurants, pubs and clubs during the evenings, and more general shopping and sightseeing during the day. Tournaments lasting several days result in considerable revenue generation for the destination, something that is appreciated particularly if the activity occurs outside of the high tourist season.

In terms of the B.C. Games, several different team cultures have emerged during observation and measurement of several Games in different venues (Carmichael and Murphy, 1996). The younger participants (those under 18 years of age), either as formal teams or individual athletes representing a provincial sport region, essentially made use of the provided free accommodation and meals. This meant most of their time was spent in and around the schools that were acting as dormitories and meal centres, with short trips to the local shops and recreation centres. In contrast, older participants and family groups often chose to decline the free accommodation and sought out nearby commercial accommodation. In their 'down time' they were more likely to frequent local restaurants and night spots, and were often more likely to engage in serious sightseeing and shopping.

The more renowned a destination is in terms of its tourism appeal, the more attractive it is to tournament organizers and participants. This is because the features and facilities that make a town or city a popular tourist destination also appeal to tournament personnel in terms of their sport and their recreation time. Therefore there is a hierarchy of tournament destinations, with the larger and more tourism-oriented towns and cities being the most desirable locations, and acting like gateway destinations because of their facilities and good transport links.

The B.C. Games tournaments do not follow the above description entirely because of the desirability to distribute the tournaments and their benefits as evenly as possible throughout the province. Even so, the attraction of the two major cities and tourism destinations within the province – Vancouver and Victoria – prove hard to resist. Within a few years the Games are likely to be drawn to these two destinations on a regular basis because of their outstanding and abundant sport facilities, their excellent air or ground transportation links, and their popularity as places to visit. In contrast, the smaller regional destinations often require some form of facility upgrade for the tournament, the transportation of more athletes and officials because most live in the two major coastal cities, and involve increased costs in getting everyone to the host destination. However, what the smaller centres lack in terms of facilities they more than compensate for with the enthusiasm of their volunteers and general welcome. This is epitomized by an experience at the Nelson Winter Games of 1989, where a local resident was observed feeding the overdue parking meters to prevent visitors from incurring parking fines.

Most tournament organizers have a checklist of desirable attributes that need to be considered in selecting destinations. The most obvious is to have sufficient venues to accommodate all teams through preliminary rounds of the competition, with a venue containing adequate spectator facilities for the finals. The next is to be assured of an adequate range of appropriate accommodation to suit all tastes and needs of participants and their supporters. It is easier to meet such needs if the tournament takes place outside the high season, and this will also assist the organizers in negotiating better rates. Another important consideration is transport availability; this again is influenced by seasonality in terms of airline seat or ferry space availability, but is also a constraint for smaller regional centres that may have a limited air passenger schedule. Finally, tournaments are meant to be fun, so recreation and entertainment facilities for participants and supporters alike are a definite plus.

Within the overall objectives of the B.C. Games all of the above destination selection criteria are considered. In every case the B.C. Games officials pay an early site visit to potential destinations. They do this to ensure the Games can be held safely and effectively, and in some cases it may mean the temporary cessation of certain sports or limits on the number of athletes. The Games organizers check what facility upgrades are needed and manageable within the budget. They work with authorities and businesses to arrange sponsorship and the organization of volunteers. To provide a special feel to its tournaments the B.C. Games has attempted to emulate certain features of hallmark sports events. Early on it developed a sponsorship deal with a natural gas provider which donates a perpetual flame facility at a prominent site over the duration of the Games. An athlete's village has been created close to the main venue or accommodation centre, where one of the prime attractions has been the official souvenir shop. More recently it has included a 'Main Stage' where local cultural activities can take place and video highlights are shown, and the (lapel) pin-trading centre has become a major feature.

Conclusion

The purpose of this chapter has been to readdress the balance of enquiry into destination attractiveness. It proposes that an often overlooked client group is that of active sport tourists – both participants and sports organizations – whose performances are critical to the success of sport events. The chapter focuses on the specific and growing needs of the modern sports person. It is noted that while significant differences can be detected between the needs of the professional and amateur active sport tourists there are still common threads in their preferences for sport tourism destinations.

Two contrasting cases illustrate the comparisons between professional and amateur sport tourist needs. One is the professional sport of rugby leading to the site selection of the New Zealand All Blacks in their preparation for the 2003 World Cup of Rugby in Australia. The other is the amateur sports tournaments of the B.C. Summer and Winter Games, where politics has a greater involvement in the selection process than does the individual athletes' need to win. Despite these different scales and emphases, both groups have some similar requirements. They need easy access to the sport venues, yet a restful and convenient base for the pre-competition preparation. Furthermore, neither the professional nor the amateur active sport tourist wants to be completely isolated from the attractions of the local destination, including the opportunity to participate in tourism activities with friends and relatives. As more cities and towns seek to host major sporting events, it is necessary for them to consider and plan for the interests and comfort of the major participants in these events – the athletes, teams and their respective professional sporting bodies.

This chapter recognizes the importance of the active pro-sport tourist as an emerging driver in sport tourist destination development. The destination needs of the active pro-sport tourist have become more specific with the advent of global professional sporting competitions. A matrix has been developed that can be used by professional sporting teams to find a strategic fit with a sport tourist destination, and can also act as a guide for destination service providers to iden-tify the type of service criteria professional sporting teams seek in a destination. This matrix is extensive, and suggests how difficult it may be to lure top quality teams to a destination. However, such considerations will need to be analysed and met if a tourist destination is to compete in global competitions where suc-cess is not only measured by victory on the field, but also by the revenue gener-ated by teams and their supporters in the host venues.

References

Amis, J. and O'Brien, D. (2001). Organizational theory and the study of sport. In B. L. Parkhouse (ed.), *The Management of Sport: Its Foundations and Application*. New York: McGraw-Hill.

B.C. Games (undated). *Performance Plan 2000/2001–2002/2003*. Victoria, B.C.: B.C. Games Society.

Carlopio, J., Andrewartha, G. and Armstrong, H. (1997). *Developing Management Skills*, Australia: Longman.

Carmichael, B. and Murphy, P. E. (1996). Tourism economic impact of a rotating sports event: the case of the British Columbia Games. *Festival Management and Event Tourism*, 4, 127–138.

Dabscheck, B. (2003). Paying for professionalism: industrial relations in Australian Rugby Union. *Sports Management Review*, Nov, 105–125.

Getz, D. (1997). *Event Management and Event Tourism*. New York: Cognizant Communication Corporation.

Goffee, R. and Jones, G. (1996). What holds the modern company together? *Harvard Business Review*, Nov/Dec.

Hall, C. M. (1989). Hallmark events and the planning process. In G. J. Syme, B. J. Shaw, D. M. Fenton and W. S. Mueller (eds), *The Planning and Evaluation of Hallmark Events*. Aldershot: Avebury, pp. 20–39.

Hall, C. M. (1992). *Hallmark Tourist Events: Impacts, Management and Planning*. London: Belhaven Press.

Herald Sun (2003). Sport city. 31 October, pp. 1–4.

Lovelock, C. H., Patterson, P. H. and Walker, R. H. (2001). *Services Marketing* (2nd edn). Frenchs Forest, NSW: Pearson Education.

Massey, M. (1996). The business of sport: playing for keeps. *Business Review Weekly*, 1 Apr, 75–78.

McDonald, M. A., Sutton, W. A. and Milne, G. R. (1995). TEAMQUAL: measur-ing service quality in professional team sports. *Sport Marketing Quarterly*, 4(2), 9–15.

McDonnell, I., Allen, J. and O'Toole, W. (1999). *Festival and Special Event Management*. Brisbane: John Wiley & Sons.

Parasuraman, A., Zeithaml, V. A. and Berry, L. L. (1985). A conceptual model of service quality and its implications for future research. *Journal of Marketing*, 49, 41–50.

Shanks, M. D. (2002). *Sports Marketing: A Strategic Perspective*. Upper Saddle River, NJ: Prentice Hall.

Shilbury, D., Quick, S. and Westerbeek, H. (1999). *Strategic Sport Marketing*. Crows Nest, NSW: Allen & Unwin.

Smith, A. and Stewart, B. (1999). *Sports Management: A Guide to Professional Practice*. St Leonards, NSW: Allen & Unwin.

Standeven, J. and De Knop, P. (1999). *Sport Tourism*. Champaign, IL: Human Kinetics.

Viljoen, J. and Dann, S. (2000). *Strategic Management*. Frenchs Forest, NSW: Longman.

Zeithaml, V. A., Parasuraman, A. and Berry, L. L. (1990). *Delivering Quality Service, Balancing Customer Perceptions and Expectations*. New York: Free Press.

Websites

www.industry.gov.au (accessed November 2003)

www.world-tourism.org/market_research/facts&figures (accessed November 2003)

www.worldtravelandtourismcouncil.org/economicresearch/recovery/background.htm.2002 (accessed August 2002)

www.worldtravelandtourismcouncil (blueprint for New Tourism, accessed November 2003)

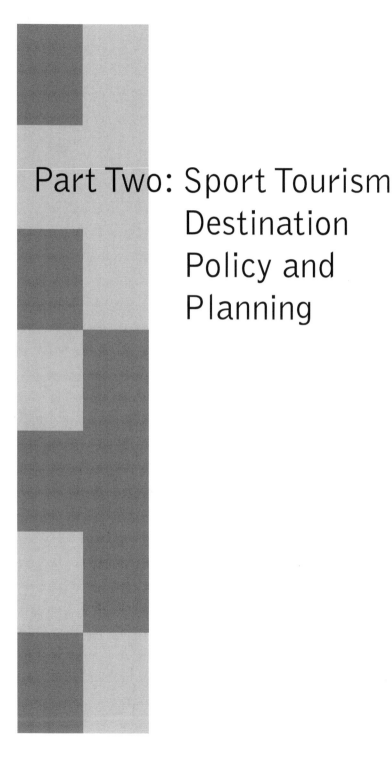

Part Two: Sport Tourism Destination Policy and Planning

7

Introduction to sport tourism destination policy and planning

James Higham

Sport tourism takes place within the social, cultural, political, economic and environmental contexts of a destination. These varied contexts require that actions are based upon a systematic planning process. However, the development and management of sport tourism destinations exist within complex policy and planning settings. While the planning process in tourism has typically been governed by the desire to perpetuate economic growth (Hall, 2000), planning interests in sport have tended to focus, at least in terms of functionalist theory, on what sports contribute to society (Coakley, 2004).

The sustainable development of sport tourism destinations, for social and economic outcomes, is a goal to which sport and tourism policy and planning agencies must aspire. The World Commission on Environment and Development (WCED, 1987: 4) definition of sustainable development is 'development that meets the needs of the present without compromising the ability of future generations to meet their own needs'. While there are many other definitions of sustainable development, most tend to focus on the sustainability of natural ecosystems. The WCED definition embraces the sustainability of cultural resources. The sustainable development of sport tourism requires the achievement of socio-cultural, economic and environment goals. A successful sport tourism economy should ideally support and enhance the social/cultural dimension of the destination community, as well as the natural and built environment, which features prominently in many types of sport tourism. However, the interaction between sport and tourism is not always positive (Hinch and Higham, 2004). Numerous examples of sport tourism demonstrate the high potential for negative impacts to influence host communities. Thus the development of sport tourism initiatives at tourism destinations necessitates constructive and integrated policy and planning approaches. Where such approaches currently exist, they are the exception rather than the rule (Weed, 2003; Weed and Bull, 2004).

Planning is a means of managing change through the taking of decisions to guide future actions. Planning in a sport tourism context is 'concerned with anticipating and regulating change in a system, to promote orderly development as to increase the social, economic, and environmental benefits of the development process' (Murphy, 1985: 156). The underlying process for planning is based on an assessment of the current situation, likely changes that will occur in the environment in which the plan is being conducted, decisions on the desired end state, formulation of some sort of action plan and its implementation, followed by monitoring, assessment and adjustment as required (Inskeep, 1991; World Tourism Organization, 1994).

Sport tourism has become widely recognized as a means by which to generate economic growth through inward investment, tourism and the development of service sector interests (Weed and Bull, 2004). Despite the potential that sport tourism offers, instances of systematic or strategic planning in sport tourism are not common. Sport tourism developments are more commonly pursued in the interests of short-term economic returns (Burgan and Mules, 1992), with long-term strategic visions in less clear focus. This is undesirable given that many sport tourism events are 'short term events with long term consequences for the cities that stage them' (Roche, 1994: 1). In many cases the long-term consequences for destinations hosting sports mega-events are negative (Olds, 1998; Shapcott, 1998). The potential for sporting events to create negative impacts increases with the scale of the event (Higham, 1999). Thus in the absence of careful planning the long-term legacies of sports events may be a burden, often financial, that is shouldered by local ratepayers.

The focus on short-term economic outcomes, largely at the expense of long-term evaluations of sport tourism and its impacts on destinations, is a consequence of a range of factors that challenge the sport tourism planning process. Planning occurs at a variety of levels, including strategic and operational. Sport tourism planning also takes place in a number of domains, including facility development, infrastructure, event planning and marketing. Each planning domain may be engineered by different public or private organizations, and the stakeholders who may influence (or be influenced by) these planning processes are varied. Furthermore, planning for sport and tourism takes place at various spatial levels ranging from international through to local site plans (Hinch and Higham, 2004). Thus planning for sport tourism may evolve in separate policy communities, in quite separate sectors, and at international, national and regional/local levels. The full range of public and private sector stakeholders must be involved in the planning process, as sport tourism plans require coordination and support if they are to be successful. As in any planning process, the likelihood of success is enhanced in situations where key stakeholders have a clear vision of the potential that sport tourism offers destinations. Such visions are becoming increasingly focused as discourses in sport tourism become more advanced (Hinch and Higham, 2004; Weed and Bull, 2004).

Thus the planning context for sport tourism is complex, and this has resulted in many cases of top-down planning and, consequently, a lack of meaningful input in the planning process on the part of destination communities. While it may be argued that this planning approach can generate significant economic development opportunities in the regional economies where sports events take place, little consideration is given to the negative impacts and feelings of disenchantment that may also result (Hodges and Hall, 1996; Hiller, 1998). The potential for such instances to give rise to tourist dissatisfaction with the destination has stimulated governments and industry to respond to this planning approach. In doing so, the focus has fallen upon sport tourism planning that seeks to achieve positive outcomes for tourism destinations and resident communities. These include enhanced access to sport and recreation, facility development, and sports event programmes that residents can contribute to as participants and/or spectators.

One recurring challenge relating to sport tourism planning is where government responsibility and institutional arrangements for sport and tourism lie. While interest in the development potential of sport tourism has increased significantly in recent years (World Tourism Organization and International Olympic Committee, 2001), the emergence of policy links incorporating the interests of government agencies, sports associations, national or regional tourism organizations and private sector interests (among others) are notable by their relative absence. The policy context for sport tourism varies considerably between countries. Weed and Bull (2004) highlight the general lack of national policy initiatives linking sport and tourism interests. Relatively few examples exist of productive sport tourism policy links at the national level. Although instances exist where sports events have been harnessed to serve national tourism interests (Whitson and Macintosh, 1996; Silk and Andrews, 2001; Silk, 2002), these are generally exceptional cases. The development of federal policy links between sport and tourism agencies is evident in the case of the 2000 Sydney Olympic Games. This Olympiad was developed as a vehicle to serve the interests of Brand Australia (Brown *et al.*, 2002), in order to maximize the economic benefits of the event associated with tourism (Chalip and Leyns, 2002).

Similarly, and perhaps part of the explanation for this, the development of favourable institutional arrangements for sport tourism is more likely at small-state, regional and urban sport tourism destinations (Bull and Weed, 1999; Weed and Bull, 2003, 2004). Meaningful collaboration between sport and tourism policy communities at the national level is complicated by the range of players involved and the primary policy functions that they perform. These factors explain the dearth of strategic collaboration between sport and tourism agencies in the pursuit of national sport tourism destination interests. Getz (1991) has shown that the scale of an event or festival will determine control and organization of the event, and that event planning is made easier and costs are minimized when events take place in smaller geographic and political arenas.

The strategic long-term planning of sport tourism is further hindered by the fragmented nature of the tourism industry. The strategic planning of sport tourism destinations requires integration between the public sector and disparate private sector interests in the tourism industry. The success of strategic planning at regional or national destinations requires that key players in the planning process recognize mutual interests in sport tourism. Achieving effective and coordinated planning between sport and tourism agencies is a considerable challenge, particularly given that business operators within the tourism industry rarely function as a coordinated unit. Effective communication between key players in the tourism sector is an important first step in any strategic planning process.

Strategic planning for sport tourism lies beyond the capacities and resources of single organizations. Partnership networks are therefore required to establish public and private sector collaboration, which may take such forms as setting common goals and objectives, and pooling human and financial resources (see Case study 7.1): 'The establishment and maintenance of strong alliances and partnerships is critical, although such initiatives may seem to be secondary to the core functions of sport and tourism managers' (Hinch and Higham, 2004: 212). Strategic planning for sport tourism destinations requires agreement on objectives and key priorities, the identification of performance indicators, and implementation.

Case study 7.1 The redevelopment and management of Telstra Stadium (Sydney, Australia)

Formerly known as Stadium Australia, Telstra Stadium was purpose-built for the 2000 Sydney Olympic Games. The stadium was reconfigured following the Olympic Games, including the relocation of the lower stadium bowl 15–17 m closer to the playing field and the reduction of its Olympic capacity (114 000) to its post-Olympic Games capacity of 83 500. The purpose of this reconfiguration was to allow the stadium to serve as a venue for major, regularly recurring sports events. The core business of the post-Olympics stadium includes sports events such as the national rugby league (NRL) preliminary finals and grand final, the Australian Rugby League (ARL) State of Origin series and Australian Rugby Union (ARU) test matches, most notably the annual Bledisloe Cup (Australia versus New Zealand). However, Telstra Stadium has been reconfigured to capture sports events ranging from the International Rugby Board (IRB) Rugby World Cup (2003), through to hosting regular season competition games in the Australian Football League (AFL), Rugby Super 12 and domestic Australian soccer competitions, as well as occasional domestic (state) cricket games.

The post-Olympic redevelopment and management of Telstra Stadium is described by Ken Edwards (CEO Telstra Stadium) as 'partnerships from the ground up'. Edwards (2003) notes that while revenue generated by venue rental is not significant, the success of the stadium hinges on multiple revenue streams such as the sale of corporate suites, corporate boxes and restaurant packages, subscriptions from Telstra Stadium club members, naming rights sponsorship, signage revenue, food and beverage, and merchandizing. Success in generating revenue from these income streams is based on effective collaboration with a range of strategic partners in both the public and private sectors. These include national sports administrations, corporate sector organizations and hospitality providers.

One such strategic partnership brings together the interests of Telstra Stadium and the Australian Rugby Union (ARU): 'Telstra Stadium has played a leading role in facilitating the growing financial health of the Australian Rugby Union since 1999 while, in turn, Telstra Stadium has benefited directly from its association with premium ARU events' (Edwards 2003: 14). Telstra Stadium featured prominently in the successful ARU bid to host the IRB Rugby World Cup (2003). The ARU was able to cover all of its tournament cost, in the vicinity of $A 120 million, from ticket sales of $A 135 million generated from the seven games (including both semi-finals, third-fourth play-off and World Cup final) played at Telstra Stadium.

Similarly, Telstra Stadium works in strategic partnership with the NRL, ARL and AFL. The annual State of Origin rugby league series and the NRL Grand Final are major domestic sport events. Within the NRL competition a 5-year partnership has been established with the Canterbury Bankstown 'Bulldogs' club, which commits the club to playing five premier games at Telstra Stadium each year. A partnership was established with the Australian Football League (AFL) in 1997 for matches to be played at Telstra Stadium. This partnership required the negotiation of spectator viewing issues relating to the design and construction of the stadium. These issues were resolved following a $A 30 million redevelopment project to allow the eastern and western lower stands to be retracted (creating an oval rather than rectangular playing surface) to accommodate cricket and AFL, thereby maximizing the spectator viewing experience associated with these sports. This partnership forms part of the AFL strategic goal of developing the Australian Football player base in Sydney and NSW.

In 2000, Telstra Stadium (then Stadium Australia) hosted 114 000 spectators for the gold medal Olympic soccer final between Spain and Cameroon. Subsequently, a strategic partnership with Soccer Australia has resulted in various soccer events taking place at Telstra Stadium, including three games involving the Australian national team – against Manchester United and Brazil, and a FIFA World Cup qualifying match against New Zealand. The Soccer Australia national administration is now based as Telstra Stadium. The redevelopment of Telstra Stadium to provide both rectangular and oval playing surfaces presents the opportunity to host domestic and international cricket. Telstra Stadium offers twice the spectator capacity of the Sydney Cricket Ground (SCG). While the traditions and heritage of the SCG remain a great asset to the Australian Cricket Board (ACB), Telstra Stadium offers additional revenue generation of particular relevance to the popular 1-day version of the game.

Telstra Stadium has a long-term naming rights sponsor (NRS) partnership with Telstra, initially for 7 years with the option of up to 15 years beyond the expiry of the original partnership. An annual business plan is produced as part of this partnership to monitor and project NRS outcomes, and identify future opportunities. The corporate hospitality facilities at Telstra Stadium include 114 corporate suites, 160 corporate boxes, four 200-seat restaurants, as well as meeting rooms and member facilities. The fact that corporate suites account for 80 per cent of all revenue generated from these sources confirms the importance of the partnerships established between Telstra Stadium and a wide range of Australian businesses. Each of these corporate partnerships generates annual revenue ranging from $A 80 000–350 000, and generally range between 3 and 5 years in duration.

(Source: Edwards, 2003)

Effective institutional arrangements, appropriate planning approaches and the formation of alliances and partnerships represent significant challenges relating to policy and planning in sport tourism. Part Two of this book (Chapters 7–10) explores these issues as they relate to sport tourism planning and policy at tourism destinations. Following this introduction, C. Michael Hall examines sport tourism planning processes in Chapter 8, highlighting various issues that pose challenges to planning for sport tourism development. Hall highlights critical issues associated particularly with long-term planning horizons for sport tourism. Despite the considerable complexity of planning for sport tourism development, Hall demonstrates that the environmental and social dimensions of sport tourism are increasingly being incorporated in the planning process, and that this is long overdue given that many forms of sport tourism development require significant public investment. Thus, planning for sustainable sport tourism development must incorporate the leisure, recreation and sports interests of those who live at the destinations where sport tourism takes place.

The fact that the institutional arrangements for sport tourism are poorly defined is highlighted by Hall as a factor contributing to the lack of strategic or long-term planning at sport tourism destinations. The success of sport tourism development interests at tourism destinations is determined by policy directions that allow planning decisions to be made systematically rather than on an *ad hoc* basis (Hinch and Higham, 2004). The institutional arrangements for sport tourism are therefore explored in detail by Mike Weed in Chapter 9. This chapter notes as a starting point that the development of links between policy-makers for sport and tourism, particularly at the national level, are in many cases weak, ineffective or non-existent. Weed then systematically explores the reasons for this. While significant variation exists between sport and tourism policy directions in different countries, some commonalities in sport tourism policy exist and apply with some consistency across national contexts. In most cases sport and tourism policy development takes place in separate departments or ministries of federal or state government. Furthermore, leadership in sport and tourism policy communities is not clearly defined. These factors, among others, contribute to a notable lack of meaningful dialogue between sport and tourism policy communities on matters of common interest and strategic importance. Thus, it clearly emerges in Chapter 9 that effective sport tourism development is more likely to exist at regional or local rather than national tourism destinations.

One exception to this rule is presented in Chapter 10, in which Steve Webb considers the development of strategic partnerships for a national sport tourism destination. Webb begins by exploring the barriers that exist in the strategic planning process at national destinations. These include the disparate and fragmented nature of the supply-side of the tourism industry, and the absence of existing networks between public and private sector interests in sport and tourism. Strategic planning for sport tourism destinations at the national level also requires visionary and leading individuals within key government agencies and private sector organizations, who might stimulate the formation of effective partnerships.

Chapter 10 provides a detailed and critical review of the formation of effective partnerships between sport and tourism agencies and organizations prior to, during and following the Rugby World Cup (RWC) hosted by Wales in 1999. The partnerships that were established between the Wales Tourist Board (WTB), Wales Rugby Union (WRU) and a range of private sector organizations in 1996 was founded on the setting, implementation and monitoring of several key objectives. The primary objectives included the development of an international brand for Wales as a tourist destination, maximizing the short-term tourism benefits of the RWC, raising the profile of Wales as a destination for several key overseas visitor markets, and sustaining levels of visitor interest following the tournament, primarily through repeat visitation. These objectives served the common interests of the various stakeholders involved in the partnerships. The intended outcomes were strategically planned prior to, and systematically evaluated during and after, the 1999 RWC. Chapter 10 demonstrates that, notwithstanding the challenges that exist in the planning and policy arenas, sport tourism destination interests at national, regional and local levels can be effectively pursued through the development of effective strategic partnerships.

References

Brown, G., Chalip, L., Jago, L. and Mules, T. (2002). The Sydney Olympics and Brand Australia. In N. Morgan, A. Pritchard and R. Pride (eds), *Destination Branding: Creating the Unique Destination Proposition.* Oxford: Butterworth-Heinemann.

Bull, C. and Weed, M. (1999). Niche markets and small island tourism: the development of sports tourism in Malta. *Managing Leisure,* 4(3), 142–155.

Burgan, B. and Mules, T. (1992). Economic impacts of sporting events. *Annals of Tourism Research,* 19, 700–710.

Chalip, L. and Leyns, A. (2002). Local business leveraging of a sport event: managing an event for economic benefit. *Journal of Sport Management,* 16, 133–159.

Coakley, J. (2004). *Sports in Society: Issues and Controversies* (8th edn). Boston: McGraw Hill Higher Education.

Edwards, K. (2003). Partners from the ground up. *Australian Leisure Management,* 41, 14–17.

Getz, D. (1991). *Festivals, Special Events, and Tourism.* New York: Van Nostrand Reinhold.

Hall, C. M. (2000). *Tourism Planning: Policies, Processes and Relationships*. Harlow: Prentice-Hall.

Higham, J. E. S. (1999). Sport as an avenue of tourism development: an analysis of the positive and negative impacts of sport tourism. *Current Issues in Tourism*, 2(1), 82–90.

Hodges, J. and Hall, C. M. (1996). The housing and social impact of mega events: lessons for the Sydney 2000 Olympics. In *Proceedings: Towards a More Sustainable Tourism, Centre for Tourism, University of Otago, 3–6 December*. Dunedin: Department of Tourism, pp. 152–166.

Hiller, H. H. (1998). Assessing the impacts of mega-events: a linkage model. *Current Issues in Tourism*, 1(1), 47–57.

Hinch, T. D. and Higham, J. E. S. (2004). *Sport Tourism Development*. Clevedon, OH: Channel View.

Inskeep, E. (1991). *Tourism Planning: An Integrated and Sustainable Development Approach*. New York: Van Nostrand Reinhold.

Murphy, P. E. (1985). *Tourism: A Community Approach*. New York: Methuen.

Olds, K. (1998). Urban mega-events, evictions and housing rights: the Canadian case. *Current Issues in Tourism*, 1(1), 2–46.

Roche, M. (1994). Mega-events and urban policy. *Annals of Tourism Research*, 21, 1–19.

Shapcott, M. (1998). Commentary on *Urban Mega-Events, Evictions and Housing Rights: The Canadian Case*, by Chris Olds. *Current Issues in Tourism*, 1(2), 195–196.

Silk, M. (2002). 'Bangsa Malaysia': global sport, the city and the mediated refurbishment of local identities. *Media, Culture & Society*, 25(4), 775–794.

Silk, M. and Andrews, D. L. (2001). Beyond a boundary? Sport, transnational advertising, and the reimaging of national culture. *Journal of Sport and Social Issues*, 25(2), 180–201.

Weed, M. E. (2003). Why the two won't tango: explaining the lack of integrated policies for sport and tourism in the UK. *Journal of Sports Management*, 17(3), 258–283.

Weed, M. E. and Bull, C. (2004). *Sports Tourism: Policy, Participants and Practice*. Oxford: Elsevier Butterworth-Heinemann.

Whitson, D. and Macintosh, D. (1996). The global circus: international sport, tourism and the marketing of cities. *Journal of Sport and Social Issues*, 23, 278–295.

World Commission on Environment and Development (WCED) (1987). *Our Common Future (the Bruntland Report)*. London: Oxford University Press.

World Tourism Organization (1994). *National and Regional Tourism Planning: Methodologies and Case Studies*. London: Routledge.

World Tourism Organization and International Olympic Committee (2001). *Sport and Tourism: Sport Activities During the Outbound Holidays of the Germans, the Dutch and the French*. Madrid: World Tourism Organization and International Olympic Committee.

8

Sport tourism planning

C. Michael Hall

Introduction

Planning is the process of preparing a set of decisions for action in the future, directed at achieving goals by preferable means (Dror, 1973). Sport tourism planning is the planning of sporting facilities (permanent and temporary) and events and related infrastructure that have been established to attract visitors and users from outside of the immediate region (destination) as well as local users. In considering planning for sport tourism, however, attention is given not only to physical considerations of planning but also to social, environmental and economic goals, and the long-term impacts of sport tourism development.

As a consequence of the considerable interest in sports, major national and international sports events attract thousands of spectators and visitors. The often extensive media broadcasting may give sports a further boost in their popularity and can provide tremendous opportunities for the marketing and imaging of destination areas (e.g. Brown *et al.*, 2002; Page and Hall, 2003). For example, mega-sports events such as the Olympic Games, Superbowl and the various World Cups of football, rugby and cricket have substantial economic impacts on host cities and regions before, during and after such events (Whitson and Macintosh, 1996; Hinch and Higham, 2004). The sporting legacy of the development of new facilities can have an impact on communities, visitors and sportspeople for many years.

The tourism benefits of a successfully developed facility or a staged event could be very valuable for the prospective increase in the number of inbound tourists. For example, in the case of hosts of Winter Olympics, the venue and hosting towns become highly identified in the winter tourist marketplace and can achieve a high degree of international awareness of their attractiveness in winter (Wall and Guzzi, 1987; Ritchie and Smith, 1991) – a time that is often low season for tourism. For example, Norway's hosting of the 1994 Olympics was perceived as an opportunity to promote activities in the country's mountainous regions, such as skiing, ski touring, and mountain climbing, which could serve to attract more domestic and international tourists (Chernushenko, 1996).

This chapter examines the means by which destinations undertake sport tourism planning. The chapter discusses some of the reasons for planning and the nature of the planning response before going on to discuss planning in the context of the maximization of environmental, social and economic benefits.

Why plan for sport tourism?

The perceived potential of sport tourism and sports events to contribute to economic growth and attract investment and tourism has been almost universally sought by government and industry (Hall, 1992; Hinch and Higham, 2004; Weed and Bull, 2004). However, in the rush to attract the tourist dollar often 'relatively little thought is generally given to the nature of the planning process with which to maximize the benefits of tourism for the host community' (Hall 1989, p. 20). Furthermore, as noted with respect to sports events:

> while the short term impact of the architecture and planning is an important element in the effective staging of a hallmark event, it is usually the long term effect of the architecture and planning that is of major consequence to the host community. Many events are now remembered by their architectural and planning legacies rather than the event itself.
> (Kelly, 1989: 263–264)

Sport tourism planning occurs in a number of forms (development, infrastructure, labour force, promotion and marketing), a number of public structures (different government and industry organizations), and a number of scales (international, national, regional, local and sectoral). The emergence of public concern over social, economic and environmental externalities resulting from tourism development have led to demands for government regulation and planning of touristic activity, including that associated with sport tourism (Hall, 2000). Therefore, from this perspective, sport tourism planning should be concerned with the anticipation and regulation of the effects of the development of sport tourism-related events, facilities and infrastructure on the host community, and the promotion of associated development in a manner that maximizes short- and long-term economic, environmental, economic and social benefits (Hall, 1989). That said, it must immediately be acknowledged that long-term evaluation of sport tourism and its impact on destinations is virtually non-existent. This may surprise many readers who believe that planning should be a rational process that includes such evaluations, particularly given the future orientation of the planning function (Hall, 2000). However, the 'messy' nature of sport tourism-related planning has been long acknowledged. For example, according to Armstrong (1986: 18), who examined 30 international mega-events and projects, many of which included sport, one of the great myths concerning such events is that they are planned according to a rational planning process:

> The planners who worked on the projects had one main role and that was to provide support for decisions already made. The planning process for prestige projects excludes the following traditional stages: recognition and definition of the problem, definition of the planning task, data collection, analysis and forecasting, determination of constraints, testing of alternatives, plan evaluation and project evaluation.

Sport tourism planning, and particularly planning for large sports events and facilities, has generally followed a top-down style of planning and promotion that has left tourism destination communities with relatively little input or control over the future of the community. Arguably, the larger the sport tourism event or facility the less input local users have, and it is only with respect to local leisure and recreational facilities that some degree of consultation seems to be engaged in. This central style of planning has had mixed outcomes. Tourism has contributed, in some circumstances, to rapid economic growth and regional development, but its accompanying impacts and spillover effects have often been ignored. One result of the failure of government, industry and planners to meet community needs and concerns can be the development of negative resident attitudes towards tourists and the tourist industry, and a level of tourist dissatisfaction with the destination. However, if government and private industry seek to use sport tourism as a mechanism to attract tourism and investment, then they simply cannot afford such negative attitudes in the longer run. This is because:

> Tourism, like no other industry, relies on the goodwill and cooperation of local people because they are part of the product. Where development and planning does fit in with local aspirations and capacities, resistance and hostility can raise the cost of business or destroy the industry's potential altogether. (Murphy, 1985: 153)

Therefore, a careful consideration of the dynamics of sport tourism planning is a necessary condition for the successful achievement of the objectives of sport tourism development at the destination level. Ideally, destinations seek to use sport tourism as a means of development not for its own sake, but because it is a means to a desired end in terms of returns to the destination. Planning is a key means by which such ends may be achieved.

The role of the state in sport tourism planning

The functions of the state will affect sport tourism to different degrees. However, the extent to which individual functions are related to particular tourism policies, decisions and developments will depend on the specific objectives of institutions, interest groups and significant individuals relative to the sport tourism policy and planning process, as well as the nature of the specific jurisdiction within which policy and planning is occurring. The state therefore performs many functions:

- As developer and producer
- As protector and upholder
- As regulator
- As arbitrator and distributor
- As organizer (Hall and Jenkins, 1995).

Each of these functions affects various aspects of planning for sport tourism, including development, marketing, policy, promotion, planning and regulation. Two important themes in tourism research that implicitly address the issue of the regulatory role of the state in tourism are those of the appropriate role of public sector tourism agencies, and the search for sustainability at different policy and planning scales (Hall and Jenkins, 1995). However, the state often fails to act in a coordinated way, with some decisions and actions being confusing to many observers. For example, while one arm of government may be actively promoting environmental conservation in a given location, another may be encouraging large-scale stadia development in order to attract employment and investment, without any consideration of the environmental impact. Furthermore, there are limits to effective state intervention in economy and society, particularly as the effects of globalization are felt by individual cities and regions at the sub-national level, also referred to as the 'local state'. Different policies in different policy arenas are often in conflict, and different levels of state action may have conflicting goals, objectives, outcomes and impacts (Hall and Jenkins, 1995), therefore raising substantial questions about the possibility of coordinating sport tourism development in the modern economy.

One significant dimension of planning is locating where in government the responsibility for sport tourism actually lies. However, one of the most significant issues here, as with tourism overall, is the definition of what sport tourism is – for how can you plan, regulate or establish policy for something unless you can define it? This has been a major issue for sport tourism for a number of years (Hinch and Higham, 2004). While several management strategies have been developed for sport tourism, there is little legislation or regulation that refers specifically to sport tourism, although legal structures may be developed for specific sports events or facilities (Hall, 1992).

Institutions are sets of rules that may be explicit and formalized (e.g. constitutions, statutes and regulations) or implicit and informal (e.g. organizational culture, rules governing personal networks and family relationships). Institutions order interrelationships between individuals or groups of individuals by influencing their behaviour (Hall and Jenkins, 1995). As a concept and as an aspect of sport tourism policy-making and planning, institutions therefore act as both active and passive influences on sport tourism development because they 'place constraints on decision-makers and help shape outcomes... by making some solutions harder, rather than by suggesting positive alternatives' (Simeon, 1976: 574). However, as the number of check points for policy increases, so too does the potential for bargaining and negotiation between interests. In the longer term, 'institutional arrangements may themselves be seen as policies, which, by building in to the decision process the need to consult particular groups and follow particular procedures, increase the likelihood of some kinds of decisions and reduce that of others'

(Simeon, 1976: 575). For example, procedures for community participation and involvement in the planning process, or even the adoption of environmental mediation procedures, constitute institutional arrangements that are often significant for sport tourism development. Similarly, new government agencies, departments or advisory groups may be established as part of the changing activities and roles of government, particularly as new demands, such as concerns over maximizing the economic benefits of sport tourism, reach a high priority on the political agenda.

The establishment of new institutional arrangements specifically for sport tourism has been relatively limited. Although new private sector organizations have been established under the sport tourism label as part of the expansion of the market and the significance of sport tourism and events as a brand, few specific sport tourism agencies have been established by the public sector. Instead, sport tourism has usually been incorporated into the activities of existing agencies that operate in the fields of sport, tourism and regional development. For example, VisitBritain established a Sports Tourism department at the beginning of 2004. The department had a three-member team and a number of objectives to fulfil:

■ To position sports as an integral part of the British tourism product alongside heritage, culture, lifestyle and the countryside
■ To raise awareness among the sports industry of the economic benefit and potential of overseas visitors
■ To contribute to the winning of major international sporting events
■ To position VisitBritain as the leading agency of an integrated approach to the development of sport tourism
■ To complement the sports strategies of the Department for Culture, Media & Sport, the Scottish Parliament and Welsh Assembly (VisitBritain, 2004).

The role taken by agencies with respect to sport tourism depends on the relevant political context in different jurisdictions. For example, in some countries tourism departments have taken the lead on developing sport tourism policies, as in Canada and Australia, while in others it has come more from sporting bodies, as in Ireland. However, the nature of sport tourism, in that it aims to integrate elements of sport with those of tourism, also means that in policy and planning terms it is often related as much to sport and leisure concerns as it is to those seeking tourism development. This situation has therefore led to the development of an extremely complex array of institutional arrangements for sport tourism, which have had a dramatic effect on policy development, planning and implementation. For example, in the case of the USA much development has occurred at the municipal or county level with the development of public–private partnerships. Kelly (2000) claimed that the first sport commission established to attract sport tourists and develop facilities and infrastructure was the Indiana Sports Corporation formed in the late 1970s. According to Kelly, by 1993 there were 30 similar organizations and by 2000 the number had grown to over 2000. In contrast, in Ireland an International Sport Tourism Advisory Group was established by Sport Ireland in 2000, when the Minister for Tourism, Sport and Recreation introduced the International Sport Tourism Initiative. The Minister's objective for the Initiative was:

to accelerate the building of Ireland's international reputation as a sports venue, and consequently to increase sports-related tourism. To achieve this objective, new funding was provided specifically to support Ireland's efforts to attract major international sports events with tourism potential for Ireland. (International Sport Tourism Advisory Group, 2001: 5)

Although a government-sponsored initiative, it is useful to note that the advisory board had substantial private sector involvement. Nevertheless, because of the political demands placed on government, a general rule will be that the greater the amount of public sector involvement in any sport tourism planning agency or initiative, the greater will be the attempt to justify sport tourism initiatives and planning processes under the realm of the public good. In the case of sport tourism, which ideally integrates marketing, development and community concerns, the problems of effective planning and administrative coordination are still being determined – although it needs to be recognized that typically there is no one perfect solution that will fit every jurisdiction. Instead, the structure of institutional roles and responsibilities for sport tourism planning will rest on the particular circumstances of the scale, location and values associated with public governance of different destinations.

The planning response

Integrated tourism planning has the potential to minimize negative impacts, and maximize economic and social returns to the host community (Hall, 2000). Nevertheless, planning may appear as a contradiction because tourism implies non-directed, voluntary and personal goal-oriented travel and 'free-enterprise' development (Gunn, 1988). However, unregulated development could poten-tially lead to the degradation of the physical and social resource base upon which sport tourism depends. Therefore, ideally, what is being planned is not the travel experience itself but the opportunity to achieve that experience within an appro-priate economic, environmental and social setting for the hosts.

While the desirability for planning for events and sport tourism is now gener-ally recognized, the form and method of the most effective method of planning remains a contested concept (Hall, 2000). Gunn (1988) identified a number of key elements in the development of an overall approach towards tourism planning that have been extremely influential in considerations of the role that planning can play in development:

1 Only planning can avert negative impacts, although for planning to be effect-ive all 'actors' must be involved – not just professional planners, government and the private sector
2 Tourism is often symbiotic with conservation values, and not a conflicting use with irreconcilably incompatible objectives or effects
3 Planning should be pluralistic, and integrate social, economic and physical dimensions and concerns
4 Planning is political, and as such there is a vital need to take into account soci-etal objectives and to balance these in the context of other (often conflicting) aspirations
5 Tourism planning must be strategic and integrative

6 Tourism planning must have a regional planning perspective; because many problems arise at the interface of smaller areas and/or impacts may spill over from one locale to another, a broader planning horizon is essential.

The elements identified by Gunn (1988) provide a valuable basis for realizing the benefits of sport tourism. However, 'the consequences of tourism development are wide ranging and often unpredictable. As a result, planning can often only articulate concerns or uncertainties, society must guide planners in assessing their acceptability' (Hall, 1992: 102), particularly given the contemporary demands for improved environmental standards for sport tourism in general. For example, in 2000 the Council of Europe recommended the adoption of a *Code of Sustainability in Sport: a Partnership Between Sport and the Environment* (Council of Europe, 2000), which explicitly recognized the significance of sustainable sport tourism. According to the Council of Europe (2000):

> The concept of sustainability in sport has already been incorporated into Article 10 of the European Sports Charter of 1992. This Article emphasizes the responsibility of everyone involved in sport to protect the environment and promotes the introduction of a model of environmentally friendly sport. However, measures are needed to address those trends and practices in sport that are currently endangering the environment. The Code indicates realistic ways to ensure environmental protection. In practical terms this entails national policies that ensure respect for sustainability in sport in urban, open country and water areas.

The linkage between sport tourism and sustainability clearly raises attention to the environmental dimensions of sports events planning, and it is to these that the chapter will now turn.

Environmental constraints

Appropriate site planning should include consideration of the environmental impacts of the event and associated facilities, not only on the immediate site but also on the associated areas (Hall and Selwood, 1989). As the majority of sport tourism events (by audience) are hosted in urban areas and/or facilities, the majority of environmental impacts are concentrated on urban resource management concerns such as sewage and effluent disposal, littering, water and air quality, and aesthetic effects, all of which have significant flow-on effects on social quality-of-life indicators (Page and Hall, 2003). For example, submissions to the Social Impact Steering Committee regarding the implications of Melbourne hosting the 1996 Summer Olympics identified the following areas of environmental concern (Economic Impact Resources Consulting, 1989: 67):

■ There may be problems of air pollution, particularly if the volume of traffic is increased
■ The storage and transport of dangerous chemicals near the Olympic Village and other venues will pose a problem

- The process for approving new projects should not circumvent existing planning guidelines
- The impact of the large number of visitors on waste disposal facilities should be assessed
- The opportunity should be taken in construction for the Olympics to implement and demonstrate energy-efficient design principles
- Any new developments should not affect existing natural habitats.

The development of sports event facilities in relatively natural areas, such as the construction of ski runs for the Winter Olympic Games at Lake Placid, Calgary, and Albertville, may have considerable physical and aesthetic impacts on a natural or semi-natural area (Wall and Guzzi, 1987). Similarly, outdoor sporting events such as whitewater rafting or endurance competitions, which attract significant amounts of spectators and competitors, may have to be closely monitored in order to ensure that environmentally sensitive areas are not damaged through littering or trampling. Unwillingness to respond to environmental demands could lead to negative attitudes to sport in general. In Alpine regions it has been observed that tourists coming from very densely populated, polluted areas have started to develop negative attitudes towards winter sports because of perceived environmental impacts (Wall and Guzzi, 1987; Hudson, 1999).

The emergence of a greater degree of environmental awareness among many communities regarding the negative impacts of tourism and the corresponding growth in conservation organizations has meant that government, sport tourism developers and event organizers can no longer ignore the environmental impacts of sport tourism. In addition, many countries now have environmental impact legislation in place which requires the proponents of large-scale projects, such as those associated with mega-events, to provide environmental impact information to legislatures or environmental protection agencies prior to final approval for the project being given. However, a major concern in the environmental impact assessment process is that the size of investment in both the impact report and the project itself is so substantial that only marginal changes, if any, will be made to projects by overseeing bodies (Hall and Selwood, 1989). Arguably, one of the significant turning points in the planning of sport tourism, and one that proved to be an important reference point for the Council of Europe's position on sport and the environment, was the 1994 Winter Games in Lillehammer (Case study 8.1).

Case study 8.1 The Lillehammer 1994 Winter Games –
meeting the environmental challenge

The Lillehammer Games are highly significant in sport tourism planning because of the extent to which environmental issues became incorporated into the planning and development process (Chernushenko, 1996). However, the reason for embedding the environment into the Games planning was not just a response to the desire to maintain the quality of the environment in the Lillehammer region, but also economic and political rationales. Key to this was the role of the Ministry for the Environment. The Ministry, after already having allocated NOK 8 million to the Games, pointed out that by considering the environment during preparations for the Olympics, Norway would be showing its willingness to follow up the recommendations of the Brundtland report (on sustainable development). The 29th report to the Stortinget, the Norwegian Parliament, stated that:

> ... development should be emphasized on adaption to natural resources, the cultural landscape and regional traditions. This is also essential to conservation and development of qualities that will attract tourism in the longer run. (Cited in Kaspar and Hall, 1993)

Not following the principles suggested by the country's own Prime Minister might have been potentially damaging both for the image of the country and the credibility of such commissions. Therefore, the Ministry played an active role in seeking to connect the environment with the potential imaging benefits of the Games. Nevertheless, the undoubted media profile of the Games represented a unique opportunity for defining and communicating environmental ideals, ideas, values, standards and knowledge across cultural, political and business barriers.

The preparation for and accomplishment of the Lillehammer Games involved many people over a short span of time: an international organization was planned, built up and disbanded within a few years. During that short interval of time the organization was responsible for many of the activities that are typical for our society – building, buying, travelling, administrating, consuming food and producing rubbish. The environmental goals for the Lillehammer Games can be seen as threefold: the first was to minimize the negative environmental impacts made by the Lillehammer Olympics; the second was to use the Olympic network to influence others to minimize their own effect on the environment; and the third was to create effective, practical solutions and develop new know-how to meet the environmental challenges.

The successful 'greening' of any organization depends on one primary condition – commitment and knowledge at the top level of the organization. Modern environmental policy must be anchored at Board level. Fortunately, the Lillehammer Olympic Organizing Committee (LOOC) assumed environmental responsibility to be one of the three pillars for the Olympic Games, together with sport and culture. Twenty-one specific environmental projects were developed (Table 8.1), most probably leading to the most environmentally conscious Olympic Winter Games ever hosted (Chernushenko, 1996).

Undoubtedly there were some major achievements. For example, all Norwegian Olympic arenas conform to the latest environmental standards. Consideration for the environment has been implemented in the selection of materials, energy consumption and transport. All suppliers had to consider the inclusion of environmental clauses in their contracts by minimizing packaging and ensuring it did not contain any harmful substances. Furthermore, there was an emphasis on recycling that had not existed before. The LOOC also required all partners

Table 8.1 Environmental initiatives associated with the 1994 Olympic Winter Games in Lillehammer

1. Managing the environment	The management team included a Director of the Controller Department, who is responsible for all environmental issues. The Controller Department also had its own Coordinator of Environmental Issues. The environmental project was designed to ensure that all staff and volunteers took environmental considerations into account when performing various other tasks. An Internal Environment Committee comprising workers from all parts of the organization was responsible for supervising and ensuring that necessary environmental steps are taken in every department of the organization. An External Committee of environmental experts and interest groups was also formed. In fact, the LOOC commissioned a local environment group to do a study on what actions the Games could and should take to best preserve the environment in its current condition
2. The Olympic profile – a choice	Four main priorities were applied when judging surroundings, architecture and the choice of materials for different construction works: upholding Norwegian traditions, conserving the environment, harmony, and aesthetic quality
3. Energy, administration, operations	The project directed building and design in such a way that annual operating costs were minimized while efforts were taken to choose environmentally friendly solutions. Two policy documents on constructing Olympic arenas were produced and provided input into the environmental audit
4. The green office	Designed to promote the use of environmentally friendly office equipment and routines
5. Waste (land)	The project concerning waste was based on what was called the sustainability scale. This was a scale regarding what is considered to be most environmentally friendly. Starting at the top of the list, the first solution is considered; if this is not feasible the second solution is considered, etc., until the most feasible solution is reached. The scale went as follows: Avoid, Minimize, Re-use, Recycle,

(Continued)

Table 8.1 (Continued)

	Utilize Residual Value, Handle Waste Responsibly
6. Temporarily erected structures	These had to achieve visual harmony with the surroundings as well as meeting environmental standards set by the LOOC
7. The green IRS	Environmental audits were carried out on both sites and staff. All the facilities were subject to audits carried out by the Controller/Environment Department in cooperation with local organizations, environmental advisers and other interest groups
8. The Birkebeiner sponsor team	Early sponsors who signed on before the environmental standards were adopted agreed to sign an additional decree which stated that they would cooperate with and promote the environmental profile
9. Top guns	The TOP III sponsors (international sponsors) had to agree to an obligation to support the Lillehammer environmental profile, and were challenged to demonstrate their concern and efforts
10. Official suppliers	Environmental standards were specified in all contracts with official suppliers
11. Cultural events	All cultural events were required to have an environmental profile
12. Green sport	The sporting community was asked to contribute to a more environmentally friendly Olympic event
13. School projects	In an attempt to involve children and teenagers in environmental issues, several school projects related to sport and outdoor activities were undertaken
14. The information age	The aim of the information project was to ensure that information given by the LOOC was printed on environmentally friendly (and sometimes even recycled) paper
15. Catering and accommodation	Living and working areas were to have a clear environmental profile
16. The services	Employees in the service of the LOOC and the Games were required to show environmental concern and express a proper environmental profile
	(Continued)

Table 8.1 (Continued)

17. The environment wheel	The project aimed to create a 'railway corridor' with as good environmental standards as possible with regard to cleanliness, forest husbandry and others
18. The environmental road	People travelling to and from Lillehammer were also made aware of the environmental challenge facing the society during the Games
19. Transport: public or private?	This project was designed to give the transport sector an environmental profile through coordination and optimum utilization of traffic and transport systems/road networks. The overall goal was to persuade as many people as possible to choose public over private transport
20. The Lillehammer Olympic Park	The Lillehammer Olympic Park had a strong environmental profile
21. EUREKA – Lillehammer 1994	This programme for European technological cooperation was established in 1987 and included a special programme covering three main environmental areas: ENSIS (Environmental Surveillance), ENVITRANS (Environmentally Friendly Transport) and WASTERED (Waste and Sewage Disposal)

Source: After Kaspar and Hall (1993).

to conform with a number of environmental standards in their preparation for the Games:

- The Olympic arenas shall have a unified, Norwegian design which is in harmony with the natural landscape
- Consideration has to be paid to the natural surroundings of the area
- Natural materials shall be preferred to artificial ones
- Energy-saving solutions shall be chosen, with regard to investment and operating costs
- Environmental audits shall be carried out in order to ensure that environmental targets are achieved. (Cited in Kaspar and Hall, 1993)

In order to evaluate the efforts in an environmental audit, the LOOC specified the conditions for the success of its ambitious targets as follows:

- Responsibility for the environment must be organized and allocated
- Environmental standards must be specified
- Cooperation with the environmental organizations is essential and use of their know-how beneficial

■ Priority must be given to environmentally conscious partners in cooperation with suppliers. (Cited in Kaspar and Hall, 1993)

The aim, of course, was to make the 1994 Olympics the most environmentally friendly Games of all time. However, in addition to minimizing and recycling waste, the Committee also achieved new solutions. Constant demands forced Norwegian suppliers to deliver chlorine-free paper (which the industry had stated could not be done, although 3 months after an order went to a Swedish paper mill all the main Norwegian suppliers offered this product) and Coca Cola to deliver paper cups, and a 96 per cent potato starch plate was developed by a Swedish company. This product dissolves fully in soil after only 3 weeks, and it can even be eaten! Spoons with 80 per cent potato starch content that degraded after 3–4 months were also used. Significantly, the LOOC environmental concept was primarily based on ecological considerations, but it also took local culture into consideration with the various measures taken being intended to:

■ Conserve and promote the diversity and special characteristics of the natural environment
■ Protect the population (humans, animals and other life forms) from the negative effects originating from 'exploitation, consumption and protection of resources'
■ Conserve and promote the parts of human well-being that arise from the well-being of the environment
■ Respect and promote traditional as well as contemporary Norwegian culture. (Cited in Kaspar and Hall, 1993)

Within Norway, networks were built by the LOOC with the Norwegian Society for the Conservation of the Nature, the Ministry of the Environment and environmental authorities of the Olympic municipalities. It has been acknowledged that mutual cooperation is a precondition for successful environmental protection. Internationally, the LOOC cooperated with EUREKA, the European programme for technological surveillance, environment-friendly transport and waste sewage disposal. In one sense the LOOC initiated an environment relay race, with the IOC coming under increased internal and external pressure to ensure that Olympic organizers and sponsors took over the baton with an aim to achieving more sustainable sport tourism development with the Olympics. Indeed, the environmental dimension became so significant that it came to be an argument for the selection of some Olympic bids over others. For example, in its August 1993 news release as to 'why Sydney would stage a great Olympics in 2000', the Sydney Olympics 2000 Bid Limited (SOB) argued that Sydney was:

pioneering environmentalism for the Olympics. Throughout Sydney's Olympic plan, from venue and residential construction to event management, the highest environmental principles are applied. Sydney's Olympic Village design, prepared in collaboration with Greenpeace, foreshadows the sustainable city of the 21st century. (SOB, 1993a: 2)

According to SOB (1993b: 2), the environmental guidelines developed for the bid, which address five major global environmental concerns (global warming, ozone depletion, biodiversity, pollution and resource depletion), 'would make Sydney's Olympic Plan a prime example of ecologically sustainable development in the 21st century', and 'integrate the latest technologies with tried and tested measures into a co-ordinated environmental protection plan for a summer Olympic Games'.

Nevertheless, while the environmental dimensions of the Games may have improved, substantial questions still remain over the social dimensions of the large-scale sport tourism development that is exemplified by the Olympics. For example, despite the LOOC's fervent claims that the organization and means of conducting the Games were the best possible, many local people started to question whether Coca Cola was really part of the Norwegian traditional culture. For any passing stranger, the most prominent features of Lillehammer in 1993 could easily have been said to be the huge billboards saying 'Coca Cola welcomes you to the site of the 1994 Lillehammer Olympics'. Although these signs were in Norwegian, they so much annoyed local citizens that a campaign to have them removed was held and the press got involved. After a public debate led by the biggest Norwegian newspaper (*Verdens Gang*), Coca Cola decided to change them for smaller, less dominant signs. Rumour has it that company executives of Coca Cola came over from the headquarters in Atlanta to take a look at the site (and create some publicity) and were shocked, stating that this was how advertising had been conducted in the United States some 15–20 years previously.

The debate over the Americanization or globalization of local culture is one dimension of large-scale sport tourism that spotlights some of the social dimensions of planning. Indeed, one of the criticisms of the Olympics is that while there is attention given to sport, culture and now the environmental dimensions of such developments, there is no formal consideration of social impacts.

Sport tourism development has usually been publicly justified because of its perceived economic benefits as well as its wider social benefits. For example, sport is often seen as a mechanism to overcome social problems. Typical of this perspective is that of the UK Policy Action Team 10 report, which suggested that sport (and the arts) can contribute to 'neighbourhood renewal by improving communities' "performance"' on four key indicators – health, crime, employment and education (Department of Culture, Media and Sport, 1999: 22). This received wisdom is often to be found as one of the keystones of government leisure and sport policies, particularly with respect to regeneration strategies (Hall, 2004). For example, the Wirral Partnership (2001) states that 'Sport brings with it benefits for the economy, for the area's health and provides a positive focus for individual and community motivation'. Nevertheless, the issue of the real social benefits that sports may bring to disadvantaged areas is increasingly under question (Long and Sanderson, 1998), particularly as unemployment and low income are at the root of social exclusion and urban deprivation (Coalter *et al.*, 2000).

An example of an attempt to include greater consideration of social impacts in sport tourism planning was the campaign of the non-profit public interest coalition, Bread Not Circuses (BNC), in Toronto's eventually unsuccessful bid to host the 2008 Olympic Games. BNC argues that given the cost of both bidding for and hosting the Olympics, the bidding process must be subject to public scrutiny: 'Any Olympic bid worth its salt will not only withstand public scrutiny, but will be improved by a rigorous and open public process' (Bread Not Circuses, 1998a). It also argued that Toronto City Council should have made its support for an Olympic bid conditional on:

- The development and execution of a suitable process that addresses financial, social and environmental concerns, ensures an effective public participation process (including intervenor funding), and includes a commitment to the development of a detailed series of Olympic standards. A time-frame of 1 year from the date of the vote to support the bid should be set to ensure that the plans for the participation process are taken seriously
- A full and open independent accounting of the financial costs of bidding and staging the Games
- A full and open independent social impact assessment of the Games.

The other key elements of the proposed public participation process included:

- A full, fair and democratic process to involve all of the people of Toronto in the development and review of the Olympic bid
- An Olympic Intervenor Fund, similar to the fund established by the City of Toronto in 1989, to allow interested groups to participate effectively in the public scrutiny of the Toronto bid
- An independent environmental assessment of the 2008 Games, with strategies being developed to resolve specific concerns
- The development of a series of financial, social and environmental standards governing the 2008 Games, similar to the Toronto Olympic Commitment adopted by City Council in September of 1989.
(Bread Not Circuses, 1998a)

In a similar vein, a BNC letter sent to the IOC President requested 'that the IOC, which sets the rules for the bidding process, take an active responsibility in ensuring that the local processes in the bidding stage are effective and democratic' and specifically address concerns regarding the 'financial and social costs of the Olympic Games', and proposed that:

1　An international network be created that includes COHRE, the HIC Housing Rights Subcommittee, academics, and NGOs (including local groups in cities that have bid for and/or hosted the Games)
2　A set of standards regarding forced evictions, etc., be developed and adopted by the network
3　A plan to build international support for the standards, including identification of sympathetic IOC, NOC and other sports officials, be developed and implemented
4　The IOC be approached with the request that the standards be incorporated into the Olympic Charter, Host City Contracts and other documents of the IOC.
(Bread Not Circuses, 1998b)

Such a social charter for the Olympics would undoubtedly greatly assist in making the Olympics more place-friendly, and perhaps even improve the image of the IOC. However, the books of the Toronto bid were never opened for full public scrutiny, and neither was there any response to the proposal for creation of a set of social standards for the Olympics (Hall, 2001).

Undoubtedly sport facilities and infrastructure can generate employment, particularly through the construction phase, and may generate some employment in the longer term – although in the case of event-related employment, much of it will be part-time or casual and low-skilled. However, integral to the successful contribution of such facilities to job recreation will be the extent to which facilities have a clear policy to train and employ people from within the target area in order to promote economic and social regeneration. An example of the use of sport and sport tourism for urban regeneration was that of the bid by Cape Town to host the 2004 Olympics. The bid was unsuccessful but nevertheless significant, as it explicitly linked the hosting of a sports mega-event to development needs (Page and Hall, 2003). The Cape Town bid sought to add a fourth 'pillar' of 'human development' to the Olympic Movement's pillars of sport, culture and the environment. The Bid Book argued that every aspect of hosting the Olympics 'should contribute to the upliftment and quality of life of the people of the city... we place special emphasis on our disadvantaged communities' (cited in Hiller, 2000: 441). Rather than merely focusing on urban regeneration through the provision of new infrastructure and an increase in city profile, the Cape Town bid sought to be transformative in a social as well as an economic sense. Therefore, the Cape Town bid introduced two innovative ideas into the role of hosting the Olympics: first, the Olympics would serve as a catalyst for improving the social and economic conditions of the historically disadvantaged; and second, they would act to redesign the apartheid city and create new linkages between people and cultures. As Hiller (2000: 455) noted:

> the idea of harnessing a mega-event to a broader urban agenda that moves beyond the interests of finance capital, developers, inner-city reclamation and the tourist city is a relatively new idea. This is especially so given the preoccupation with winning IOC votes internationally and the minimization of local costs and dissent.

However, it is notable that Cape Town did not win its bid (coming third in the final vote). Therefore, the Cape Town Bid Company's argument that in awarding the bid to Cape Town the International Olympic Committee would have demonstrated that the Olympic Movement was not 'beholden to gigantism and commercial exploitation' and was instead 'devoted to the progress of all people and must therefore also offer opportunity to those still struggling for their place in the economic sun' (1996: 38, cited in Hiller, 2000: 442) holds considerable weight in judging why events are located where they are. Nevertheless, what is also significant about the Cape Town bid is that it demonstrated that the hosting of sporting events can be utilized as much for the broader public good as for the regeneration of cities as places of consumption, entertainment and leisure (Page and Hall, 2003).

Conclusions

Planning for sport tourism is inherently complex and difficult. It is an ill-defined area with poorly defined institutional frameworks and, importantly, multiple stakeholders. Perhaps most significantly, sport tourism planning is about much more than sport and tourism; it is also concerned with economic, social, environmental and political impacts. Indeed, arguably the larger the sport tourism event or facility, the more important these other considerations become. Historically, and as evidenced in this book, the prime focus of sport tourism development has been maximizing economic returns to destinations, particularly to the urban growth coalitions who promote such ventures (Hall, 2001). Nevertheless, the fact that environmental and social considerations are gradually being brought into the policy and planning mix of the largest sport tourism development of all, the Olympic Games, however imperfectly, is important – particularly because of its influence on other policy avenues, such as those of the Council of Europe, who now highlight the need for sustainable sport tourism.

Yet if sustainable sport tourism is to be a destination goal, one of the other main elements of tourism planning, public participation, needs to become incorporated in sport tourism development. Indeed, one of the most significant aspects of mega-sports events and facility development is that they often exclude participation while at the same time requiring such large public investments that if they do not work as revitalization or re-imaging strategies, then their actual and opportunity costs are substantially modified (Page and Hall, 2003). Successful planning is a process that involves the formulation of strategies based on conceptual models of places which are, in turn, founded on notions of civic life (Hall, 1991). Sustainable sport tourism destinations require more than just the development of product and image. Instead, destinations are fundamentally about the people who live and play there. Most fundamentally of all, from a destination perspective, planning for sport tourism is not just about building another sports facility or hosting an event; it is about maximizing the benefits of sport tourism to the people that live in the destination.

References

Armstrong, J. (1986). International events and popular myths. In *International Events: The Real Tourism Impact, Proceedings of the 1985 Canada Chapter Conference*. Edmonton: Travel and Tourist Research Association (Canadian Chapter), pp. 7–37.

Bread Not Circuses (1998a). *Bread Alert!* (E-mail edition) 2(2), 20 February.

Bread Not Circuses (1998b), *Bread Alert!* (E-mail edition) 2(3), 26 February.

Brown, G., Chalip, L., Jago, L. and Mules, T. (2002). The Sydney Olympics and Brand Australia. In N. Morgan, A. Pritchard and R. Pride (eds), *Destination Building: Creating the Unique Destination Proposition*. Oxford: Butterworth-Heinemann, pp. 163–185.

Chernushenko, D. (1996). Sports tourism goes sustainable: the Lillehammer experience. *Visions in Leisure and Business*, 18(1), 34–44.

Coalter, F., Allison, M. and Taylor, J. (2000). *The Role of Sport in Regenerating Deprived Urban Areas*. Edinburgh: Centre for Leisure Research, University of Edinburgh, The Scottish Executive Central Research Unit.

Council of Europe (2000). *Council of Europe Committee of Ministers, Recommendation Rec(2000)17 of the Committee of Ministers to Member States on the Code of Sustainability in Sport: A Partnership Between Sport and the Environment* (Adopted by the Committee of Ministers on 13 September 2000 at the 720th meeting of the Ministers' Deputies), Council of Europe (available at http://cm.coe.int/ta/rec/2000/2000r17.htm).

Department of Culture, Media and Sport (1999). *Policy Action Team 10: Report to the Social Exclusion Unit – Arts and Sport*. London: HMSO.

Dror, Y. (1973). The planning process: a facet design. In A. Faludi (ed.), *A Reader in Planning Theory*. Oxford: Pergamon Press, pp. 323–343.

Economic Impact Resources Consulting (1989). *1996 Melbourne Olympic Games: A Preliminary Social Impact Assessment*, a report for the Social Impact Assessment Steering Committee prepared by Economic Impact Resources Consulting, Melbourne.

Gunn, C. A. (1988). *Tourism Planning* (2nd edn). New York: Taylor & Francis.

Hall, C. M. (1989). Hallmark events and the planning process. In G. J. Syme, B. J. Shaw, D. M. Fenton and W. S. Mueller (eds), *The Planning and Evaluation of Hallmark Events*. Aldershot: Avebury, pp. 20–39.

Hall, C. M. (1992). *Hallmark Tourist Events: Impacts, Management, and Planning*. London: Belhaven Press.

Hall, C. M. (2000). *Tourism Planning*. Harlow: Prentice-Hall.

Hall, C. M. (2001). Imaging, tourism and sports event fever: the Sydney Olympics and the need for a social charter for mega-events. In C. Gratton and I. P. Henry (eds), *Sport in the City: The Role of Sport in Economic and Social Regeneration*. London: Routledge, pp. 166–183.

Hall, C. M. (2004). Sports tourism and urban regeneration. In B. Ritchie and D. Adair (eds), *Sports Tourism: Impacts, Issues and Interrelationships*. Clevedon, OH: Channel View.

Hall, C. M. and Jenkins, J. (1995). *Tourism and Public Policy*. London: Routledge.

Hall, C. M. and Selwood, H. J. (1989). America's Cup lost, paradise retained? The dynamics of a hallmark tourist event. In G. J. Syme, B. J. Shaw, D. M. Fenton and W. S. Mueller (eds), *The Planning and Evaluation of Hallmark Events*. Aldershot: Avebury, pp. 103–118.

Hiller, H. (2000). Mega-events, urban boosterism and growth strategies: an analysis of the objectives and legitimations of the Cape Town 2004 Olympic bid. *International Journal of Urban and Regional Research*, 24(2), 439–458.

Hinch, T. D. and Higham, J. E. S. (2004). *Sport Tourism Development*. Clevedon, OH: Channel View.

Hudson, S. (1999). *Snow Business: A Study of the International Ski Industry*. London: Casell.

International Sports Tourism Advisory Group (2001). *International Sports Tourism Initiative 2000–2005, Report of the International Sports Tourism Advisory Group for the Year Ended 31 December 2000*. Dublin: Sport Ireland.

Kaspar, R. and Hall, C. M. (1993). *Tourism and the Olympic Games*. Tourism and the Environment Conference, Vienna, September.

Kelly, I. (1989). The architecture and town planning associated with a hallmark event. In G. J. Syme, B. J. Shaw, D. M. Fenton and W. S. Mueller (eds), *The Planning and Evaluation of Hallmark Events*. Aldershot: Avebury, pp. 263–273.

Kelly, J. (2000). Event planning: looking to sport for development dollars. *American City and Country*, 1 October.

Long, J. and Sanderson, I. (1998). Social benefits of sport: where's the proof? In *Sport In The City: Conference Proceedings Volume 2*, Sheffield, 2–4 July. Sheffield: Sheffield Hallam University, pp. 295–324.

Murphy, P. (1985). *Tourism: A Community Approach.* New York: Methuen.

Page, S. and Hall, C. M. (2003). *Managing Urban Tourism.* Harlow: Prentice-Hall.

Ritchie, J. R. B. and Smith, B. H. (1991). The impact of a mega-event on host region awareness: a longitudinal study. *Journal of Travel Research,* 30(1), 3–10.

Simeon, R. (1976). Studying public policy. *Canadian Journal of Political Science.* 9(4), 558–580.

Sydney Olympics 2000 Bid Limited (1993a). *News Release: Why Sydney would Stage a Great Olympics in 2000.* Sydney: Sydney Olympics 2000 Bid Limited.

Sydney Olympics 2000 Bid Limited (1993b). *News Release: Sydney's Plans for an Environmental Olympics in 2000.* Sydney: Sydney Olympics 2000 Bid Limited.

The Wirral Partnership (2001). *Economic Regeneration Strategy 2001–2002, Priority 4 Infrastructure and the Environment* (available at http://irdss.wirral.gov.uk/ecregen/prior4.asp, accessed 1 April 2002).

VisitBritain (2004). *Sports Tourism* (available at www.visitbritain.com/corporate/sports_tourism.htm, accessed 25 January 2004).

Wall, G. and Guzzi, J. (1987). *Socio-economic Analyses of the 1980 and 1988 Winter Olympics* (draft). Waterloo, Ontario: University of Waterloo.

Weed, M. and Bull, C. (2004). *Sports Tourism: Participants, Policy and Providers.* Oxford: Elsevier Butterworth-Heinemann.

Whitson, D. and Macintosh, D. (1996). The global circus: international sport, tourism, and the marketing of cities. *Journal of Sport and Social Issues,* 23, 278–295.

9

Sport and tourism policy: the national and regional policy contexts for sport tourism destinations

Mike Weed

Introduction

While there has been increasing interest in the development of the sport–tourism link in recent years – as this volume and an increasing range of other publications show – this is rarely matched by significant liaison among policy-makers for sport and tourism at national and regional level. Weed and Bull (1997a) identified the lack of liaison among regional policy-makers in England, and suggested a policy matrix of areas where it might reasonably be expected that sport–tourism policy liaison might take place. Since Weed and Bull's (1997a) review there have been some examples of strategy and policy initiatives aimed at developing a collaborative sport–tourism policy in several countries around the world. However, there has been little evidence of any sustained strategic policy collaborations. The reasons for this general lack of liaison have been the subject of a range of previous papers and articles (Weed and Bull, 1997a,b, 1998; Weed, 2001, 2002, 2003) that have addressed both policy structures and factors that influence policy development. The focus of this chapter is on the way in which a number of countries around the world formulate sport and tourism policy, and the implications this has for sport–tourism policy development. It provides an understanding of the national and regional level policy contexts within which local destination planning and development takes place.

Policy communities

Policy development for sport and for tourism can be conceptualized as taking place within sectorized arenas called policy communities. A policy community refers to those groups sharing an interest in a policy sector that interact with each other on a regular basis to maximize the benefits of their relationships with each other. They include government departments and agencies, voluntary clubs and associations, commercial sector firms, charities, and any other group or individual with an interest in the development of policy in a particular sector.

The policy communities for sport and tourism exist within a broader leisure policy universe that includes the large number of organizations, groups, associations and individuals which share a common interest in the leisure policy area, and may attempt to contribute to policy development on a regular or irregular basis. A simple Venn diagram (Figure 9.1) illustrates the location of sport and tourism policy communities within a leisure policy universe, and shows the area of overlap where a policy network to deal with sport–tourism issues should emerge.

Wright (1988: 606) describes a policy network as 'a linking process, the outcome of those exchanges within a policy community or between a number of policy communities'. Furthermore, Wilks and Wright (1987) argue that a major advantage of the policy network concept is that it allows for the possibility that members may be derived from different policy communities. This is particularly useful in examining the type of cross-sectoral policy liaison that is necessary for collaborative

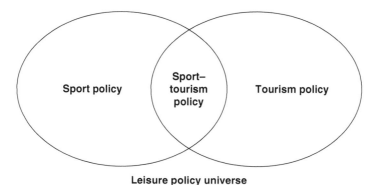

Leisure policy universe

Figure 9.1 Sport and tourism policy interactions

sport–tourism policy development (for greater detail on the policy network/ policy community model, see Weed, 2001 or Weed and Bull, 2004).

A further strength of the model illustrated in Figure 9.1 is that it allows for an examination of the influence of structural issues within the individual policy communities for sport and for tourism on the emergence and development of collaborative sport–tourism policy. A number of other texts and papers have dealt with specific factors relating to sport–tourism policy networks (see Weed and Bull, 1998; Weed, 2003; Weed and Bull, 2004), and this chapter will not seek to repeat this material. Rather, the chapter will discuss the structure and operation of policy communities for sport and for tourism in both the UK and a number of other countries around the world, highlighting in the process a number of key differences between the way in which policy is developed for sport and for tourism, and the implications of such differences for sport–tourism policy development. As the substantive content of this chapter, this examination of policy development at national and regional levels provides an understanding of the policy contexts that affect the development of sport–tourism destinations, and thus provides a backdrop for the discussions in a number of other chapters in this book. However, the final section of this chapter also briefly discusses, by way of illustration, the development of sport–tourism collaborations on the island of Malta and in the UK city of Sheffield. These examples highlight the more favourable conditions that exist for the development of collaborative policy, first at the smaller-scale sub-national region or small-state levels and secondly at the city level.

The operation of policy communities for sport and tourism

There is a number of common salient issues in the structure and operation of policy communities. These relate to leadership, membership, resource dependencies and structural relationships. The issue of leadership in sport and tourism policy communities around the world is often not clear-cut. In the UK, the lead government department would be expected to be the Department for Culture, Media and Sport; however, historically policy issues for sport and tourism have been devolved to partially autonomous, 'arms-length' government agencies, namely the Sports Council (restructured into Sport England and UK Sport in 1997) and VisitBritain (formed by the merger of the English Tourism Council and the British Tourist Authority in 2003). In 1997 the Department for Culture, Media and Sport established a Tourism Advisory Forum, made up of prominent figures from the tourism industry, to advise it on tourism matters, which is the exact role the English body was set up to fulfil in 1969. The establishment of the Tourism Forum was a clear first step towards the replacement of the old English Tourist Board with the English Tourism Council in 1999, and the later subsumation of the English body into the British organization in 2003. The Department has also increasingly restricted the autonomy of the Sports Council, to the point where its drawn-out restructure into United Kingdom and English Sports Councils has resulted in the new Sport England spending much of its time focusing on distributing Lottery Sports Fund grants in accordance with principles established at government department level. The Department for Culture, Media and Sport now exerts a much greater level of control over Sport England direction, and consequently the organization has become an agent rather than an instigator of national sports policy. In both sport and tourism policy communities this situation creates tensions between governments (which ultimately control the purse strings) and national agencies (where, in theory, expertise is invested).

In other countries around the world the situation is often less complex because tensions are not created by any formal 'arms-length' principle. Consequently, while tensions may exist between government departments and national agencies, these tensions are often resolved by the power or resource superiority of the government, or the status of national agencies as a branch of the government. In France, for example, there is no national agency for sport, and sports policy is developed directly by the Ministry of Youth and Fitness. In respect of tourism, the Loi Mouly (a new law for tourism administration passed in 1992) made provision for regional contributions to tourism policy, albeit under strict central control by the federal government who, as might be expected given France's formal economic planning system (Jeffries, 2001), maintains tight control over the registering and classification of resorts, and the sub-sectors of accommodation and catering. In Canada, both Sport Canada and the Canadian Tourism Commission (CTC) are branches of the federal government, which obviously prevents any tensions between government and national agency. The Australian system is perhaps most similar to that of the UK, with the Australian Sports Commission and the Australian Tourism Commission reporting to separate departments of the federal government. However, a significant difference exists in that both the ASC and the ATC accept that they are subject to direction over policy by the government, and thus while tensions may emerge there is little question as to where the power of veto lies. The one major country where government control over both sport and tourism is slight is the USA. The general ideological commitment in many areas of life in the USA to the supremacy of the free market means that the majority of sport and of tourism provision is dictated by market forces. This obviously leaves little room for government agencies and, in line with such thinking, the country's National Tourism Organization, the United States Travel and Tourism Association (USTTA), was abolished in 1996, leaving the operation of the industry to the private sector. Similarly, the United States Olympic Committee (USOC), although having a legislatory base, receives no government funding but funds its activities through the significant share of monies it receives from the International Olympic Committee's television contracts.

In some policy communities it is possible to identify primary and secondary communities (Laumann and Knocke, 1987). The primary core contains the key actors, who set the rules of the game and determine membership and the main policy direction of the community, whilst the secondary community contains the groups that, although abiding by the rules of the game, do not have the resources or influence to greatly affect policy. It would appear that this distinction of a primary and a secondary community is useful in examining the differences between structures of sport and tourism policy sectors. In the UK, although neither community could be said generally to have stable restricted membership, the nature of the primary and secondary communities does vary. The sports policy community has a fairly stable primary community which includes the Department for Culture, Media and Sport, Sport England and the other national Sports Councils, and UK Sport. The secondary community, the membership of which is fairly open, contains a wide range of interest groups, sports organizations and clubs, and local authorities. It might be argued that local authorities, or at least their representative organizations, form part of the primary community, although evidence suggests (Weed, 1999) that they have little input into the development of national policy. Similar situations can be found in other countries. In Australia, for example, a fairly tight group of organizations exists around the Australian Sports Commission (ASC), although the primary focus of Australian sports policy tends to be elite sport (Green, 2002). The Australian government, the ASC, the Australian Institute of Sport (AIS) and, to a certain extent, the Australian Olympic Committee (AOC) constitute a fairly closed primary community for elite sport in Australia. The position of the AOC in this primary group has been boosted by the recent hosting of the Olympics in Sydney. Although Australia has a federal system of government, sport, particularly elite sport, is seen as something that is too important to be managed by the states, who are expected to follow the lead given by the federal government and the ASC (Houlihan: personal communication, 2002).

The situation in tourism policy communities is often different, and it may not be possible clearly to define primary and secondary communities. This is often due to the nature of tourism as a primarily commercial concern. In England, as in many other countries, there has been a government sponsored tourism agency, but the recent subsumation of the English Tourism Council into the new Visit-Britain, which primarily has a marketing-oriented role, means that there is no key group of organizations to comprise a primary core. This tends to be the case in many other countries around the world – for example, as mentioned above, the USA abolished its government-funded national tourism organization in 1996, and now the commercial sector, under the auspices of the entirely privately funded Travel Industry Association of America, conducts any overseas marketing that takes place (Jeffries, 2001). In some countries, such as France, there is a greater public sector involvement due to a tradition of providing for *social tourism* (subsidized development for the benefit of low-income groups). However, this does not mean that there is an identifiable group of agencies that comprise a primary core across the full range of issues (which in tourism sectors around the world are particularly diverse), and consequently tourism policy communities tend to lack the division between primary and secondary communities. This leads to the conclusion that tourism policy communities tend to be more loosely constituted, with an unstable membership and groups joining or leaving the community according to the issues being discussed. This often contrasts with sports policy communities, which, while having fairly open secondary communities, appear to have relatively tightly constituted primary communities of which membership is fairly stable and restricted.

These differences in the basic structures of the communities can clearly cause problems for sport–tourism liaison. In the UK, the lack of an identifiable lead agency in the tourism policy community means that there is no organization with which sports agencies can liaise on strategic matters. In the past it might have been argued that the Regional Tourist Boards could have fulfilled this lead role at subnational level. However, alongside the incorporation of the English Tourism Council into VisitBritain, the Department for Culture, Media and Sport has also devolved responsibility for the distribution of regional tourism funding to Regional Development Agencies, which largely have an economic development remit. The Regional Tourist Boards must submit detailed business plans to justify such funding, which may be distributed to Regional Tourist Boards, or to other agencies, at the Regional Development Agencies' discretion. It is too early to assess the impact of these changes, but early indications are that the relationships between development agencies and tourist boards vary considerably from region to region. In some regions the Regional Tourist Boards appear to have retained a pivotal role in tourism policy and development, whilst in others it appears that the Regional Development Agencies have preferred to bypass Regional Tourist Boards altogether, particularly in regions where city tourism is the main product. However, notwithstanding the evolution of these new relationships, the regional nature of these agencies means that they cannot provide a lead for the tourism policy community at national level.

Consequently, while in the past this situation has resulted in some liaison taking place at regional level (Weed and Bull, 1997a), there has been a dearth of initiatives nationally. In countries with federal systems of government, such as France, Canada, the USA and Australia, it might be expected that there would be a greater focus on this regional level. In Australia, as discussed above, while the states are expected to follow the lead of the federal government in relation to elite sport, they do have a freer reign in relation to recreational participation. Furthermore, in many states there are specific government departments and statutory agencies with a tourism promotion remit. This may mean that, as has previously been the case in the UK, the regional level is likely to be where most productive sport–tourism partnerships can be established. The exception is in relation to what has become known as 'leveraging' major events, which refers to a range of strategies employed to maximize the economic effects of events such as the Sydney Olympic Games (Chalip and Leynes, 2002). Here, a national lead has been taken by the federal government. In the USA, given the independence of the USOC and the entirely commercial operation of the TIAA, and the variation in the ideological commitment to state involvement among the 52 states, it is not surprising that it is difficult to provide any sort of general characterization of structures for sport and for tourism in the USA. However, whilst at national and state level this may be the case, it should be noted that over 100 'sports commissions' have been established, often under a Convention and Visitor Bureau umbrella, in cities and regions across the USA (Standeven and De Knop, 1999). The range of studies of the use of sport in 'city marketing' in the USA (see, for example, a number of papers in Gratton and Henry, 2001), further highlight that the city level is perhaps the most important for sport–tourism partnerships in this country.

In Canada, the provinces and municipalities are often quite fierce about their independence. It might be argued that this has affected Canadian sports policy over the last 30 years. During this time there has generally been an overt or underlying emphasis on 'National Unity' in sports policy at the federal level (Green, 2002) and as such, particularly in relation to elite sport, the federal government and Sport Canada have taken a controlling lead role, based on historical precedence, legislation and funding. There has been a fairly overt split in responsibility for sports policy in Canada, with the provinces/municipalities being asked to take responsibility for recreational sport, while the federal government takes responsibility for elite sport. However, the more militant provinces, such as Quebec, have developed their own elite programmes, based on developing provincial identity. In relation to tourism, the Canadian Tourism Commission has been promoting 'product clubs' that are based on tourism niches rather than particular regions or destinations. It would seem, therefore, that the adoption of 'product clubs' based on sport tourist niches would appear to be a significant opportunity for the promotion of provincial identity, and serves to make the regional provincial level an important level for sport–tourism liaison in Canada.

One of the major issues facing both sport and tourism policy communities in many countries is the extent to which they are susceptible to interference from other policy areas. Houlihan (1991) highlights the inability of the sports policy community in the UK to insulate itself from other more powerful policy areas. An example of this is the response to the problem of football hooliganism in the 1980s, where the sports policy community was overridden by the law and order policy community in defining responses to that problem. Another example would be the inner city policy area, which in the UK and in many other countries often impinges on the work of sports policy communities. Whilst the 'city marketing' emphasis was identified above as being important in the USA, there may still be a worry about the extent to which initiatives are for the benefit of sport, or for marketing purposes. Of course, the market-oriented ideology of many US states means that often no distinction is made between the two.

The changing priorities of the inner cities also impinge considerably on the work of tourism policy communities. In the UK, the funds that are now to be offered to Regional Tourist Boards by the government, via Regional Development Agencies, are subject to the submission of a detailed business plan. In this way the government, via Regional Development Agencies which have an economic development remit, is able to direct the Regional Tourist Boards' activities towards the government's broader policy priorities by ensuring such funding is stipulated in business plans as being focused on the economic and social regeneration of communities. In the UK such regeneration projects have often been directed at urban areas, although this is not necessarily typical. The programme for the regeneration of the Languedoc Roussillon region of France focused on an area of coast running 180 kilometres from the south of Montpellier to the Spanish border. This programme, initiated in 1963, had the personal and powerful backing of the then French President, General de Gaulle. While this initiative was largely successful in developing a tourism product, it was undoubtedly driven by the need to restructure the regional economy and provide employment opportunities for an area where income was significantly lower than the national average (Jeffries, 2001). The French emphasis on social tourism was also incorporated into this development, as it aimed to provide subsidized recreational outlets for the French population (Ferras *et al.*, 1979). The conclusion to be drawn in the instances of both sport and tourism policy communities is that they cannot insulate themselves from other, more powerful and politically important, policy communities. Perhaps the reason for this is that, in all but the smallest minority of cases, political ideologies for both sport and tourism are often linked to other policy areas rather than seeing the provision of sport and tourism as an end in itself.

The extent to which this occurs can perhaps be best illustrated by a consideration of the effect the European Union has had on tourism. Jeffries (2001) suggests that a superficial examination would indicate that the Union's involvement has been virtually negligible if the focus is on the work of the Tourism Directorate within the Directorate Generale for Enterprise (DGE). The part played by the DGE is slight because the EU has no formal competence in tourism. However, the EU has considerable powers to decide policies and allocate funding to shape development in areas which are also bound to shape tourism. The European Commission's Paper 'Tourism and the European Union' (1995) lists over 20 such areas, which include: regional and social development, competition policy, transport policy, environmental protection, economic and monetary union (single currency), and employment and social policy. Thus tourism policy at the European level is clearly and overtly derived from other policy areas. Furthermore, the situation for sport is little different (Henry and Matthews, 1998), and this European example reflects, although perhaps to a more extreme degree, the situation in many countries throughout the world. Deriving policies from other policy areas clearly makes long-term strategic planning difficult because political objectives for sport and tourism are liable to change in the short to medium term. This obviously does not assist in the creation of links between the sport and tourism agencies, as each is dealing with more specific aims and objectives laid down by the political thinking of the time.

The distribution of resources often affects dependencies and influence within policy communities. Resources come in a range of forms; the most obvious are financial resources, but also important are knowledge, information, legitimacy and the goodwill of other groups (Smith, 1993). Tourist agencies, as discussed above, may often have to forego their independently established strategic plans in order to access funds offered by governments which often have specific conditions attached – control over direction is exchanged for financial resources. To a certain extent this has also occurred in the sports policy community in the UK, where Sport England has sacrificed much of its independence (although not necessarily willingly) in exchange for a central role in the distribution of Lottery funds.

Although a complex pattern of resource dependencies often exists in tourism policy communities between commercial sector organizations, and between the commercial sector and semi-public sector bodies, governments tend to retain a privileged position due to their greater economic resources (Rhodes, 1988). This means that governments are often able to wield considerable influence in the areas they consider to be important. However, the open and unrestricted nature of tourism communities' membership means that, with the exception of that with government, there are no major resource relationships upon which such communities are dependent. The relationships are complex, but they are small, and the loss of any one of them would not greatly affect the operation of the community as a whole.

In contrast, sports policy communities do tend to have a range of resource relationships upon which the community is dependent. In the primary community the resource relationships between government and national agencies are important because such national agencies could not survive without government grant aid. In the UK, this relationship helps ensure that Sport England accepts the lead of the Department for Culture, Media and Sport over general policy direction. However, the government in general does not wish to involve itself with the detail of all aspects of sports policy, and thus Sport England's expertise is required to convert general policy direction into implementable specifics. It is this exchange relationship that ensures these agencies comprise the primary core of the sports policy community. Their relationship with the secondary community is as a result of the dependence of much of that secondary community on Sport England grant aid and Lottery Sports Fund money. The actors in the secondary community do not have anything to exchange for these resources, and as a result have to accept the general policy directions and terms and conditions under which they are offered. The primary cores of the sports policy communities in the Canadian and Australian cases described earlier are similar to the UK situation, with the distinction between primary and secondary communities being largely, although not exclusively, based on the resource dependence of much of the secondary community on the primary actors. In addition, in the USA, the USOC, apart from its legislative base in the 1978 Amateur Sports Act, is able to wield a powerful influence over the rest of the sports policy community due to its significant resource base derived from the large proportion of the television rights money it receives from the International Olympic Committee.

The nature and features of sport and tourism policy communities can be summarized as follows. In tourism policy communities, membership is often unstable and open with no clear leadership and few major resource dependencies. Furthermore, there is often virtually no insulation from interference by other policy sectors, and member interests are mainly commercial, although governments often retain a privileged position as a result of their resource position. By contrast, sports policy communities often have a primary core, the membership of which tends to be stable and restricted, although the secondary community is usually fairly open. There is also often a number of major resource dependencies, both in terms of finance and expertise, that dictate the structure of, and relationships in, sports communities, while member interests, particularly in the primary community, are mainly governmental, supplemented by professional connections.

Clearly, as the above discussion indicates, these varied structures and operating norms for sport and tourism policy communities have implications for sport–tourism policy development. It appears to be the case that it is unrealistic to expect any sustainable strategic collaboration at national level because it is often difficult to identify the range of actors and areas of common interest necessary to sustain such collaboration. The area of major events may be the one exception to this generalization, as central government often has a considerable appreciation of the contribution such events can make to a range of national policy areas, and is keen to ensure the various agencies collaborate to both win and support such events. The less high-profile areas of the sport–tourism link may be better served by regional or state level liaison, for which the conditions and prospects for collaboration would appear to be more favourable. Furthermore, there appears to be a more recent trend, particularly in the USA, towards policy collaborations at city level. The final section of this chapter briefly illustrates these two levels of liaison in relation to two very different Case studies (9.1 and 9.2).

Case study 9.1 The island of Malta: sport tourism policy and destination development

The Mediterranean island of Malta has been seeking to counter its reputation for providing a low-quality mass-tourism product by upgrading its facilities and also by introducing new markets that will reduce its dependence on traditional mass tourism. As part of this process it has been encouraging diversification and the development of niche markets. A key area which has clearly been identified by the Maltese authorities as an important market is that of sport tourism (UNDP & WTO, 1989; Inskeep, 1994; Brincat, 1995; Lockhart, 1997), with the Maltese National Tourist Organization promoting a wide range of sports events and activities – both for participation and spectating – to foreign tourists (National Tourist Organization – Malta, 1997). Diving, yachting, power boating, golf, football and swimming are just a few examples from a wide range of sports that are seen as having a great deal of potential in this respect.

However, as the discussion here suggests, the future direction and success of sport tourism can in part be determined by the policies and commitment of the relevant government departments. Whilst Malta can clearly be identified as a tourism destination, it is also an independent 'small-island state'. Malta's size means that many of the structural forces affecting policy collaboration are similar to those that exist at the state or regional level in many other countries. Furthermore, the roles the government plays in a number of areas are similar to those of state or regional governments and agencies in many larger countries. First, the Maltese government is responsible in large measure for some of the key infrastructural requirements of sport tourism, such as the quality of transport facilities and provision of an adequate water supply. Secondly, through its environmental planning policies it can influence both the quality of the physical environment (and thus the attractiveness of the places in which sport tourism operates) and, through its development control mechanisms, the extent to which sports facilities are permitted to develop. Thirdly, through both its sports and tourism policies it can specifically encourage sport tourism development; and finally, through its relevant agencies it can promote its sport tourism attractions.

For several decades successive Maltese governments have attempted to promote tourism but, while espousing the principles of effective tourism planning, policy goals have not always been realized. Since the late 1980s a clearer recognition of the problems has emerged and, according to Lockhart (1997), evidence of recent progress has been made regarding diversification, niche markets and an improvement in the seasonal spread of arrivals. However, as the discussions above have shown, the development and implementation of policies involving the integration of sport and tourism may be more difficult to achieve. In particular, it appears that problems may be associated with the historical and continuing separate development of the two sectors.

The administrative arrangements in Malta are similar to those at regional/state level in many other countries, with sport and tourism being the responsibility of separate government departments and agencies. Tourism responsibility in Malta rests with the Ministry of Tourism, whilst responsibility for sport is located in the Secretariat for Youth, Sport, Art and Culture within the Education Ministry. Obviously, as a result of its small size, Malta has no regional structure of sport or tourism agencies; nor does it need the large-scale bureaucracy that exists in many other countries to coordinate matters at a national level. In this respect the historically separate development of the two spheres may not be as problematic, as large-scale readjustment would not be required for greater integration. Furthermore, the small-scale nature of the Maltese administration should make it easier and simpler to coordinate things on an informal level between the individuals involved, as has been shown to be the case at regional level in England (Weed and Bull, 1997a).

However, during discussions with officials of the Maltese government in the course of preparing this case study, it became apparent that in a number of cases such informal coordination did not appear to be occurring. Informal lines of communication between the planning department (responsible for the Ta'Qali Development Plan, which covers the National Recreation Centre) and officials in the government responsible for sport had not even reached the point where the officials concerned knew the names of their colleagues in the other department. This example appears to be indicative of the situation across the Maltese government. Weed (2003) identifies the inclinations of individuals to develop links across sectors as one of a number of important factors affecting sport–tourism liaison, and it may be the case that the attitudes of key staff are of greater importance in the Maltese situation, where there is greater latitude to develop links through informal coordination as a result of its smaller scale. Given Malta's potential to develop its sport tourism market (Bull and Weed, 1999), a key future challenge is to make the most of the advantages offered by its small size, typical of many other small states or sub-national regions around the world, in developing a collaborative and supportive policy for its develop-ment as a sport tourism destination.

Case study 9.2 The city of Sheffield, United Kingdom: sport tourism policy and destination development

The UK city of Sheffield is a large urban centre with a population of 530 000. As such, it possesses a variety of sports facilities consistent with its size and boasts a number of stadia linked to domestic sports teams. It contains a range of world-class spectator sports venues, including Bramall Lane and Hillsborough, the respective homes of the city's two football teams, Sheffield United and Sheffield Wednesday; the Sheffield Arena, for ice hockey and bas-ketball; the Don Valley Stadium, for athletics and rugby league; Ponds Forge International Sports Centre, for ice hockey, basketball, swimming and aquatic sports; and Owlerton Stadium, for speedway, stock cars and greyhound racing. In addition to spectator sports the city also possesses various facilities for active sport, including various leisure and sports centres, climbing centres, an ice centre with facilities for ice skating and speed skating, ski village (Europe's largest artificial ski resort), golf courses, tenpin bowling venues and a laserzone. Furthermore, the new Phoenix Centre, being built with the help of a Lottery award, will include a 200-m indoor athletics track and straight, a sports hall, dojo, sports science and medicine services. Sports competitions not only attract substantial numbers of spectators to the city, but a range of sports facilities is thus also available to general tourists.

However, it is the way sport has been utilized in conjunction with tourism as part of Sheffield's regeneration process that is particularly interesting. As such, it is illustrative of many of the potential linkages identified by Weed and Bull (1997a) in their Policy Area Matrix for Sport and Tourism. It also provides an example of city level partnerships generated by the specific 'regional context' of Sheffield's decaying manufacturing industry and employment base. As such it is an example of the way in which the specific factors identified by Weed (2003), of which regional contexts is one, can overcome many of the structural barriers to collaborative sport–tourism policy development at national level identified in this chapter. Furthermore, it is indicative of the trend towards city level policy partnerships.

In recent years Sheffield has developed a substantial array of sports venues linked to mega-events as part of a regeneration process involving a conscious effort to promote itself on the basis of a new image linked to sport, leisure and tourism. This was not an automatic process, and it involved key decisions being made by city councillors and other prominent players, considerable risks being taken both economically and politically, specific organizations (and especially partnerships) being established to facilitate the process, and a considerable amount of marketing and promotion. This showed that many of the structural problems that work against the development of collaborative sport–tourism policy identified in this chapter can be overcome, particularly if there is a specific focus for liaison. In the Sheffield case, as noted above, this was provided by the 'regional context' (Weed, 2003) of urban decay and unemployment, and became strategically focused in the mid-1990s following the hosting of the World Student Games in 1991. While these policy directions did not attract universal support and clearly involved some problems, not least the £147 million cost of hosting the World Student Games and the lack of an initial strategy to capitalize on this event, there are many who would now admit the overall idea has been a success. This has largely been the result of the somewhat belated strategization of Sheffield's sport event tourism efforts. Following a report by Friel, a consultant employed to advise on Sheffield's marketing in the mid-1990s, strategies were formulated specifically linking the Games investment with the development of tourism as a means of promoting city development (Bramwell, 1997a). Friel's report also led to greater cooperation between sport event organizers and tourism staff in the Visitor and Conference Bureau, with the Events Unit moving into the same building as the Bureau. The formal strategic plan of 1995 (Destination Sheffield, **An Event-Led City and Tourism Marketing Strategy for Sheffield**) involved the use of 'profile' events utilizing the venues built for the 1991 Games (Bramwell, 1997a), and was developed within the context of a strategic plan for Sheffield's wider economic regeneration, **The Way Ahead**, published in 1994, which also contained elements of sport, tourism and city marketing (Bramwell, 1997b). The conventional wisdom of the urban regeneration process (see Law, 2002) suggests that a city with high-profile sport and leisure facilities marketed as key elements of a vibrant and exciting place in which to live is one means of attracting inward investment, and Sheffield has clearly adopted this thinking in its approach to its development as a sport tourism destination.

Conclusion

It has been the aim of this chapter to provide a context for the consideration of policy and planning issues in sport tourism destinations. Consequently, the focus has been on the generic structural problems faced in developing strategic partnerships between the sport and tourism sectors at national and regional levels. The chapter shows that it is unlikely that sport tourism destinations will be working within a context where any policy collaboration has taken place at national level. In fact, it is often the case that there is a range of structural forces working against such national level policy liaison. However, as the Malta case shows, there may be a greater potential for the development of collaborative policy at sub-national or small-state level, although such potential is not always realized. Furthermore, as has been the case in Sheffield and many other cities, it is increasingly at the city level that the most useful collaborations can occur. This is usually in spite of, rather than the result of, the way in which policy for sport and tourism is developed nationally.

Acknowledgement

The commentary on policy community structures is derived from material previously published in Weed and Bull (2004).

References

Bramwell, B. (1997a). User satisfaction and product development in urban tourism. *Tourism Management*, 19(1), 35–47.

Bramwell, B. (1997b). A sport mega-event as a sustainable tourism development strategy. *Tourism Recreation Research*, 22(2), 13–19.

Brincat, I. (1995). Sport tourism. *Cobweb, Business Journal*, Special Issue on Sustainable Tourism in Malta, AIESEC.

Bull, C. J. and Weed, M. E. (1999). Niche markets and small island tourism: the development of sports tourism in Malta. *Managing Leisure*, 4(2), 142–155.

Chalip, L. and Leynes, A. (2002). Local business leveraging of a sport event: managing an event for economic benefit. *Journal of Sport Management*, 16(2), 132–158.

Destination Sheffield (1995). *An Event-Led City and Tourism Marketing Strategy for Sheffield*. Sheffield: Destination Sheffield.

European Commission (1995). *Tourism and the European Union: A Practical Guide*. Luxembourg: Office for Official Publications of the European Communities.

Ferras, R., Picheral, H. and Vielzeuf, B. (1979). *Languedoc Roussillon*. Famot: Flammarion et Editions.

Gratton, C. and Henry, I. P. (eds) (2001). *Sport in the City: The Role of Sport in Economic and Social Regeneration*. London: Routledge.

Green, M. (2002). Western approaches to sport policy. Loughborough: Loughborough University, Unpublished Review Paper.

Henry, I. P. and Matthews, N. (1998). 'Sport policy and the European Union: the post-Maastricht agenda'. *Managing Leisure*, 4(1), 1–17.

Houlihan, B. (1991). *The Government and the Politics of Sport*. London: Routledge.

Inskeep, E. (1994). Tourism planning approach of Malta. *National and Regional Tourism Planning*. London: Routledge, Ch. 11.

Jeffries, D. (2001). *Governments and Tourism*. Oxford: Butterworth-Heinemann.

Laumann, E. O. and Knocke, D. (1987). *The Organizational State*. Madison, WI: The University of Wisconsin Press.

Law, C. M. (2002). *Urban Tourism: The Visitor Economy and the Growth of Large Cities*. London: Continuum.

Lockhart, D. G. (1997). Tourism to Malta and Cyprus. In D. Lockhart and D. Drakakis-Smith (eds), *Island Tourism: Trends and Prospects*. London: Cassell, pp. 152–178.

National Tourist Organization – Malta (1997). *Malta Sports Calendar*. Valletta: NTO – Malta.

Rhodes, R. A. W. (1988). *Beyond Westminster and Whitehall*. London: Unwin Hyman.

Smith, M. J. (1993). *Pressure, Power and Policy*. Hemel Hempstead: Harvester Wheatsheaf.

Standeven, J. and De Knop, P. (1999). *Sport Tourism*. Champaign, IL: Human Kinetics.

UNDP & WTO (1989). *The Maltese Islands Tourist Development Plan*. Madrid: WTO.

Weed, M. E. (1999). *Consensual Policies for Sport and Tourism in the UK: An Analysis of Organizational Behaviour and Problems*. PhD Thesis, Canterbury: University of Kent at Canterbury/Canterbury Christ Church College.

Weed, M. E. (2001). Towards a model of cross-sectoral policy development in leisure: the case of sport and tourism. *Leisure Studies*, 20(2), 125–141.

Weed, M. E. (2002). Organizational culture and the leisure policy process in Britain: how structure affects strategy in sport–tourism policy development. *Tourism, Culture and Communication*, 3(3), 147–164.

Weed, M. E. (2003). Why the two won't tango: explaining the lack of integrated policies for sport and tourism in the UK. *Journal of Sports Management*, 17, 258–283.

Weed, M. E. and Bull, C. J. (1997a). Integrating sport and tourism: a review of regional policies in England. *Progress in Tourism and Hospitality Research*, 3(2), 129–148.

Weed, M. E. and Bull, C. J. (1997b). Influences on sport–tourism relations in Britain: the effects of government policy. *Tourism Recreation Research*, Sport and Tourism Special Edition, 22(2), 5–12.

Weed, M. E. and Bull, C. J. (1998). The search for a sport–tourism policy network. In M. F. Collins and I. S. Cooper (eds), *Leisure Management: Issues and Applications*. Wallingford: CAB International, pp. 277–298.

Weed, M. E. and Bull, C. J. (2004). *Sports Tourism: Participants, Policy and Providers*. Oxford: Elsevier Butterworth-Heinemann.

Wilks, S. and Wright, M. (eds) (1987). *Comparative Government–Industry Relations*. Oxford: Clarendon Press.

Wright, M. (1988). Policy community, policy network and comparative industrial policies. *Political Studies*, 36(4), 593–612.

Strategic partnerships for sport tourism destinations

Steve Webb

Introduction

Tourism remains a major global growth industry, and the key drivers of demand – world population increase, rising prosperity among the major post-industrial nations and more accessible and affordable forms of transport – will continue to stimulate international tourism arrivals. Tourism, however, does not perform a global balancing act between the developed and developing economies of the world. Most international tourists come from the developed market economies and go to countries at a similar stage of economic development. Governments throughout the world have become increasingly aware of the contribution tourism can make in securing economic prosperity. Tourism stimulates income generation, employment, investment and changes in land use, and can make a positive contribution to a host country's balance of payments. The essential reason why countries promote themselves as tourist destinations is for economic benefit. Individual tourism businesses and national governments are driven by the same basic imperative – economic gain. However, whereas the commercial sector will understandably focus on short-term profitability, governments are obliged to operate to a longer, more strategic timeframe. While economic growth may remain the primary objective, tourism's pervasive ability to influence societies, cultures and environments places a clear obligation on the public sector to set guidelines for growth within a strategic context.

A strategic approach to the development of tourism needs to reflect not only current problems and concerns, but also future aspirations (Jenkins, 1991). A haphazard, *ad hoc* approach to tourism development is not a viable option, given the growing acknowledgement of the importance of sustainability. It follows that those who shape and steer the industry must accept a wider responsibility for their actions, and adopt a more rounded and strategic approach. Tensions exist, however, between operationally driven motivations (short term) and strategically determined aspirations (long term), and the fragmentary nature of tourism does little to facilitate a strategic approach. Demand for tourism is inherently volatile and is subject to a melting pot of possible influences. In turn, demand is satisfied by a destination area where supply of the product or tourism experience is fragmented and variable. The dynamic nature of tourism leads many to contend that any balance that is achieved between the generating and destination countries (i.e. supply and demand) is the result of serendipity rather than strategy. Understandably, individual tourism businesses, concerned primarily with considerations of continued survival, will make independent, self-contained investment decisions. Few will have the inclination or the need to consider their actions from any longer-term strategic standpoint.

Left to market forces alone, the benefits associated with tourism are unlikely to be optimized. Government intervention is needed to enable the tourism industry to achieve its full potential and also to manage its environmental and socio-cultural impacts. At the point of delivery to the consumer, tourism tends to be a localized activity. Consequently, the positive and negative impacts generated by tourism activity will be concentrated in the local area, at least in the short term. Whether these impacts are spread more widely or extended over a longer timeframe will depend on many factors, including size and economic structure of the destination area, diversity and sphere of the influence of tourism activity, and the existence of appropriate control or management systems. It is in this context that government intervention is an appropriate response. On behalf of the tourism industry, it is incumbent on governments or their agencies to provide strategic leadership. A strategic approach can provide a framework for clarifying future direction, establishing priorities and stimulating effective working relationships within a fragmented industry over a definite timescale. A range of measures can be put in place to influence demand and supply in tourism, to ensure sustainable, long-term outcomes (Bramwell, 1998). Partnerships between the public and private sectors have increasingly been seen as an effective way to identify and implement the necessary controls, incentives and investment to optimize the beneficial effects of tourism within a destination area.

Partnerships in tourism

The concept of community involvement in tourism development, first described in Murphy's (1985) seminal work on this subject, provides an early reference point for partnerships in tourism. The common link between the community approach to tourism development and the partnership approach can be expressed in one word – 'collaboration'. Partnership is based on cooperation and integration of effort between the public and private sector to achieve a common end result. The success of any strategy will, in no small measure, be determined by the industry's ability to collaborate and cooperate through effective partnership working to turn 'words' into 'action'.

Gray (1989) developed a three-stage model to explain the process of collaboration. The first stage consists of problem-setting (identifying key stakeholders and issues), followed by a second stage of direction-setting (identifying a framework of common purpose) and a third stage of implementation, which may or may not be required depending on the goals of the exercise. The development of a model to describe the concept of partnerships was examined by Snape and Stewart (1995) in their evaluation of the business partnership structures that operated in the Bristol business community. They carried out an in-depth study of the strengths and weaknesses of partnerships, and attempted to identify examples of good practice that could inform future collaborative ventures. One of the main findings to emerge from their work in this area was the difference that existed between the relative importance attached to the 'process' compared with the 'output' performance of partnerships. In overall terms, there was greater emphasis placed on establishing partnership processes or on the formation of working structures and in establishing partnerships than on the measurement of substantive, quantifiable outputs. Disappointing progress was reported in establishing sound monitoring and evaluation systems that could measure the achievements/outputs of the partnerships under review.

While partnership structures have become inherent to tourism as an integral tool for implementation, there remains a lack of rigorous evidence to demonstrate that partnerships are an appropriate delivery mechanism. Conceptual work to monitor the performance of partnerships as delivery tools was undertaken by Saleem (1992), who concluded that, without agreement on the objectives and priorities at the outset, the subsequent evaluation of performance will be unstructured and lacking a point of reference. Programme targets or performance measures are essential, and need to be defined within a strategic framework of partnership goals and objectives to facilitate the monitoring of performance during the intended lifetime of the partnership. Unless a partnership defines what it is setting out to achieve, how will it be able to monitor its progress?

Gunn (1988) suggests that all the components that are essential to a properly functioning tourism system are in a delicate dynamic balance where changes to one element can have far-reaching and unpredictable effects on others, upsetting the equilibrium and requiring continuous monitoring. The development of a new attraction (such as a major sporting event), for example, can expect to generate new demand that will need to be serviced at the point of delivery. In turn, this may require supplementary investment in new and improved tourism facilities and amenities in the vicinity. However, not all impacts will be beneficial. Some existing attractions may well be affected by the displacement of visitors to the new attraction. The delicacy of the point of equilibrium in any functioning tourism system emphasizes the case for integrated strategic planning to achieve optimum benefits for the destination, by balancing supply with demand.

Tourism in the UK, and particularly in Wales, is characterized by its small business unit structure. Most of these units act independently even when they form part of a larger grouping or consortium. Decisions that are independently made by guesthouse owners, hotel managers, restaurateurs, attraction operators and event organizers will directly influence the quality of the tourism experience. These industry players who supply the tourism product in the destination region seldom work together, and usually have only a vague idea of the activities of neighbouring suppliers in the industry.

The public sector adds yet a further layer of potential distortion on the supply side of the tourism equation. Expansion and development programmes in tourism are heavily influenced by the role of the public sector in securing resources for infrastructure and facility improvements, providing a positive framework for land-use planning and adopting an entrepreneurial attitude towards marketing and investment activities. Regular communication between the major stakeholders on the supply side of tourism is a pre-condition for effective collaborative action. It is necessary to establish mechanisms that inspire, stimulate and support the process of communication. Partnership structures can form an effective tool for facilitating the process of active communication and for stimulating collaboration among the public and private sectors.

Acknowledging that destinations make up the supply side of the basic tourism system, as conceived by Leiper (1990), it is within destination areas that most operational partnerships will be formed. The formation of partnerships will depend in great part upon a range of relevant variables including, among others, the traditional networks existing within the tourism community, resource availability, the organizational structures of tourism, the strength of the local commercial and entrepreneurial consortia, and the existence of a lead player to stimulate partnership formation.

Imperfections in the tourism market lead to problems affecting both supply and demand. Economic growth will largely be achieved through private sector activity. The essential role of the public sector is to create the appropriate environment and the right conditions that will allow private enterprise to prosper. The need for effective coordination between the industry and all public sector bodies involved in the organization of tourism is crucial in order to achieve equilibrium in the tourism system and support the optimum contribution of tourism to economic prosperity. No single organization has the skills, resources or ability to work in isolation. Tourism is a fragmented industry, and it is essential for people, organizations and businesses to work together in an effective way to get things done and make things happen. Partnership networks can stimulate the necessary collaboration between the public and private sectors and provide value-added benefits by:

- Pooling of resources
- Pooling of talent
- Agreeing common goals and priorities
- Focusing investment on market needs
- Raising the status and profile of tourism
- Agreeing output targets.

A tourism strategy for Wales

Achieving Our Potential

The tourism product in Wales is fragmented and made up of predominantly small-scale business units which are economically vulnerable and do not have a strong or cohesive marketing voice. Government has a key role in setting a strategic direction for the industry. The strategic approach has proved itself a useful way to identify the most effective responses to the main challenges that confront the tourism industry by identifying priorities for coordinated action.

The setting up of a devolved Welsh Assembly Government in 1999 resulted in a higher profile for tourism and increased funding support for the industry, channelled through the Wales Tourist Board. Devolution also provided impetus for the preparation of a national tourism strategy for Wales, *Achieving Our Potential* (2000), which set out a framework for coordinated action through partnership working. *Achieving Our Potential* (2000) is integrated closely with the national economic development strategy, *A Winning Wales* (2002).

The Wales Tourist Board (WTB) consulted with all parts of the industry to produce a strategy that would provide a framework for future direction. It establishes strategic priorities and provides a sound framework for coordinated action between organizations, agencies and individual businesses to help secure long-term prosperity and sustainable growth for the industry and increase its contribution to a more diverse Welsh economy. Four key strategic themes are identified in *Achieving Our Potential*: competitiveness, quality, sustainability and partnership.

A strategic approach to tourism is important for the following reasons:

1 *Setting priorities*. Tourism is a fragmented, piecemeal industry that can result in random, *ad hoc* and inefficient responses by the industry and disequilibrium between the demand and supply sides. Acknowledging that tourism is an industry that can have negative and harmful effects on the environment, culture and quality of life of destination areas, as well as offering positive economic benefits, it is important to set priorities for action which promote and develop tourism in ways that minimize the detrimental and maximize the beneficial impacts of the industry.

2 *Responding to market needs*. The tourism industry must understand and be able to adapt to changing market behaviour. A strategic approach facilitates a more considered appreciation of changing trends in market demand, and the identification of product gaps or inefficiencies. Investment in new and improved facilities and skills can be targeted accordingly.

3 *Target-setting*. A strategy can set targets of growth for the industry and allow monitoring of performance over pre-determined timescales. The definition of quantifiable targets can help to channel industry efforts, avoid duplication and improve efficiency. If they are to be meaningful, however, targets must be realistic and achievable, measurable and specifically defined.

4 *Sustainable development*. A strategic approach can provide the framework for a positive commitment by all decision-makers to the principles of sustainability.

5 *Partnership action.* A strategy needs to be action-focused. The essentially fragmented nature of tourism means that it will be essential for people, businesses and organizations to work together in an effective way to get things done and to make things happen. Securing future success and prosperity depends on effective working relationships being established between willing partners.

Developing an international image/brand for Wales

Achieving Our Potential (2000) acknowledges that developing a distinctive and attractive national identity for Wales will bring significant political, social, cultural and economic benefits. The lack of a strong identity in international markets has been a barrier to growth, constraining attempts to sell Wales as an attractive destination for tourism and for inward investment. In this context, the promotion of Wales as a venue for first-class sporting events was viewed as an effective strategic response to boost awareness and develop positive perceptions of Wales as a tourism destination.

Wales' share of international tourism arrivals in the UK is low – it attracts 3 per cent of all international visits to the UK, and less than 2 per cent of all international spending. Wales depends heavily on the domestic (UK) market. International visitor spending accounts for only 15 per cent of all overnight visitor spending in Wales. At the UK level, the international share is closer to 50 per cent. In many overseas markets, the awareness of Wales is low and is often based on out-of-date perceptions. Wales lacks a distinctive separate identity (Pride, 2000) and is often synonymous with at best Britain, at worst England. Wales' hosting of the Rugby World Cup (RWC) in 1999 was timely because it provided a unique opportunity for public and private sector organizations in Wales to work in partnership to redefine and strengthen its 'branding' in overseas markets.

The RWC 1999 was seen as a platform for an image-building exercise that would not only increase awareness of Wales throughout the world, but also enable the tourism industry to communicate a strong, modern and attractive image of Wales to potential visitors. Wales was the focus of considerable media attention prior to and during the tournament. A strategic approach was devised by a partnership of organizations to optimize the short-term and longer-term benefits of the RWC 1999. This Team Wales initiative involved the development of an integrated programme of activities, including marketing and promotion, accommodation upgrading, infrastructural improvements, visitor management and customer care initiatives (see Case study 10.1).

Case study 10.1 'Team Wales': evaluating the impact of the Rugby World Cup 1999

The Rugby World Cup ranks as the fourth largest sporting event in the world on the basis of income generated and the number of spectators and viewers it attracts. It was the largest sporting tournament to take place anywhere in 1999. The RWC 1999 took place during the 5-week period from 1 October to 6 November 1999.

The Welsh Rugby Union (WRU) was the official host, and was responsible for the on-the-ground delivery of the tournament in partnership with the RWC tournament office. As the host union, the WRU had agreements with the rugby unions for England, Ireland, Scotland and France to stage pool matches in these countries. Wales hosted one of the five group sections of the tournament, as well as one of the quarter-finals, the third and fourth place play-off and the RWC final – nine games in total. Seven games were held at the Millennium Stadium in Cardiff, and one each was held in Llanelli (South West Wales) and Wrexham (North Wales).

The role of the Wales Tourist Board in the RWC

The Wales Tourist Board (WTB) had a crucial role in relation to marketing and promotion of the tournament. It led the formation of a 'Team Wales' partnership approach to support the implementation of a coordinated marketing strategy and associated activities. As early as 1997, the WTB recognized the opportunity presented by the hosting of the RWC in Wales. Consequently it put in place a series of project teams to handle a wide range of activities in relation to the tournament, including:

■ Marketing and promotion
■ Press and PR
■ Business support.

In June 1997, the WTB received confirmation of a successful bid for funds amounting to £600 000 from the National Sector Challenge Programme (NSCP). These funds were provided to support a marketing and promotional strategy to maximize the benefits of the RWC to the tourism sector in Wales. The WTB, in partnership with a number of other organizations (Welsh Development Agency, Cardiff Bay Development Corporation, Arts Council of Wales, Cardiff International Airport, Cardiff Marketing Limited, Cardiff County Council, Tourism South and West Wales – which represented the interests of a number of local authorities), also secured European Union funding to promote Wales and Cardiff 'around' the tournament. Table 10.1 shows the funds made available from the core budgets of public sector 'partners'.

A total of just over £5 million was spent in relation to the tournament. This includes almost £3 million of public sector funds, including NSCP, which was matched by £275 000 from private sector and over £1.9 million from the EU. These public agencies, together with the private sector, provided substantial support for RWC in Wales. This was not only in the form of marketing and advertising, but also in the delivery of suitable infrastructure – including transportation, provision of information, community events, environmental activity (such as street dressing) and generally encouraging participation among the community.

The overall aim of the WTB's Rugby World Cup marketing programme was:

To maximize the economic and tourism benefits of the Rugby World Cup 1999, using the tournament as an opportunity to attract additional visitors during the

Table 10.1 Direct financial support for Rugby World Cup 1999

Organization	Source (£'000)				
	Public sector	EU	NSCP	Private sector	Total
Wales Tourist Board	824	476	600	70	1970
Cardiff Bay Development Corp.	172	172	–	–	344
Cardiff Marketing Limited	723	602	–	–	1325
Welsh Development Agency	75	75	–	–	150
Arts Council of Wales	111	93	–	–	204
Tourism South & West Wales	123	267	–	190	580
Cardiff Airport Limited	–	13	–	15	28
Cardiff County Council	299	251	–	–	550
Wrexham County Borough Council	20	–	–	–	20
'Public sector' total	2347	1949	600	275	5171

event to raise the profile and image of the host nation in order to secure lasting tourism benefits.

The specific objectives of the marketing programme were:

1 To maximize the short-term tourism benefits of the tournament both for Wales and the UK by seeking to maximize the number of visitors and their spending levels.
2 To enhance the competitive position of Wales as a destination for overseas visitors by using the tournament as an opportunity to raise the profile of Wales and improve its image overseas, thereby securing lasting economic and tourism benefits.
3 To evaluate and disseminate the findings of a research project in order to demonstrate the competitive benefits which can be gained from the hosting of a large-scale, international event.

The marketing strategy sought, therefore, to spread the benefits of the tournament as widely as possible, encouraging visitors to travel to various parts of Wales during their stay. The staging of the RWC offered both short- and long-term economic benefits to Wales. The short-term benefits were associated with the expenditure generated by large numbers of participants, spectators and media attending the event. The long-term benefits were twofold. First, the RWC provided an opportunity to present a positive image of Wales on the world stage, to change attitudes and raise the awareness and the profile of Wales as a tourist destination. Secondly, the tournament would act as a catalyst to secure associated infrastructure improvements, which would improve quality and levels of competitiveness within the industry.

The following strategic targets were set by the partnership:

Target	Rationale
T1	To achieve an increase in the volume and value of tourism to Wales in 1999 – an additional 55 000 visitors (20 000 domestic and 35 000 overseas) and associated spend of £12 million A key objective was to maximize the tourism benefits of the tournament to Wales; the proposed target increase was approximately one-third on top of the forecast annual increase expected between 1998 and 1999 It was not appropriate to set similar targets for the UK as a whole, since the impact of the event on tourism at this level was likely to be far more diffuse and difficult to trace back to the RWC and the marketing programme
T2	Following the tournament, to sustain the increase in overseas visitors in 2000 – an anticipated increase of 45 000 overseas visitors with associated spend of £12 million The provision of additional resources to market and promote Wales overseas will enable an increase in the rate of growth of overseas markets – the target was twice the annual increase in overseas visitors observed between 1992 and 1995. The target assumes that this higher rate of growth will be sustained in the future
T3	The creation of 1000 additional short-term jobs in the tourism industry associated with the tournament, and 600 jobs in the longer term as a consequence of the improved competitiveness of the sector. The increase in the volume and value of domestic and overseas tourism will inevitably support employment in the tourism industry in Wales. The employment creation targets are consistent with the forecast increases in tourism anticipated

Evaluation of the RWC

A key partnership objective was to put in place a long-term programme of research to evaluate the tourism and wider economic benefits that were secured for Wales by the hosting of the RWC 1999. In September 1997 a competitive brief was issued, inviting research proposals to assist and advise the WTB in the monitoring and evaluation of the impacts and effects of the RWC 1999 on tourism and the economies of Cardiff, South East Wales and Wales. Segal Quince Wicksteed Limited (SQW) together with System Three were appointed to undertake an integrated programme of research (Figure 10.1).

The research started a full year before the event, with a series of baseline surveys:

1 Self-completion questionnaires were sent to 1000 businesses to determine plans for improvement or investment in time for the RWC and baseline information on tourism activity during October 1998.
2 Supplementary questions were added to the WTB's existing occupancy survey – e.g. details of tourism origin, businesses turnover and employment.
3 UK/overseas images and perceptions surveys were used to provide baseline information for subsequent benchmarking research.

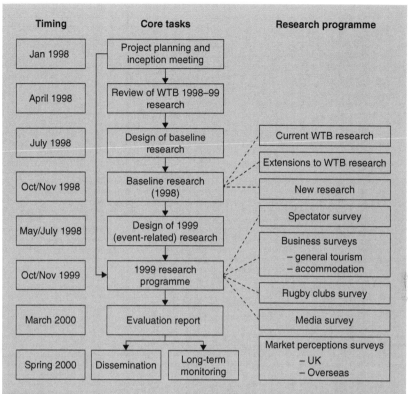

Figure 10.1 Overview of the RWC 1999 study method

During the event these baseline surveys were repeated, along with a supplementary survey:

1 The Rugby Club Survey (a self-completion questionnaire) was sent to 400 clubs to find out about details of overseas rugby clubs who may be staying/playing in the area.
2 A media survey was performed – telephone interviews were held with members of the media to measure their economic impact.
3 A spectator survey was carried out, consisting of 1100 face-to-face interviews with spectators throughout Wales. This was crucially important primary research, and provided essential information on visitor spending, visitor origin, travel patterns and overall economic impact.

The starting point for the evaluation of the economic impact of the RWC was the survey of spectators, which provided information on gross expenditure and travel patterns. In order to measure the net effect of RWC on the Welsh economy it was important to exclude anything that was not directly attributable to it. Adjustments

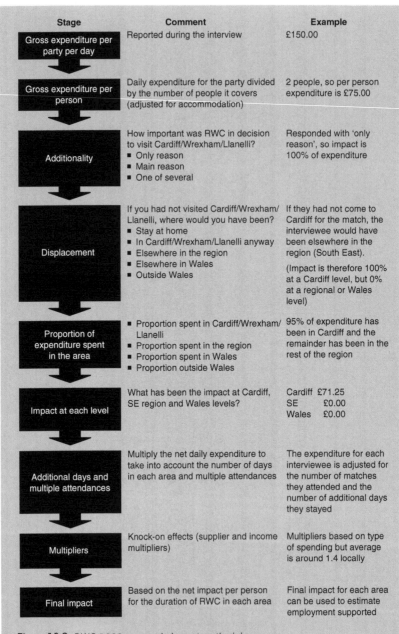

Stage	Comment	Example
Gross expenditure per party per day	Reported during the interview	£150.00
Gross expenditure per person	Daily expenditure for the party divided by the number of people it covers (adjusted for accommodation)	2 people, so per person expenditure is £75.00
Additionality	How important was RWC in decision to visit Cardiff/Wrexham/Llanelli? ■ Only reason ■ Main reason ■ One of several	Responded with 'only reason', so impact is 100% of expenditure
Displacement	If you had not visited Cardiff/Wrexham/Llanelli, where would you have been? ■ Stay at home ■ In Cardiff/Wrexham/Llanelli anyway ■ Elsewhere in the region ■ Elsewhere in Wales ■ Outside Wales	If they had not come to Cardiff for the match, the interviewee would have been elsewhere in the region (South East). (Impact is therefore 100% at a Cardiff level, but 0% at a regional or Wales level)
Proportion of expenditure spent in the area	■ Proportion spent in Cardiff/Wrexham/Llanelli ■ Proportion spent in the region ■ Proportion spent in Wales ■ Proportion outside Wales	95% of expenditure has been in Cardiff and the remainder has been in the rest of the region
Impact at each level	What has been the impact at Cardiff, SE region and Wales levels?	Cardiff £71.25 SE £0.00 Wales £0.00
Additional days and multiple attendances	Multiply the net daily expenditure to take into account the number of days in each area and multiple attendances	The expenditure for each interviewee is adjusted for the number of matches they attended and the number of additional days they stayed
Multipliers	Knock-on effects (supplier and income multipliers)	Multipliers based on type of spending but average is around 1.4 locally
Final impact	Based on the net impact per person for the duration of RWC in each area	Final impact for each area can be used to estimate employment supported

Figure 10.2 RWC 1999: economic impact methodology

were required, therefore, for additionality, displacement and geographical location of expenditure. A further adjustment was necessary because many people attended more than one match, and it was necessary to gross up the figures to include the effects of additional days and attendance at multiple matches. A final adjustment involved the application of multiplier values. Figure 10.2 summarizes the methodology used to measure economic impact.

Summary of findings

The RWC well exceeded the original visitor targets. Over 330 000 people were estimated to have visited the country as a result of the RWC, at a time of the year when leisure travellers were not normally so abundant. This level of activity gave rise to an estimated 480 000 bed-nights in the country. Residents of Wales comprised 66 per cent of total visitors, 13 per cent coming from the rest of the UK and 21 per cent from overseas. Many of the visitors were on their first trip to the country, and there were indications of very high levels of satisfaction with their experience of Wales.

Figure 10.3 provides details of the spatial dimensions of the economic impact. As might be expected, Cardiff and the South East region were the main beneficiaries. In total, the RWC generated a net expenditure of £77.1 million for Wales. Including media expenditure and additional investment generated, the total short-term impact on Wales was £83.2 million. The longer-term impact generated from return trips was estimated at £4.4 million from a subsequent piece of follow-up research conducted in 2001.

In impact studies of this nature, it is usual to convert the net impact on expenditure into jobs. The usual convention is to apply multiplier figures to the total estimated expenditure. On this basis, it was estimated that the net additional spending generated 1700 full-time equivalent jobs for one year. This 'jobs created' figure is meaningless in practical terms. The new revenue that was generated is predominantly absorbed by businesses, suppliers to businesses and existing staff, who may work longer hours or be paid overtime. In fact, 15 per cent of businesses took on additional part-time staff (2000 in total), and in 32 per cent of businesses staff worked longer hours (4000 in total).

Public sector expenditure of £4.8 million generated £83 million additional spending for the economy — a return ratio of 1:17.

In terms of the RWC's impact on the competitiveness of the tourism industry, based on the survey of businesses, £3 million of investment in improved tourism was stimulated by the RWC. Exploring changes in perceptions towards Wales is a difficult area to research, and in this case visitors were asked a series of attitudinal statements about Wales before and after the event. There was very little measurable change, although positive perceptions were higher amongst those who had attended the matches and there was some measurable effect that Wales was seen as more of a 'cosmopolitan and dynamic place'. The event did demonstrate conclusively that Cardiff had the ability to host large-scale sporting events. This effect may be difficult to quantify in terms of its future residual impact. It is worth noting, however, that the Millennium Stadium in Cardiff was subsequently awarded the FA Cup Final in 2001, and will continue to host this prestigious event until such time as the new Wembley Stadium has been constructed.

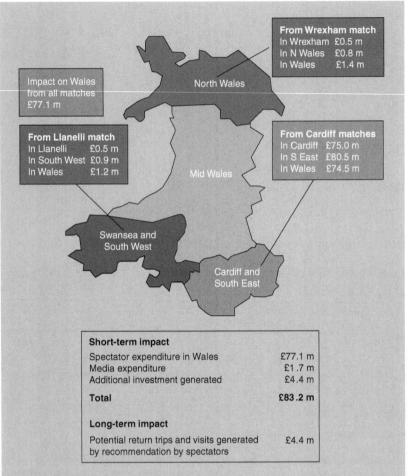

From Wrexham match
In Wrexham   £0.5 m
In N Wales   £0.8 m
In Wales   £1.4 m

Impact on Wales
from all matches
£77.1 m

North Wales

From Llanelli match
In Llanelli   £0.5 m
In South West £0.9 m
In Wales   £1.2 m

From Cardiff matches
In Cardiff   £75.0 m
In S East   £80.5 m
In Wales   £74.5 m

Mid Wales

Swansea and
South West

Cardiff and
South East

Short-term impact	
Spectator expenditure in Wales	£77.1 m
Media expenditure	£1.7 m
Additional investment generated	£4.4 m
Total	**£83.2 m**
Long-term impact	
Potential return trips and visits generated by recommendation by spectators	£4.4 m

Figure 10.3 RWC 1999: economic impact distribution

The WTB's marketing activities

It seems clear that the overall aims of the marketing programme was achieved. What is less evident is the success in spreading the benefits of the tournament or encouraging visitors to travel to various parts of Wales during their stay. Although the tournament impacted positively on North Wales and in the South West region, this was considerably overshadowed by the level of visitor numbers, expenditure and resultant net economic benefit experienced in Cardiff and the South East region. This is perhaps to be expected, given the focus of the tournament in this area.

Given the widespread international awareness of the event and the many influences that would contribute to visitors' decisions, it is difficult to isolate the specific role which WTB marketing had on visitor behaviour. This was examined in the spectator survey by probing recall and the influence of WTB advertisements and brochures. Although the number of spectators who claimed that they had been influenced in some way by this marketing (decision to visit Wales, decision to visit other parts of Wales, realization that there was more to do and see, likelihood of returning) is small, it is estimated that the impact, measured in terms of spectator expenditure, might be in the region of £2 million.

Events such as the RWC do not occur very often. It will be many years before Wales is invited to host the RWC again. It was important, therefore, to seek to maximize the tourism benefits of staging the RWC, both in the short and longer term. The Team Wales approach adopted in Wales required collaboration between willing partners in the private and public sectors to achieve commonly agreed objectives and mutual benefits. This partnership structure ensured that all major stakeholders were involved in not only marketing the event but also 'delivering the promise'.

Conclusions

Partnerships in tourism are an effective way to deliver strategic imperatives but they are a means to an end rather than end in themselves. It is important to put in place appropriate tools to measure the performance of partnership approaches. The setting of clear objectives and targets are a necessary discipline and it is essential to monitor and evaluate the outputs achieved in order to critically appraise the success of the partnership. All too often, the formation of a partnership is seen as being more important than measuring the quality of its output. The Team Wales case study is a good example of a partnership arrangement which gave a high priority to evaluating its role in maximizing the economic benefits of RWC 1999. The programme of research was carefully planned to ensure that adequate time was given to the task of setting realistic baseline measures well in advance of the actual event which could be subsequently benchmarked against – during and post-event. It is more common to find that the evaluation of the economic impact of major sporting events is planned in haste and rarely is enough preparation time given to planning pre-event baseline research.

Sport today is a big business phenomenon and it is a major contributor to global tourism activity. RWC 1999 stimulated significant economic benefits for Wales in terms of visitor numbers, increased visitor spending and job creation. It also had a major impact on changing perceptions of Wales. These are important measures to demonstrate the short-term and long-term benefits of the tournament. Just as importantly perhaps, RWC 1999 was a success at the social or community level. As host country, Wales took the tournament to its heart. The research findings confirmed that the feeling was reciprocated by the visitors from around the globe. High levels of visitor satisfaction demonstrated that the partnership approach succeeded in achieving a fundamental strategic priority for Wales — to exceed the expectations of the market and to achieve an effective balance between the dynamic forces of supply and demand.

References

A Winning Wales — The National Economic Development Strategy of the Welsh Assembly Government (2002). Cardiff: Welsh Assembly Government.

Achieving Our Potential – A Tourism Strategy for Wales (2000). Cardiff: Wales Tourist Board.

Bramwell, B. (1998). Selecting policy instruments for sustainable tourism. In W. F. Theobald (ed.), *Global Tourism*. Oxford: Butterworth-Heinemann, pp. 361–380.

Gray, B. (1989). Conditions facilitating interorganizational collaboration. *Human Relations*, 38, 911–936.

Gunn, C. A. (1988). *Tourism Planning* (2nd edn). New York: Taylor & Francis.

Jenkins, C. L. (1991). *Developing Tourism Destinations – Policies and Perspectives*. London: Longman.

Leiper, N. (1990). *Tourism Systems*. Department of Management Systems, Occasion Paper 2, Massey University, New Zealand.

Murphy, P. E. (1985). *Tourism: A Community Approach*. London: Methuen.

Pride, R. (2002). Brand Wales: 'Natural Revival'. In N. Morgan, A. Pritchard and R. Pride (eds), *Destination Branding – Creating the Unique Destination Proposition*. Oxford: Butterworth-Heinemann, pp. 109–124.

Saleem, N. (1992), Monitoring and evaluation of area based tourism initiatives. *Tourism Management*, 22(4), 844–856.

Snape, D. and Stewart, M. (1995). *Keeping Up the Momentum: Partnership Working in Bristol and the West*. Conference Paper to the Bristol Chamber of Commerce and Initiative – The Continuing Partnership Challenge, October. Bristol: School of Policy Studies, University of Bristol, pp. 22–25.

Wales Tourist Board (2000). *Rugby World Cup 1999, Economic Impact Evaluation*. Cardiff: Segal Quince Wickstead/System 3.

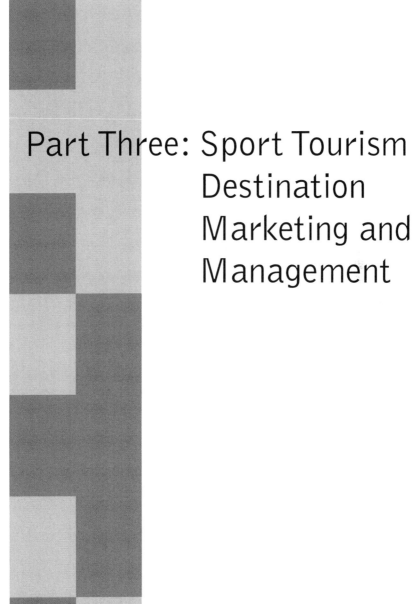

Part Three: Sport Tourism Destination Marketing and Management

11

Introduction to sport tourism destination marketing and management

James Higham

National and regional tourism organizations are confronted by a range of challenging issues associated with the marketing and management of sport tourism destinations. Various issues that are central to destination marketing relate, for example, to branding and destination image. Hinch and Higham (2004) note that the success of the tourism industry hinges on the uniqueness of tourism destinations. As such, destination marketing organizations face the challenge of constructing destination imagery that is unique or differentiated in some way from competing destinations. This process involves the construction of a competitive brand or destination image. In cases where destinations are associated with vague or negative images, destination marketing becomes a particularly important challenge (Page and Hall, 2003).

Destination marketing has assumed heightened importance as destinations have confronted increasing competition from other places (Hall, 1998). Kotler *et al.* (1993) employ the term 'place wars' to explain that globalization and technological change has intensified competition between places to attract and retain investment, commercial interests, products and markets. This scenario applies equally to competition between sport tourism destinations. Page and Hall (2003: 309) recognize that in order to compete in this environment, 'marketing practices, such as branding, rely upon the commodification of particular aspects of place, exploiting, reinventing or creating place images in order to sell the place as a destination product for tourists or investment'.

Hinch and Higham (2004) highlight various approaches that utilize sports to create differentiated destination imagery. These include the development of unique sports resources (Belanger, 2000), harnessing sport events to re-image destinations (Brown *et al.*, 2002), capitalizing upon strong associations between sports and specific countries or regions (Rooney and Pillsbury, 1992), and the development of sports-related leisure services, usually in association with urban redevelopment strategies (Porteous, 2000). These approaches may be adopted individually or collectively as part of a strategy to re-image tourism destinations.

These are examples of sport opportunities that can contribute significantly to the image or brand with which destinations may actively develop an association (see, for example, Case study 11.1). The role of the media is critical in achieving destination branding outcomes. Sports are unique in the media attention that they generate (Hinch and Higham, 2004). The media markets associated with sports include media reporting of sports (elite and non-elite), live television broadcasting, sports marketing and advertising. The growing trend towards commercial sponsorship in sport through, for example, the endorsement of sports stars (Andrews and Jackson, 2002) serves to heighten these interests. As the media play such a critical role in building the image or brand of sport tourism destinations, it is important to consider approaches to incorporating media into destination branding activities, and the effectiveness of approaches to doing so.

Understanding the visitor experience and manifestations of tourist behaviour at a destination are also important challenges facing sport tourism destination managers. These aspects of sport tourism are not well understood (Gibson, 1998), yet are linked closely to visitor satisfaction, perceived value and repurchase intentions (Petrick, 2002). Furthermore, experiences and behaviours vary considerably between niche sport tourism markets. The visitor experience is a combination of tangible (physical attributes) and intangible (emotions and feelings) elements. The experiential approach to studying the visitor experience involves understanding the emotions and feelings associated with sport tourism. Understanding the visitor experience also requires consideration of the manifestations of sport tourist behaviour. The theory of planned behaviour states that tourist behaviour can be predicted based on attitudes and subjective norms (Ajzen and Driver, 1992). Tourist behaviours are evaluated based on instrumental costs and benefits, as well as the positive or negative feelings that behaviours may bring about. Studies that investigate the motivational characteristics of sport tourism niche markets illustrate the broad diversity of motivations and desired experiences that may be related to the pursuit of individual sports (Klenosky *et al.*, 1993; Richards, 1996; Millington *et al.*, 2001; see also Case study 11.1).

Case study 11.1 Diversifying sport participant experiences and behaviours: City Marathons

The London City Marathon was first contested in 1981. This urban sports event was the initiative of Chris Brasher, following his participation in the New York Marathon. Brasher, a former Olympic champion, did not establish the event to serve solely as an elite competition. Instead he envisaged a formula similar to the race that he had completed in New York, which included 11 532 men and women from 40 countries in what he described as 'the greatest folk festival the world has seen'.

To date more than half a million people have completed the London Marathon, and each year more than half a million people line the city streets of London to support the competitors. In 1981, over 20 000 applications to compete in the inaugural race were received. A total of 7747 were accepted, of which 6255 completed the course. In 2003, a capacity of 46 500 entrants was accepted from a record 80 500 applicants. With this growth in numbers has come a diversification in the motivations underpinning participation in the event. In addition to elite championship runners who compete to win, and in some cases aim to break world record times, the event provides for domestic and overseas runners, clubs, corporate teams and wheelchair athletes. Increasingly the event has been linked to charity causes, allowing runners to raise money for the charities of their choice. Pubs on the race course work alongside specific charities providing entertainment for spectators and runners. A festival atmosphere is fostered through bands, street entertainers and the design of marathon banners by local schools. The intention is to create a 26.2-mile long street party. This diversity brings with it spectator interests that are similarly diverse. The 26.2-mile course is designed to follow the river Thames as closely as possible and finish in the Mall, in the heart of the city of London, so as to promote and encourage spectatorship.

The product is an event that generates a carnival atmosphere. It also now serves a wide range of motivations and desired sport experiences. A similar course of development has continued with the New York Marathon. The New York Marathon itself is now one part of a week-long series of events, including a 5-mile race in Central Park, the Marathon Health and Fitness Expo, the Continental Airlines International Friendship Run, a ceremony to post results, and their publication in a special edition of The New York Times. In 2004 the National Track and Field Hall of Fame featuring the Fred Lebow Marathon Hall opened at the New Balance Track and Field Center at the Armory in New York City. The facility is New York City's first national sports hall of fame. The Fred Lebow Marathon Hall features displays of marathon memorabilia, an inlaid floor of the New York City Marathon route, and photographic murals from marathons across the USA. These attractions, activities and festivities are a response to the diversifying interests that have developed in association with the New York Marathon.

(Sources: London Marathon: http://www.london-marathon.co.uk/; New York Marathon: http://www.nycmarathon.org/)

Tourist behaviour is a critical element for sustainable sport tourism development. Individual sports are characterized by sport tourist behaviour profiles that may or may not benefit the tourist destination. Active sport tourism is generally constructive in the immediate outcomes of participation, including exertion, fitness, camaraderie, social contact and subcultural identity (Hinch and Higham, 2004). The behaviours associated with sports team fans and spectators are highly varied (Giulianotti, 1995, 1996; Getz and Cheyne, 1997; Weed, 2002). Bale (1989) notes that 'ritualized conflict' is an apt description of spectator responses to some team sports. He also highlights the intensity of atmospheres generated in sports stadiums and arenas. In some sports such atmospheres can trigger situations of confrontation and aggression. It is noteworthy, however, that some sports teams have over time generated loyal groups of followers, who collectively may bring an atmosphere of celebration to the destinations that their teams visit. The Barmy Army (England cricket) and the Tartan Army (Scotland football) are examples of colourful supporter groups that have developed in association with the teams that they follow (Giulianotti, 1991). The Brazilian football team also has a unique and longstanding association with carnival fandom.

Understanding the motivations, experiences and behaviours of tourists travelling in support of sports teams is important to destination managers. The behaviours associated with the supporters of sports teams may greatly enhance, or significantly damage, the tourism interests of destinations where sports take place. The manifestations of sport tourism behaviour are not readily predicted, and are in fact in many cases a consequence of a range of factors, at least some of which are impossible to manage (e.g. competition draws, quality of refereeing and the outcomes of important contests). Thus, while the Italia 1990 Federation Internationale de Football Association (FIFA) World Cup was marred by acts of hooliganism, the USA 1994 FIFA World Cup was notable for the absence of football hooliganism, and the emergence of carnival fandom (Giulianotti, 1996). Four years later, the circumstances surrounding France's victory in the 1998 FIFA World Cup prompted 'an outpouring of joy and sentiment that was unprecedented since the liberation of 1944' (Dauncey and Hare, 2000: 331). Individual sports such as tennis, golf and surfing generally offer demonstrations of individual skill, and these sports are less likely to be associated with collective spectator behaviour.

Sport tourists can heavily influence tourism destination interests through individual and collective behaviours. They may create a sense of carnival and bring colour, excitement and atmosphere to a destination that is attractive to tourists. Alternatively, sports may generate social impacts and security risks, and create offence, that may be repulsive to tourism (Higham, 1999; Weed, 2002). The resumption of international cricket tours between India and Pakistan in 2004 provides evidence of the feelings that may be expressed, positively or negatively, through the medium of sports. Sports may therefore generate inward flows of visitors during and after sports events or, equally, create aversion effects (Faulkner et al., 1998) that may displace leisure, business and conference travel. The varied and contrasting manifestations of tourist behaviour confirm the need to understand the motivations and desired experiences associated with niche sport tourism markets.

In addition to managing visitor experiences, it is important for tourism organizations to consider and, where possible, manage the relationship between sports and tourism *vis-à-vis* seasonal patterns of tourist activity. Seasonality is an inescapable reality of tourism. Natural and institutional factors contribute to regular temporal variations in travel patterns (BarOn, 1975; Hartman, 1986; Frechtling, 1996). The availability of seasonal sports at a destination contributes to seasonal travel flows (Butler, 2001). Winter sports such as skiing, snowboarding and snowmobiling are perhaps the most obvious examples of seasonal sports. While institutionalized sports such as golf, tennis and ice hockey are characterized by clearly defined seasons, even independent sports such as surfing, cycling and fishing are generally characterized by distinct patterns of seasonal participation.

The evolution of many elite sports competitions over the past 30 years has resulted in the expansion of competition seasons. Technological innovations, changing social conditions and commercial interests have resulted in the expansion of existing sports seasons (Higham and Hinch, 2002). Related to this, the professionalization of many sports at the elite level of competition has resulted in the initiation of new levels of professional and amateur competition, as well as qualification tours, that take place in new competition seasons (McPherson *et al.*, 1989). The expansion of professional golf and tennis circuits to cater for various levels of elite competition is an example of new sports seasons. Recent developments in the New Zealand representative rugby calendar further illustrate this point. The addition of new competitions such as Super 12, Tri-Nations and end of year international tours has considerably extended the playing calendar (Higham and Hinch, 2002). The New Zealand Rugby Union now administers a series of overlapping seasons for local, provincial, regional and international competitions. Collectively these competitions will, from 2005, extend across all 12 months of the calendar year. Under this system different players will be eligible for some but not all levels of competition, as a safeguard against player burnout. As players are selected for higher levels of competition, their eligibility for participation in different competitions changes.

The expansion of competition seasons and the emergence of new competitions offer new opportunities for sport tourism destinations. However, seasonal patterns still exist in many sports. Notwithstanding the development of new technologies, snow sports remain dependent upon seasonal weather conditions, as do many other outdoor sports such as tennis, golf and the proliferating range of water sports. These sports continue to offer the challenges of seasonality at sport tourism destinations. Higham and Hinch (2002) argue that the relationship between sport and tourism seasons can be actively influenced with destination management goals in mind. Thus changes to the sport product mix, the use of sports events and the development of niche sport tourism markets are among some of the responses that destination organizations may pursue in an attempt to manage seasonal travel flows.

Changes to the product mix in the urban sport tourism context have in many cases been based on stadium developments, which increasingly exist as a focal point for entertainment facility development. Entertainment consumption now centres on 'creating a new urban landscape filled with casinos, megaplex cinemas, themed restaurants, simulation theatres, stadia and sports complexes' (Belanger, 2000: 378). In many cases this new urban landscape exists in nodal entertainment enclaves that function as 'tourist precincts' (Leiper, 1990). 'These group-specific combinations of spatially related attractions and facilities are called complexes' (Dietvorst, 1995: 165). The competitiveness of sport tourism destinations is enhanced when facility developments are planned in coordination with entertainment, tourism and service sector interests. The development of the modern stadium features prominently in advancing the status of sport centres that function as tourist destinations. The Astrodome (Houston) and Superdome (New Orleans) are examples of stadiums that have been developed alongside hotel and convention centre complexes as part of urban regeneration and inner-city tourist-based development programmes (Stevens, 2001). They have also stimulated development of the service industry, including travel agents specializing in sport tourism, to accommodate the needs of tourists. These developments, in combination with ancillary tourism services such as accommodation, transport, dining and entertainment, enhance the status of sport tourism destinations.

Such developments offer significant potential to generate tourist activity at a destination. The modern stadium contributes in numerous ways to the advancement of tourism and service sector interests. Stadium facilities that meet stated requirements (e.g. covered seating, corporate suites, media facilities and ticketing/ financial yield outcomes) are a prerequisite to hosting large-scale stadium sports events. Such facilities serve the additional purpose of attracting/retaining professional sports teams (e.g. premier league football, major league baseball, national basketball league teams). The tourism and service sector interests associated with professional sports teams are not well understood, but, as an example, the city of Manchester receives up to 15 000 international visitors when Manchester United plays premier league games at Old Trafford (Law, 2002). Law (2002) reinforces that argument, stating that the greatest contribution of the stadium to tourism will be felt in cases where stadiums are developed in close proximity to attractions, tourism services and infrastructure. It is not surprising, therefore, that there is a trend to integrate contemporary stadium developments with entertainment facilities such as sports theme parks, halls of fame and sports museums (Stevens, 2001).

Part Three of this book is comprised of five chapters (Chapters 11–15) which examine in detail various important aspects of sport tourism destination marketing and management. In Chapter 12, Laurence Chalip presents a critical analysis of the functions performed by sports in relation to marketing, media and place promotion at tourism destinations. Chalip highlights the important roles that sports events may perform in developing a destination brand. This requires community support for the event, a point of difference that differentiates the event and therefore the destination, clear articulation of what the brand will communicate, and systematic planning of media coverage associated with the event in order to achieve media exposure that will serve the interests of the destination brand. It is noted in Chapter 12 that while sports may generate significant media exposure, it cannot be assumed that the effects of any such coverage will be positive or effective in building the destination brand. This highlights the importance of developing media liaison that is effective in communicating brand attributes and marketing communications for which media coverage may function as a vehicle. The planning, coordination and facilitation of media coverage that will be effective in serving destination brand interests is an important outcome of this chapter.

In Chapter 13, Chris Ryan and Birgit Trauer explore the sport tourism experiences associated with competition in Masters games events. Masters sports competitors represent a desirable niche market for sport tourism destinations. Masters athletes demonstrate a strong propensity to travel for competition events, generate significant expenditures, and are relatively less constrained in the timing, frequency and duration of visits (Ryan and Lockyer, 2001). Given the distinct demographic profile of Masters participants, these events have become increasingly attractive to sponsors seeking to communicate with the growing numbers of fit, active and competitive Masters athletes. In this chapter, Ryan and Trauer position participation in Masters sports competitions in terms of high–low involvement and social sport–pure sport orientation. This allows them to identify quite different types of Masters competitors, including 'novices/dabblers', 'games enthusiasts' and 'serious competitors'. The authors demonstrate that Masters sports events receive a range of quite distinct types of competitors. In describing the desired experiences relating to different types of Masters competitors, Ryan and Trauer are able to provide valuable insights into how Masters sports organizers and destination managers can meet the needs of these sport tourists.

Chapter 14, by Simon Hudson and Peter Cross, addresses the challenges associated with managing seasonality at winter sports destinations. This chapter recognizes that in most parts of the world the ski industry has stagnated, and that responding effectively to seasonality has become an important element in the management and survival of ski resorts. Hudson and Cross present a discussion of the causes and consequences of seasonality in the ski industry, and then critically analyse the multitude of responses to seasonality that have, in varying contexts, been attempted at winter sports destinations. Such responses include short-term solutions, such as investment in snow-making technologies, and long-term responses to global climate change. Product enhancement and diversification, modification of the sports product mix, market diversification, differential pricing and yield management are some of the strategic responses to sport tourism seasonality explored in this chapter. These responses form part of a broader strategy to reposition ski resorts as resort destinations in their own right. These avenues of response to high seasonality in winter sports provide sport tourism operations and destination organizations with valuable insights into managing the seasonal fluctuations that are, to varying degrees, universally associated with tourism.

Chapter 15, by Terry Stevens, explores the significant and diversifying functions of the modern sports stadium as they relate to urban sport tourism destinations. Traditionally, the stadium has been a venue of occasional sports events that may generate significant inward flows of visitors to a destination. More recently, the roles performed by the sports stadium have diversified far beyond hosting large-scale (but often infrequent) sports events that attract tourists as sport spectators. Stevens explains that the stadium may be a vehicle for projecting urban destination imagery, thus enhancing the status and profile of urban tourism destinations. While stadium developments may generate significant employment during the construction phase, they are also increasingly associated with inward investment and sponsorship. Most notably, stadiums are essential to hosting one-off events and retaining or attracting professional sports teams. With these things come media attention, investment, inward flows of spectators and service sector development.

However, stadium interests relating to tourism extend beyond the immediate benefits of hosting sports contests and events. New stadium developments have become a central feature of major urban regeneration schemes, and in such cases stadia are being developed as a centrepiece of new urban entertainment precincts. Increasingly the stadium is an iconic symbol of urban tourism destinations, and a visitor attraction that may be complemented by stadium tours, sports museums and sports halls of fame. More recent stadium developments have, by necessity,

Giulianotti, R. (1996). Back to the future: an ethnography of Ireland's football fans at the 1994 World Cup Finals in the USA. *International Review for the Sociology of Sport*, 31(3), 323–347.

Hall, C. M. (1998). Imaging, tourism and sports event fever: the Sydney Olympics and the need for a social charter for mega-events. In C. Gratton and I. P. Henry (eds), *Sport in the City: The Role of Sport in Economic and Social Regeneration*. London: Routledge, pp. 166–183.

Hartman, R. (1986). Tourism, seasonality and social change. *Leisure Studies*, 5(1), 25–33.

Higham, J. E. S. (1999). Sport as an avenue of tourism development: an analysis of the positive and negative impacts of sport tourism. *Current Issues in Tourism*, 2(1), 82–90.

Higham, J. E. S. and Hinch, T. D. (2002). Sport, tourism and seasons: the challenges and potential of overcoming seasonality in the sport and tourism sectors. *Tourism Management*, 23, 175–185.

Hinch, T. D. and Higham, J. E. S. (2004). *Sport Tourism Development*. Clevedon, OH: Channel View.

Klenosky, D., Gengler, C. and Mulvey, M. (1993). Understanding the factors influencing ski destination choice: a means-end analytic approach. *Journal of Leisure Research*, 25, 362–379.

Kotler, P., Haider, D. H. and Rein, I. (1993). *Marketing Places: Attracting Investment, Industry, and Tourism to Cities, States and Nations*. New York: The Free Press.

Law, C. M. (2002). *Urban Tourism: The Visitor Economy and the Growth of Large Cities*. London: Continuum.

Leiper, N. (1990). Tourist attraction systems. *Annals of Tourism Research*, 17(3), 367–384.

McPherson, B. D., Curtis, J. E. and Loy, J. W. (1989). *The Social Significance of Sport: An Introduction to the Sociology of Sport*. Champaign, IL: Human Kinetics.

Millington, K., Locke, T. and Locke, A. (2001). Adventure travel. *Travel and Tourism Analyst*, 4, 65–97.

Page, S. J. and Hall, C. M. (2003). *Managing Urban Tourism*. Harlow: Prentice-Hall.

Petrick, J. F. (2002). Experience use history as a segmentation tool to examine golf travellers' satisfaction, perceived value and repurchase intentions. *Journal of Vacation Marketing*, 8(4), 332–342.

Porteous, B. (2000). Sports development: Glasgow. *Leisure Manager*, 18(11), 18–21.

Richards, G. (1996). Skilled consumption and UK ski holidays. *Tourism Management*, 17, 25–34.

Rooney, J. F. and Pillsbury, R. (1992). Sports regions of America. *American Demographics*, 14(10), 1–10.

Ryan, C. and Lockyer, T. (2001). An economic impact case study: the South Pacific Masters' Games. *Tourism Economics*, 7(3), 267–276.

Stevens, T. (2001). Stadia and tourism-related facilities. *Travel and Tourism Analyst*, (2), 59–73.

Weed, M. (2002). Football hooligans as undesirable sports tourists: some meta-analytical speculations. In S. Gammon and J. Kurtzman (eds), *Sport Tourism: Principles and Practice*. Eastbourne: Leisure Studies Association, pp. 35–52.

12

Marketing, media, and place promotion

Laurence Chalip

Introduction

Sport tourism opportunities are elements of the destination's overall product and service mix. As attributes of the destination, sport opportunities contribute to the destination's image and brand (Brown *et al.*, 2002). Consequently, the roles of sport tourism in destination marketing need to be evaluated not merely with reference to sport as an attraction, but also with reference to the ways in which opportunities for tourists to enjoy sport can contribute to the destination's marketing communications mix (Chalip, 2001). This includes publicity that sport may generate for the destination, advertising for sport that mentions or highlights the destination, and destination advertising that includes mentions or visuals of sport.

It is heuristically useful to differentiate three forms of sport tourism: tourism to watch sport events, tourism to participate in sport, and tourism to visit famous sport attractions (Gibson, 1998). Each of these can contribute to the destination's overall product and service mix. The vast majority of research has focused on sport events as tourist attractions. This includes events at which visitors spectate, such as a World Cup or a motor race, as well as events that visitors attend for purposes of participation, such as a triathlon or a Masters championship. The focus on sport events has resulted from two distinctive aspects of their role in destination marketing. One feature of events is that they can attract a large number of visitors over a relatively short period of time, thus helping to fill room nights during periods when tourist demand would otherwise be relatively light (Higham and Hinch, 2002). The other significant feature of sport events is that the media they generate can play a useful role in building the image or brand of the destination (Chalip *et al.*, 2003; Jago *et al.*, 2003).

This chapter explores the roles and value of sport events and their associated media in helping to build the brand of the host destination. It concludes by considering implications for incorporating events into destination branding activities, and notes that the same principles apply to other forms of sport tourism (i.e. tourism to participate in sport outside the context of events and tourism to visit sport attractions). Opportunities for further research are also noted.

Destination image versus destination brand

In order to understand the potential for sport events to play a role in building the destination's brand, it is useful to specify the link between destination image and destination brand. The notion that tourists form an image of destinations and that the image may affect visitation has played a significant role in tourism theory and practice since Hunt's (1975) seminal work. Over the same period, marketing researchers built on the work of consumer behaviour theorists (e.g. Herzog, 1963) to formulate models of the ways that consumers relate to brands. In recent years models of branding have found their way into destination marketing, although much of the discussion about destination branding has continued to be grounded in notions of image development. Thus, Nickerson and Moisey (1999: 217) define a (state's) destination brand as 'what images people have of the state and what kind of relationship they have with it'. Similarly, Hall (1999) uses such phrases as 'image building' and 'image construction' to describe development of the destination's brand.

In fact, there is a logical link between destination image and destination brand. Models of product branding are often described with reference to the product's 'brand image'. For example, marketing theorists (e.g. Aaker, 1996; Keller, 1998; de Chernatony, 2001) describe brand image in terms of the associations that consumers have with brands. These include product attributes (including price) and benefits. Models of destination image similarly emphasize such characteristics as destination attributes (including price) and the benefits that tourists expect to derive from a visit (e.g. Echtner and Ritchie, 1993; Gallarza *et al.*, 2002).

This is not to suggest that models of destination image and models of destination brand are identical, as the literatures on destination image and branding have developed separately. Nevertheless, there has been some convergence as tourism researchers have begun to bring the literatures together and embrace the brand concept (*cf.* Cai, 2002; Morgan and Pritchard, 2002). The key advantage of the brand concept is that it has been strongly theorized, and theories of branding are well grounded in cognitive psychology. Further, research has demonstrated that strong brands – those for which the consumer associates well-defined attributes and favourable benefits – are more positively evaluated and more likely to be purchased, to enjoy repeat purchase and to benefit from advertising (Hoeffler and Keller, 2003). For the purposes of this chapter, the phrases 'destination brand' and 'destination image' refer to the attributes and benefits that consumers associate with a destination. Although the latter phrase is used when describing studies that have been framed in terms of destination image, the phrase 'destination brand' is preferred because it permits exploration of co-branding effects, which are important when considering the effects that events can have when promoting a destination (Brown *et al.*, 2002).

Experts' views on events and destination branding

Any discussion of the role of events in building the destination's brand begins from the premise that events are, in fact, useful tools for destination branding. This assumption was put to the test in a series of six half-day workshops run throughout Australia (Jago *et al.*, 2003). Each workshop brought together leading event marketers and destination marketers to examine and compare their opinions regarding the roles and efficacy of events in destination branding. The experts were unanimous in their view that events can play a useful role in building a destination's brand, but they also felt that many events fail to do so. They agreed that five conditions need to be met in order for an event to make a contribution to its host destination's brand.

First, they agreed that there must be community support for the event. Indeed, they felt that this is the single most significant factor in determining whether an event can contribute to the destination's brand. They noted that local residents' support for an event favourably impacts the way that visitors experience an event, and consequently the way they experience the host destination. Positive local support gives an event a friendly feel, which can foster positive feelings about the destination and favourable word-of-mouth. This may even be noted by the media, as it was in the case of the Sydney Olympics.

A second criterion is that the event has a point of differentiation. Event visitors may come to associate the benefits they experience at the event (be they cultural, experiential, social or financial) with the destination itself, thus helping to differentiate the destination from others. Thus, it is important for event and destination marketers to be clear about the specific nature of benefits that an event is providing to event visitors. However, there has been a rapid proliferation of events as destination marketers have endeavoured to attract or create them in order to build their destination's brand (Janiskee, 1994; Getz, 1997). Thus it is necessary to position each event uniquely – that is, to make the event and its consequent benefits distinctive. This may include the ways in which marketing communications link the event to its host destination.

Despite the need for each event to be distinctive, workshop participants felt that each event's culture, values and requisite infrastructure should be consistent with what the community wishes to communicate through its brand. In order to retain local support and also to build a desired brand image, it was noted that the event should be consistent with the way a community sees itself and the way it wants to be seen by others. This was seen to be important not merely for the host destination but also for the event, because the host destination's culture, values and infrastructure affect the experience that event visitors obtain and that event media communicate.

Workshop participants felt that effective use of events in destination branding requires cooperative planning by event managers and destination marketers. Event managers (including event marketers) are typically concerned with hosting a successful event – one that attracts visitors and runs smoothly. They are not concerned with marketing the destination itself. Conversely, each event occurs only for a short period of time and is only a small piece of the destination's total product and service mix. Consequently, destination marketers do not typically devote substantial marketing attention to integrating each event into destination's marketing communications strategy. Thus events have not been used systematically in destination marketing, but have instead been haphazard (and therefore inconsistent) contributors to their host destination's brand.

Media attention is the fifth element that participants in the workshop deemed necessary in order for an event to contribute to the host destination's brand. Although large events generally obtain more publicity (i.e. news stories, features, telecasts) than small events, event advertising and mentions of events in destination advertising also constitute valuable media exposure. Thus, the media value of an event needs to be understood with reference to the reach and frequency of its advertising as well as the reach and frequency of its publicity.

The experts agreed that the five conditions described above are essential if an event is to make a contribution to its host destination's brand. The experts also felt that a long association of an event with a destination – one lasting several years – may help an event become synonymous with its host. The experts noted, however, that events that occur only once at a destination (e.g. the Olympic Games, America's Cup) can contribute to the destination's brand. Consequently, they felt that longevity is not necessary, although it was thought to be helpful in securing and capitalizing upon the five conditions they deemed to be essential.

The experts' views raise three important issues that have been discussed elsewhere in the literature: the vital role of media, the need for a match between the event's brand and the destination's brand, and the challenges of co-branding. These, in turn, point to particular challenges in leveraging events to optimize their impact on the destination's brand. They also suggest the utility of determining how each event fits with the overall product and service mix – including other events – that the destination has to offer. Each of these matters is discussed below.

The role of media

The suggestion that event media will help to build the destination's brand has an intuitive appeal. The publicity that events obtain and their presence in advertising messages should help to raise the profile of the host destination, thereby adding salience to its brand. This assumes, of course, that event publicity supports the destination's association with the event. In order for event publicity to promote the destination, the destination must be shown or mentioned. This also assumes that event publicity and event advertising will convey messages that are consistent with the destination's desired brand. In order for the destination's brand to be promoted, the messages that are delivered must foster a brand image that is consistent with the image that the destination seeks. There has been scant research testing these two assumptions, but two recent studies are not encouraging.

Green *et al.*'s (2003) content analysed telecasts of the 2002 National Collegiate Athletic Association (NCAA) Women's Final Four. They examined the extent of the host city's exposure during the telecast and the kinds of mentions and images the host city (San Antonio) obtained. They found that throughout the 11 hours and 45 minutes of the event telecast, visuals of the city appeared for a total of less than 3.5 minutes. Further, they noted that visuals were not accompanied by mentions of the city name, and that many of the visuals were sufficiently generic in nature that they could not have been distinguished by viewers as images of San Antonio. The researchers also found that the host city was never mentioned in any promotional spot for the event. San Antonio did, however, obtain a few mentions as the broadcast segued from commercial break to the event telecast. The vast majority of the host city's exposure during the event – 28.6 minutes – came as a consequence of the event logo being caught by the camera during games, or being shown on the screen at other times. The logo provided some exposure for the city because it had incorporated both the city name and the silhouette of the Alamo (San Antonio's primary icon). Had the logo not referenced the host city (as many event logos do not), San Antonio would have obtained exposure in less than 0.005 per cent of the telecast. Even with the logo exposure included, San Antonio obtained exposure in less than 0.05 per cent of the telecast. Although disappointing from a destination branding perspective, this finding makes intuitive sense – after all, the media's focus is on the event, not the destination. Unless there is a compelling reason for them to do so, there is no reason to expect the media to highlight the destination.

A related problem has to do with what is communicated and what consumers perceive as a consequence of event media. The coverage of the host destination – whether via publicity or advertising – is not built from a targeted message controlled by destination marketers. In the case of event advertising, marketers are promoting the attributes and benefits that they expect will bring people to the event, even if those attributes and benefits are not compatible with the destination's desired brand. In the case of publicity, the images and messages audiences obtain are a haphazard collage selected and edited by broadcasters and journalists.

In order to explore the effects of sport event media, Chalip *et al.* (2003) experimentally tested the effects of advertising for the Honda Indy 300, a telecast of the Honda Indy 300, and destination advertising on nine dimensions of destination image and on intention to visit the host destination (Gold Coast, Australia). The experiment was conducted in New Zealand (short-haul market) and the USA (long-haul market). Since the destination obtained substantially more advertising in its short-haul market than in its long-haul market, it was expected that event media effects would be less pronounced in the short-haul case. The higher level of advertising for the destination in the short-haul market was expected to dilute the effects of event media.

Although the range of effects was consistent with expectations, the nature of effects was not. In the short-haul market, only two (of the nine) dimensions of destination image were affected by event advertising or the event telecast. Further, the joint effects of these two forms of event media were negative. That, is when both event advertising and event media were viewed, New Zealanders' perceptions of the value and the quality of the natural environment at the Gold Coast were lower than if no event media were seen. In the long-haul market, event advertising affected five dimensions of destination image and the event telecast affected three. Both improved Americans' views of the Gold Coast as a developed and novel destination. The event telecast improved Americans' views about the climate on the Gold Coast. The event advertisement improved Americans' perceptions of safety on the Gold Coast and the convenience of the Gold Coast, but substantially depressed their perceptions of the quality of the natural environment on the Gold Coast. Regression showed that perception of the quality of the natural environment was one of the dimensions of destination image to affect Americans' expectations that they might visit the Gold Coast. Thus, there was an indirect negative effect of event advertising on intention to visit.

Taken together, these studies suggest that event media provide far less volume or value to destination marketers than has heretofore been assumed. From a practical standpoint, the findings clearly demonstrate that destination marketers will need to take a more proactive role than in the past if they are to obtain marketing value from event media. Iconographic images of the destination need to be brought into event media – both advertising and publicity. Descriptions and visuals of the destination need to be consistent with the brand that the destination seeks to project. In order for these things to occur, destination marketers must take an active role in planning event advertising, designing the event logo, working with event journalists and negotiating rights with event broadcasters.

The match-up hypothesis

Even if an event becomes an effective platform for generating media exposure for the destination, this does not imply that the effects of the exposure will be positive or effective. The notion that there needs to be a fit between an event and its host destination has some theoretical and empirical support. It has been shown that the greater the perceived match between a sport event and its sponsor (Gwinner and Eaton, 1999; McDaniel, 1999), a product and its spokesperson (Till and Busler, 2000), or a service and the characteristics of the service provider (Koernig and Page, 2002), the more positive the attitude toward the sponsor, the product or the service. The reason for these effects, it has been argued, is that a match-up facilitates processing of the association between the product (in this case the event) and its host. In other words, the more similar the attributes of the two are, the easier it is for the consumer to process an association between the two.

This notion derives from schema-based models of learning and memory (e.g. Fiske and Linville, 1980; Anderson, 1983). A schema is an associative network consisting of patterns of concepts that represents knowledge about a type of object, such as an event or a destination. Schema theory derives from research showing that memory is a blend of general abstractions and specific memories (e.g. Bartlett, 1932; Lynch and Schuler, 1994). The effect of general abstractions is to facilitate functioning in new and complex situations. Instead of having to recall the best response to every possible situation, the individual can use general knowledge having to do with situations of the type encountered. Misra and Beatty (1990) argue that schemas help the consumer to filter information. They showed, for example, that characteristics of a spokesperson that were incongruent with the consumer's schema for a brand were filtered out. Extending the model, if a consumer's schema for an event were inconsistent with their schema for the destination then the association would be filtered out. The event would not build or reinforce the destination's brand.

However, from the standpoint of both theory and practice, the match-up hypothesis suffers two deficiencies. First, it provides no basis upon which to determine which attributes or benefits render a match or a mismatch. Second, by demanding a close match from the outset, the theory implies that it is only feasible to enhance an existing brand, but not to change it. Since schemas incorporate abstractions, they are relatively flexible (Martindale, 1991). Since they are learned, they can be changed (Klein, 1991). This is encouraging insomuch as destinations often use events to elaborate or change their brand (Bramwell, 1997; van den Berg *et al.*, 2000). Co-branding is the appropriate technique.

Co-branding

When a destination makes use of an event to build its brand, it is seeking to associate its brand with that of the event. In fact, cooperative branding of this type has been used with increasing frequency in a number of industries. Cooperative branding (i.e. co-branding) enjoyed a 40 per cent growth during the latter years of the twentieth century (Spethmann and Benezra, 1994), which is an indication of its apparent utility for building brand equity.

From a co-branding perspective, the issue is not one of match-up but one of relative contribution (Simonin and Ruth, 1998). In other words, what does one brand add to the other? This brings us back to schema-based models of learning and memory which hold that knowledge is represented by associative networks (e.g. Collins and Loftus, 1975; Anderson, 1983; Halford *et al.*, 1998) – that is, a set of concepts that are connected through a network of associations called an 'association set'. The concepts in an association set for a brand can include both attributes and benefits (Keller, 1993). The particular attributes and benefits in a brand's association set, and the relationships among those attributes and benefits, have been shown to be useful descriptors of brand image (Henderson *et al.*, 1998).

The association set model is a useful one for understanding what happens when two brands are paired, as when an event's brand is paired with that of its host destination. When two brands share similar association sets, pairing one with the other will strengthen the association set of each by adding saliency to shared attributes and benefits (Gwinner and Eaton, 1999). However, when events are used in destination branding, the typical objective is not merely to reinforce a particular set of attributes and benefits; the objective is to transfer perceived attributes and benefits from the event to the destination, thus enhancing the destination's image (Brown *et al.*, 2002; Jago *et al.*, 2003). Research has shown that pairing two brands can cause the attributes or benefits from one to be transferred to the other (Till and Shimp, 1998; Levin and Levin, 2000). Thus, an event can reinforce perceptions of attributes and benefits that are already established in the destination's brand, and events can add new attributes and benefits to a destination's brand. It is not necessary that there be a strong *a priori* match-up between the event and its destination. Rather, marketing communications need to enable a linkage between the event's attributes and benefits and those of the destination. Two steps are required in order to mobilize a transfer of perceived attributes or benefits from the event to the destination (Grossman, 1997):

1   At least one attribute or benefit common to the event and the destination needs to be asserted
2   The attributes or benefits that are to be transferred from the event then need to be stated and paired with the destination.

In other words, links between the event and the destination need to be communicated explicitly in event and destination media, and the attributes and benefits that marketers seek to transfer from the event to the destination brand need to be explicitly articulated in marketing communications.

The process is not, however, always benign, particularly if it is not strategically managed. The transfer of attributes or benefits from an event to a destination can include negative associations (Stuart *et al.*, 1990), or might mobilize incompatible imagery (McDaniel, 1999; Koernig and Page, 2002). This clearly explains Chalip *et al.*'s (2003) finding that Indy Car race media depressed American consumers' image of the host destination's natural environment, although it elevated their perceptions of the quality of its developed environment. Motor racing is an outgrowth modern technology, and is thus readily associated with developed settings. On the other hand, the noise and technology of a motor race are not readily associated with natural environments.

This example is instructive because it demonstrates the need for management of marketing communications associated with an event. Australia's Gold Coast, which hosts the Honda Indy 300, boasts 20 kilometres of white sand beaches, undeveloped hills to the west, and nearby pristine rain forest. The quality of its natural environment is an important part of the Gold Coast's brand (Chalip and Fairley, 2002; Harrison-Hill *et al.*, 2002). Yet its natural environment was never featured in event advertising or the event telecast. Nonetheless, it would have been relatively simple to do so. Much of the course for the event runs along the beach; a simple adjustment of camera angles during the event telecast could have showcased the beach. Many of the racing teams and event attendees tour the hills or visit the rainforest. Mentions or visuals of the rainforest in event advertising or at interludes during the event telecast could have made the quality of the host destination's natural environment more salient. However, without guidance or contractual stipulations from destination marketers, event organizers focused their advertising on the event, with scant attention to the image it was transferring to the Gold Coast. Meanwhile, the event broadcaster chose commentary and tight camera angles at track level that obscured the beach, and that never highlighted the hills to the west or the rainforests nearby.

Media leverage

The review so far demonstrates that the value of event advertising and event publicity for the destination can be trivial or negative. In order to optimize the volume and quality of exposure that a destination receives via events that it hosts, the destination marketer must take an active role in the design and implementation of event marketing communications. This represents a subtle but profound shift in orientation. The traditional orientation has focused on each event's media impact. Thus, the reach and frequency of destination exposures through event media have been the primary concerns (Green *et al.*, 2003). However, optimization of event media requires that the marketer plans and executes strategies designed to maximize exposure of images and messages that are consistent with the brand that the destination seeks to build.

In recent years, marketing dogma has stressed the value of integrated marketing communications (Hutton, 1996; Cornelissen, 2003). The essential insight is that each marketing medium – whether advertising, promotions or publicity – communicates something about the brand to the consumer. In order to build a consistent brand image, each marketing communications activity needs to convey a consistent message, and each use of the media needs to be coordinated and synergized with all others. Although this seems a fairly commonsensical prescription, marketers have found it challenging to implement (Hartley and Picton, 1999; Fill, 2001). Nevertheless, organizations that implement integrated marketing communications obtain greater promotional effectiveness at lower cost (Raulas and Vepsalainen, 1995), and are consequently more likely to grow their market share (Low, 2000). Implementing a proactive strategic approach to leveraging event media for destination promotion is a requisite step for integrating a destination's marketing communications mix.

In order to develop the communications mix in a manner that manages the co-branding impact of an event, it is first necessary to identify consumers' association sets for the destination and the event (Grossman, 1997; Henderson *et al.*, 1998; Brown *et al.*, 2002). This will identify the attributes and/or benefits via which to create a meaningful link between the event and the destination. It will also identify those attributes and benefits consumers associate uniquely with the event that the destination marketer wants to transfer to the destination's brand, as well as those the destination marketer does not wish to transfer. These then establish the basis for formulating the messages and visuals at the heart of the destination's strategic leverage of event media.

Once the target messages are formulated, the next step is to maximize the reach and frequency those messages obtain. Media management techniques have rarely been used to optimize the contribution events make to the host destination's brand. Yet one of the most significant lessons from the Sydney Olympic Games was that strategies designed to leverage event media for purposes of destination branding can make a significant difference in the impact that an event makes on the destination's brand (Chalip and Green, 2001). There are two strategic elements: first, make the fullest possible use of event advertising and publicity; and second, build the event into destination advertising, publicity and promotions.

Building the event into destination advertising, publicity and promotions simply requires that event visuals and descriptions be incorporated into the destination's marketing communications. The choice of visuals and descriptions is dictated by the attribute or benefit that the marketer seeks to reinforce or to transfer from the event to the destination's brand. Event visuals or descriptions are appropriate when their inclusion is likely to pique the interest of the communication's target audience, and when the event is superior or complementary to alternative inclusions from the destination's product or service mix.

Building the event into the destination's marketing communications is relatively straightforward because destination marketers have some control over those communications. It is somewhat more challenging to manage the destination's brand in the context of the event itself because destination marketers have less direct control. Seven tactics have proven to be useful when leveraging event advertising and publicity (Brown, 2000; Chalip and Green, 2001; Green *et al.*, 2003):

1 Identify those aspects of the host community that are likely to appeal to the event's target market segments, and then build those into event advertising
2 Assist journalists at the event to locate and research background stories and anecdotes about the host community
3 Provide photographs and video postcards of local scenes (particularly local icons) to journalists and broadcasters for inclusion in their stories and telecasts
4 Work with event organizers, journalists and broadcasters to design the event so that its locations will best showcase the destination, and then establish camera locations and angles that will take in the most favourable backdrops and scenery
5 Place signs advertising the destination at the event in locations that are likely to be picked up by photographers and television cameras
6 Work with the event organizers to design a logo that incorporates the destination name and/or visuals that represent local icons
7 Work with event sponsors to assist them to use destination imagery, mentions and awards in their advertising and promotions.

The destination's event portfolio

No matter how well event media are managed or leveraged, the mere fact that audiences have been exposed to event media does not necessarily render an effect on the destination's brand. This was well demonstrated by Mossberg and Hallberg's (1999) study of the effect that hosting the World Athletics Championships had on the images that English, Dutch and German travellers had of the host city (Göttenberg, Sweden). After surveying travellers *en route* to the city before and after the event, Mossberg and Hallberg found no discernable impact of the event on any dimension of destination image.

The reasons for this finding are unclear. However, from the standpoint of classic marketing communications theory it is not particularly surprising that a single event had little impact, despite its stature and its consequently high volume of media. The key issue is how many meaningful exposures the destination obtained via the event (i.e. frequency), and how many people obtained a sufficient number of exposures to have had an effect on their image of the destination (i.e. reach). It is generally expected that repetition of a marketing message (frequency) to its target audience (reach) is required in order for it to have an effect (Sissors and Baron, 2002). Events are short-lived, which restricts the frequency of any associated destination marketing messages, and events typically have a narrow (though often avid) audience, which restricts the reach of its marketing communications.

Consequently, in order to strengthen the impact of destination-relevant messages associated with event media, it is useful for destinations to build a portfolio of events designed to increase the reach and frequency of destination-relevant messages. The normal practice has been to build a portfolio of events that take place at different times of the year and that appeal to consumers across the range of psychographic profiles to which the destination seeks to appeal (*cf.* Schreiber and Lenson, 1994; Getz, 1997). The discussion in previous sections of this chapter suggests three additional criteria that should be applied when bringing events into the portfolio – at least when one purpose of building the portfolio is to build the destination's brand. First, consumers' perceptions of the event's brand should include attributes and/or benefits that allow destination marketers to fashion a marketing message that affirms a logical link between the event and the destination. Second, the event's brand should incorporate attributes or benefits that the destination marketer wants to reinforce in the destination's existing brand, or that the destination marketer seeks to import into the destination's brand. Third, the event's brand should not include attributes or benefits that are likely to become linked to the destination's brand, but that are incompatible with the brand that the destination seeks to promote.

Conclusions

Although events have come to play an increasingly significant role in destination branding, there are grounds to be cautious about their application. If event advertising and publicity play a key role in the effect that events have on a destination's brand, then events are both blunt and double-edged. Even a high-profile mega-event may generate negligible exposure for the destination (Green *et al.*, 2003) and have no discernible impact on the destination's brand (Mossberg and Hallberg, 1999). Further, when there is a measurable impact, it may be negative or may affect only those aspects of the brand that are not relevant to the audience's destination choice (Chalip *et al.*, 2003). Clearly the application of events to destination branding requires a much more analytic and proactive strategy than has heretofore been applied. The event's brand, the utility of that brand for strengthening or elaborating the host destination's brand, the event's fit with other events in the destination's portfolio, and the means to formulate and implement marketing communications that exploit the event's relevance all need to be identified and employed.

That effort requires collaboration between destination marketers and event marketers. Although both groups recognize the potential benefits of a marketing alliance (Jago *et al.*, 2003), the two have typically functioned in separate spheres (Weed, 2003). More work is needed to understand factors that facilitate or impede cooperation between event and destination marketers. This includes research that explores the means to secure the relationships and organizational learning that are engendered by cooperation between event organizers and destination marketers.

Much of what has been said here can be applied to other elements of the destination's sport tourism mix, such as recreational sport opportunities, sport museums and sport facilities. These can also become relevant inclusions in the destination's marketing communications mix. Like events, their utility depends on the brand associations they provide and their capacity to lend narratives and/or visuals that reinforce or enhance the brand that marketers seek to build for the destination. More importantly, non-event sport tourism opportunities may complement events in the overall marketing communications mix. Tourists who attend events – whether to participate or to watch – are demonstrating a particular sporting interest. Recent work suggests that sport interests are frequently associated with distinctive patterns of consumption (Schouten and McAlexander, 1995; Yoder, 1997; Green and Chalip, 1998; Wheaton, 2000). Yet we know very little about the profiles of sport tourists' interests, or the mix of a destination's products and services that is most likely to appeal to tourists, particularly those with an interest in sport. More work is needed that explores the ways in which sport amenities and other features of the destination can complement one another in terms of their functionality for the tourist, their symbolic value or the quality of experience they enable.

There are comparable knowledge gaps regarding the media uses of event portfolios. There has been little work that explores the efficacy of alternative means to incorporate events into an integrated marketing communications strategy. Nor do we understand how best to create synergies among events in order to optimize their combined impact on the host community's brand. Each of these matters warrants further research.

This chapter's emphasis on media may give the impression that small sport events – those with a primarily local appeal or that are unlikely to obtain media attention – have no role to play in branding the destination. That is not the case. Indeed, destination marketers and event organizers insist that small-scale events can play a vital role in fostering a community's enthusiasm for events and building its capacity to host larger events (Jago *et al.*, 2003). Thus the value of an event portfolio is not measured by the media its events create; rather, the portfolio's value derives from the contribution that each event makes to the destination's capacity to build its brand for residents and visitors alike. Media can play a role, but that role is by no means the only one that matters.

References

Aaker, D. A. (1996). *Building Strong Brands*. New York: Free Press.

Anderson, J. R. (1983). A spreading activation theory of memory. *Journal of Verbal Learning and Verbal Behavior*, 22, 261–295.

Bartlett, F. C. (1932). *Remembering: A Study in Experimental and Social Psychology*. Cambridge, MA: Cambridge University Press.

Bramwell, B. (1997). Strategic planning before and after a mega-event. *Tourism Management*, 18, 167–176.

Brown, G. (2000). Emerging issues in Olympic sponsorship: implications for host cities. *Sport Management Review*, 3, 71–92.

Brown, G., Chalip, L., Jago, L. and Mules, T. (2002). The Sydney Olympics and Brand Australia. In N. Morgan, A. Pritchard and R. Pride (eds), *Destination Branding: Creating the Unique Destination Proposition*. Oxford: Butterworth-Heinemann, pp. 163–185.

Cai, L. A. (2002). Cooperative branding for rural destinations. *Annals of Tourism Research*, 29, 720–742.

Chalip, L. (2001). Sport and tourism: capitalising on the linkage. In D. Kluka and G. Schilling (eds), *The Business of Sport*. Oxford: Meyer and Meyer, pp. 71–90.

Chalip, L. and Fairley, S. (2002). *Positioning the Gold Coast in International Tourist Markets*. Altona: Common Ground.

Chalip, L. and Green, B. C. (2001). Leveraging large sport events for tourism: lessons from the Sydney Olympics. In R. N. Moisey and N. P. Nickerson (eds), *A Tourism Odyssey* (Suppl.). Boisey, ID: Travel and Tourism Research Association, pp. 11–20.

Chalip, L., Green, B. C. and Hill, B. (2003). Effects of event media on destination image and intention to visit. *Journal of Sport Management*, 17, 214–234.

Collins, A. M. and Loftus, E. F. (1975). Theory of semantic processing. *Psychological Review*, 82, 407–428.

Cornelissen, J. P. (2003). Change, continuity and progress: the concept of integrated marketing communications and marketing communications practice. *Journal of Strategic Marketing*, 11, 217–234.

de Chernatony, L. (2001). *From Brand Vision to Brand Evaluation: Strategically Building and Sustaining Brands*. Oxford: Butterworth-Heinemann.

Echtner, C. M. and Ritchie, J. R. B. (1993). The measurement of destination image: an empirical assessment. *Journal of Travel Research*, 31(4), 2–12.

Fill, C. (2001). Essentially a matter of consistency: integrated marketing communications. *Marketing Review*, 1, 409–425.

Fiske, S. T. and Linville, P. W. (1980). What does the schema concept buy us? *Personality and Social Psychology Bulletin*, 6, 543–557.

Gallarza, M. G., Gil Saura, I. and Calderón García, H. (2002). Destination image: towards a conceptual framework. *Annals of Tourism Research*, 29, 56–78.

Getz, D. (1997). *Event Management and Event Tourism*. Elmsford, NY: Cognizant Communication.

Gibson, H. (1998). Sport tourism: a critical analysis of research. *Sport Management Review*, 1, 45–76.

Green, B. C. and Chalip, L. (1998). Sport tourism as the celebration of subculture. *Annals of Tourism Research*, 25, 275–291.

Green, B. C., Costa, C. and Fitzgerald, M. (2003). Marketing the host city: analyzing exposure generated by a sport event. *International Journal of Sports Marketing and Sponsorship*, 4, 335–352.

Grossman, R. P. (1997). Co-branding in advertising: developing effective associations. *Journal of Product and Brand Management*, 6, 191–201.

Gwinner, K. P. and Eaton, J. (1999). Building brand image through event sponsorship: the role of image transfer. *Journal of Advertising*, 28(4), 47–57.

Halford, G. S., Bain, J. D., Maybery, M. T. and Andrews, G. (1998). Induction of relational schemas: common processes in reasoning and complex learning. *Cognitive Psychology*, 35, 201–245.

Hall, D. (1999). Destination branding, niche marketing and national image projection in Central and Eastern Europe. *Journal of Vacation Marketing*, 6, 227–237.

Harrison-Hill, T., Fairley, S. and Chalip, L. (2002). *Positioning the Gold Coast in Domestic Tourist Markets*. Altona: Common Ground.

Hartley, B. and Pickton, D. (1999). Integrated marketing communications requires a new way of thinking. *Journal of Marketing Communications*, 5, 97–106.

Henderson, G. R., Iacobucci, D. and Calder, B. J. (1998). Brand diagnostics: mapping branding effects using consumer associative networks. *European Journal of Operational Research*, 11, 306–327.

Herzog, H. (1963). Behavioral science concepts for analysing the consumer. In P. Bliss (ed.), *Marketing and the Behavioral Sciences*. Boston, MA: Allyn and Bacon, pp. 76–86.

Higham, J. E. S. and Hinch, T. D. (2002). Sport, tourism and seasons: the challenges and potential of overcoming seasonality in the sport and tourism sectors. *Tourism Management*, 23, 175–185.

Hoeffler, S. and Keller, K. L. (2003). The marketing advantages of strong brands. *Brand Management*, 10, 421–445.

Hunt, J. (1975). Image as a factor in tourism development. *Journal of Travel Research*, 13(3), 1–7.

Hutton, J. G. (1996). Integrated marketing communications and the evolution of marketing thought. *Journal of Business Research*, 37, 155–162.

Jago, L., Chalip, L., Brown, G., Mules, T. and Ali, S. (2003). Building events into destination branding: insights from experts. *Event Management*, 8, 3–14.

Janiskee, R. (1994). Some macroscale growth trends in America's community festival industry. *Festival Management and Event Tourism*, 2, 10–14.

Keller, K. L. (1993). Conceptualizing, measuring, and managing customer-based brand equity. *Journal of Marketing*, 57, 1–22.

Keller, K. L. (1998). *Strategic Brand Management*. Upper Saddle River, NJ: Prentice-Hall.

Klein, S. B. (1991). *Learning: Principles and Applications*. New York: McGraw-Hill.

Koernig, S. E. and Page, A. L. (2002). What if your dentist looked like Tom Cruise? Applying the match-up hypothesis to a service encounter. *Psychology and Marketing*, 19, 91–110.

Levin, I. P. and Levin, A. M. (2000). Modeling the role of brand alliances in the assimilation of product evaluations. *Journal of Consumer Psychology*, 9, 43–52.

Low, G. S. (2000). Correlates of integrated marketing communications. *Journal of Advertising Research*, 40(3), 27–39.

Lynch, J. and Schuler, D. (1994). The match-up effect of spokesperson and product congruency: a schema theory interpretation. *Psychology and Marketing*, 11, 417–445.

Martindale, C. (1991). *Cognitive Psychology: A Neural-network Approach*. Pacific Grove, CA: Brooks/Cole.

McDaniel, S. R. (1999). An investigation of match-up effects in sport sponsorship advertising: The implications of consumer advertising schemas. *Psychology and Marketing*, 16, 163–184.

Misra, S. and Beatty, S. E. (1990). Celebrity spokesperson and brand congruence: an assessment of recall and affect. *Journal of Business Research*, 21, 159–173.

Morgan, N. J. and Pritchard, A. (2002). Contextualising destination branding. In N. J. Morgan, A. Pritchard and R. Pride (eds), *Destination Branding: Creating the Unique Destination Proposition*. Oxford: Buterworth-Heinemann, pp. 11–41.

Mossberg, L. L. and Hallberg, A. (1999). The presence of a mega-event: effects on destination image and product-country images. *Pacific Tourism Review*, 3, 213–225.

Nickerson, N. and Moisey, R. (1999). Branding a state from features to positioning: making it simple. *Journal of Vacation Marketing*, 5, 217–226.

Raulas, M. and Vepsalainen, A. P. J. (1995). Integrated marketing communications management: a promotion process portfolio approach. *European Journal of Marketing*, 29(5), 36–47.

Schouten, J. W. and McAlexander, J. H. (1995). Subcultures of consumption: an ethnography of the new bikers. *Journal of Consumer Research*, 22, 43–61.

Schreiber, A. and Lenson, B. (1994). *Lifestyle and Event Marketing: Building the New Customer Partnership*. New York: McGraw-Hill.

Simonin, B. L. and Ruth, J. A. (1998). Is a company known by the company it keeps? Assessing the spillover effects of brand alliances on brand attitudes. *Journal of Marketing Research*, 35, 30–42.

Sissors, J. Z. and Baron, R. B. (2002). *Advertising Media Planning* (6th edn). Chicago, IL: McGraw-Hill.

Spethmann, B. and Benezra, K. (1994). Co-brand or be damned. *Brandweek*, 35(45), 20–25.

Stuart, E. W., Shimp, T. A. and Engle, R. W. (1990). Classical conditioning of negative attitudes. *Advances in Consumer Research*, 17, 539–540.

Till, B. D. and Busler, M. (2000). The match-up hypothesis: physical attractiveness, expertise, and the role of fit on brand attitude, purchase intent and brand beliefs. *Journal of Advertising*, 29(3), 1–13.

Till, B. D. and Shimp, T. A. (1998). Endorsers in advertising: the case of negative celebrity information. *Journal of Advertising*, 27(1), 67–82.

van den Berg, L., Braun, E. and Otgaar, A. H. J. (2000). *Sports and City Marketing in European Cities*. Rotterdam: euricur.

Weed, M. (2003). Why the two won't tango! Explaining the lack of integrated policies for sport and tourism in the UK. *Journal of Sport Management*, 17, 258–283.

Wheaton, B. (2000). 'Just do it': consumption, commitment, and identity in the windsurfing subculture. *Sociology of Sport Journal*, 17, 254–274.

Yoder, D. G. (1997). A model for commodity intensive serious leisure. *Journal of Leisure Research*, 29, 407–429.

13

Sport tourist behaviour: the example of the Masters games

Chris Ryan and Birgit Trauer

Introduction

Masters games have emerged as significant sporting events capable of attracting large numbers of competitors from many parts of the globe. Like other sporting events, they exist at varying levels of scale and importance, from being primarily regional to international. This chapter looks at such events from the viewpoint of analysing the motives of competitors, and offers a conceptualization derived from three theoretical stances as advanced by Trauer and Ryan (2004) in the context of adventure tourism. It also briefly considers some of the management implications of such a motivational conceptualization. It is argued that these issues are applicable regardless of location of the games, and indeed the internationalization of the Masters games movement makes the analysis applicable to many destinations.

The nature of Masters games

Ryan and Lockyer (2002) trace the development of the modern generation of Masters games to the jogging boom of the 1970s and 1980s. The core of the Masters games has been the traditional sports of the modern Olympic Games, with athletics and swimming events very much to the fore. Nonetheless, like the modern Olympiad, the numbers of sports being offered continue to expand. For example, the 2005 World Masters Games in Edmonton, Canada, offers 17 core sports that include golf, and an additional 10 optional sports that include ten-pin bowling. The reasons for such an expansion are both economic and social. The economic rationale is that promoting cities, organizers and sponsors wish to attract as many out-of-region competitors as is possible in order to maximize revenues and economic impacts. Masters games attract potentially large-spending competitors, whose nature is also perceived not only as being economically beneficial but also as posing few problems for law enforcement agencies and possessing little potential for being controversial. This is not always true of other events. For example, the Canberra V8 Australian Super Saloon series, while perhaps bringing a high-octane event to Canberra that attracted significant television coverage, was generally not approved by local residents, who resented the intrusion on traffic flow, the noise and a perceived 'petrolhead' image. Masters games, on the other hand, are seen as attracting above-average income and educated groups who are drawn not only by feelings of competition but also by friendly social environments to which, in turn, they contribute. The ability of such games to attract large numbers of competitors is demonstrated by the 20 000 competitors attending the 2002 Melbourne World Masters Games.

A second reason for the development of Masters games lies in the need for commercial interests in sportswear and associated goods to both respond to and confirm trends that extend the market for their products. Essentially, the interest of older groups in sustaining their sporting activities well into old age represents an extension of a market that in past decades would have ceased with the onset of the third decade of a person's life. Masters games represent a combination of commercial interests by the sporting and tourism industries, combined with the growth in the public sector of an administrative class of sports promoters. The public sector often possesses the facilities of stadia and sports centres, and an administrative class that develops its own career and importance by achieving higher rates of utilization of such resources and attracting commercial sponsorship that defrays the costs of such facilities. Masters games are thus driven by a nexus of individual interest and changing personal lifestyles that emphasize fitness and a commercial and public sector interest. They are therefore an interesting example of 'foot-free' sporting events in that while, as other chapters in this book demonstrate, location has significance, in this instance location has arguably a secondary role while the nature of involvement and means of management adopted are primary. This would be consistent with past work – for example, that of Ryan and Lockyer (2002), who found that the location of Hamilton, New Zealand, while important, was less so when compared to other factors.

The third reason for the extension of the Masters games programme lies in the wish to facilitate participation across all age groups and levels of fitness in the belief that active participation is beneficial to older members of society. This is perhaps exemplified in the welcome message on the web pages of the New Zealand Masters Games, which describes the Games as:

> an annual multi-sport event attracting some 8,000 participants mostly between the ages of thirty and ninety something in up to seventy sports, alternating between the cities of Wanganui and Dunedin. At the New Zealand Masters Games, participation comes before competition, entry being open to anyone from any country who meets the age criteria for their particular sport, no matter what their level of ability or skill. An atmosphere of friendliness and camaraderie is reflected in the comprehensive social programme, which is an integral part of the event.

Consequently, the line-up of sports includes not only major sports such as athletics and minor sports like windsurfing and mountain biking, but also a range of other activities such as twilight petanque, line-dancing, dog-handling, marching, bridge and croquet.

The nature of participation in Masters games

Given the popularity of Masters games and their potential for beneficial economic and social impacts, there is a comparative scarcity of academic literature upon the subject. What does exist might be divided into two components; economic impact assessments and studies of participants. Economic impact studies, by their nature, are specific to an event, time and place. Results of such studies (e.g. Ritchie, 1996; Ryan and Lockyer, 2001) would seem to imply that the determinants of economic impacts include scale of event, the ability to attract out-of-region visitors, the duration of visitor stay, pricing structures, types of accommodation used and merchandising policies. What also appears to be evident is that such events attract a hard core of Masters games enthusiasts who devote considerable amounts of time to such events and more generally to their sports. Therefore, within any one such event, there will exist a group of athletes who will have competed at many such games on previous occasions, and at different locations. The more mature an event is, the more likely it will be that it attracts experienced participants. Experienced competitors will fall into two different groupings; those who have previously competed in several different games at different locations and those who have solely competed in their local games. An intermediate third categorization might also be identified, namely those who will have started their career paths with their local games and have subsequently enjoyed the event so much that they have used this as a springboard to experience events elsewhere. Lockyer (2003), in a study of the South Pacific Masters Games of 2002, found that the proportion of such experienced participants had notably increased between the first and second hosting of the Games in Hamilton, New Zealand.

It can be hypothesized that participants form a degree of involvement with games participation that in part is a confirmation of self-identity as an exponent of a particular sport. This is particularly true of those athletes who travel away from home to attend events. Such athletes may well be a key group in determining the longer-term economic success of an event. For example, in the first South

Pacific Masters Games Ryan and Lockyer (2002) report that 69 per cent of those who travelled from outside the Waikato region to attend the Games had previously competed in such events. In this study, in some instances, recorded participation rates had been very high (that is, more than 10 different Masters games had been attended, including overseas events in Australia). What, therefore, might be the nature of this involvement?

Involvement studies in the recreation and sports literature now possess antecedents that include scale construction of more than a quarter of a century. Consequently, by 1993 Havitz *et al.* (1993a) were able to identify 25 studies for the period 1988 to 1992 that had sought to measure degrees of involvement in various recreational and sporting pursuits. Indeed, by 1993 attempts were being made to compare the rigour of three main scales that had emerged as means of measurement, these being the Involvement Profile (IP) of Kapferer and Laurent (1985), the Personal Involvement Inventory (PII) of Zaichkowsky (1985) and the McQuarrie and Munson Revised Personal Involvement Inventory (RPII) of 1987. Initially these scales emerged from a generalized consumer theory literature concerned with consumer loyalty, and can be associated with an emergent market research emphasis at that time with the determinants of repeat purchasing. In one sense it might be argued that such concepts provided a motivational base for the statistics associated with Markov models that could trace brand share over time. However, scholars in the leisure domain such as McIntyre (1989), Havitz and Dimanche (who used these concepts within his original doctoral studies, 1990) quickly appreciated the wider importance of the concept in terms of leisure pursuits and began to adapt them to the sporting and leisure fields. For example, Havitz *et al.* (1993b) used the scales to test the levels of involvement of downhill skiers, while of particular interest to this chapter is the work of McIntyre *et al.* (1992), who used the concept of involvement to study the motivation of participants in an Australian Masters Games. As stated, a series of studies then commenced to test the stability of the scales and the items within them, and the degree to which they were context specific. Such studies were notably associated with a group of Canadian-based researchers and are, in part, described by Havitz *et al.* (1993a, 1993b) who, among other ploys, changed the order of items within scales to assess the underlying factor dimensions. Similarly, Havitz and Howard (1995: 98) contextualized the items within the sports of windsurfing, golf and downhill skiing, only to conclude that 'importance-pleasure scores were stable over time as predicted ... whereas sign and risk consequence scores showed situational variability in activity contexts ... {and} product involvement scores were relatively stable'.

This brief review therefore prompts three questions – what is actually being measured by the involvement scale, why are situational aspects of importance, and does the theory help to explain participant motivation in Masters games? Given the nature of the answers to these questions, a fourth question subsequently emerges: what are the implications for the management and promotion of Masters games?

The initial scales were developed around five dimensions, these being importance, pleasure, sign, risk probability and risk consequence, to which was added a sixth by leisure researchers, that of centrality. In a review of these dimensions Havitz and Dimanche (1990) paid specific attention to the facets of pleasure, sign value and risk. Within the context of sporting leisure, it can be argued that pleasure can be derived from three sources, the actual physical activity, the subsequent sense of well-being and achievement, and camaraderie derived from sharing the experience with others. Ryan (1997) specifically draws attention to the success of a white-water rafting operation because of the way in which the operator generated opportunities for that social interaction to occur, through which participants relived and enhanced their experience through the telling of the story. Sign value, in the sporting context, also has considerable importance. Trauer and Ryan (2004) argue that the media have a number of influences on adventure, one of which is not only the familiarization of product, place and activity, but also the means by which participants can locate themselves within the activity and derive meaning from it. In a sense, this may be said to be consistent with the notion of cultural capital. Such capital signifies membership of a group or significant others with whom values are shared. According to Trauer and Ryan, risk in adventure tourism is necessarily context specific as a participant assesses the situation with reference to the perceived dangers and the competency of themselves and others.

By the latter part of the 1990s, the debate had moved on to utilize degrees of involvement and commitment as a means of segmenting markets. Indeed, by 1998 Iwasaki and Havitz (1998) offered a multi-dimensional model in which importance and evaluation were collapsed into the dimension of attraction; the other dimensions being those of sign, centrality, risk assessment and risk consequence. However, sign and centrality were more strongly located within a social framework – where sign conveyed signals about a participant, while centrality of a pursuit occurred within the social setting of family and friends because of the impact that it had on those relationships.

The implications of these frameworks for an understanding of the motives for participants in Masters games are significant. Skill acquisition in sporting endeavours requires time spent in training, which intrudes upon family relationships. The degree of commitment to that training is justified by the attraction of the pursuit, which is both physical and psychological, and must, at least, compensate for time not spent in other activities. An integrated whole exists wherein personal attributes, activity specifics, family and social setting all combine to determine the degree of participation in a chosen sport. For many entrants, participation in Masters games combines all of these factors. In their analysis of participants in the South Pacific Masters Games, Ryan and Lockyer (2002) report the results of a cluster analysis where two types of competitors were identified. These were labelled the 'Sports Purists' and the 'Games Enthusiasts'. There were no statistically significant differences on items relating to 'challenging themselves' or 'challenging others' within their sports between the two groups – both were 'serious' in their athletic pursuits. Rather, the difference lay in their orientation toward the social aspects of the Games. The latter group (who formed two-thirds of the sample) valued much more highly the social events and the 'signs' as represented, for example, by their willingness to buy merchandise related to the Games. It can also be hypothesized that this latter group is much more likely to involve their whole family in such events – itself an aspect that helps determine the overall economic impact of such games (Murphy and Carmichael, 1996).

Trauer and Ryan (2004) suggest a model of participation in adventure tourism that possibly might be amended to include an explanation of sport tourism in this particular context of Masters games. They argue that participation in adventure tourism is determined by a macro- and a micro-system. The former comprises the demand for and supply of the product. In that sense the model differs little from

Leiper's (1990) model of the tourism system, with its tourist-generating and tourist-receiving zones. However, they locate adventure tourism in a Venn diagram within three dimensions, the third being that of the role of media. It is argued that the promotion of place and activity has an important role in shaping familiarization with those places and activities, enabling the tourist as actor to imagine and locate him- or herself in the locale or adventure. The tourist is truly a participant acting out roles and expectations. This line of argument has significant linkages with the importance attributed to 'sign' in the involvement models discussed above. In the case of Masters games, the sign is conveyed in the many specialist magazines that meet the needs of the athlete. Particularly in the English language market of the northern hemisphere, the commodification of leisure and the creation of niche markets is symbolized by the racks of newsagents where, among other magazines, can be found *Runners World*, *Running Fitness* and *Inside Triathlon* for the sport of athletics alone. These magazines carry news, advice and details of Masters sports. Supporting this is the associated advertising of sports shoes manufacturers, who convey messages of achievement and image. However, for the purpose of this chapter it is the micro-system model that is of interest. Trauer and Ryan (2004) locate adventure tourism within three dimensions, these being involvement, the hard vs soft dimension of the adventure product concerned, and finally the degree of flow. It is here argued that, by replacing the hard vs soft dimension of the adventure product with the 'social sport' vs 'sports purist' orientation of Ryan and Lockyer (2002), it becomes possible to create a framework that explains the motives of Masters games competitors and to do so in a way consistent with the modelling suggested by the framers of the involvement concept.

Figure 13.1 reproduces the framework. The two dimensions of the sports/social orientation and the degree of involvement create a matrix of four cells.

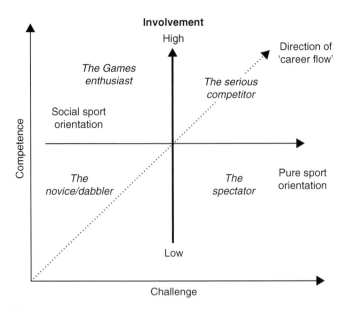

Figure 13.1 The nature of participation in Masters games

Theoretically it becomes possible to identify four types of competitor as against the two derived by Ryan and Lockyer (2002). These are:

1 *The games enthusiast*. This repeats the characterization by Ryan and Lockyer (2002) as being someone who demonstrates high levels of involvement in their sport, but is motivated not solely by the intrinsic rewards of a sense of physical well-being but also by the social interaction that the sport brings. In consequence, while a sense of challenge is important to games enthusiasts, they may, at times, mitigate their performance by a wish to be with others – a factor that can perhaps be best seen by middle- and long-distance runners in 'fun runs'.

2 *The serious competitor*. Again this replicates the cluster identified by Ryan and Lockyer (2002) and locates this type of person as being highly motivated by a wish to compete successfully and by being very involved in their chosen sport.

3 *The novice/dabbler*. This type of entrant may engage in sport as a means of acquiring a degree of fitness, but is not as involved as the above two categories. This may be by choice, or alternatively he or she may be at the commencement of a 'career' as a games participant. In terms of theoretical perspectives, Trauer (2003) suggests a continuum in the sports/leisure recreation literature that posits serious competition in opposition to games playing, and it might be said within the context of Figure 13.1 that the dabbler is orientated toward the 'playing' end of any such continuum.

4 *The spectator*. This type of person has a serious attitude to sports, but a low involvement. This appears to be a paradoxical position to take, but is explicable if the perspective of a passive involvement is adopted. From one stance the stereotype of the couch potato sports enthusiast emerges – someone who is perhaps knowledgeable but is not (yet) motivated to actually participate.

To this model can be added the third dimension suggested by Trauer and Ryan (2004), and this is the flow dimension derived from the theory of Csikszentmihalyi (1975, 1990). Essentially Csikszentmihalyi argued that human motivation could not be explained by external motivators such as pay or peer approval alone. Rather, intrinsic motivation was important, and people sought a state of 'flow', which was experienced where an individual's level of competence permitted him or her to deal successfully with challenges inherent in a given situation. In circumstances where competence (i.e. an individual's skills and abilities) was not sufficiently challenged, then the resultant emotion could be boredom. On the other hand, where a participant had insufficient skill to meet a challenge, frustration and annoyance would be felt.

In terms of the framework of Masters games participation that is being conceptualized here, it can be argued that the *Serious competitor* would be frustrated by levels of competition that were felt inappropriate, particularly, it might be said, if the level of competition was thought insufficient. However, Figure 13.1 also illustrates a modification of Csikszentmihalyi's theory of flow in the case of the *Games enthusiast*. Here, the extrinsic social orientation that results from involvement and personal preference might mean that the levels of frustration that might otherwise be felt from a lack of a situation where challenge < competency would be mitigated by a sense of sharing. In their original work, Trauer and Ryan indicate, through the 45-degree line representing flow, that an adventure tourism career might be discernable in the manner in which Hall and Weiler (1992) conceptualize 'serious leisure'. In the instance of the Masters games, the interesting perspective arises that the participants can be 'serious' about their leisure, but the sense of leisure remains predominant.

What perhaps the proposed framework does not fully catch is the nature of the involvement. Involvement, as described in the literature, is a behaviour derived from an attitude and, as conventionally described, attitudes possess an affective as well as cognitive component. High levels of involvement might be hypothesized as engaging significant levels of emotion. An example of such emotion is shown by the World Masters Games participant Mary, in her web pages, www.marysadventures.com. Mary can be described as a serious competitor, being the US National Masters 40 W 800-metre champion in 2002. This is how she described her feelings after the Melbourne 2002 World's Masters Games:

> My plane left Australia at 11:30 a.m. on Saturday and I arrived home about the same time in Eugene, Oregon. It's an odd feeling, but a happy one. The flight was long and uncomfortable, but worth every minute. I would do it again in a heartbeat. My sincerest thanks goes out to all the people of Australia who went out of their way to make this adventure the experience of a lifetime for me.

> Sharing lifetime experiences with friendly people in distant lands has brought me ever closer to discovering who I really am. I am leaving my adventure to the 2002 World Masters Games knowing a part of me will always remain with the people and places of Melbourne, Australia.

Mary's commentary perhaps also reveals a further reason for the attraction of Masters games for both competitors and promoters. König (1995) criticizes the ethics of professional sport as containing an inherent paradox in that it condones practices by which competitors push themselves to the breaking point, but condemns the use of performance-enhancing drugs. Such views, he argues, represent an antiquated and dangerous code of ethics by which athletes damage their bodies in pursuance of the commercial gain of winning. While Masters games attract commercial notice, at present their participants engage in an ethos that represents a return to a perceived 'golden age' where participation is the rationale. The organization of the games by 5-year age-bands reinforces the notion of participation, and for any given event can generate numerous medal winners. For example, the 100-metre sprint could generate 11 gold medal winners from the age-bandings 40 to over 90. As yet, such winners do not sign lucrative advertising endorsements (but one wonders for how much longer if television coverage of such games were to occur), and thus the issues of doping and drug usage are not pertinent in such games. Additionally, given that several competitors might be on medication of some form or another, the introduction of drug testing could conceivably be a minefield of litigation. Hence, from the perspectives of participation motivation and resultant ethos, and limited commercial exploitation, Masters games retain an amateur athletic spirit that evokes a spirit of yesteryear which is attractive to both promoters and competitors.

The management and promotional implications

While the proposed framework is not directly supported by empirical evidence, it is not inconsistent with the findings reported by Ryan and Lockyer (2001) and McIntyre *et al.* (1992). The framework is also consistent with one of the major findings of both these studies, namely that while Masters games participants may well be regarded as enthusiasts, amateur sports people or 'fun sports people', they are in fact very serious about their sport, and hence the measurement of performance is of significant importance to them. Therefore one of the management implications of both conceptual framework and data is that refereeing, time-keeping and other aspects of recording performance need to be at the highest level possible.

Another implication of Figure 13.1 is that many Masters games athletes will develop a 'career' as such an athlete. One of the consequences of entering several different events over time and space is that participants develop criteria by which to judge how well a game is being run. While performance assessment is a key component, the games enthusiast will also evaluate the social functions of the games. It is notable in the histories of games that have sustained repeated events that the performance arena and the concept of a games village appears to acquire increasing importance. This may be particularly so when the games establish a loyal following of competitors who enjoy one another's company. In some ways the situation is akin to camp-grounds where, summer after summer, families who do not otherwise see or visit each other nonetheless meet and anticipate meeting 'old friends'.

Figure 13.1 implies that the social aspect of the games might be important in acquiring future 'loyal' games participants from the 'novice/dabbler' segment of the market. For this market segment it can be hypothesized that the social aspect of the games may diminish concerns about not having sufficient athletic skill.

Figure 13.1 also indicates how there might be a hierarchy and differentiation of Masters games events or products, and it is of interest to assess the role of the World Masters Games from this perspective. The degree of seriousness with which the World series of Masters Games is held is indicated by the fact that some sports publish 'world rankings'. For example, those of the laser class in sailing can be found on the web page www.jdecm.com/lasermasters/masters_news.htm. From a tourism industry viewpoint, three implications of such serious degrees of leisure come to the fore. The first is the high levels of willingness shown by participants to travel, sometimes quite considerable distances. Perusing the lists of winners for different sports and age groups for different World Masters Games indicates a veritable list of nationalities. Second, the willingness of these competitors to spend, and their ability to spend, means that such events attract high levels of sponsorship. For example, in 1998 in Oregon, the main sponsor was Nike. Third, the level of professionalism of organization grows, and the Games become bigger over time. These factors lead to a fourth conclusion, that the World Masters Games has become so attractive that cities are now beginning to bid to host them in much the same way as the Olympics.

Consequently, while not perhaps of the class of Getz's 'mega-event', a classification of Masters games can be observed, from the regional to the national to the supra-national to the pinnacle of the World Masters Games. There is also an ancillary and associated type of sporting event emerging, and that is the single sports code events designed for the 'older sports person'. This is exemplified by the 'Golden Oldies' Rugby series. The Golden Oldies Rugby Festivals commenced in Auckland in 1979, and since then have been generally held once every 2 years, with the 2003 event being hosted by Brisbane. Like the Masters games, regional events are held, such as European Festivals. In 2004 the European Golden Oldies Rugby Festival was hosted jointly by Alicante and Benidorm, but it is indicative of the growth of this type of sport tourism that six cities vied to be the host.

The increasing commercialism and professionalism of hosting and organizing Masters sports at different levels is increasingly becoming apparent, yet organizers, even at World Masters Games level, have to retain an awareness of the different types of competitors as described by the cells of Figure 13.1. Athletes are serious, but possibly their seriousness is tempered by growing age and maturity. Involvement is important as a source of identity, but arguably, following the humanistic psychology of writers like Maslow, the person with a strong sense of identity becomes less dependent upon the recognition of others. In short, Masters athletes may work hard to achieve, continue to challenge themselves and others, but the participation is the winning. It is nice to cross the line first, but it is no longer essential in order to prove oneself.

References

Csikszentmihalyi, M. (1975). *Beyond Boredom and Anxiety*. San Francisco, LA: Jossey-Bass.

Csikszentmihalyi, M. (1990). *Flow – The Psychology of Optimal Experience*. New York: Harper & Row.

Dimanche, F. (1990). *Measuring Involvement in Recreational and Touristic Contexts with the Involvement Profile Scale*. Unpublished doctoral theses, University of Oregon.

Hall, C. M. and Weiler, B. (1992). *Special Interest Tourism*. London: Belhaven.

Havitz, M. E. and Dimanche, F. (1990). Propositions for testing the involvement construct in recreational and tourism contexts. *Leisure Sciences*, 12(2), 179–195.

Havitz, M. E. and Howard, D. R. (1995). How enduring is enduring involvement in the context of tourist motivation? *Journal of Travel and Tourism Marketing*, 4(3), 95–100.

Havitz, M. E., Dimanche, F. and Howard, D. R. (1993a). A two-sample comparison of the Personal Involvement Inventory (PII) and the Involvement Profile (IP) scales using selected recreation activities. *Journal of Applied Recreation Research*, 17(4), 331–364.

Havitz, M. E., Green, T. R. and McCarville, R. E. (1993b). Order effects and the measurement of enduring leisure involvement. *Journal of Applied Recreation Research*, 18(3), 181–196.

Iwasaki, Y. and Havitz, M. E. (1998). A Path Analytic Model of the relationships between involvement, psychological commitment and loyalty. *Journal of Leisure Research*, 30(2), 256–280.

Kapferer, J. and Laurent, G. (1985). Consumer involvement profiles: a new practical approach to consumer involvement. *Journal of Advertising Research*, 25(6), 48–56.

König, E. (1995). Criticism of doping: the nihilistic side of technological sport and the antiquated view of sports ethics. *International Review for the Sociology of Sport*, 34(3/4), 247–261.

Leiper, N. (1990). *Tourism Systems: An Interdisciplinary Perspective*. Palmerston North: Department of Management Systems, Massey University.

Lockyer, T. (2003). The South Pacific Games 2002 – Final Report. Hamilton: Department of Tourism Management, University of Waikato Management School.

McQuarrie, E. and Munson, J. (1987). The Zaichkowsky involvement inventory: modification and extension. *Advances in Consumer Research*, 14, 36–40.

McIntyre, N. (1989). The personal meaning of participation: enduring involvement. *Journal of Leisure Research*, 21: 167–179.

McIntyre, N., Coleman, D., Boag, A. and Cuskelly, G. (1992). Understanding Masters sports participation: involvement, motives and benefits. *ACHPER National Journal*, 138, 4–8.

Murphy, P. and Carmichael, B. (1996). Tourism economic impact of a rotating sports event: the case of the British Columbia Games. *Festival Management and Event Tourism*, 4(3/4), 127–139.

Ritchie, B. W. (1996). How special are special events? The economic impact and strategic development of the New Zealand Masters Games. *Festival Management and Event Tourism*, 4(3/4), 107–116.

Ryan, C. (1997). Rafting in the Rangitikei, New Zealand – an example of adventure holidays. In D. Getz and S. J. Page (eds), *The Business of Rural Tourism – International Perspectives*. Wiley, pp. 162–190.

Ryan, C. and Lockyer, T. (2001). An economic impact case study: the South Pacific Masters' Games. *Tourism Economics*, 7(3), 267–276.

Ryan, C. and Lockyer, T. (2002). Masters' games – the nature of competitors' involvement and requirements. *Event Management*, 7(4), 259–271.

Trauer, B. (2003). *The Sport Tourism Phenomenon in Contemporary Society*. Unpublished paper. Department of Tourism, University of Queensland.

Trauer, B. and Ryan, C. (2004). Adventure tourism – a conceptualisation. Submitted to the *Journal of Travel Research*.

Zaichkowsky, J. (1985). Measuring the involvement construct. *Journal of Consumer Research*, 12, 341–352.

14

Winter sports destinations: dealing with seasonality

Simon Hudson and Peter Cross

Introduction

Seasonality is one of the most widely recognized yet least researched features of tourism. The innovatory work of BarOn (1975) stood as virtually the only significant contribution to research on seasonality until about 1980, with seasonality regarded as an inevitable feature of the industry rather than a problem to be resolved. However, enough material now exists to indicate that patterns of seasonal fluctuation in the tourism industry have nothing inevitable about them, and that the emergence of seasonal patterns, the degree of their intensity and their historical durability are all variables that can both merit and repay research, especially at the local level. This chapter focuses on the issues of seasonality in winter sports destinations. In most parts of the world the ski industry has stagnated, with many resorts facing severe financial difficulties. It could be argued that the industry is witnessing the onset of a mature phase of development, as envisaged by Butler (1980) in the tourist area lifecycle. If resorts are not to face inevitable decline, adaptation is essential. Coping with seasonality is an important part of that adaptation.

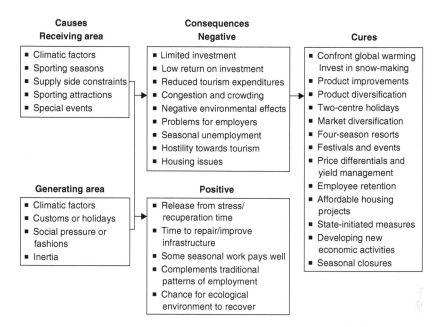

Figure 14.1 Seasonality in winter sports destinations: causes, consequences and cures

The chapter is divided into three distinct sections and is based on a framework presented in Figure 14.1. The first section looks at the causes of seasonality in winter sports destinations – causes that can be attributed to eight factors. The second section of the chapter moves on to discuss the consequences of seasonality for winter sports destinations, both positive and negative. The third and largest part of the chapter is more applied, and shows how winter sport tourism destinations around the world have attempted to cure or alleviate the problems associated with seasonality.

Definition of seasonality

Seasonality of demand has been defined generally by Moore (1989: 49) as 'movements in a time series during a particular time of year that recur similarly each year', and in the tourism context as 'the tendency of tourist flows to become concentrated into relatively short periods of the year' (Allcock, 1989: 92). Seasonality is rarely a simple phenomenon, and takes a number of forms that display different patterns of visitation. Butler and Mao (1997) identified three basic patterns, single peak, two-peak and non-peak. Single-peak seasonality occurs where the seasonal pattern of demand in a generating region matches the seasonal attractiveness of a destination, leading to extreme seasonality. An example would be the French Riviera, where visitors in July and August vastly outnumber tourists during any other month of the year. Two-peak seasonality occurs when there are two seasons, most commonly a summer one and a winter one, reflecting two seasons of attractiveness in the destination region. Mountainous regions experience this kind of seasonality, as they attract both summer tourists and winter sports enthusiasts. Finally, non-peak patterns occur mostly in urban destinations such as Hong Kong and Singapore, where seasonality indices of peak to non-peak visitation are extremely low.

Causes of seasonality

Figure 14.1 suggests that tourism seasonality at winter sport tourism destinations can be attributed to many factors, caused by both generating and receiving areas. The cause common to both, and probably the key reason for seasonality, is a natural factor – climate. Climate and weather conditions have led to the appearance of distinct seasonal variations in sport tourism visitation in a significant number of mountain destination areas across the globe (Kreutzwiser, 1989). Sporting activities specifically relating to snow, such as skiing, snowboarding and snowmobiling, have clear seasonal patterns due to the weather. In fact, a major challenge to future development of such sports is global warming. Most scientists tend to agree that winters will be shorter and warmer (Rosa, 2001; Best, 2003), meaning the economic viability of many winter sports destinations will be in doubt (Harrison et al., 1999; Viner and Agnew, 1999).

The remaining causes of seasonality tend to be classified as institutional factors (BarOn, 1975), and from the generating area include customs and holidays, (Frechtling, 1996), social pressures or fashion, and inertia (Butler, 1994). The scheduling of school and statutory holidays are common forms of institutionalized seasonality, and have a significant impact on the winter tourism season. In Europe, for example, holidays are taken primarily in the summer months, so that the skiing trip is seen as a 'second' and even 'luxury' holiday. Social pressure or fashion can also cause institutionalized seasonality. In the past, in many societies the privileged elite frequently divided their year into specific 'seasons' during each of which it was considered socially necessary to participate in selected activities and visit certain locations. For example, late in the nineteenth century the British upper classes made skiing into a fashionable winter pursuit, with the first winter mountain holidays starting in St Moritz, Switzerland (Hudson, 2000).

Inertia or tradition can also cause seasonality. Many people take holidays at peak seasons because they have always done so, and such habits are hard to break. Even without children, many tourists prefer the traditional holiday months as they often have the best weather, and transportation and other services may not be available out of the traditional season. In Europe, the end of the skiing season is traditionally Easter, regardless of whether Easter falls at the end of March or mid-April. Failure to recognize the importance of this tourist behaviour in maintaining seasonality may be a major cause of the apparent continued inability to change or reduce seasonality (Butler, 1994).

Institutional factors at work in the receiving area include sporting seasons (Butler, 1994), supply-side constraints (Baum and Hagen, 1999), and special events and sporting attractions (Butler, 2001). The sporting season reflects the changing patterns of recreational and tourist activity. In the twentieth century, the sporting attributes of winter sports, for example, replaced the social aspects in terms of importance to most participants and particularly spectators. Sporting activities related to snow, including skiing and snowboarding, are clearly confined to distinct seasons in mountain regions. For mountain resorts, mountain biking has emerged as a major summer activity, with over 20 million participants, and has helped the sport achieve Olympic designation (Frost and McCullough, 1995).

The supply side is also a potential cause of seasonality, such as where constraints in labour availability, the restriction of services or the alternative uses of facilities lead to closures or altered target markets. In Europe, for example, many tour operators from the United Kingdom do not package skiing holidays in April even though snow conditions are often very good. This is because the aircraft that they have been chartering all winter are used for the summer season, which begins at the beginning of April. The types of sporting attractions are also likely to impact seasonality for winter sports destinations. The most specialized destinations are the most seasonal (World Tourism Organization, 1999), and examples later on in this chapter will show how winter sports destinations are attempting to reduce seasonality by offering a wider variety of sporting attractions. Finally, special events can lead to seasonality in winter sports destinations. Such events may have long traditions, like the Inferno Cup first held in 1928 in Murren, Switzerland, or they may be more contemporary, such as the World Ski and Snowboard Festival in Whistler referred to later in this chapter.

Consequences of seasonality

From a review of the literature on seasonality, there is a general consensus that seasonality is a problem, that it has a number of facets and implications, and that it is a disease to be cured – or at least modified and reduced in effect. Figure 14.1 lists the negative consequences of seasonality applicable to winter sports destinations, but it also reflects the notion that there may well be economic or social benefits that flow from seasonality, and these are listed as positive consequences.

Negative impacts

BarOn (1975: 45) coined the term 'seasonal loss' to refer to costs that may be attributed to the negative effects of seasonality. The viewpoint that seasonality is a problem is primarily taken from an economic position, and reflects concerns with the difficulty of ensuring efficient utilization of resources. The seasonal nature of the tourism industry is often blamed for *limited investment* and *low returns on investment*, and a key reason that winter sports destinations attract limited investment is that they are perceived as operating a strictly seasonal business. Fifteen years ago there were 727 ski resorts in the USA, almost all backed by private investors. Now there are approximately 490, dozens of which are teetering on the edge of bankruptcy (Sullivan, 2002). Linked to these impacts is *reduced tourism expenditures* off-season. In Canada, for example, there is a very sharp and pronounced seasonal pattern in Canadian tourism expenditures. Seasonality explains 75 per cent of the statistical variation in tourism expenditures, with recreation expenditures having a severe degree of seasonality (Wilton and Wirjanto, 1998).

Congestion and crowding are also closely linked to issues of seasonality. The threshold or saturation level of visitor use of a destination usually is reached only during the peak periods of use and not during the low season or on an annual average basis. Therefore peak tourist demand must be considered in calculating carrying capacities. As a generalization, southern Europeans will tolerate more congestion and closer interpersonal spaces than do northern Europeans and most North Americans (Inskeep, 1991). However, in France, congestion within resorts in the form of long queues for ski lifts has developed as a major constraint to skiing (Tuppen, 2000).

There has been much discussion about the *environmental effects* of seasonality, focusing on the intensity of pressure on often fragile environments because of crowding and overuse during the peak season. In many parts of the world the mountains are a threatened wilderness, with skiing central to the crisis. In fact, a major deterrent to the further development of the ski market comes in the form of growing environmental concerns about human and traffic congestion in the mountains, and the intensive use of natural resources by skiers in a concentrated period (Hudson, 2000).

It is often suggested that the seasonal nature of tourism presents *problems for employers*, making it difficult to recruit full-time staff and to retain them (Mathieson and Wall, 1982; Krakover, 2000). A consequence of not being able to attract qualified staff is the variable quality of product and service delivery. In addition, Mill and Morrison (1985) have argued that seasonal work is less meaningful, and that this will have a negative impact on productivity. Seasonal unemployment is also often cited as a negative consequence of seasonality, and it is frequently implied that unemployment in the off-season is an involuntary state in which seasonal workers are regarded as victims (Mill and Morrison, 1985).

Jafari (1974) has linked seasonal fluctuations to the hostility towards tourism that is sometimes generated within local communities. More specifically, several studies have noted the association between tourism and crime. The late Jost Krippendorf (1994) blamed mass tourism in the Swiss Alps for the resident hostility towards tourists, particularly amongst the younger generation. He suggested that seasonal workers are over-saturated with contacts and sooner or later the symptoms of overkill will come to the surface. The overstressed worker will then react in an irritated and aggressive way. Krippendorf (1994) also linked the seasonality of tourism with negative impacts on the housing market in mountain resorts. He referred to the 'unpaid social costs' for the host population associated with tourism development in the mountains (Krippendorf, 1994: 49). First the locals sell their land for building at low prices to non-residents, losing control of economic development. When land prices start to rise the locals are left out in the cold, because it is others who make a profit. Ultimately the locals can no longer afford to live, let alone build a house, in their own district because of high land prices and rents paid by non-residents. This kind of situation can be observed in various tourist districts in the Swiss mountain areas, but affordable housing problems also exist in many winter sport tourism destinations in North America.

Positive impacts

Murphy (1985) suggests that seasonality is not necessarily bad for everyone, and for some communities the end of the tourist season is looked forward to. This is because individuals need release from stress, and some populations would not be capable of experiencing (or at least not content to experience) the stress of catering for tourists throughout the year. The off-season may represent the only time that the local population can operate in what to it is a 'normal' manner, and engage in traditional social and cultural activities (Butler, 2001). Krippendorf (1994) points to evidence in the Swiss mountains that shows residents are glad when the season is over. 'They need the intervening time between each invasion of holiday-makers to recuperate from the last lot' (Krippendorf, 1994: 46). There is also evidence in some destinations that a proportion of tourism operators seek a period of recuperation outside the main tourism season because they operate their business for lifestyle reasons (Commons and Page, 2001). Finally, destinations might welcome a period of rest so that infrastructure can be repaired or improved (Twining-Ward and Twining-Ward, 1996). Ski lifts, for example, are usually replaced or upgraded in the summer months.

Others have argued that many employees choose seasonal tourism employment because it pays better than alternative work that is available, and also because it allows those who wish to pursue other activities during the off-season to do so (Mourdoukoutas, 1988). Flognfeldt (1988) found evidence that employment in the tourism industry, particularly in remote and small communities, may complement traditional patterns of employment rather than compete with them. Ball (1989) has raised the possibility of the development of long-term 'symbiotic' relations between areas that have contrasting periodic demands for labour. This certainly exists in France, where the demand for seasonal labour is high during the winter for winter sport destinations, and correspondingly high during the summer months in the coastal resorts. Finally, Hartmann (1986) has argued that a dormant period for the environment is the only chance for an ecological environment to recover. While areas may experience heavy use in peak seasons, a lengthy rest period may allow almost complete recovery, or at least a new level of stability, to be achieved.

Cure for seasonality

The complexity of factors that give rise to seasonal impacts is not easily addressed by tourism destinations, and many attempts to reduce seasonality fail (Butler, 2001). This section of the chapter discusses how winter sport tourism destinations around the world have attempted to cure or alleviate the problems associated with seasonality.

Confront global warming

The main cause of seasonality – climate – is a major challenge. A study in Canada found that a temperature rise of one degree Celsius above the seasonal norm in the winter months would have an estimated $116 million negative effect on tourism domestic expenditures in the first quarter (Wilton and Wirjanto, 1998). In the past few years ski area operations have begun to acknowledge their vulnerability and the need to confront global warming. The National Ski Areas Association's (NSAA) 'Keep Winter Cool' programme coalesced several dozen ski areas in 2003 into explaining their efforts to reduce greenhouse gases as well as other environmental accomplishments (Best, 2003). The NSAA's campaign seeks to strike a balance between raising awareness of global warming and raising alarms about the possibly detrimental effects on snow conditions.

Investing heavily in snow-making

The invention of snow-making in the 1950s actually gave an impetus to the growth of ski facilities – a technological development that not only lengthened the ski season in the snow-belt states, but also made the sport possible in areas where natural snowfall was less than abundant. These days operators are investing heavily in snow-making equipment just to survive, but it is an expensive investment for many resorts (Bender, 2000). Buying the machinery and accessing the water – a process than can require protracted negotiations with state authorities and installing dozens of wells and miles of pipes – can cost tens of millions of dollars. In addition, low-altitude resorts do not always receive low enough temperatures to make snow.

Product improvements

Product improvements can help alleviate the problems caused by seasonality. The ski runs and related lift systems clearly represent a prime attraction of resorts, and therefore have long been the object of continuous improvements. For example, the process of linking ski areas has now become commonplace in France, following the initial lead given by resorts such as Tignes and Val d'Isere, which combined to form 'Espace Killy', and Courchevel, Meribel, les Menuires and Val Thorens, which created the 'Trois Vallées'. With these changes, skiing areas have been expanded to higher altitudes, giving better snow conditions, increasing resorts' capacities and extending their season. A special effort is also underway in France to improve accommodation, particularly in many of the apartment blocks that became a universal feature (and eyesore) of high-altitude resorts (Tuppen, 2000).

Product diversification

A commonly advocated strategy for the achievement of a more balanced flow of trade is product diversification (BarOn, 1975; Manning and Powers, 1984). Many ski resorts have started to attract summer tourists by developing a wide range of sports and activities. Chairlifts and cable cars are operating for walking holidays, or for mountain bikers. The majority of ski resorts now have swimming pools, skating rinks, tennis courts, guided walks and bike hire, and some – about 30 resorts in Europe – offer glacier skiing. In Vail, the creation of 'Adventure Ridge' – a four-acre entertainment complex at the 10 350-foot level of Vail Mountain – has succeeded beyond expectations. Although detractors have called it the Disneyland of the Rockies, the wide range of activities and a choice of restaurants, all available via a free (after 4 p.m.) gondola, have allowed the resort to extend the season and to offer evening employment to hundreds of staff (Best, 1997).

Another success story in diversification comes from Camelback in Pennsylvania, which spent US$ 6 million on Camelbeach Waterpark and has seen overall attendance increase from 100 000 during its inaugural 1998 summer season to more than 300 000 in 2002 (Devlin, 2003). Water slides are not the only way ski resorts are expanding and diversifying summer business. To its petting zoo, playgrounds, water slide, wading pools and other activities, Smuggler's Notch, Vermont, has added night-spiker volleyball. Ski Roundtop, Pennsylvania, has added paintball, and Northstar-at-Tahoe, California, has had great success with its ropes course. Another activity Northstar added recently was fly-fishing, but the ski resort best known for this is Sun Valley, Idaho. Its two busiest months of the year are July and August, and fly-fishing and ice-skating are the two biggest and most unusual summer draws.

Two-centre holidays

A sub-variety of this approach to countering seasonality developed by several tour companies has been the 'two-centre' holiday. This attracts the customer to a well-established resort with an accepted reputation, which may be suffering from excessive demand, but links a part of the holiday spent there to a less well-used resort or one with different types of attractions. In Spain, for example, the Sierra Nevada – the most southerly ski resort in Europe – appeals to tourists in search of both skiing and the beaches of the Costa del Sol. Many packages from the UK combine the two destinations in one two-centred holiday. The development of 'ski safaris', where ski trips are customized to visit a variety of resorts, may also help to make seasonality more manageable. While these strategies may do nothing to reduce the overall seasonal skew in demand for the product, they may serve to provide a better spatial distribution of demand.

Market diversification

Understanding market segmentation and differing demand motives permits recognition of those segments that are less tied to traditional vacation structures and are, therefore, more likely to travel during the shoulder and off-season. Such groups, widely recognized in the tourism industry, include senior travellers, conference delegates, incentive travellers, 'empty nesters', affinity groups and special interest groups (CEC, 1993). In the ski areas of Canada, resorts have achieved reasonable success targeting ski clubs to build visitor volumes during the 'off-peak' periods of the winter season (Williams and Dossa, 1998), and other resorts like Whistler have been successful in attracting conference business in the shoulder season. Canmore in Canada is counting on the ageing baby boomers to help eliminate the shoulder season. Plans have been drawn up for a health and wellness resort offering a myriad of traditional and non-traditional health services (Picard, 2003).

It has been suggested that to defeat seasonality the destinations should focus on yield rather than volume (Getz and Nilsson, 2003). In the Banff region of Canada, for example, the ski areas have been aggressively targeting European skiers over the last few decades. They are known as 'destination skiers' – the longer-stay tourists. Although they represent only 50 per cent of the market, non-resident skiers account for 77 per cent of tourism expenditures. Other resorts are taking a more targeted approach to development (Forstenzer, 2003). Tamarack Resort in Idaho, for example, is limiting the number of skiers and boarders to 3500 a day, despite capacity to accommodate 7000. The idea is to create a 'boutique' resort with a private club, with a focus on yield rather than volume.

Some ski resorts have used a combination of product and target market diversification to deal with seasonality. In 1996 Snow Valley in California lagged far behind competitors as a ski area, but with a focus on youth marketing and a diversification of the products and services offered, Sun Valley has become 'The Mountain of Youth' (Gerard, 1998). Having traditionally targeted the family market, the resort made a dramatic move away from the norm in the late 1990s and targeted the youth market. Opening new marketing channels, addressing skateboarders, inline skaters and the music industry, the resort built a unique mountain sports park for youths with activities and features that appeal to a whole new lifestyle.

Four-season resorts

One strategy for coping with seasonality in winter sports destinations is the development of four-season resorts, in which skiing is not the only activity, where sporting and entertainment facilities are open throughout the year rather than just in the winter months. Vancouver-based Intrawest is perhaps the most successful company in North America in developing four-season resorts. One of its resorts, Panorama, is profiled in Case study 14.1, but the most successful Intrawest destination is Whistler in British Columbia. Over the past decade, Whistler has experienced unprecedented growth and rising stature as a world-class year-round destination. Strong growth in visitor numbers has consistently been achieved in both summer and winter, and for the first time in the summer of 1996 the actual number of summer visitors exceeded the number of winter visitors. This trend has continued to date.

It is not just in North America that mountain resorts are seeking to develop all-round centres. In Australia, mountain resorts have traditionally been promoted as winter resorts, but a directive from the state government to the resort management boards in Victoria is to investigate the promotion of tourism to these resorts year round (Russell and Thomas, 2004). Alpine resorts in Europe have also been investing heavily in developing all-year round attractions. Verbier in Switzerland, for example, offers over 400 km of hiking paths, and mountain biking and golf are increasingly popular in the summer months. The *Hameau de Verbier* includes a large 300-seat conference room, plus several smaller conference venues. Resorts in France are also looking to attract the corporate market. The provision of purpose-built conference facilities in Val d'Isere and l'Alpe d'Huez is attracting a very different clientele to normal, and not necessarily during the peak season.

Festivals and events

Festivals and events are often introduced to cope with seasonality and boost tourism receipts during normally quiet times of the year. In 1996, Whistler in

British Columbia held its first World Ski and Snowboard Festival in April in order to increase occupancy rates in its quietest week at the end of the winter season. Now in its eighth year, the event is North America's largest snow sport and music event and attracts thousands of young enthusiasts from all over the world. Hotel rooms are fully booked during the event, which spans two weekends in order to maximize occupancy rates. In addition to ski and snowboard competitions, film events, parades and a lively club scene at night, more than 30 acts are booked for the Outdoor Concert Series. The concerts usually attract audiences of up to 10 000 revellers. According to an independent research study commissioned by the festival organizers, the 2003 festival resulted in a $26 million impact on the resort (Hudson, 2004).

The growth of adventure racing, spurred on by the popularity of the international Eco-Challenge, has given resorts another way of boosting summer revenue (Skinner, 2002). As athletes ranging from weekend enthusiasts to world-class endurance fanatics have broadened the scope of the sports they play, the standard Saturday 'fun run' has evolved into an adventure race ideally suited for many mountain resorts. Mountain resorts provide perfect venues, with a combination of facilities, existing recreation permits and the variety of terrain. In Durango Mountain Resort in Colorado, the first AdventureXtreme Series improved occupancy rates in the resort's hotels by 50 per cent compared to the same weekend the year before.

Case study 14.1 Panorama, British Columbia, Canada

Create memories for our guests and staff as the best mountain and resort experience . . . again and again. (The Intrawest mission)

Vancouver-based Intrawest is perhaps the most successful company in North America in countering seasonality by developing resort destinations as opposed to ski resorts. The company invests heavily in real estate developments and tourism infrastructure, adding retail, lodging and restaurants to attract people to the resort and keep them there. Involved in 15 mountain resorts in North America and Europe, Intrawest has developed a business model consisting of four distinct 'waves'. Wave 1 is the starting point when Intrawest first becomes involved in a resort, and Wave 2 is characterized by increasing development and longer-staying guests. In Wave 3, the village is well established and there is a dramatic increase in the number of destination visitors. Finally, in Wave 4 the resort is transformed and destination visitors are visiting year-round, maximizing the use of shops, hotels, convention facilities and restaurants. Currently, Whistler is the only Intrawest resort that has evolved into a true four-season destination resort, with Tremblant, Quebec, not far behind in the development cycle.

One Intrawest resort that is currently positioned in 'Wave 2' of the business model is Panorama. Located 2 hours southwest of Banff in British Columbia, and 18 km west of Invemere, Panorama boasts the highest vertical descent in the Canadian Rockies, with over 4000 vertical feet and more than 2700 acres of skiing terrain. In the village, four distinct neighbourhoods with 3110 beds are linked by pedestrian pathways and a village gondola, and guests have the use of 6000 square feet of heated hot pools at the bottom of the ski hill. 'We are in the development stage so we have to build incrementally' says Gord Ahrens, former General Manager of the resort and now consultant to Intrawest. However, development is pushing ahead, and already the resort has an 18-hole championship golf course and many other summer activities, including mountain biking, hiking, tennis, horseback riding, kayaking and rafting, bungee jumping and mini-golf.

Despite this proliferation of summer activities, winter at Panorama is still the busiest season. Ahrens says that in the summer Panorama operates at very low margins – sometimes even at a loss – to fill units and bring the place alive. 'We look at events that will sell rooms – so we may have two or three events over a weekend to keep people up for the whole weekend.' For example, at the end of the winter season in April 2003, Panorama hosted the 'Spring Fiesta', the 'Sunpit Safari' and 'Easterfest', all on consecutive weekends. That summer, the resort hosted the 1000 Peaks Triathlon, the Mad Trapper BC Cup Mountain Bike Race, the Sea2Summit adventure race, and the Shimano Dirt Series Women's Skill Camp.

Other attempts to increase business during the off-season include a newly renovated conference facility as an attempt to capture the corporate market. Different facilities are available for the business market, depending on needs: the Great Hall is suited for banquets and events for groups of up to 300 people; the Conrad Kain and Earl Grey room is best equipped for a board-style meeting of 10 to 25 people; and the Copper Crown meeting rooms are ideal for classroom-style gatherings. Panorama is also being groomed into an official national alpine ski-racing training centre, established via enhanced early season snow-making capabilities and permanent safety equipment. The upgrades ensure Panorama can make available early-season training space for the Canadian Alpine Ski Team prior to opening to the public in December.

Panorama employs about 450 employees in the wintertime. 150 are full-time employees, and of the seasonal workers about 120 return every year, so they are re-hiring about 180 each year. 'It is not hard to keep our year-round staff' says Ahrens. 'It is a pretty attractive job in the region as logging is depressed and mining has almost finished. So to find a full-time job with benefits is quite attractive and staff can live in Invemere and own a home – as opposed to higher-priced resorts like Whistler where employees cannot find affordable housing. But still, employee housing is always a challenge.'

'To keep our employees I make sure that they are having fun' says Rusty Noble, Director of People. 'Certainly for the 18–26-year-olds this is crucial. The challenge of the job is not so important – neither is the money. For our year-round people job security is a big attraction, and they will be looking for more job satisfaction and progress. We have an annual survey that is done by an outside company to measure employee satisfaction, and this is completed by all staff. We are also going through a process called "Fireside chats", where a director will sit down with a group of employees and say "how are things going?" and "how can we make this a better place for our employees and guests?".'

Both Ahrens and Noble agree that, operationally, people are the biggest challenge, but financing the resort is also a key focus for managers. 'Financially we have a number of assets tied up that don't produce income for a great chunk of the year. The golf course is an example. It cost nearly $16 million to build, and with operating revenue of just 4 months, the window of opportunity to gain income is very small' says Ahrens.

Financial reporting is very focused on room nights, golf rounds and skier visits – depending on the season – so as soon as they drop off managers are expected to drop expenses. 'If you can keep your rooms full, you can keep all your people year-round, but seasonality doesn't allow this' says Noble. 'September, October and November are traditionally slow so we have to keep the gap between revenue growth and cost growth stable. We gain incentives when we increase revenue at a greater percentage than our costs. That drives management at all levels to keep costs down when things get quiet.'

Panorama uses yield management for pricing golf and accommodation, but not so much for ski-lift tickets. 'With golf we are constantly looking at how we get more golfers on the course at prime times – and how do we fill all the other times with people who want to pay a lower price? Yield management is all about finding the right price for the right people at the right time' says Ahrens. Packaging is also used during low-demand periods to generate additional business. Most of the packages at Panorama include unlimited skiing, and children aged 8 and under ski and stay free when accompanied by parents.

As for the future, Panorama is looking toward moving into 'Wave 3' of the Intrawest business development model, where year-round facilities emerge along with village expansion. 'We need a critical mass in order to move on to the next stage' says Ahrens. Until then, dealing with seasonality and smoothing out the troughs will remain a management challenge for Ahrens and his management team.

(Sources: Personal interviews with Gord Ahrens, Vice President and General Manager; and Rusty Noble, Director of People, 14 August 2003; **Resort Life**, Intrawest Corporate Magazine, 2003; Panorama Mountain Village brochures for 2003.)

Websites
Panorama website, www.panoramaresort.com
Intrawest website, www.intrawest.com
Intrawest job openings, www.wework2play.com

Price differentials and yield management

The use of price differentials as stimuli to the market in periods outside the main season might be thought an obvious corrective to excessive seasonal concentration, but pricing has not been excessively examined in relation to seasonality (Allcock, 1989). Pricing may work in two directions in relation to seasonal congestion. Price reductions can attract visitors during the low season, and higher prices can discourage trade during the peak season. Grouse Mountain in British Columbia used a short-term pricing strategy to develop a loyal market that would ski throughout the season. In 1999 it slashed season ski passes for children and seniors to CDN\$ 20, and sold adults passes for CDN\$ 2000. A total of 13 700 passes were sold, and overall snow visits went up 192 per cent (Lazarus, 2000). However, there are suggestions that discounts do not necessarily help problems of seasonality. In a study of seasonality in English hotels, Jeffrey and Barden (2001) found that practising yield management helped but deep price discounts did not.

Yield management is the practice of developing strategies to maximize opportunities for the sale of an organization's perishable products, such as airline seats, hotel rooms and tour seats, and therefore improving its long-term viability. It was initiated by the airline industry in the 1980s as a way to increase revenue from existing routes and aircraft, and the practice of yield management is now common in other sectors of tourism, from hotels to ski resorts. Different rates are offered for different groups of customers, with restrictions on the use of rates by other groups. Withiam (1999) reported that switching to a yield management system at the Vail Resort, Inc. properties at Keystone Resort and the Great Divide Lodge in Breckenridge, Colorado, resulted in more than US\$1 million in incremental revenue, and Perdue (2002) found that the use of yield management for setting season passes in Colorado ski resorts significantly influenced skier loyalty to the respective resorts.

Employee retention

Retaining employees can help with some of the problems for employers caused by seasonality, and can reduce seasonal unemployment. A study of ski industry employees in Colorado and New Mexico by Ismert and Petrick (2003) found that satisfaction with money and job challenge were best at predicting intention to return, while satisfaction with management attitude, level of camaraderie and job challenge were the best predictors of seasonal employees' overall job satisfaction. One of the greatest benefits of a successful summertime business for a ski resort is the opportunity to offer employees more work for longer periods of time. Employees from all departments – food services, lift operations, ski patrol – can be cross-trained to do different jobs in summer and winter. For example, Camelback's ski patrol manager becomes the aquatics manager in the summertime.

Affordable housing projects

Providing reasonable housing options (whether rental units or home ownership) for those who live and work in mountain resorts has been the most challenging issue facing many communities over the last few decades. Affordable housing projects have emerged as a solution to the problems of employees unable to rent or purchase property in winter sports destinations. In North America (more so than Europe) there are many mountain communities that have made efforts to address resident housing, including the Banff Housing Corporation, the Aspen/Pitkin County Housing Authority, the Town of Vail Housing Division, and the Mountainlands Community Trust in Utah. Whistler – through The Whistler

Housing Authority – has found that creating an inventory of price-controlled units that are only available to resident employees is the best means of reducing the impact of market forces that are driving the price of housing out of reach for locals.

State-initiated measures

Considerable effort has been applied (especially in European countries) to influence the pattern of seasonal concentration through various state-initiated measures directed at its institutional roots (Allcock, 1989). For example, attention was applied systematically in the francophone countries during the 1980s to the possibility of staggering the main school and industrial holidays over a longer period. In fact, winter rather than summer holidays are staggered in France, as the popularity of skiing holidays caused substantial peaking problems (McEniff, 1992). The French authorities have also addressed themselves to the possibilities of utilizing seasonal patterns in employment, rather that trying to eliminate them. The employment of seasonal workers in the peak season is now linked to periods of education and professional training in the low season. The scheme aims to benefit employees in giving them greater security and chances for both career advancement and higher status; to give employers the benefit of a better trained labour force which is more committed to the industry; and to improve the quality of service offered to the customer.

Developing new economic activities

More recently there have been certain resort-level strategies to offset seasonality that focus on developing new economic activities that encourage people to relocate. These people will move into mountain communities, often for lifestyle reasons, but they will generate income (often using new technologies) from sources that have nothing to do with tourism. For example, Leysin in Switzerland is encouraging a 'learning resort' concept. Leysin is only 30 minutes from Montreux, but is a struggling ski resort constrained by low altitude, a small, antiquated lift system, and south-facing slopes. As a result it is embarking on a strategy of evolving into an educational environment to attract schools and colleges. Switzerland's largest English-speaking hospitality education provider is creating a campus with state-of-the art facilities designed for the specific needs of students. In so doing, it will double its capacity of 1600 students per year.

Seasonal closures

Finally, seasonal closures might sometimes be the most appropriate strategy to deal with seasonality. Flognfeldt (2001) suggests that some destinations must learn how to live with strong seasonality, and his idea is to fit different types of tourism production into the seasonal patterns of other production activities, including an adjustment of some public services. He noted a number of business strategies in place in Norway, such as mixing employment (tourism and agriculture), using student and migrant workers, or just taking long holidays.

Conclusions

A primary growth target of the tourism industry today is the off-season. Alaska is aggressively touting winter because of high demand in the summer; Montana is advertising autumn, its slowest season; while New York City is focusing on its weakest months, January and February. This chapter has focused specifically on the issues of seasonality in winter sports destinations. Causes of seasonality in these destinations can be attributed to eight factors, and these factors can have both positive and negative consequences for destinations. The chapter suggests that there are a number of 'cures' or strategies in place to deal with the negative consequences of seasonality. Whilst there are some examples of the development of four-season resorts, more common than 'overcoming' seasonality are plans to extend the existing season into shoulder periods at either end of the demand period, based primarily on utilization of the same resources as the main season, but often targeted at alternative market segments. In a perfect world, all stakeholders would reap the benefits of a long-term strategy that reduced the peaks and troughs of seasonal tourism in winter sports destinations. However, in reality only business models like those of Intrawest (see Case study 14.1) can hope to develop such a strategy efficiently and effectively.

References

Allcock, J. B. (1989). Seasonality. In S. F. Witt and L. Moutinho (eds), *Tourism Marketing and Management Handbook*. Englewood Cliffs, NJ: Prentice-Hall, pp. 387–392.

Ball, R. M. (1989). Some aspects of tourism, seasonality and local labour markets. *Area*, 21(1), 35–45.

BarOn, R. R. V. (1975). *Seasonality in Tourism: A Guide to the Analysis of Seasonality and Trends for Policy Making*. London: Economist Intelligence Unit, Technical Series No. 2, London.

Baum, T. and Hagen, L. (1999). Responses to seasonality: the experiences of peripheral destinations. *International Journal of Tourism Research*, 1(5), 299–312.

Bender, C. (2000). Snowmaking survey. *Ski Area Management*, 39(6), 52.

Best, A. (1997). That's entertainment. *Ski Area Management*, 36(3), 66–67.

Best, A. (2003). Is it getting hot in here? *Ski Area Management*, 42(3), 57–76.

Butler, R. W. (1980). The concept of a tourist area life cycle of evolution: implications for management of resources. *Canadian Geographer*, 24(1), 5.

Butler, R. W. (1994). Seasonality in tourism: issues and problems. In A. V. Seaton, C. L. Jenkins, R. C. Wood et al. (eds), *Tourism: The State of the Art*. Chichester: Wiley, pp. 332–339.

Butler, R. W. (2001). Seasonality in tourism: issues and implications. In T. Baum and S. Lundtorp (eds), *Seasonality in Tourism*. New York: Pergamon, pp. 5–22.

Butler, R. W. and Mao, B. (1997). Seasonality in tourism: problems and measurement. In P. E. Murphy (ed.), *Quality Management in Urban Tourism*. Chichester: John Wiley, pp. 9–23.

CEC (1993). *All-season Tourism: Analysis of Experience, Suitable Products and Clientele*. Brussels: Commission of the European Communities and Fitzpatrick Associates.

Commons, J. and Page, S. (2001). Managing seasonality in peripheral tourism regions: the case of Northland, New Zealand. In T. Baum and S. Lundtorp (eds), *Seasonality in Tourism*. New York: Pergamon, pp. 153–172.

Devlin, I. (2003). Sliding into summer. *Ski Area Management*, 42(2), 40–59.

Flognfeldt, T. (1988). *The Employment Paradox of Seasonal Tourism*. Paper presented at Pre-Congress meeting of International Geographical Union, Christchurch, New Zealand, 13–20 August.

Flognfeldt, T. (2001). Long-term positive adjustments to seasonality: consequences of summer tourism in the Jotunheimen area, Norway. In T. Baum and S. Lundtorp (eds), *Seasonality in Tourism*. New York: Pergamon, pp. 109–117.

Forstenzer, M. (2003). Solving the resort puzzle. *Ski*, 68(4), 45–48.

Frechtling, D. C. (1996). *Practical Tourism Forecasting*. Oxford: Butterworth-Heinemann.

Frost, J. and McCullough, J. (1995). Biking trails: the ins and outs, the ups and downs. *Ski Area Management*, 34(3), 78–91.

Gerard, M. (1998). A mountain of youth. *Ski Area Management*, 37(1), 69.

Getz, D. and Nilsson, P.A. (2003). Responses of family businesses to extreme seasonality in demand: the case of Bornholm, Denmark. *Tourism Management*, 25(1), 17–30.

Harrison, S. J., Winterbottom, S. J. and Sheppard, C. (1999). The potential effects of climate change on the Scottish tourism industry. *Tourism Management*, 20(2), 203–211.

Hartmann, R. (1986). Tourism, seasonality and social change. *Leisure Studies*, 5(1), 25–33.

Hudson, S. (2000). *Snow Business: A Study of the International Ski Industry*. London: Continuum International Publishing Group.

Hudson, S. (2004). *Marketing Tourism and Hospitality: A Canadian Perspective*. Toronto: Nelson Thomson.

Inskeep, E. (1991). *Tourism Planning: An Integrated and Sustainable Development Approach*. New York: Van Nostrand Reinhold.

Ismert, M. and Petrick, J. F. (2003). Indicators and standards of quality related to seasonal employment in the ski industry. Proceedings of the 34th Annual Conference of the Travel and Tourism Research Association, St. Louis, MO. TTRA.

Jafari, J. (1974). The socio-economic costs of tourism to developing countries. *Annals of Tourism Research*, 1, 227–259.

Jeffrey, D. and Barden, R. R. D. (2001). Multivariate models of hotel occupancy performance and their implications for hotel marketing. *International Journal of Tourism Research*, 3(1), 33–44.

Krakover, S. (2000). Partitioning seasonal employment in the hospitality industry. *Tourism Management*, 21(5), 461–471.

Kreutzwiser, R. (1989). Supply. In G. Wall (ed.), *Outdoor Recreation in Canada*. Toronto: Wiley, pp. 19–42.

Krippendorf, J. (1987). *The Holidaymakers*. London: Heinemann.

Lazarus, E. (2000). Not just a ski hill. *Marketing Magazine*, 105(40), 15.

Manning, R. E. and Powers, L. A. (1984). Peak and off-peak use: redistributing the outdoor recreation/tourism load. *Journal of Travel Research*, 23(2), 25–31.

Mathieson, A. and Wall, G. (1982). *Tourism: Economic, Physical and Social Impacts*. Harlow: Longman.

McEniff, J. (1992). Seasonality of tourism demand in the European Community. *Travel & Tourism Analyst*, 3, 67–88.

Mill, R. C. and Morrison, A. M. (1985). *The Tourism System: An Introductory Text.* Upper Saddle River, NJ: Prentice-Hall.

Moore, T. W. (1989). *Handbook of Business Forecasting*. London: Gower.

Mourdoukoutas, P. (1988). Seasonal employment, seasonal unemployment and unemployment compensation: the case for the tourist industry of the Greek Islands. *American Journal of Economics and Sociology*, 47(3), 314–329.

Murphy, P. E. (1985). *Tourism: A Community Approach*. New York: Methuen.

Perdue, R. R. (2002). Perishability, yield management, and cross-product elasticity: a case study of deep discount season passes in the Colorado ski industry. *Journal of Travel Research*, 41, 15–22.

Picard, C. (2003). TGS shifts gears. *Rocky Mountain Outlook,* 3(4), 1, 3.

Rosa, B. (2001). Skiing's end? *Skiing Winter Adventure*, 53(6), 32.

Russell, R. and Thomas, P. (2004). Destination image: Victorian mountain parks and resorts in the summer. In M. Hall and S. Boyd (eds), *Nature-based Tourism in Peripheral Areas: Development or Disaster*. Clevedon, OH: Channel View.

Skinner, M. (2002). Adrenaline junkies. *Ski Area Management*, 41(2), 46.

Sullivan, A. (2002). Downhill risks for ski resorts. *Financial Times*, 12 March, XXII.

Tuppen, J. (2000). The restructuring of winter sports resorts in the French Alps: problems, processes and policies. *International Journal of Tourism Research*, 2(5), 227–344.

Twining-Ward, L. and Twining-Ward, T. (1996). *Tourism Destination Development: The Case of Bornholm and Gotland*. Research Centre of Bornholm, Denmark. Report 7/1996.

Viner, D. and Agnew, M. (1999). *Climate Change and its Impacts on Tourism*. Report Prepared for WWF-UK by the Climate Research Unit, University of East Anglia, Norwich.

Williams, P. W. and Dossa, K. B. (1998). Ski channel users: a discrimination perspective. *Journal of Travel and Tourism Marketing*, 7(2), 1–29.

Wilton, D. and Wirjanto, T. (1998). *An Analysis of the Seasonal Variation in the National Tourism Indicators*. Report prepared for the Canadian Tourism Commission, Ottawa: CTC.

Witham, G. (1999). Better ideas? *Cornell Hotel and Restaurant Administration Quarterly*, 40(4), 12.

World Tourism Organization, (1999). *World Tourism Statistics*. Madrid: WTO.

15

Sport and urban tourism destinations: the evolving sport, tourism and leisure functions of the modern stadium

Terry Stevens

Introduction

Sports stadia, especially those with the potential for multiple use, help create a vibrant image for a destination. 'Stadia' is used here as the generic term to describe public assembly facilities providing amenities for spectator viewing of sporting events, but it also includes covered arenas where the primary purpose may be entertainment rather than sporting. The stadium is now part of the tourism infrastructure and appeal of a city. Events in the stadium, especially when they involve major league sports teams or competitions, attract tourists. These landmark buildings, the 'cathedrals of sport', have now become attractions in their own right. Iconic symbol of a city's vitality, the stadium is often used as the anchor for major regeneration schemes. Realization of the power of sport to generate tourism is prompting many national, regional and city tourism organizations to re-evaluate the interrelationships between sport and tourism. The conclusion of much of this analysis is that modern, aesthetic, comfortable, technically superb stadia are often the key to unlocking this potential.

The sport–tourism interface

The sports stadium is becoming more readily integrated and accepted as a fundamental component of the leisure industry and tourism in general. The word 'stadium' is derived from the ancient Greek name for a footrace observed by spectators (Stevens, 1994). The appreciation of the importance of stadia in civic life is an ancient phenomenon, but one that was confined to a small part of Europe until the mid-twentieth century. Inglis (1993) speculates as to why this is the case, highlighting that many cities in Europe had no classical stadia as 'at Olympia or Delphi'; no 'Coliseum as in Rome'; no 'arena as in Arles, Nimes or Verona'. Ironically, today these heritage *stadia* are also part of the tourism resources of these destinations (Luciani, 1990).

Exploiting the interface between tourism and sport is set to become a major focus for tourism development on a global basis over the next 20 years (Stevens, 2003). It is surprising, however, how few destinations around the world have yet fully embraced sport-related tourism. In Britain, the British Tourist Authority, together with the four national tourist boards, only established a sport–tourism initiative in 2000. The genesis of this approach was rooted in the government's goal of attracting major global sports events to Britain, including the Olympic Games in 2012, and ensuring that the 2002 Commonwealth Games in Manchester established a springboard for wider tourism benefits.

The economic impact and global exposure of high-profile sporting events have prompted much of the clamour amongst cities and countries to compete to host these events. The positive experience of Sydney in hosting the XXVII Olympiad in 2000 typified the ambitions of many destinations. The Australian Tourism Commission secured A$ 6.7 million from the Australian government over the period of 1997–2000 to maximize the tourism opportunities presented by the Games, the aim being to add depth and dimension to Australia's international tourism image for long-term gain.

Destination image is a decisive factor in influencing the choice of location for a holiday or for business tourism (Seaton and Bennett, 1996), and because potential tourists have limited knowledge about a destination, their perceptions are strongly influenced by the media as well as their social networks (Crompton, 1992). Clearly, destination image and place marketing are inextricably linked with sport and sports stadia providing vibrant, exciting images to provide the platform for tourism marketing strategies (Neill, 1993). In this context, it is pertinent just how many well-known tourism destinations are associated with sport and sporting venues – Henley, Wimbledon, Ascot, Manchester, Le Mans, Monaco, Lausanne, Indianapolis, Melbourne. At a time when tourism commentators are describing 'place wars', with cities and territories competing for economic survival, sport, especially stadium sports, has a fundamental role to play in the post-industrial marketing of tourism (Kotler, 1993).

Significantly, stadia and arena development holds the key to a country or a city being able satisfactorily to host a major sporting event and to position themselves as a sport tourism destination (Whitson and Macintosh, 1993). It is within these 'cathedrals' of sport that the key events take place, including the increasingly important opening and closing ceremonies. Unless competing cities can demonstrate that their sports stadia are technically superb and have the appropriate spectator capacity, then they are unlikely to be successful in their bids. As a result, prospective contenders for these events invest heavily in their stadia real estate even before their candidatures have been adjudicated (Andranovich *et al.*, 2001).

For example, the Stadium Australia Trust, together with the Olympic Co-ordinating Authority and the Sydney Organizing Committee for the Olympic Games, identified Homebush Bay as the location for the majority of the sporting venues for the Olympic Games. This included the 110 000 capacity Stadium Australia (at a cost of $A 480 million, and now the Telstra Stadium, host to the 2003 Rugby World Cup Final), the State Hockey Centre, and Novotel and Ibis Hotels.

Similarly, prior to the 1999 Rugby World Cup in Wales the Welsh Rugby Union, together with Cardiff County Council, created the 73 000 capacity, £130 million Millennium Stadium at the heart of the city with £40 million funding from the Millennium Commission. The Wales Tourist Board's high-profile promotional campaign alongside the 1999 Rugby World Cup resulted in a range of benefits from over 100 000 tourists (including 40 000 overseas tourists), with spending valued at over £83 million and a long-term significant uplift in tourism, including repeat visitations (see Chapter 10).

Without modern, safe, comfortable and aesthetically attractive stadia there could be no modern global sporting events. Equally, without these quality stadia it would be impossible for cities satisfactorily to attract and retain major league sports teams. The presence of these 'hallmark' teams regularly attracting large spectator crowds has now become synonymous with tourism place promotion as well as short-break leisure tourism packages (Stevens, 2001). For example, in Baltimore (USA) the Orioles baseball team regularly attracts some 46 per cent of all fans from out of town, with 24 per cent (or 11 000) of people staying overnight in the Baltimore area for at least 1 night when attending games at the new Camden Yards Stadium, built adjacent to the waterfront regeneration area.

Sports stadia, especially those with a genuine multipurpose capability, have a significant, often fundamental, role to play in creating the opportunities to exploit the interrelationship between sport and tourism. They are the venues for events (sporting and non-sporting); they can be the architectural icons that create place promotion images; and they are the focal point for much leisure-related investment. As the UK National Heritage Committee (1995) stated: 'It is clear that bids to stage major sporting events can operate as a catalyst to stimulate economic regeneration even if they do not ultimately prove successful'. The Committee continued:

> ... once the initial redevelopment has taken place, the existence of high
> quality facilities means that the cities concerned are able to attract other

sports events. The impact however does not stop there. Many of the facilities are suitable for other uses such as conferences and concerts. In addition the favourable publicity which can follow from a successful event may increase the attractiveness of a city, raise its profile overseas, and enable it to attract an increasing number of tourists. (UK Sports, 1998)

Stadia – a major focus of investment

Throughout the 1990s, for reasons good and bad, stadia were rarely out of the news. In Europe, as a result of a series of fatal accidents (notably in the Heysel Stadium in Brussels in 1985 and at Hillsborough in Sheffield in 1989), there were calls for major investment to make these large-scale venues safe and comfortable. In Britain, the report by Lord Justice Taylor on the Hillsborough disaster (HMSO, 1990), at which 95 people died, led directly to the government's insistence that soccer clubs take proper responsibility for their properties. This resulted in a major overhaul of stadia within the soccer league system in England, Scotland, Wales and Northern Ireland. In the first four years following the Taylor Report, some £800 million was invested in soccer stadia in England and Wales. In the period 1994–2000 the figure increased to twice that amount.

These tragic events and their implications have reverberated around the wider world of sport, drawing attention to the issues of design, safety, amenity and management of public assembly facilities. As a result, improvements have taken place at numerous other sporting venues throughout the UK and Europe. In North America the primary driver of change appears to have been the recognition of the significance of major league franchise teams, playing in well-designed stadia, capable of generating significant media interest (Lipsitz, 1984; Bale, 1989; Getz, 1992) and attracting corporate investment (Petersen, 1990). More recently, in the Asia-Pacific region the motivation has been to host mega-sporting events, especially the 2002 Soccer World Cup in Korea and Japan; the 2002 Olympic Games in Australia, followed by the 2003 Rugby World Cup also in Australia and future bids to host the Olympic Games.

A number of these new generation stadia in North America, notably Toronto's Skydome, Houston's Astrodome and Baltimore's Oriole Park at Camden Yards were producing evidence to demonstrate a strong correlation between the successful regeneration of urban areas and the enhancement of civic pride associated with successful major league teams and sporting events. The construction of sports stadia was emerging as a tool for stimulating public and private investment aimed at solving problems of urban development.

Although there is inconclusive support for the notion that a new stadium can bring about economic regeneration on its own, it is widely accepted that the development of a stadium can act as a catalyst to regenerate an area (Ladd and Davis, 2003). This is especially the case when the stadium is located in deprived areas and/or new development centres such as at Milton Keynes new town in England, which in 2003 became the 'home' of Wimbledon Football Club (Gray, 2003). The range of planning, design and locational considerations for stadia development in the UK fail, however, to include tourism-related matters. This is compounded because, unless such matters are specifically linked in the statutory development plan system, they tend to be ignored (Maison, 2003).

This lack of connectivity experience between the physical planning design and development of stadia with the realization of the tourism potential of the project is endemic in other aspects of the tourism and sport equation (Weed and Bull, 2004), but is particularly prevalent in the case of stadia (Stevens, 2003). As a result, the public sector has recognized the added value of investment in stadia and increasingly accepts that they can rarely be expected to make a profit. The political risk involved in supporting these schemes is considerably outweighed by the wider economic gains to the community. As the catalyst for urban regeneration, the stadium is a seductive tool.

The Urban Land Institute in North America estimates, for example, that 65 per cent of the projects being developed or refurbished in the USA in the mid-1990s were public sector funded. Despite this safety net, there is increasing pressure on stadium operating companies to become financially viable. This has resulted in stadia designers incorporating more tourism and leisure facilities into their plans in order to attract year-round use and generate new sources of revenue income.

The importance of Oriole Park at Camden Yards extends beyond the major uplift of the tourism economy of Baltimore's Waterfront and the immediate environs, with the City's tourism business reporting an average 25 per cent uplift in trade on game days (Stevens, 2001). Many observers recognize the non-pecuniary benefits of stadia development for cities and regions as being an essential part of the justification for investment. These benefits give rise to other outcomes, such as civic pride, investment in infrastructure and place profile, that underscore the efforts to create a strong tourism destination. In this way, the stadium is inextricably part of the tourism infrastructure and marketing proposition.

It is for these reasons that Humphreys (2003) has identified some 26 new stadia being constructed in 21 different cities across 16 states in the USA between 1998 and 2003. This represents a total investment of $US 7.84 billion (average $302 million), of which 65 per cent ($5.09 billion) resulted from some form of public subsidy that recognized the importance of the stadium for city profiling from hosting major league sports teams. Of the 26 stadia developed in the USA between 1998 and 2003, 8 were for baseball, 11 for American football and 7 for basketball. In all but two cases the new stadium was replacing an existing facility, one of which was just 3 years old, but on average the age of the replaced facility was 32 years (i.e. the original facility was built in the 1970s).

The contribution of stadia-based events to the local economy is now becoming well documented. The Rugby World Cup, for example, is the fourth largest sporting event in the world, and in 1999 the finals were held in Cardiff, Wales. The Wales Tourist Board secured a gross marketing budget of £5.2 million to promote the event. This resulted in over 330 000 tourists to Wales in November 1999, 480 000 net additional bednights and a short-term economic impact of £83.2 million with a further £4.4 million predicted from return tourist trips. A similar scale of impact was identified following the Euro '96 soccer competition held in England. As stated in the English Tourism Council's *Insights* Tourism Intelligence Papers in 1999:

> the economic importance of major sports events became an increasingly important issue following the economic success of the Euro 96 football championships, which attracted 280 000 overseas visiting supporters, spending around £120 million in the eight host cities and surrounding regions. If we include the impact of spending by domestic visitors not

resident in the host cities, the total economic impact generated in the host cities by all spectators and media/officials to Euro 96 was £195 million. (Gratton *et al.*, 2000)

Euro '96 was estimated to have increased Britain's net earnings from travel and tourism in the second quarter of 1996 by 3 per cent and generated an extra 0.25 per cent of UK exports of goods and services. The impact on the whole economy was estimated at an added 0.1 per cent on British Gross Domestic Product in the period from April to June – a quarter of the total growth of 0.4 per cent. The tourist boom during the championships helped to push Britain's trade balance into its first surplus since the beginning of 1995.

According to estimates from Deloitte & Touche, the government also experienced £64 million gains as a result of England hosting the tournament: £40 million from the tournament through VAT on ticket sales, merchandising, corporate hospitality and other Euro '96 spending; £5 million from betting tax from the £80 million wagers on Euro '96 matches; £3 million from taxation on the incomes of competition organizers; and £16 million from companies paying corporation tax on commercial profit.

In a recent paper to the European Travel and Tourism Research Association in Glasgow, Cosgrove (2003) challenged tourism planners to 'think out of the box' and beyond the obvious in terms of developing sport tourism. This thesis is that sport tourism must more explicitly and willingly embrace stadia sports. Football tourism in Europe, for example, represents a strong tourism consumer base, represented by a post-Heysel fan who is in full-time employment and affluent, and includes 40 per cent who are women. These are potential returners for other types of tourism experiences.

Cosgrove highlighted the power of the traditional 'Old Firm' matches between Glasgow Rangers and Glasgow Celtic soccer teams in generating some 12 000 bednights from overseas tourists (estimated at 3000–4000 from Ireland and 1200–2000 from Scandinavia) and injecting £1.8 million into the city's economy for each game. These figures are comparable to those for each Manchester United Premiership match played at Old Trafford, which generates some £76 million of spending by overseas tourists each season (Trafford Metropolitan Borough Council, 2000).

In addition, it is estimated that each of Glasgow's two clubs' Champions League soccer games attracts up to 20 000 away fans from the opposing team and is worth £3–£5 million to the city's tourism industry (Friel, 2003). The 2002 UEFA Champions' League Final at Scotland's National Stadium, Glasgow's Hampden Park, generated an estimated £25 million for the city's economy. The match was screened in Germany (which represents 11 per cent of Scotland's overseas tourism market) and in Spain (which accounts for 4 per cent of the overseas market). Friel is adamant that 'football tourism is booming, the positive images of Scottish football must be embraced in mainstream tourism planning and promotion' (Dyer, 2002).

The ability for these facilities to host non-sporting events such as pop concerts, religious conventions and trade shows greatly enhances their asset value to a destination's tourism industry. Strategically programmed, these events can generate tourism trips at times when there is spare capacity in hotels and attractions. Travel agents and ground handling companies are now gearing up to manage these new event-led packages.

The current scale of investment worldwide

It is impossible to provide a comprehensive schedule of development on a world-wide basis. Many schemes are kept under wraps until land assembly and funding are in place, whilst other projects are more speculative than real.

In March 2001 there were at least 70 new stadia currently in their development phase, with a further 48 existing facilities undergoing major refurbishment world-wide (see Tables 15.1–15.3). This new development is equally distributed across North and South America, Europe and Asia. These lists are not exhaustive and do not, for example, include those existing stadia in Japan and South Korea, Portugal and Germany that were upgraded for the World and European Cup competitions in 2002, 2004 and 2006 respectively.

Much of the stimulus for these new developments is directly related to the increasing global competition to host the mega-sporting events. For example, the New York Jets American Football Team's new owner has recently announced an

Table 15.1 Number of stadia by continent, 2000–2003

Continent	New	Existing/refurbished
America and Canada	24	29
Europe	26	13
Asia Pacific	20	6
Total	70	48

Source: Stevens & Associates (2003).

Table 15.2 Number of stadia by country

Country	New	Existing/refurbished
USA	23	25
Canada	1	4
Brazil	1	–
UK	15	7
Germany	3	2
Portugal	6	–
Russia	1	–
Croatia	–	1
Norway	–	1
Switzerland	1	–
Netherlands	–	1
Spain	–	1
Korea	11	–
Japan	7	1
Dubai	1	–
Australia	–	2
Singapore	–	2
China	–	1
Total	70	48

Source: Stevens & Associates (2003).

Table 15.3 Completion of stadia, 2001–2008

	2001	2002	2003	2004	2005	2006	2007	2008	Total
New (56 known out of 70 new)	28	13	5	7	1	1	–	1	56
Refurbished*	1	1	1	1	–	–	–	–	4
Total	29	14	6	8	1	1	–	1	60

Notes: * Six other projects have confirmed refurbishment, but the completion dates are unknown: Barcelona, Parc del Barca; Brighton Centre; Charlotte Hornets Arena; Rosenborg FC; Sydney Cricket Club; Wisconsin, Camp Randall University.
Source: Stevens & Associates (2001).

ambitious scheme to establish a 75 000 capacity stadium with one million square feet of exhibition halls and a convention hotel in Manhattan as part of a long-term scheme to attract the Olympics to the City in 2012. The project could be completed by 2008, and involves costs of $US 2 billion.

It is estimated that the current programme of investment represented by the developments totals some $18.7 billion. Capital investment across these developments is in excess of $169 million per stadium. Clearly, therefore, this represents one of the most significant areas of leisure investment in the world. Indeed, as Radley (former Editor of *Panstadia*) said in an editorial: 'a modern city is not a global player unless it has at least two, modern, 50 000 capacity stadia'.

Each country has a different model of capital funding for its schemes. In the USA, municipal and private bonds, tourism/hotel taxes, sponsorship and private funds are the typical range of sources. In Europe the ownership of stadia is more complex, with many still in public ownership (as in Germany and France) whilst in Britain and Spain stadia are owned by the sports clubs – few of whom are actually publicly quoted companies, or publicly owned. Under these circumstances there is more scope for public sector investment and investment from Lottery funds as well as from sponsors. In Asia there appears to be a stronger public sector involvement with new projects. These increasingly engage the private sector in joint venture schemes, but are driven by the desire to capture the global events whilst realizing real estate investment opportunities.

Without doubt, the primary motivation for stadia owners and operators to develop visitor facilities is directly related to the need to generate non-sporting income revenue as well as use of the facilities and the staff. As a result, stadia are actively developing new business models that incorporate conference and meetings facilities along with restaurants and other methods of attracting casual visitors. It is widely recognized that, in a European context, the major soccer clubs in Britain have developed a business model that has transformed stadia into profit centres, with much of the £1 billion that has been spent on Premiership stadia over the past 11 years being geared to this new business model.

In the excellent *Annual Review of Football Finance*, Deloitte & Touche (2003) analyse the financial performance of England's '92 Premiership and Nationwide League Clubs. The *Annual Review* identifies English football as the most financially powerful football leagues in Europe. One of the reasons for this powerbase is that:

> in recent years, the ability of football clubs to diversify their revenue
> profile has been perhaps their greatest success, and it will be critical to

future success ... the key is in developing stadia that are flexible enough to maximize non-match day income.

Stadia as the tourist attraction

Increasingly, it is not simply a stadium's role as the venue for events that attract tourists on an occasional basis that is of interest. It is the potential for the stadium to become an attraction in its own right and to provide the core of a mixed leisure and tourism development trading on a year-round basis that interests operators (Stevens, 1992, 1994).

The potential for sports stadia to be developed as all-year-round, 18-hours-a-day visitor attractions is closely linked to the growth in the day visitor market and in special interest tourism, as well as urban tourism marketing, which includes travel to watch sport. In the USA, the remarkable transformation achieved by the Indiana Sports Movement, translating 'Indiana-no-place' to 'The Star of the Snowbelt', is testimony to an integrated tourism and sport strategy featuring world-class sports stadia and arenas. A similar approach also prevails in Lausanne in Switzerland. The emergence of successful tourism programmes centred on stadia and arena development is also evidenced in St Louis, Chicago and Calgary. Sheffield, Barcelona, Cardiff, Manchester and Vancouver have also restructured (or intend to restructure) their tourism product, based upon their stadia infrastructure.

Domed facilities in Atlanta (Georgia Dome and Philips Arena), Amsterdam (ArenA) and Tokyo (Fukuoka Dome) extend this concept by providing real multiple-use options, especially for convention and conference markets. Consequently, there should be a much closer relationship between sport, the stadium and tourism. Rarely, however, has the potential of the stadium location been exploited as it has, for example, in the case of FC Barcelona (Spain), where the existing museum attracts 500000 and where the club is now proposing a multi-million pound sports theme park wrapped around the Nou Camp.

Whilst stadium tours are commonplace and feature in most venues, most potential exists in the development of stadia as sports-based visitor attractions, especially since the attractions industry is dynamic and anxious to find new applications and settings in which to create exciting visitor experiences. The inherent appeal of stadia as special places where heroes play and legends are made gives them the type of attributes on which more recognized visitor attractions are based – atmosphere, sense of occasion, evocation and emotion.

It is apparent that an important part of the appeal of the stadium as a visitor attraction is its potential to give visitors a real experience of 'Sport as heritage' (Stevens, 2003). This concept has been explored in academic terms (see Filger, 1981; Holt, 1989; Taylor, 1991) and has found its way into popular literature, as evidenced in Dylan Thomas' *Boys of Summer*, Paul Gallico's *Goodbye to Sport* and Nicholas Princes' 1950s thriller *Cup Final Murder*. More recently stadia have been given a place of honour in the literature of sport in, for example, *The End* by Tom Watt (1993) and *From Hendford to Huish Park* by Kerry Miller (1999).

This link between sport, stadia and popular culture has developed an interesting new dimension in Europe in the past 3 years. This relates to the growth of the low-cost airlines such as Ryanair, easyJet and bmibaby. These services, which have already captured 35 per cent of all outgoing air travel from the UK into Europe, are reporting significant levels of business based upon customers taking weekend breaks to their Italian, Spanish and German destinations to watch soccer.

It is surprising, therefore, that since sport makes a significant contribution to cultural identity and heritage, there are very few sports-based visitor attractions outside the USA. In the UK, for example, these are limited to museums at Manchester United, Chelsea, Liverpool, Bolton, Aston Villa and Arsenal football clubs; the recently opened National Football Museum at Preston; the Wimbledon Tennis Museum; the Newmarket Horseracing Museum; and the British Golf Museum, which opened at St Andrews in 1990, joining the number of traditional-style, rather staid presentations (Table 15.4).

Examples from North America illustrate the most advanced application of the visitor attraction concept; that is 'the sports hall of fame', which uses sport as the dominant theme. Even here, however, the attractions are often traditional museum-style presentations, yet there is considerable scope to develop and apply techniques, designs and technologies from the wider leisure industry (especially theme parks) to create a new generation of sports attractions offering exciting visitor potential and generating significant and commercially viable levels of attendance. However, this does not appear to have been an important consideration; rather, the genesis for their location tends to be non-market related criteria, such as the location of administrative offices or the owners' desire to convert a hobby into a public display. Most are located outside the main metropolitan areas, and when compared

Table 15.4 A selection of European sports visitor attractions

Attraction	*Location*
The Olympic Museum	Lausanne, Switzerland
National Sports Museum	Paris, France
National Sports Museum	Helsinki, Finland
Sports Museum	Tartu, Estonia
Swiss Sports Museum	Basle, Switzerland
Flemish Museum of Sport	Louvain, Belgium
Museum of Sport	Prague, Czech Republic
National Ski Museum	Oslo, Norway
National Rowing Museum	Limerick, Ireland
Cricket Museum	London, England
Tennis Museum	Wimbledon, England
Horseracing Museum	Newmarket, England
Rugby Museum	Edinburgh, Scotland
Gaelic Athletics	Thurles, Ireland
Musée de la Pelote	Bayonne, France
Barcelona FC Museum	Barcelona, Spain
Manchester United FC Museum	Manchester, England
Liverpool FC Museum	Liverpool, England
Golf Museum	St Andrews, Scotland
Museum of Physical Culture	Poland
Museum Nacional do Desporto	Lisbon, Portugal
Museum of the Olympic Games	Olympia, Greece
Museum of Olympics	Lisbon, Portugal

Source: Stevens & Associates (1998).

to the geography of major league franchises (and hence major stadium developments) it is apparent that the opportunity physically to link sports stadia with visitor attractions has largely been missed. Consequently, only a handful of the sports halls of fame have visitor figures in excess of 150 000 per annum (Table 15.5). This will change.

A new generation of sporting visitor attractions is now emerging. For example, at Turner Field in Atlanta, 'Home of the Braves', a new interactive plaza entertains fans before games and at other times. A similar concept has been deployed to a lesser extent at Chelsea FC in London, and in the master plan concept for a number of other stadia. The potential for modern visitor attractions offering broad market appeal is an obvious development for stadia. A 'World of Rugby' at Cardiff Millennium Stadium, Newcastle's Helix Centre, the Dallas Cowboys' Experience and the Olympic Spirit in Toronto are forerunners of a new and exciting trend.

The stadium as a potential host venue for these developments is a logical proposition to meet the criteria for a new sports visitor attraction, and should be reviewed positively for this purpose. The infrastructure is generally in place or put in place; space, facilities and services are available, the site is an appropriate setting, often steeped in history, and, given the desire amongst owners to achieve optimum use, the current momentum to build and rejuvenate stadia could embrace the potential to include wider, year-round visitor attractions. It does not automatically follow, however, that the location is capable of optimizing visitor markets, and the emphasis must be on identifying locations likely to achieve high levels of attendance and where the public's awareness of the attraction is underpinned by exposure to large numbers.

Table 15.5 United States halls of fame and annual visitor numbers

Sport	Stadium	State	Average annual visitors
General	College Campus	Alabama	25 000
Sport Car	Knoxville Raceway	Idaho	25 000
Baseball	Cardinal Stadium	Missouri	40 000
Horseracing	Churchill Downs	Kentucky	200 000
Football	Lambeau Field	Wisconsin	60 000
Trapshot	Ohio State Shoot	Ohio	2 000
Horseracing	Kentucky Horse Park	Kentucky	42 000
Swimming	Ft Lauderdale Complex	Florida	250 000
Lacrosse	Homewood Field	Maryland	10 000
Trotting	Goshen Track	New York	15 000
Tennis	Newport Casino	Rhode Island	50 000
Horseracing	Kentucky Horse Park	Kentucky	175 000
Baseball	Camden Yards	Maryland	61 000
Golf	Sheraton Hills	California	30 000
Softball	Fame Stadium	Oklahoma	28 000
Motor Racing	Talladega Speedway	Alabama	98 000
Motor Racing	Daytona Int. Speedway	Florida	Unknown
Motor Racing	Indy 500	Indiana	120 000
Track & Field	Hoosier Dome	Indiana	10 000
General	Hoosier Dome	Indiana	10 000

Source: Stevens & Associates (2000).

At the same time, schemes must build upon the physical and psychological sense of place essential to creating the right environment to enhance the visitor experience. However, the 'real' potential of a stadium or arena depends much more on the interrelationship between other factors, such as location; catchment area; the nature, structure and organization of the sports that are played in them; the characteristics and demands of spectator and market trends; and the stage of the stadium's development.

Tourism-related developments at new stadia

A high percentage of the new generation of stadia being developed are purposely embracing this tourism potential (Table 15.6). The mix of development is varied, but includes a typical range of urban-based leisure products such as family entertainment centres with interactive games, halls of fame/museums, multiplex cinemas and/or large-screen format cinemas (IMAX), and theme parks. All include entertainment and hospitality facilities as well as multiple-use spaces for exhibitions, conferences and conventions.

Increasingly, hotels are becoming an important component of the development, often being incorporated into the design and structure of the stadium itself. This is the case with De Vere's Hotel at Bolton Wanderers' Reebok Stadium (England), the Marriott Renaissance Hotel in Toronto's Skydome, the proposed hotel in the North Stand of Bayer Leverkusen football stadium (Germany) and the new Shanghai Stadium. Elsewhere, the Singapore Turf Club and the Sydney Cricket Ground are also considering hotel schemes.

Within this broad spectrum of real estate investments, some highly innovative tourism schemes have emerged. These include:

- Interactive game-day experiences (e.g. Cincinnati, Anaheim, MCI Washington)
- Theme parks (e.g. Turner Field, Atlanta and Coamerica Park, Detroit)
- Entertainment centres (e.g. Gaylord Center, Nashville and Seattle Center)
- Multiple sports campus (e.g. Homebush in Sydney, Cardiff in UK, Freiburg in Germany and Dublin in Ireland)
- Comprehensive leisure destinations (e.g. New York Meadowlands, Chicago Lakefront First Initiative, Milwaukee's Miller Park, Columbus Nationwide Arena and Amsterdam ArenA).

Table 15.6 Type of tourism-related facilities

	Mall/ plaza	Hotel	Theme park	Interactive games	Museum HOF	Park/ gardens	Cinema/ IMAX	Ents	Education facility	Other sport
Number	34	20	6	7	18	18	8	15	5	9
Integrated into stadia	22	12	2	4	13	–	–	7	2	–
Located on same site/ adjacent	12	8	4	3	5	18	8	8	3	9

Source: Stevens & Associates (2001).

All the evidence suggests that stadium investors will demand that the facilities are capable of generating higher operating revenues and that the developments lever out significant added value by attracting leading-brand tenants. Architects and designers are rising to these challenges by creating comprehensive leisure and tourism destinations in attractive settings around the stadia. City planners are anxious to ensure these developments are integrated with regional transport networks, and positively contribute to the city and regional economic regeneration. For tourist boards and the tourism industry these new destinations are a fundamental part of urban tourism in the new Millennium. Disney's entry into the sport tourism market, with its Florida-based 'Wide World of Sports' complex, has galvanized the market's interest in this interrelationship.

An analysis of the current range of stadia projects reveals three major development trends relevant to the evolving concept of the stadium as a tourist attraction. These three trends echo some of the innovation witnessed over the past 5 years (with the Amsterdam ArenA and the Dallas Cowboys' Experience), but serve to consolidate the merger of tourism interests with stadia developments. The trends are:

1   The creation of multi-use destination areas based upon a major stadium of 50 000 plus capacity. Examples include:
    – in Spain, Real Madrid's 'Cuidad del Madridisimo', a 1.25 million square metre development with a museum and football-based attractions
    – the Sportcity development at Manchester in England, where a 146-acre site includes the City of Manchester Stadium (built for the 2002 Commonwealth Games) as the anchor for a cluster of sports attractions
    – the Bergamo Sport Park in Northern Italy, which will include the new stadium for Atalanta, together with extensive tourism and entertainment facilities, close to the rapidly-growing Seriate Airport
    – the San Diego Padres' baseball stadium in California, which will become the centrepiece of a major baseball district, including a hall of fame, amphitheatre, artificial beach and hotels
    – Chicago's 'Soldier Field', one of the key venues in the 1994 Soccer World Cup, which is being redeveloped as part of the Lakefront First Initiative and will combine with existing attractions (Field Museum, Shedd Aquarium and the Adler Planetarium) to form a $US 587 million leisure sub-destination in the city
    – in Seattle, the Washington State Stadium, which is being built next to the Seattle Central Retail Mall to establish a major visitor destination that will include a multipurpose arena (home to the Sonics Basketball Team), a theme park and an IMAX theatre.
2   An investment in the aesthetics of stadia and their settings (architecture and design) as well as their amenities in order to reflect heritage, create visual icons and/or generate visitor interest and curiosity, as well as media coverage. Oriole Park in Baltimore was one of the first of the new generation of stadia to be designed to capture the atmosphere of the traditional baseball stadium. The current developments of this nature include:
    – the Detroit Tigers' Joker Marchant Stadium in Lakeland Florida for their summer training programme, which reflects the region's architectural style and includes echoes of the original World War II flying school at the site,

217

with watch towers and the retention of a picnic berm for casual enjoyment of the game
- the Green Bay Packers' Lambeau Field Stadium, which is a 72 500 capacity stadium originally built in 1959 but where, in 2002, renovation works at a cost of $295 million created 'The Atrium', a multipurpose 1400 capacity hospitality venue
- the Charlotte Ericsson Stadium in Carolina, which is a 73 200 capacity stadium that has been specifically designed for American Football at the heart of the city centre; the design includes unique architectural features such as towers and massive arches clad in materials accenting the team's colours of black, silver and panther blue
- the Seoul World Cup Stadium, which was designed to represent the Korean kite, representing spirit and hope
- Istanbul's Ataturk Stadium (completed in 2001 in readiness for Turkey's proposed bid to host the 2012 Olympics), which has a crescent-shaped roof, representing the country's national symbol.

3   Investment to make the stadium itself an attraction, with developments within the fabric of the building that go beyond what has become expected (such as conference facilities, museums, tours and hotels). Recent innovations related to tourism include:
- a proposed casino at the Montreal Expos Park in Canada
- a mini-theme park at Detroit's Coamerica Park
- a theatre and cabaret at Dortmund's Westfalenstadion in Germany
- a sun and pool spa pavilion at the Arizona Diamondbacks' new Bank One Ballpark in the USA.

Conclusions

Stadia and future tourism developments: the next 10 years

The promotional literature for the Amsterdam ArenA describes the arena as being at the heart of a new urban concept for the twenty-first century. 'ArenA Boulevard' will be a 300 000 square metre complex that embraces leisure, tourism, work and residential developments wrapped around the sports complex. Developed by a joint public/private venture, the tourism offer includes a 14-screen multiplex, a music concert hall, a health and entertainment complex, and an 80 000 square metre retail provision. This model of urban development has wider application when associated with stadium developments.

The key to harnessing this potential is the shared use of infrastructure, capturing significant volumes of visitors attending events and sporting occasions in the stadium, and using the stadium as the physical landmark (or icon) within the cityscape. All stadia have their own restaurants, bars, conference and meeting rooms that need to be used year round. There is therefore a synergy that binds this form of mixed development. The competition amongst countries to host the mega-sporting events shows no sign of abating. Decisions will soon be made to allocate the Olympics and the World Cup competitions until 2016 and beyond. This automatically creates a requirement to invest in the stock of sports facilities in each host country.

Consequently, major investment in sports stadia will continue for the next 10–15 years.

There will be increasing pressure upon the governing bodies of sport and event organizers to take these events to emerging economies. Consequently, the next phase of stadia investments will take place in South America, Africa and Eastern Europe. At the same time, cities in America and Western Europe with stadia stock that is already ageing (even though some of the developments are less than 20 years old) will redevelop or build anew. In every instance, there will be a requirement to examine how the stadium can contribute to the tourism appeal of the destination. This requirement will emerge from the need to capture a share of the special interest and urban tourism markets, and to achieve greater utilization of the facilities. At the same time, destinations are increasingly in need of strong images and icon buildings upon which to base their tourism promotions. Stadia can help to meet this challenge.

References

Andranovich, A., Burbank, M. J. and Heying, C. H. (2001). Olympic cities: lessons learned. *Journal of Urban Affairs*. 23(2), 113–131.

Bale, J. (1989). *Sports Geography*. London: E & FN Spon.

Cosgrove, S. (2003). Think out of the box. *Proceedings of the European Travel and Tourism Research Association Meeting*, August, Glasgow. Glasgow: TTRA.

Crompton, J. (1992). The role of image and perceived constraints in the tourist's destination decision process. *Journal of Travel Research*, 30(3).

Deloitte & Touche (2003). *Annual Review of Football Finance 2002–2003*. Manchester: Deloitte & Touche.

Dyer, M. (2002). New plans to target growth in tourism. *The Journal*, 17, 2–4.

Filger, S. (1981). *Sport and Play in American Life*. Philadelphia, PN: Saunders Press.

Friel, E. (2003). *Personal Correspondence*. CEO, Greater Glasgow and Clyde Valley Tourist Board.

Getz, D. (1992). *Special Event Tourism and Festivals*. New York: Van Doren Rheinhold.

Gratton, C., Dobson, N. and Shibli, S. (2000). The economic importance of major sports events: a case study of six events. *Managing Leisure*, 5(1), 17–28.

Gray, D. (2003). A new stadium for Milton Keynes. In J. Ladd and L. Davis (eds), *BURA Guide to Best Practice in Sport and Regeneration*. London: British Urban Regeneration Association, pp. 41–51.

HMSO (1990). *The Taylor Report: The Hillsborough Stadium Disaster*. Cmnd 962. London: HMSO.

Holt, R. (1989). *Sport and the British*. London: Clarendon Press.

Humphreys, B. (2003). The final comment. In J. Ladd and L. Davis (eds), *BURA Guide to Best Practice in Sport and Regeneration*. London: British Urban Regeneration Association, pp. 75–78.

Inglis, S. (1993). *New Directions in Stadium Design*. London: Building Centre.

Kotler, P. (1993). *Marketing Places*. New York: The Free Press.

Ladd, J. and Davis, L. (2003). *BURA Guide to Best Practice in Sport and Regeneration*. London: British Urban Regeneration Association.

219

Lipsitz, G. (1984). *Sports Stadia and Arenas*. New York: Urban Land Institute.

Luciani, R. (1990). *The Colosseum*. Rome: De Agostini.

Maison, P. (2003). Football stadia relocations and development: town planning, design and transport considerations. In J. Ladd and L. Davis (eds), *BURA Guide to Best Practice in Sport and Regeneration*. London: British Urban Regeneration Association, pp. 59–73.

Miller, K. (1999). *From Hendford to Huish Park*. Yeovil: Yeovil Town FC.

Neill, W. (1993). Physical planning and image enhancement. *International Journal of Urban and Regional Research*, 17(4).

Petersen, D. (1990). *Convention Centres, Stadia and Arenas*. New York: Urban Land Institute.

Seaton, A. and Bennett, M. (1996). *Marketing Tourism Products – Concepts, Issues and Cases*. London: Thompson Business Press.

Stevens, T. (1992). *Stadia – The Sleeping Giants of Tourism*. Washington, DC: CHRIE Conference Proceedings.

Stevens, T. (1994). Sports stadia and arenas. In A. Seaton, C. Jenkins, R. Wood, P. Dieke, M. Bennett, R. MacLellan and R. Smith (eds), *Tourism: State of the Art*, pp. 238–245. London: John Wiley & Son.

Stevens, T. (2001). Stadia and tourism related facilities. *Travel and Tourism Analyst*, 2, 59–73.

Stevens, T. (2003). *Sport and Tourism: The Essential Partnership*. Inaugural Professorial Lecture, Dundee Business School.

Taylor, R. (1991). *Football and its Fans*. Leicester: Leicester University Press.

Trafford Metropolitan Borough Council (2000). *Seize the Opportunity: Tourism Strategy*. Manchester: Trafford MBC.

UK Sports (1998). *Major Events: A Blueprint for Success*. London: UK Sports.

Watt, T. (1993). *The End*. London: Mainstream Publishing.

Weed, M. and Bull, C. (2004). *Sports Tourism: Participants, Policy and Providers*. Oxford: Elsevier Butterworth-Heinemann.

Whitson, D. and Macintosh, D. (1993). Becoming a world-class city: hallmark events and sport franchises in the growth strategies of western Canadian cities. *Sociology of Sport Journal*, 12, 21–40.

Part Four: Sport Tourism Impacts and Environments

16

Introduction to sport tourism impacts and environments

James Higham

Sport tourism, like any other form of tourism, brings both positive and negative impacts to bear upon tourism destinations. The impacts associated with sport tourism are inevitably viewed subjectively by different stakeholder groups (Mathieson and Wall, 1987; McKercher, 1993; Hunter and Green, 1995). This inevitability arises from the fact that the social, cultural, economic and environmental contexts of a destination are complex and interconnected. The sustainable development of sport tourism destinations necessitates that destination planners, tourism organizations and industry players are aware of the social, cultural, economic and environmental impacts of sport tourism (Hunter, 1995; Cantelon and Letters, 2000). The following chapters explore the economic, socio-cultural and physical manifestations of sport tourism, and how these manifestations evolve over time at sport tourism destinations.

It has been noted in Part Two (Chapter 8) that the rationale for the planning and development of sport tourism initiatives is generally economic. The economic impacts of sport tourism are multifaceted. They include interests in return on government investment in sports facilities, construction, expenditures generated by professional sports teams, media- and sport-related business travel, and visitor expenditures associated with sports institutes and other training facilities. Despite these wide-ranging economic interests in sport tourism, much attention has hitherto focused on the expenditures generated in association with sports events, and most particularly with spectator travel.

The Sport Industry Research Centre (Sheffield Hallam University) has been at the forefront of research into the economic impacts generated by different sports. Gratton *et al.* (2000) present an economic impact study of six sports events hosted in British cities and towns in 1997. Their research highlights the varied visitor experiences and expenditure patterns that are associated with different sports. Sports vary in the extent to which they are competitor and/or spectator driven. The manner in which different sports generate different types of sport tourists is highly relevant to the development interests of tourism destinations. The duration and timing of sports events and competitions also influence economic outcomes (Gratton *et al.*, 2000). Thus sports contested at different levels of competition offer different degrees of opportunity for both competitors and spectators to engage in visitor activities at a destination. The profile of sport tourists, which varies considerably between sports, is also of interest to destination managers. The market profiles of spectators associated with sports such as polo, equestrian, tennis and golf on one hand, and surfing, club football and adventure sports on the other, offer stark contrasts in terms of demographic and psychographic characteristics, travel patterns and economic impacts.

Some sports markets are typically gender-based (e.g. club football – male; netball – female), while others may be dominated by niche markets that centre on youth (e.g. surfing, snowboarding), family (e.g. cricket, baseball), mature markets (e.g. golf, tennis), affluence (e.g. polo, equestrian) or commercial interests (e.g. Superbowl American football, America's Cup yachting). These sports offer the contrasts of quite distinct participant and spectator markets (Loverseed, 2001), with important implications for tourist experiences and expenditure patterns (Gratton *et al.*, 2000). It is also evident that different tourist expenditures are associated with different levels of sports competition (Reeves, 2001). Professional sports attract a wider catchment of sports fans as well as media, commercial and sponsors' interests. Similarly, competitive sports are usually pursued with a single-minded focus, although touristic/leisure activities may be an important part of preparations for competition or may be pursued at the conclusion of competition. By contrast, recreational participation in sports is often free of rigid time constraints, which offers wider possibilities for engagement in tourist activities at the destination. The timing, pacing and duration of an event or sport contest may also facilitate or inhibit engagement in tourist activities at a destination. Thus the spatial and temporal planning of sports events may strongly influence gate receipts and visitor expenditures (Jones, 2001).

While the defining qualities of different sports will inevitably mediate the expenditure patterns associated with those sports, a range of circumstances relating to the tourist experience will also influence the economic impacts of sport tourism (Hinch and Higham, 2004). The investment of discretionary time and money in accessing a destination influences length of stay and, therefore, many aspects of the visitor experience (Collier, 1999). While proximity to sports resources offers the advantages of market access, this will also mediate the duration of visits to the destination. Length of stay is closely related to visitor experiences at a destination and, therefore, visitor expenditures (Nogawa *et al.*, 1996). The distinction between excursionists (or day visitors) and tourists (those who remain at the destination for a minimum of one night) is particularly relevant to the visitor experience. Levels of engagement in non-sport activities at a destination vary significantly between tourists and excursionists, but will also be influenced by factors such as first-time or repeat visitor status. Godbey and Graefe (1991) provide clear evidence of changing (and generally declining) visitor expenditures among repeat visitors. This would indicate that in cases where sports markets are highly loyal (e.g. Masters games competitors, see Chapter 13), event managers, sports organizations and tourism managers must innovate to promote novelty and retain the loyalty of participant and spectator markets.

Sport tourism development interests are also closely tied to the physical resource base, both natural and built. The existence of most sports at a destination is determined by specific resource requirements. Tourism destinations may achieve a distinct advantage over competing destinations through investment in modern world-class sports facilities. Furthermore, destinations may be managed and promoted to develop new or exploit existing links to specific sports. The intensive development of integrated golf resorts in Spain, ski resorts in Eastern Europe, Nordic ski facilities in Finland and facilities and services to serve adventure sport pursuits in New Zealand are examples that illustrate the development of specific facilities and services to cater for niche sports markets. Event sport tourism development at a destination requires, in most cases, constructed resources, including sport facilities and tourism infrastructure. Sports may require the use of facilities that are purpose-built, such as stadia, marinas, sports halls and gymnasiums. Alternatively, sports may take place at venues/locations that are used temporarily (Hinch and Higham, 2004), and here, again, specific impact issues need to be carefully considered.

An understanding of the impacts of sport tourism, and management techniques appropriate to those impacts, is critical to the development interests of sport tourism destinations. Growth in demand for sports, and the changing resource requirements of sports, may place considerable demands upon built and natural environments (Bale, 1989). Many sports are associated with both short-term and long-term impact issues. Sports that attract significant groups of spectators may generate immediate impacts, including traffic congestion and crowding, vandalism, anti-social behaviour, littering and breaches of security. These impacts may disrupt the lives of community residents, generate host community resentment or antagonism, and contribute to aversion effects that can detract from tourism interests at a destination (Faulkner *et al.*, 1998). Longer-term impacts include degradation of natural landscapes, which may also be associated with long-term damage to tourism interests. May (1995), for example, reports upon the long-term environmental implications, including permanent and irreversible environmental damage, associated with the 1992 Albertville (France) Winter Olympic Games. This sports event may in fact be implicated in the stagnation of international ski markets in response to the unsustainable management of environmentally sensitive alpine environments (Hudson, 1999; Flagestad and Hope, 2001).

The impacts associated with sport tourism in urban and natural destination contexts vary considerably. The latter centre in many cases upon the management of environments that are fragile and sensitive to disturbance. The speed with which new sports emerge and develop poses considerable planning and management challenges. The transition from an emerging sport pursued by relatively few to a mass participation phenomenon may take place in a short space of time (Standeven and De Knop, 1999). The potential consequences that may be associated with the rapid rise in popularity of sports such as mountain biking, snowboarding and scuba diving need to be understood and managed by destination organizations. The establishment and implementation of appropriate policies and management strategies are also required to protect the natural resources at activity sites, particularly where sports take place in fragile environments. The impacts of sport tourism in alpine ecologies may, due to extremes of altitude and climate, require extended recovery and regeneration timeframes, long-term monitoring and appropriate management interventions (Holden, 2000; Flagestad and Hope, 2001). Unless the impacts of sports are carefully managed, the long-term viability of sport tourism destinations will be compromised.

The socio-cultural context of sport tourism is also susceptible to impact. The experiences of sport tourists are a function of interactions with the place where sports take place, and the communities of people who reside in those places (Standeven and De Knop, 1999). Sports may contribute to a unique visitor experience, and sports may also contribute in important ways to the uniqueness of the destinations where tourism takes place. Hinch and Higham (2004) observe that the evolution of many sports in recent decades has involved a general trend towards the standardization of venues for sports. This trend has been driven by demands to maximize spectator and participant comfort and safety, and to standardize playing conditions. Such trends counter interests in developing tourism destinations that are unique and differentiated from competing destinations. Sports may contribute significantly to the uniqueness of tourism destinations through cultural programmes aligned with sport events, sport as a form of popular culture and sport subcultures. Each of these cultural dimensions influence place identity and, potentially, place marketing for tourism. The careful management of sports and sports events is required in order for this outcome to be achieved.

The relationships that exist between sport tourism and the social, cultural, economic and environmental contexts of a destination are constantly evolving. The success with which these impacts are understood and managed influences the sustained success or failure of sport tourism destinations. Destination and product lifecycles are dominant features of tourism (Christaller, 1963/1964; Plog, 1972; Doxey, 1975; Stansfield, 1978). Butler's (1980) tourist area lifecycle model captures the idea that tourism destinations evolve through stages. Central to this theory is the notion that increasing visitation and the development of tourism products takes place in association with the various resources for tourism that are available at a destination. At some point those resources, be they physical, financial, infrastructural or human, may be adversely affected. This model confirms the importance of informed and deliberate management of tourism development if tourism resources are to be sustained.

Sport may play a significant role in the evolution of destinations through the stages of the destination lifecycle. For instance, sports are increasingly being used in tourism strategies that aim to develop or rejuvenate tourism destinations (Case study 16.1). The constant evolution and adaptation of sports gives rise to changing allocation preferences and resource requirements associated with specific sports. As participant and spectator demands change, so new opportunities emerge for sport tourism destinations (Keller, 2001).

Case study 16.1 Queenstown, New Zealand: the use of sports to perpetuate the sustained success of a tourism destination

Queenstown is New Zealand's premier international resort destination. Situated on Lake Wakatipu within the wider Central Otago (South Island) lakes district, the landscape of the region is predominantly alpine in character, and Queenstown is located in close proximity to Mount Aspiring and Fiordland national parks. The sustained success of this destination has been built for over half a century upon sport-related tourism developments. A sequence of nature-based sport developments and innovations in the domain of adventure sports has entrenched Queenstown's undisputed status as New Zealand's premier domestic and international tourism destination.

The evolution of Queenstown as an international tourism resort dates to the development of ski facilities, initially at Coronet Peak, in 1953. At that time tourism in Queenstown was primarily domestic, summer-based and highly seasonal. Rapid tourism development took place due to the transformation of Queenstown into an all-season domestic and international tourism destination (Hall and Kearsley, 2001). Subsequent alpine ski field developments in the Queenstown Lakes region at the Remarkables and Cardrona, and nordic ski facilities at Waiorau have emphasized the status of Queenstown as a winter sports destination. The Queenstown Winter Festival (QWF), inaugurated in 1974, was developed specifically to cement this status. QWF was the first event in New Zealand to be developed specifically to serve regional economic development and tourism functions (Higham and Ritchie, 2001). It now marks the opening of the winter sports season with a 2-week celebration that includes concerts, extreme ski events (e.g. Air New Zealand big air event), multi-sport races and media and celebrity events.

It is important to note that in addition to facility and event development, this success has been achieved through constant innovation and responsiveness to changing technologies and evolving tourist demands. Responsiveness to new technologies is demonstrated through the adoption of snow-making facilities, investment in high-speed detachable quad chair lifts, and floodlighting to allow for night skiing during the height of the ski season (July–September). Evolving consumer demands have resulted in the development of wide trails and purpose-built half pipes to cater for the emergence of the snowboarder phenomenon, and the designation of slow zones to meet the needs of new participants in skiing and snowboarding. The development of base facilities, including restaurants, bars and cafés, equipment rentals, a licensed crèche and guest services, aim, once again, to satisfy desired visitor experiences.

The emergence of Queenstown as a sport tourism destination was further advanced through the development of adventure sports in the 1970s. Jet boating began on the Shotover River in 1963, but the commercial development of jet boating as a tourist activity took place in the 1970s, on both the Shotover and Kawarau Rivers, catering initially for 'thrill seekers' who were predominantly aged between 20 and 35 and principally Australian (Kearsley, 1992). Rafting was commercially introduced on the Shotover River in 1973, catering for a similar visitor profile. In the 1970s, no Asian tourists were carried by either commercial jet boat or rafting operations. During the 1980s the jet boat and rafting markets expanded considerably to include the major Asian inbound visitor markets, as these activities became major attractions within the Queenstown region, and as a new generation of adventure sports was spawned.

In the 1980s a new wave of innovation in the adventure sports industry was centred upon the Queenstown region, giving rise to the reputation of Queenstown as the 'adventure capital of the world'. The commercial development of bungy jumping was innovated by A. J. Hackett and Henry van Asch in the mid-1980s. They achieved international prominence in 1987, when Hackett bungy jumped from the Eiffel Tower. The Kawarau Bridge (43 m) was established as the first commercial bungy site in the world in November 1988, to which the Bungy Dome multi-media experience was added in 2003. Subsequent variations of the bungy experience have been innovated, including Skippers Canyon bungy (71 m), the Nevis high-wire bungy (at 134 m, the highest in Australasia) and heli-bungy. More recent has been the introduction of the ledge bungy and ledge swing, which take place from the summit of Bob's Peak (400 m above central Queenstown) at the Skyline Gondola terminus, which stands immediately overlooking the town centre of Queenstown and Lake Wakatipu. The development of commercial bungy operations is mirrored by the proliferation of other adventure sports in Queenstown, such as parapenting, tandem hang gliding, white water kayaking, wilderness rafting, heli-skiing, the 'swoop and soar' controllable 'rocket' and the Coronet Peak luge. These developments, but most particularly the innovation and commercial development of bungy jumping, have further perpetuated sport-related tourism development in this region.

Since 1990 the sustained success of Queenstown as a sport tourism destination has continued with the development of Millbrook resort as a world-class international golf resort, guided wilderness fishing and the successful bidding and hosting of world championship sports events, most notably the 2003 World Triathlon championships. Bidding to host the Winter Olympic Games (with Christchurch, New Zealand) and the hosting of Masters winter sports events continues this trend. Queenstown's status as a tourism destination is due in large part to the intrinsic beauty of the alpine lakes environment, and in more recent years the growing film-making and wine industries have contributed significantly to this success. However, through the last five decades a sequence of sports-related developments and innovations has established and entrenched the status of Queenstown as New Zealand's premier tourism destination.

Like tourism destinations, the popularity of different sports evolves over time. While the popularity of sports such as recreational running and skiing has waned since the 1970s, the sport of skateboarding was rejuvenated in the 1990s, during which time new sports such as mountain boarding, ultimate frisbee and kite surfing also emerged and increased in popularity. As skiing has entered into a period of decline, so snowboarding and extreme skiing have emerged. Snowboarding, once an alternative minority sport, has been rapidly commodified and indeed professionalized in recent years (Heino, 2000). The dynamics of modern sport have been typified in recent times by the stagnation of power and performance sports, which are typically structured and organized individual and team sports (Coakley, 2004). These have been succeeded in popularity by pleasure and participation sports, which are characterized by individualized, aesthetic and autonomous qualities (Murray and Dixon, 2000; Thomson, 2000; de Villiers, 2001; Keller, 2001). Pleasure and participation sports are also subject to social and economic forces that may cause them to become increasingly mainstreamed (Hinch and Higham, 2004). As the popularity of sports such as beach volleyball, snowboarding and windsurfing increases, so structures and rules begin to form to ensure the activity is managed in a way that facilitates measurements of performance and commodification (Hoffer, 1995). These sports are, at least initially, relatively free of the formal organizational structures of power and performance sports which are generally governed by national or international sports organizations (e.g. the International Rugby Board, International Cricket Council and Federation Internationale de Football Association). These sports may evolve rapidly, or develop hybrid forms that may complement the particular natural or built resources of specific tourism destinations. These dynamics obviously influence the fortunes of tourism destinations where sports take place.

Part Four of this book addresses, in Chapters 16–20, the impacts, environments and resource constraints of sport tourism. In Chapter 17, Chris Gratton, Simon Shibli and Richard Coleman examine the economics of sport tourism relating to international and world championship sports events. They highlight the fact that as governments have implemented national sports policies that seek to attract major sports events, so competition has intensified to host international events relating to an increasing range of sports that differ in the extent to which they attract participants, spectators, sponsor interests and media. With this course of development in sport tourism has emerged heightened interest in understanding the economic consequences of 'lower-order' sports events. It is noteworthy that even sports mega-events are by no means an inevitable economic success story. Similar interests apply to professional sports teams. As cities have competed to attract and/or retain professional sports franchises, so public subsidization of professional sport, through stadium and training facility development, has increased. While government investment in sports stadiums has taken place without direct return on public investment, such public expenditures have been predicated on the assumption that significant economic benefits return to the local economy through service development and tourism.

Chapter 17 explores these issues, focusing particularly on the economics of sport tourism associated with major sports events. It is argued in this chapter that the economic impacts of sports events, particularly those generated by competitors, officials and media (less so spectators), can be accurately forecasted in advance of bidding to host sports events. Given the levels of local, regional or national government investment required to host international sports events, and the diversity of sports events that destinations seek to host, insights into the economics of sports events warrant close attention.

In Chapter 18, Mark Orams observes that the impacts of sport tourism on the natural environment have received remarkably little attention, particularly given the scale and importance of the sport and tourism industries. It is somewhat surprising that research dedicated to the specialized study of sport and tourism impacts on natural systems has been so neglected. To address the dearth of published material in the field, Orams applies concepts, approaches and theories established in the study of tourism in a consideration of the impacts of sport tourism upon natural environments. In doing so, Chapter 18 highlights the complexities inherent in understanding the impacts of sport tourism, and the causes of those impacts. This complexity arises in part from the diversity of sports and sport-related activities that take place in natural areas. Furthermore, the demands placed upon natural areas vary considerably between the developmental/facility requirements associated with sports (which are often long-term or irreversible), and the impacts that arise (through participation and spectatorship) when sports are actually being contested. While the former may be immediately observed, the latter may contribute long-term incremental changes to natural systems, which are no less significant in terms of the sustainable development of sport tourism destinations.

Sport tourism attractions, including stadia, sports facilities and nature-based venues for sport (e.g. ski slopes and mountain bike trails), represent the most obvious and tangible manifestations of sport tourism destination resources. However, Tom Hinch and Suzanne de la Barre argue in Chapter 19 that the cultural dimensions of sport may, if recognized, respected and appropriately managed, contribute in important ways to the uniqueness of tourism destinations and the authentic experience of sport tourism destinations. For sports organizations, destination managers and host communities this poses both a valuable opportunity and a considerable challenge. While the forces of professionalization and globalization have contributed to the homogenization of many sports, Hinch and de la Barre identify an entrenchment of heterogeneity in many regional and national sports. Despite changing circumstances in sport and tourism associated with commodification, globalization and control/partnership, there is considerable potential for sports organizations and tourism destination managers to achieve collaborative goals relating to sport tourism. Thus the competitiveness of sport tourism destinations may be enhanced where visitor experiences combine active or passive involvement in sports with elements of the culture of unique places.

The last chapter in Part Four considers the influence of sports on the development of tourism destinations. In Chapter 20, Richard Butler notes that tourism destinations have traditionally been developed based on specific environmental, climatic or cultural features that attract visitors. The development of destinations that lack conventional tourism resources may also be advanced, intentionally or otherwise, due to the uniqueness of specific places. Butler presents a detailed analysis of the case of St Andrews (Scotland), demonstrating that, while the economy of the town is diverse, tourism interests have been based largely upon the unique status of the town in terms of the historical development of the sport of golf. The manifestations of this association have included the diversification and expansion of sport and tourism facilities, the emergence of a recreational business district (RBD), and development of the retail and service functions of the destination. This chapter demonstrates the significant role that sports may play in the development of tourism destinations. However, it also highlights resource constraints and impact issues that may pose a considerable challenge to the sustainable development of sport tourism destinations.

References

Bale, J. (1989). *Sports Geography*. London: E & FN Spon.

Butler, R. W. (1980). The concept of the tourist area lifecycle of evolution: implications for the management of resources. *Canadian Geographer*, 24(1), 5–12.

Cantelon, H. and Letters, M. (2000). The making of the IOC Environmental Policy as the third dimension of the Olympic Movement. *International Review for the Sociology of Sport*, 35(3), 294–308.

Christaller, W. (1963/1964). Some considerations of tourism location in Europe: the peripheral regions – underdeveloped countries – recreation areas. *Papers, Regional Science Association*, 12, 95–105.

Coakley, J. (2004). *Sports in Society: Issues and Controversies* (8th edn). Boston: McGraw Hill Higher Education.

Collier, A. (1999). *Principles of Tourism: A New Zealand Perspective* (5th edn). Auckland: Longman.

de Villers, D. J. (2001). Sport and tourism to stimulate development. *Olympic Review*, 27(38), 11–13.

Doxey, G. (1975). *Visitor-Resident Interaction in Tourist Destinations: Inferences from Empirical Research in Barbados, West Indies and Niagara-on-the-Lake, Ontario*. Paper presented at the Symposium on the Planning and Development of the Tourist Industry in the ECC Region, Dubrovnik, Yugoslavia, 8–11 September.

Faulkner, B., Tideswell, C. and Weston, A. M. (1998). *Leveraging Tourism Benefits from the Sydney 2000 Olympics*. Paper presented at the Sport Management Association of Australia and New Zealand, Gold Coast, Australia, 26–28 November.

Flagestad, A. and Hope, C. A. (2001). Strategic success in winter sports destinations: a sustainable value creation perspective. *Tourism Management*, 22(5), 445–461.

Godbey, G. and Graefe, A. (1991). Repeat tourism, play and monetary spending. *Annals of Tourism Research*, 18(2), 213–225.

Gratton, C., Dobson, N. and Shibli, S. (2000). The economic importance of major sports events: a case-study of six events. *Managing Leisure*, 5(1), 17–28.

Hall, C. M. and Kearsley, G. W. (2001). *Tourism in New Zealand: An Introduction*. Melbourne: Oxford University Press.

Heino, R. (2000). What is so punk about snowboarding? *Journal of Sport and Social Issues*, 24(1), 176–191.

Higham, J. E. S. and Ritchie, B. W. (2001). Strategic management and rural event tourism in Southern New Zealand. *Event Management*, 7(1), 39–49.

Hinch, T. D. and Higham, J. E. S. (2004). *Sport Tourism Development*. Clevedon, OH: Channel View.

Hoffer, R. (1995). Down and out: on land, sea, air, facing questions about their sanity. *Sports Illustrated*, 83(1), 42–49.

Holden, A. (2000). Winter tourism and the environment in conflict: the case of Cairngorm, Scotland. *International Journal of Tourism Research*, 2(4), 247–260.

Hudson, S. (1999). *Snow Business: A Study of the International Ski Industry*. London: Cassell.

Hunter, C. (1995). Key concepts for tourism and the environment. In C. Hunter and H. Green (eds), *Tourism and the Environment: A Sustainable Relationship?* London: Routledge, pp. 52–92.

Hunter, C. and Green, H. (eds) (1995). *Tourism and the Environment: A Sustainable Relationship?* London: Routledge.

Jones, I. (2001). A model of serious leisure identification: the case of football fandom. *Leisure Studies*, 19(4), 283–298.

Kearsley, G. W. (1992). Tourism and resource development conflicts on the Kawarau and Shotover Rivers, Otago, New Zealand. *Geojournal*, 29(3), 263–270.

Keller, P. (2001). *Sport and Tourism: Introductory Report.* Paper presented at the World Conference on Sport and Tourism, Barcelona, Spain, 22–23 February. Madrid: World Tourism Organization.

Loverseed, H. (2001). Sports tourism in North America. *Travel and Tourism Analyst*, 3, 25–41.

Mathieson, D. and Wall, G. (1987). *Tourism: Economic, Physical and Social Impacts.* London: Longman.

May, V. (1995). Environmental implications of the 1992 Winter Olympic Games. *Tourism Management*, 16(4), 269–275.

McKercher, B. (1993). Some fundamental truths about tourism: understanding tourism's social and environmental impacts. *Journal of Sustainable Tourism*, 1(1), 6–16.

Murray, D. and Dixon, L. (2000). Investigating the growth of 'instant' sports: practical implications for community leisure service providers. *The ACHPER Healthy Lifestyles Journal*, 47(3/4), 27–31.

Nogawa, H., Yamaguchi, Y. and Hagi, Y. (1996). An empirical research study on Japanese sport tourism in sport-for-all events: case studies of a single-night event and a multiple-night event. *Journal of Travel Research*, 35(2), 46–54.

Plog, S. (1972). *Why Destination Areas Rise and Fall in Popularity.* Paper presented at the Southern California Chapter of the Travel Research Bureau, San Diego, USA, 10 October.

Reeves, M. R. (2001). *Evidencing the Sport–Tourism Relationship: A Case Study Approach.* Unpublished PhD thesis, Loughborough University.

Standeven, J. and De Knop, P. (1999). *Sport Tourism.* Champaign, IL: Human Kinetics.

Stansfield, C. J. (1978). The development of modern seaside resorts. *Parks and Recreation*, 5(10), 14–46.

Thomson, R. (2000). Physical activity through sport and leisure: traditional versus non-competitive activities. *Journal of Physical Education New Zealand*, 33(1), 34–39.

17

The economics of sport tourism at major sports events

Chris Gratton, Simon Shibli and
Richard Coleman

Introduction

The study of hallmark events or mega-events became
an important part of tourism literature in the 1980s.
Since then, the economics of sport tourism at major
sports events has become an increasing part of this
event tourism literature. Many governments around
the world have adopted national sports policies
that specify that hosting major sports events is a
major objective. A broad range of benefits has been
suggested for both the country and the host city
from staging major sports events, including urban
regeneration legacy benefits, sporting legacy benefits, tourism and image benefits, and social and
cultural benefits (DCMS/SU, 2002), as well as the
economic benefits which will be the main focus of
this chapter. It is well known that cities and countries compete fiercely to host the Olympic Games
or the soccer World Cup. However, over recent years
there has been increasing competition to host less
globally recognized sports events in a wide range of
other sports where spectator interest is less assured
and where the economic benefits are not so clear cut.
In this chapter we will analyse the benefits generated

across a wide range of sports events, from large spectator events staged as part of domestic professional team sports to World and European Championships. In this review we will concentrate on the economic benefits generated, but will also consider the economic and tourism implications of the broader benefits outlined above. To begin, we discuss the literature associated with hosting major sports events.

Literature on the economic benefits of hosting major sports events

The literature on the economics of major sports events is relatively recent. One of the first major studies in this area was the study of the impact of the 1985 Adelaide Formula 1 Grand Prix (Burns *et al.* 1986). This was followed by Brent Ritchie's in-depth study of the 1988 Calgary Winter Olympics (Ritchie, 1984; Ritchie and Aitken, 1984, 1985; Ritchie and Lyons 1987, 1990; Ritchie and Smith, 1991). In fact, immediately prior to these studies it was generally thought that hosting major sports events was a financial liability to host cities following the large debts faced by Montreal after hosting the 1976 Olympics. There was a general change in attitude following the 1984 Los Angeles Olympics, which made a clear profit.

Mules and Faulkner (1996) point out that even with such mega-events as Formula 1 Grand Prix races and the Olympics, there is not always an unequivocal economic benefit to the cities that host the event. They emphasize that, in general, staging major sports events often results in the city authorities losing money, even though the city itself benefits greatly in terms of additional spending in the city. Thus the 1994 Brisbane World Masters Games cost the city $A 2.8 million to organize but generated a massive $A 50.6 million of additional economic activity in the state economy. Mules and Faulkner's basic point is that it normally requires the public sector to finance the staging of the event, and incur these losses, in order to generate the benefits to the local economy. They argue that governments host such events and lose taxpayers' money in the process in order to generate spillover effects or externalities.

It is not a straightforward job, however, to establish a profit and loss account for a specific event. Major sports events require investment in new sports facilities, and often this is paid for in part by central government or even international sports bodies. Thus some of this investment expenditure represents a net addition to the local economy, since the money comes in from outside. Also such facilities remain after the event has finished, acting as a platform for future activities that can generate additional tourist expenditure (Mules and Faulkner, 1996).

Sports events are increasingly seen as part of a broader tourism strategy aimed at raising the profile of a city, and therefore success cannot be judged on simply profit and loss basics. Often the attraction of events is linked to a re-imaging process, and in the case of many cities is invariably linked to strategies of urban regeneration and tourism development (Bianchini and Schwengel, 1991; Roche, 1992; Bramwell, 1995; Loftman and Spirou, 1996; Collins and Jackson, 1999). Major events, if successful, have the ability to project a new image and identity for a city. The hosting of major sports events is often justified by the host city in terms of long-term economic and social consequences, directly or indirectly resulting from the staging of the event (Mules and Faulkner 1996). These effects are primarily justified in economic terms, by estimating the additional expenditure generated in the local economy as the result of the event, in terms of the benefits injected from tourism-related activity and the subsequent re-imaging of the city following the success of the event (Roche 1994).

Cities staging major sports events have a unique opportunity to market themselves to the world. Increasing competition between broadcasters to secure broadcasting rights to major sports events has led to a massive escalation in fees for such rights, which in turn means broadcasters give blanket coverage at peak times for such events, enhancing the marketing benefits to the cities that stage them.

Measuring the economic impact of major sports events

The economic impact of major sports events is normally assessed using multiplier analysis. Multiplier analysis converts the total amount of additional expenditure in the host city to a net amount of income retained within the city after allowing for 'leakages' from the local economy. As an example, the total amount of money spent in a hotel will not necessarily all be recirculated within a given city. Some of the money will be spent on wages, food suppliers, beverage suppliers, etc., the recipients of which may well be outside the city. Thus the multiplier is a device that converts total additional expenditure into the amount of local income retained within the local economy.

The ultimate purpose of multiplier calculations is that they can be used as the basis for further economic analysis, such as making estimates of job creation attributable to a given inflow of income into a local economy. Sustained additional income into a local economy will lead to the creation of additional jobs within that economy.

There are many different multipliers, but the one used most commonly for studies of events is called the proportional income multiplier. The proportional income multiplier is expressed as:

$$\frac{\text{Direct} + \text{Indirect} + \text{Induced income}}{\text{Initial visitor expenditure}}$$

Once the initial visitor expenditure has been measured, economic impact in terms of additional local income can be estimated by multiplying this initial expenditure by the local multiplier.

Direct income is the first-round effect of outside visitor spending. It represents additional wages, salaries and profits to local residents working in businesses that were the direct recipients of the additional visitor expenditures. Indirect income is the income to other businesses and individuals within the local economy as a result of the additional expenditures of the visitors, but who were not the direct recipients of this visitor expenditure (e.g. local suppliers to the shops, restaurants, hotels, etc. that were the recipients of visitor expenditures). Induced income is the income resulting from the re-spending of additional income earned directly or indirectly on locally produced goods and services.

By dividing additional local income by an average annual full-time wage for the sector where the income is received (e.g. hotel and catering), then the additional jobs created can be obtained and expressed in full-time equivalent job years. One full-time equivalent job year is the employment equivalent of one full-time job for one year.

Crompton (1995, 2001) argued that there have been many examples where this relatively simple approach to estimating the economic impact of events was applied incorrectly. Most of these misapplications are due to employing inappropriate multipliers. In particular, sales multipliers (which are considerably larger than income multipliers) are often used in impact studies since they exaggerate the economic benefit. A sales multiplier measures the direct, indirect and induced expenditure generated by visitor spending in the host community as a result of the event, whereas an income multiplier measures the additional income retained in the community as a result of that expenditure. Sales multipliers are often in the region of 2–3, meaning the indirect and induced expenditures are two to three times larger than the direct expenditure. Income multipliers are normally less than 1, and often in the region 0.3–0.6. The economic impact would therefore be considerably overestimated by using sales multipliers rather than income multipliers.

Crompton also indicated that many economic impact studies of events overestimate the impact by including local residents' expenditures and/or expenditures by visitors who would have visited the city anyway even if the event did not take place. These expenditures should not be included, since they do not represent additional expenditure in the city as a direct result of the event. Crompton's main argument is that there is often pressure on researchers carrying out economic impact studies for events to come up with the highest figure possible, since the clients paying for the study are normally the event organizers – who wish to maximize the economic benefit for advocacy purposes.

Economic impact of major sports events

In the USA, Indianapolis, Cleveland, Philadelphia, Kansas City, Baltimore and Denver are examples of cities that have adopted sports-oriented economic regeneration strategies. Most of these strategies have been based on attracting sports events associated with the main professional team sports, in particular American football, baseball, ice hockey and basketball. Unlike the situation in most of the rest of the world, professional teams in the USA frequently move from city to city, so cities often compete to attract a team.

Over the last decade cities have offered greater and greater incentives for these professional teams to move by offering to build new stadia to house them, costing hundreds of millions of dollars. The teams just sit back and let cities bid up the price. They either move to the city offering the best deal, or they accept the counter-offer invariably put to them by their existing hosts. This normally involves the host city building them a brand new stadium to replace their existing one, which may only be 10 or 15 years old.

This use of taxpayers' money to subsidize profit-making professional sports teams seems out of place in the context of the USA economy. The justification for such public expenditure is an economic one: the investment of public money is worthwhile since it is clearly outweighed by the stream of economic activity that is generated by having a major professional sports team resident in the city.

The amount of stadium construction in the USA in the 1996–2000 period exceeded the level of that in any 5-year period in US history. It is estimated that the total cost of stadium construction in the USA in the 1990s alone could exceed $US 9 billion. At the end of the 1990s there were 30 major stadium construction projects in progress, around one-third of the total professional sports infrastructure, but around a half of all professional teams in the USA expressed dissatisfaction with their current facilities (Baade, 1999). Stadium construction costs increased substantially during the 1990s. Escalating construction costs have also generated an increase in the size of public subsidies to stadia.

As cities compete to use public money to satisfy the demands of these professional teams in terms of more state-of-the-art facilities, there has been much controversy in recent years over whether the economic benefits generated justify such high levels of public subsidy to professional sport (Baade, 1999). Crompton's (2001) criticism of the misapplication of multiplier analysis in the estimation of the economic impact of sports events related to the situation in professional team sports in the USA. He argued that, in many cases, external consultants carrying out economic impact studies to demonstrate the economic benefits on investing in a new stadium to hold major professional team sports events considerably overestimate such benefits. These overestimations may be the result of a genuine misunderstanding of the procedure for calculating economic impact, but Crompton suggests that on many occasions it is a deliberate attempt to mislead by generating very high values for economic impact in order to provide advocacy for those arguing for the need to invest in a new stadium. It is certainly the case that most sports economists in the USA have taken the view that the economic benefits associated with staging major professional team sports events do not justify the level of investment in new stadia to host such events that has taken place over the recent past.

Outside of the USA, research has concentrated on estimating the benefits associated with major sports events such as World or European Championships that move from country to country and city to city. Cities compete to host such events, again mainly driven by the argument that they will generate sufficient economic benefits to justify government funding of the hosting of the event. Although it is generally accepted that for two events (the summer Olympic Games and soccer's World Cup) the benefits do exceed the costs, it is not clear that this will be true of other major sports events, even at World Championship level. In the rest of this section, we report the results of a study of six major sports events held in the United Kingdom between June 1996 and December 1999. The research was carried out on behalf of the UK, English and Scottish Sports Councils by the Sport Industry Research Centre. The study aimed to evaluate the economic impact of these events on the local economies of host cities and towns, as well as to investigate the complicated economics of staging major sports events. Each of the events was hosted by one of the UK's National Cities of Sport – Sheffield, Glasgow and Birmingham. Four of the events were World Championships, with the other two being European Championships. The sports involved included football, swimming, badminton, judo and climbing.

The six events studied were:

1 9–20 June 1996   Group D Matches, Euro '96, Hillsborough
                         Stadium, Sheffield
2 22 June–3 July 1996   World Masters Swimming Championships,
                         Ponds Forge International Sports Centre, Sheffield
3 19 May–1 June 1997   World Badminton Championships and
                         Sudirman Cup, Scotstoun Leisure Centre, Glasgow
4 11–13 December 1998   European Short Course Swimming
                         Championships, Ponds Forge International Sports
                         Centre, Sheffield
5 7–10 October 1999   World Judo Championships, Indoor Arena,
                         Birmingham
6 3–5 December 1999   World Indoor Climbing Championships, Indoor
                         Arena, Birmingham

Figure 17.1 shows the wide variety in the economic impact generated by the six events. The Euro '96 matches in Sheffield generated by far the highest additional expenditure in the host city, even though this event involved only three football matches lasting in total four and a half hours. Euro '96 was also the highest-profile event with the widest media coverage. The next in economic impact terms was the World Masters Swimming Championships, also taking place in Sheffield, just a few days after the Euro '96 event had finished in the city. Although there was very little media coverage of this event, it involved over 4000 competitors from all over the world staying for a considerable period in the city. These competitors also brought along friends and family, who were the main spectators of the event. Given the large number of competitors there was also a considerable number of coaches and officials, making a total of 6500 visitors to the city as a result of the event. In contrast, Euro '96 attracted 61 000 visitors to the city but the majority of

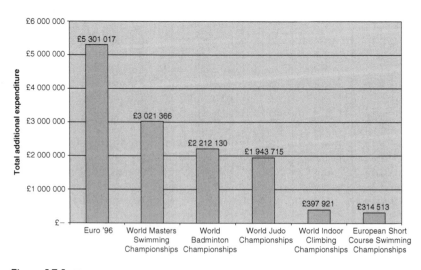

Figure 17.1 The economic impacts of major sports events

these were day-visitors, not overnight stays. However, given the large number of visitors, the economic impact was still considerable.

Table 17.1 shows that, when the number of event days is taken into account, the dominance of Euro '96 over the World Masters Swimming becomes greater, since there were 12 event days for the Masters but only 3 for Euro '96. The spend per event day of £1.77 million for Euro '96 is way ahead of any of the other events, probably establishing this event as the third largest in the world in economic terms after the Olympics and football's World Cup.

The World Masters Swimming and Euro '96 both illustrate that certain events are more attractive economically than others because of the number and type of 'sport tourists' they attract. The type of sport tourist associated with the Masters event was typically from the more affluent sections of society, more likely to stay overnight in the city (an average stay in the city of 5.82 nights for all visitors), with greater disposable income and with an increased ability to inject money into the local economy (£100 000 was generated through the sale of merchandise to visitors related to the event). The tourists' impact stretched beyond the days of competition, as a result of a further vacation in Sheffield, its surrounding region or other parts of the UK. This type of event is an ideal type of sporting event upon which to base sporting regenerative strategies. Unfortunately, like all similar sports events, there is fierce competition to secure such events.

Figure 17.1 shows that the World Badminton Championships and the World Judo Championships were similar in overall impact, with the badminton generating just over £2 million in additional expenditure and the judo just less than £2 million. However, the badminton lasted for 2 weeks whereas the judo took place over 4 days, and hence Table 17.1 shows that judo generated over three times as much on a per event day basis than badminton.

The World Indoor Climbing and the European Short Course Swimming Championships were the events generating the smallest impacts, with the former generating nearly one-third more additional expenditure than the latter. Since the number of event days (3) is identical, the relationship is also identical in Table 17.1. The additional expenditure in Sheffield generated by Euro '96 is nearly 17 times greater than that generated in the same city by the European Short Course Swimming Championships, even though both events consisted of 3 event days. This illustrates the considerable variation in the contribution major sports events make to economic regeneration.

Figure 17.2 shows the relative contribution to economic impact of spectators on the one hand and competitors, officials and media representatives on the

Table 17.1 Average additional visitor expenditure per event day

	Average additional expenditure per event day (£)
Badminton	158 009
Climbing	132 640
Euro '96	1 767 006
Judo	485 928
Masters Swimming	251 781
Short Course Swimming	104 838

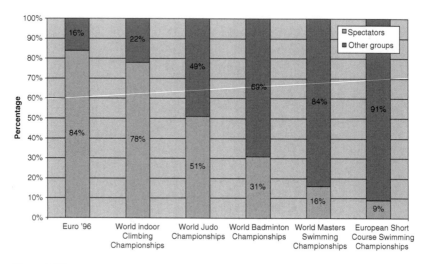

Figure 17.2 The continuum from spectator- to competitor-driven events

other. Euro '96 is at one end of the spectrum, with 84 per cent of additional expenditure generated by spectators. At the other end is the European Short Course Swimming Championships, with 91 per cent of additional expenditure in the city generated by competitors, officials and media. This is the typical picture for a major swimming championship, and the World Masters proportions confirm this. What is perhaps more surprising is that the World Indoor Climbing Championships is at the Euro '96 end of the spectrum whereas the World Badminton Championships is closer to the picture for swimming. The World Judo Championships have almost a 50:50 split between additional expenditure generated by spectators, and that generated by competitors, officials and media.

The level of additional expenditure generated by competitors, officials and media should be relatively easy to forecast in advance, since it depends on the numbers of competitors and officials visiting and the number of event days. Hence, forecasting the economic impact of competitor-driven events is not a major problem. In Sheffield, for the European Short Course Swimming Championships, it was possible to build up a profile of expenditure on the main items of accommodation and food by investigating the terms offered by the hotels to the visiting teams and officials. There was little additional expenditure in addition to that on accommodation and food. In such circumstances it is possible to build up a very accurate forecast of the economic impact of the event prior to bidding for the event by investigating the number of competitors, officials and media present at previous stagings of the same championships, and the number of days for which the championships ran.

Predicting the impact of spectators is much more difficult. In general, those cities bidding for events such as World or European Championships tend to overestimate the number of spectators that will attend. For instance, the predicted attendance for the World Badminton Championships in Glasgow was 35 000–40 000, whereas the actual attendance was 21 642. This illustrates the danger of staging special 'one-off' events. Projected attendances have a high error margin, and mistakes can have a dramatic effect on the final budget out-turn for the event organizers as well as on the economic impact of the event in the local economy. A detailed analysis of an event generating substantial economic impact, the London Marathon, is included in Case study 17.1.

Case study 17.1 The economic impacts of the Flora London Marathon 2000

The London Marathon was the brainchild of Chris Brasher and was first run on 29 March 1981, with 7747 runners accepted (from 20 000 applicants). The event has proved to be increasingly popular in the intervening years, so much so that for the Millennium Flora London Marathon (FLM) there were over 99 000 applicants with almost 42 000 runners accepted and 32 620 starters. The event is now such a major part of the UK sporting calendar that it is screened in over 100 countries around the world. Up to and including the 1999 event, over 413 000 runners had completed the course, raising £110 million for charities.

From its humble beginnings, the FLM has developed into one of the largest mass participation events of its kind in the world. Notwithstanding this, the FLM also attracts some of the top distance runners from around the world, making it a world-class international event.

The economic impact model developed by the Sport Industry Research Centre (SIRC) is capable of producing an accurate estimate of the additional expenditure made in a given locality as a result of an event being staged. The model has shown that the extent of the economic impact is dependent upon the number of visitors (especially spectators and participants from outside the locality) attracted to the event (see Shibli, 2001), and as a result the FLM was expected to have a major impact on London. Apart from the net economic change in the London economy as a result of staging the FLM, the total economic activity generated in the UK as a result of the FLM taking place was also estimated.

The project utilized desk research and primary data collection, which amounted to 3228 survey questionnaires completed by a variety of groups attending the FLM (e.g. runners, spectators and media) both prior to and during the event on Sunday 16 April 2000. In order to quantify the economic importance to the UK of the FLM, changes were made to the runners' questionnaire such that they were asked about their expenditure in preparation for the event. Categories of preparatory spend were developed in conjunction with the London Marathon Limited, and included (for example) expenditure on running shoes and apparel, on other races, fitness regimens; magazines/books, and on diet and food supplements.

The total economic activity generated in the UK (economic importance, see Table 17.2) as a result of the FLM taking place was almost £58.3 million. Spectators (£14.7 m) and runners (£8.8 m) accounted for 40 per cent of this sum, with charity fund-raising of £22.8 m (39 per cent), sponsors £5.8 m (10 per cent) and entry fees £3.5 m (6 per cent) accounting for much of the remainder. Local hotels enjoyed high occupancy levels, based on the considerable number of

Table 17.2 Summary of the economic importance/impact of the Flora London Marathon 2000

	Spectators	Volunteers	Media	Runners	Importance
Commercial Bed-Nights	97 398	–	292	17 577	115 265
Number of	282 600	7,000	241	32 620	
Accommodation	£7 177 964	£ –	£27 743	£1 220 099	£8 425 807
Food & drink	£3 855 233	£18 690	£9 608	£449 791	£4 333 324
Entertainment	£930,798	£ –	£1,375	£92 049	£1 024 221
Programmes/Merchandise	£80,696	£ –	£166	£155 620	£ 236 482
Shopping/Souvenirs	£905 149	£ –	£9,869	£138 452	£1 053 469
Travel	£1 413 943	£ –	£3,276	£204 512	£1 621 730
Other	£320 448	£ –	£577	£55 338	£376 363
Preparation spend				£6 445 265	£6 445 265
Sub total	£14 684 230	£18 690	£52 613	£8 761 126	£23 516 660
Exhibition staff spend					£26 840
Exhibitors spend					£921 548
Sponsors					£5 803 500
Entry fee					£3 490 750
Charity					£22 768 000
Organizational spend (inc profit)					£1 745 500 on UK
Total expenditure re Marathon					£58 272 797

runners and spectators (from outside London) who required accommodation for the event. In total, 115 267 commercial bed-nights were generated in London, equivalent to additional expenditure of £8.4 m in London hotels and guesthouses. Spectators spent £7.2 m on accommodation, and the runners themselves spent an additional £1.2 m. Expenditure by spectators, the media and runners on food and drink was £4.3 m, which represents a significant financial injection to London's catering industry. Runners spent £6.4 m in preparation for the Marathon, equivalent to £198 each (excluding entry fees). This included £2.6 m spent on running shoes; equivalent to 1.34 new pairs per runner at a cost of £60 per pair. Nearly £1 m was spent on running apparel and a further £0.75 m on entry fees for other races as part of training programmes for the FLM.

In order to calculate the net increase in the London economy (the economic impact), the importance figure was reduced to include only the expenditure in London directly attributable to the FLM. Excluding charity fund-raising this figure amounted to £27.4 m, and represents the economic activity generated in London by non-residents, most notably by spectators (£13.8 m) and runners (£4.2 m), who accounted for almost 66 per cent of the additional expenditure. The £8.4 m spent on 115 267 commercial bed-nights in London amounted to almost 31 per cent of the total economic impact, sponsors accounted for over 14 per cent (£4 m), spending on food and drink in excess of 13 per cent (£3.7 m), and combined expenditure on travel, shopping and entertainment a further 12.5 per cent (£3.4 m) of the impact on London. The economic impact figure of £27.4 m included the FLM's net profit of approximately £1.5 m (within organizational spend), because the London Marathon Charitable Trust uses this surplus to support recreational projects in London. In addition, the expenditure (£0.14 m) of 80 trade exhibitors and their staff who took part in the FLM Exhibition between 12 and 15 April 2000 has been included.

Major events involving either direct or indirect trade with other nations have an effect on the UK's balance of trade, with Euro '96 credited with contributing 25 per cent of the total GDP growth achieved in the second quarter of 1996 (Dobson et al., 1997). The FLM is not of the same scale; however, it did generate a net export effect of £1.2 m, largely due to visitors from overseas spending £2.5 m in the London economy.

Although not included in the calculations, of the 91 businesses surveyed along the route 58 per cent revealed that they were busier than a normal Sunday, with 56 per cent reporting an increase in their normal takings. Moreover, 24 per cent of the 38 publicans surveyed said that the Sunday of the FLM was their busiest day of the year, with an average of 20 extra staff hours incurred per pub. Furthermore, 63 per cent of all business proprietors on the route felt that the FLM had a positive effect on their business, compared to only 16 per cent who reported negative effects linked mainly to road closures and disruptions to routine.

This case study has demonstrated that one of the most prestigious and high-profile events in the UK sporting calendar leaves a significant economic legacy in its wake. Not only is the Flora London Marathon a great sporting spectacle and a celebration of the human spirit, it is also a successful business venture that generates in excess of £58 m in associated expenditure, of which over £27 m impacts directly upon London through sport tourism. Such information contributes to the growing body of knowledge linked to major sports events, and is likely to be of interest to authorities that are formulating strategic plans around sport tourism. In particular, the secondary spend in London on accommodation (£8.4 m) and subsistence (£3.7 m) coupled with the net export effect from overseas trade (£1.2 m) are likely to be of the greatest interest.

Longer-term benefits of hosting major sports events

The previous section concentrated on the economic benefits generated by major sports events at the time the events are staged. It is often argued, however, that such events generate a longer-term legacy of economic benefits. One example that is often quoted to support this argument is the case of the Barcelona Olympics in 1992.

Sanahuja (2002) provided evidence on the longer-term economic benefits of hosting the Olympics in Barcelona in 1992. The paper analysed the benefits to Barcelona in 2002, 10 years after hosting the games. Table 17.3 shows an increase of almost 100 per cent in hotel capacity, number of tourists, and number of overnight stays in 2001 compared to the pre-Games position in 1990. Average room occupancy had also increased from 71 per cent to 84 per cent. In addition, the average length of stay had increased from 2.84 days to 3.17 days. In 1990, the majority (51 per cent) of tourists to Barcelona were from the rest of Spain, with 32 per cent from the rest of Europe and the remainder (17 per cent) from outside Europe. By 2001 the absolute number of Spanish tourists had actually risen by 150 000, but, given the near doubling in the number of tourists overall, this higher total only accounted for 31 per cent of the total number of tourists. The proportion of tourists from the rest of Europe went up from 32 per cent to 40 per cent (representing an absolute increase of around 800 000) and from the rest of the world from 17 per cent to 29 per cent (representing an absolute increase of around 600 000).

Table 17.3 Legacy tourism benefits of the Barcelona Olympics

	1990	2001
Hotel capacity (beds)	18 567	34 303
Number of tourists	1 732 902	3 378 636
Number of overnights	3 795 522	7 969 496
Average room occupancy (%)	71	84
Average stay	2.84	3.17
Tourist by origin (%)		
Spain	51.2	31.3
Europe	32.0	39.5
Others (USA, Japan, Latin America)	16.8	29.2

Source: Turisme de Barcelona (Barcelona's Tourist Board) and Sanahuja (2002).

Table 17.4 The best cities to locate a business today

City	Rank		
	1990	2001	2002
London	1	1	1
Paris	2	2	2
Frankfurt	3	3	3
Brussels	4	4	4
Amsterdam	5	5	5
Barcelona	11	6	6
Madrid	17	8	7
Milan	9	11	8
Berlin	15	9	9
Zurich	7	7	10
Munich	12	10	11
Dublin	–	13	12

Source: Sanahuja (2002).

Overall infrastructure investment prior to the Games was $US 7.5 billion, compared to a budget of around $US 1.5 billion for the Olympic Committee to stage the games. The Olympics in Barcelona were the most expensive ever staged. However, Barcelona's use of the Games as a city marketing factor is generally regarded as a huge success.

This is evidenced by Barcelona's rise in Cushman and Wakefield Healey Bakers European Cities Monitor of the best European cities in which to locate a business; Barcelona was eleventh in 1990 and sixth in 2002 (Table 17.4).

Conclusions

The evidence presented above indicates that major sports events can generate substantial economic impact in the local economy of host cities. Although the events contribute to economic activity in the local area, local, regional and national governments are often called upon to cover the costs of staging the events since many of the economic benefits flow to leisure, tourism and hospitality industries rather than as direct income streams to the city authorities that host the events. However, city authorities do benefit from the media coverage given to the event and the place marketing benefits to the venues and the city itself, which are discussed in other chapters of this book. The longer-term benefits of hosting major sports events such as the Olympics can be huge, as the data from Barcelona illustrate.

References

Baade, R. (1999). An analysis of why and how the United States Judiciary has interpreted the question of professional sports and economic development. In C. Jeanrenaud (ed.), *The Economic Impact of Sports Events*. Neuchatel: CIES, pp. 41–62.

Bianchini, F. and Schwengel, H. (1991). Re-imagining the city. In J. Comer and S. Harvey (eds), *Enterprise and Heritage: Crosscurrents of National Culture*. London: Routledge, pp. 214–234.

Bramwell, B. (1995). *Event Tourism in Sheffield: A Sustainable Approach to Urban Development?* Unpublished paper, Centre for Tourism. Sheffield Hallam University.

Burns, J. P. A., Hatch, J. H. and Mules, T. (eds) (1986). *The Adelaide Grand Prix: The Impact of a Special Event*. Adelaide: The Centre for South Australian Economic Studies.

Collins, M. F. and Jackson, G. A. M. (1999). The economic impact of sport. In J. Standeven and P. W. Kopf (eds), *Sport Tourism*. Champaign, IL: Human Kinetics.

Crompton, J. (1995). Economic impact analysis of sports facilities and events: eleven sources of misapplication. *Journal of Sports Management*, 9(1), 14–35.

Crompton, J. (2001). Public subsidies to professional team sport facilities in the USA. In C. Gratton and I. Henry (eds), *Sport in the City: The Role of Sport in Economic and Social Regeneration*. London: Routledge, pp. 15–34.

DCMS/SU (2002). *Game Plan: a Strategy for Delivering Government's Sport and Physical Activity Objectives, a Joint Department of Culture, Media and Sport/Strategy Unit Report*. London: Cabinet Office.

Dobson, N., Gratton, C. and Holliday, S. (1997). *Football Came Home: The Economic Impact of Euro '96*. Sheffield: Leisure Industries Research Centre.

Loftman, P. and Spirou, C. S. (1996). Sports, stadiums and urban recreation: the British and United States experience. Paper presented at the conference *Tourism and Culture: Towards the 21st Century*, University of Northumbria, Longhirst, Morpeth, September 14–19.

Mules, T. and Faulkner, B. (1996). An economic perspective on major events. *Tourism Economics*, 12(2), 107–117.

Ritchie, J. R. B. (1984). Assessing the impact of hallmark events: conceptual and research issues. *Journal of Travel Research*, 23(1), 2–11.

Ritchie, J. R. B. and Aitken, C. E. (1984). Assessing the impacts of the 1988 Olympic Winter Games: the research program and initial results. *Journal of Travel Research*, 22(3), 17–25.

Ritchie, J. R. B. and Aitken, C. E. (1985). OLYMPULSE II: evolving resident attitudes towards the 1988 Olympics. *Journal of Travel Research*, 23, 28–33.

Ritchie, J. R. B. and Lyons, M. M. (1987). OLYMPULSE III/IV: a mid term report on resident attitudes concerning the 1988 Olympic Winter Games. *Journal of Travel Research*, 26, 18–26.

Ritchie, J. R. B. and Lyons, M. M. (1990). OLYMPULSE VI: a post-event assessment of resident reaction to the XV Olympic Winter Games. *Journal of Travel Research*, 28(3), 14–23.

Ritchie, J. R. B. and Smith, B. H. (1991). The impact of a mega event on host region awareness: a longitudinal study. *Journal of Travel Research*, 30(1), 3–10.

Roche, M. (1992). Mega-event planning and citizenship: problems of rationality and democracy in Sheffield's Universiade 1991. *Vrijetijd en Samenleving*, 10(4), 47–67.

Roche, M. (1994). Mega-events and urban policy. *Annals of Tourism Research*, 21(1), 1–19.

Sanahuja, R. (2002). *Olympic City – The City Strategy 10 years after The Olympic Games in 1992.* Paper delivered to the International Conference on Sports Events and Economic Impact, Copenhagen, April.

Shibli, S. (2001). *Using an Understanding of the Behaviour Patterns of Key Participant Groups to Predict the Economic Impact of Major Sports Events.* Book of Proceedings for the 9th EASM Congress, Vitoria-Gasteiz, Spain, pp. 294–298.

Sport tourism and natural resource impacts

Mark Orams

Introduction

Moves to put boaties in poo

Sweeping powers to ban boaties and ferries dumping untreated sewage in Waitemata Harbour – similar to that seen in the recent America's Cup incident – are currently before the Auckland Regional Council. A report by ARC officers has suggested a review of sewage disposal regulations and a complete ban on the dumping of raw sewage. The report was sparked by a public outcry when raw sewage from the America's Cup spectator fleet began washing up on North Shore beaches. (Saunders, 2003: 10)

Media and anecdotal reports like this from yachting's America's Cup, hosted in Auckland, New Zealand in March 2003, are not unusual when large sporting events are held. Large numbers of visitors to an area, whether for sport or some other reason, often impact the local environment. It is therefore a little surprising that the issue of the impacts of sport tourism on the natural environment has received so little attention in the literature. However, sport tourism is a relatively recent area of specialization in the tourism management field and so, while it is certainly well understood that tourism of any kind can (and often does) have significant influence over the natural environment (Inskeep, 1991; Ward and Beanland, 1996), there has been little focus on the environmental impacts of sport tourism specifically. Despite few specific examples reported in the literature, there is no doubt that sport tourism can and does impact nature (Keller, 2001). Not all of these impacts are negative, however. Sport tourism has provided the impetus for host communities to improve natural settings, particularly when the quality of that setting is important for the sporting activity itself or when the poor quality of the local area could reflect badly on the image of the host community. This chapter will provide a general overview of some of the important issues surrounding the effects of sport tourism on natural resources. In particular, it will examine some of the challenges inherent in assessing the impacts of human activities on natural ecosystems and consider relevant research methods that may render such assessments more accurate. Typical types of environmental impacts resulting from sport tourism will be outlined, and finally the chapter will use Case study 18.1, of Auckland, New Zealand's hosting of the America's Cup, to illustrate some of these impacts.

Sport tourism and its impacts

Earlier chapters in this volume have discussed in depth the issues surrounding the variety of definitions that have been given for sport tourism (see Chapter 1). There is little point in repeating that discussion here. However, it is important to recognize that sport tourism occurs in a variety of settings and modes, each of which has implications for considering impacts on natural ecosystems. Figure 18.1 represents a simplified model of issues related to environmental impacts in the sport tourism realm.

Sport tourism is generally considered to include travel for both competitive and recreational sport activities (Gibson *et al.*, 1997). In addition, support staff such as coaches, trainers, physiotherapists, doctors, sport psychologists, equipment technicians and so on also form a significant component of sports groups travelling for certain activities or events. In many cases family, friends, fans and spectators add a significant number of tourists travelling for a particular sport (especially for mega-events, such as the Olympic Games). Administrators and organizers, as well as sponsors and ancillary business people, may also be involved. Thus the number and diversity of sport tourists can be extremely large. It is certainly not a homogeneous group. An additional important, and relatively recent, component of sport tourism is those travellers who are visiting facilities or sites that have historic or heritage significance related to sport – sport museums, halls of fame and memorials are becoming increasingly significant as tourism attractions (Delpy Neirotti, 2003).

As a consequence of this diversity sport tourism is conducted in a variety of settings, including those that are nature-based (for example, as with game fishing contests, river kayaking or surfing competitions), those that are dependent on human built structures (such as sport stadia hosting a multitude of sports and their spectators) and some that are heritage/history based (for example, the International Swimming Hall of Fame in Ft Lauderdale, Florida). In many circumstances, sport attractions are a combination of natural settings and human influence or modification. In more recent times, structures and settings have been specifically built to replicate nature-based sport settings (for example, as with indoor 'wave pools'

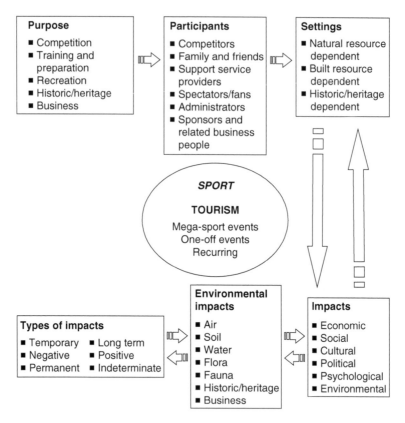

Figure 18.1 A model of sport tourism and its potential environmental impacts

that host surfing contests and with the white water kayaking venue built for the Sydney Olympic Games).

Thus, understanding the impacts of sport tourism on the environment is complicated by the wide variety of settings, the diversity of activities and the complexity of nature itself. Nevertheless, it is widely accepted that tourism and sport tourism does impact the natural environment. What is more difficult is to determine exactly what impacts occur and what causes those impacts.

Understanding impacts

Cause and effect issues

One of the significant challenges in assessing the impacts of sport tourism (or any tourism for that matter) is in isolating the causal factors behind observed environmental changes. Natural ecosystems are dynamic, and respond to a wide variety of 'drivers' responsible for change. Some changes are the result of dramatic natural events such as earthquakes, hurricanes, lightning strikes and fire;

however, most are small incremental changes that are part of the fundamental evolutionary process. Thus natural life is always in a state of change, and human activities such as tourism are part of that process and can influence it in a variety of ways. What is difficult is determining which changes are as a result of human activities and which are simply a normal part of 'natural' environmental change.

A second complicating factor is that human-induced change in nature may only be temporary – natural ecosystems are remarkably robust and can (and fortunately often do) 'bounce back' from negative human influence. This tendency is particularly relevant to sport tourism because many sport tourism activities are periodic, seasonal or 'one-off' events.

Effect, impact and disturbance

It is useful to classify impacts in a way that recognizes that not all of them are necessarily negative or permanent. Findlay (2001) categorized the influence of human activities on natural ecosystems as a response, impact or disturbance. A 'response' is when an element of the natural environment shows a reaction or change as a consequence of tourism activity or development, an 'impact' is the resultant effect of that response, and a 'disturbance' is an assessment that the impact is detrimental. This classification is helpful because it counters the common conclusion that any observed response in the natural environment to tourism activities is a detrimental impact. This is often not the case. Most natural ecosystems are extremely adaptable and robust, as evidenced by the wide variety of habitats and situations where they are influenced by human activities. Thus in many situations natural ecosystems are already affected by human influences. Therefore, responses to tourism activities may be short term and temporary or even adaptive, but not necessarily detrimental.

The role of research and potential research methods

Inevitably, any attempt at quantifying or understanding the effects of tourism (or more specifically sport tourism) on nature requires research. Environmental impact research is now well established and widely practised (at least in the developed world). Environmental Impact Assessment (EIS) and Environmental Impact Reporting (EIR) are, in many cases, required by law as part of the approval process for large-scale development projects and activities that have potential to harm the natural environment. While such approaches are widely accepted (especially for construction projects), they are not as commonly applied to activities or events themselves. Thus the construction of a new sport stadium typically would likely require an EIS/EIR, but the hosting of a major multi-sport event with many thousands of participants may not.

Before and after studies

Ideally, research on impacts on natural ecosystems should be conducted on a temporal–comparative basis. That is, research that results in a thorough understanding of the working of the natural ecosystem should be conducted *before* the sport tourism event, development or activity takes place. A replicate study can

251

then be carried out *during* and/or *after* the sport tourism activity, and comparisons made. This kind of approach engenders much more confidence when attributing changes to tourism activities. Moreover, the understanding of the workings of the natural ecosystem in the absence of the human activity ('before' data) allows the development of appropriate management strategies to minimize or mitigate the effects of the tourism. Unfortunately 'baseline' studies before tourism are rare; the great majority of research tends to be carried out either during or after the tourism activity or development, and, as a result, uncertainty always exists with regard to cause and effect determination.

Control-experiment studies

A second methodological approach is for researchers to manipulate or create a comparative study that compares a natural ecosystem impacted by tourism with a similar replicate system that is not exposed to tourism. This allows for comparisons to be made and conclusions regarding the impact of tourism to be reached. Such studies are often complicated by the differences that are inherent in two ecosystems (no two are identical), and thus changes observed in the 'experiment' system may not be directly attributable to the tourism but could be related to the nature of the ecosystem being monitored.

The Limits of Acceptable Change model

The 'carrying capacity' concept has been widely reported in the literature (Manning, 1999), and has an attractive, simplistic logic. That is, if the threshold can be determined at which the number of tourists to an area unduly impacts that ecosystem, then management strategies based on managing tourist numbers can be developed and implemented. The problem with this concept is that it is most frequently the behaviour of tourists rather than the absolute number of tourists that impacts nature. Simply put, one person doing the wrong thing is far more detrimental than 100 people doing the right thing. As a reaction to the inability of carrying capacity approaches to successfully manage tourism (and recreation), the concept of determining the 'limits of acceptable change' (LAC) was developed (Prosser, 1986). Rather than attempting to answer the question 'how much is too much?' (as the carrying capacity approach does), the LAC model attempts to determine 'how much change are we prepared to accept?'. Such an approach is predicated by a need to understand the dynamics of the natural ecosystem in order to determine how much change is normal (and natural) and then decide how much additional change the ecosystem can cope with. Measurement of change based on criteria such as what levels or types of change might be permanent or fundamentally damaging to the long-term health and integrity of the ecosystem are, therefore, important. Arriving at an agreement on such criteria and their measurement is seldom easy; however, the model does provide a useful framework for researching and considering the impacts of tourism on nature.

Temporary, short-term, long-term and permanent impacts

Probably the most important judgment with regard to sport tourism impacts pertains to the temporal nature of those impacts. In most cases, if impacts are temporary or short term (i.e. they only occur for the duration of the event and disappear soon after) then they are of little importance from an ecological point of view. Ironically, these are often the type of impacts that produce the most outrage and condemnation from the wider public (fuelled by dramatic images in the media) – an example might be the death of a deer fawn from a car strike in a motor-sport race, or the case of the sewage washing up on the beaches from America's Cup spectators as reported in the foreword to this chapter. From an ecological perspective such effects of tourism are of little consequence because, while they are dramatic, they have no long-term effect on the health and viability of the ecosystem. Impacts that are serious are those that typically are 'silent'. Examples include small incremental changes to the balance of predator–prey relationships in ecological food chains (such as that often produced by hunting or fishing of predator species), the introduction of foreign pathogens that indigenous fauna have no natural immunity to, the release (accidentally or otherwise) of invasive foreign plant species, or the loss of fertile topsoil due to accelerated erosion. All have significant long-term implications for natural ecosystems.

Typical negative impacts of sport tourism for nature

It is not possible to compile a comprehensive list of all environmental impacts that arise from sport tourism. Nor is it possible to discuss such impacts in detail within the constraints of one chapter. However, a brief list that is illustrative of some of the main impacts is helpful in providing an overview of some of the negative environmental consequences of sport tourism. Elements of the natural environment that can be negatively impacted by sport tourism include the following:

1 *Climate.* The issues surrounding global warming and climate change have been widely reported and debated. Sport tourism contributes to climate change only indirectly; however, it is still important to recognize that any activity that includes, facilitates or promotes the emission of increased levels of 'greenhouse gases' is part of the problem. Thus sport tourism can and does contribute to global climate change and the consequent 'downstream' environmental effects.
2 *Air.* A deterioration in the quality of air is often a result of a major sport tourism event when environmental conditions are conducive (for example, when temperature inversion occurs and on still, windless days) and when large numbers of vehicles are involved. This is often the case when large numbers of spectators are transiting to and from stadium-based events. It can also occur during the construction phase for sporting facilities – emissions from diesel-powered construction machines and the suspension of fine dust, silt and sand during 'earth-moving' works can all contribute to air pollution.
3 *Soil.* The removal of topsoil for the construction of facilities can change the geological structure of an area. Erosion can be accelerated by trampling, vehicle damage and 'run-off'. In some cases, the siting and building of sporting facilities (including associated infrastructure such as roads, drains and parking lots) can be at the expense of fertile areas that were once the basis of agriculture and horticulture. Spillage and drainage of petrochemicals and the deliberate application of herbicides and pesticides (as used frequently on golf courses, for example) can compromise the biological viability of soils and the food chains that they support.

4 *Water*. Because water is such a fundamentally important element for all life, compromises to its quality and quantity always have consequences for nature. Many sporting activities are extremely consumptive of fresh-water resources; in particular, turf-dependent activities such as golf, lawn bowls, football, rugby and the multitude of other sports played on grass can place excessive demands on fresh-water resources. It should also be noted that even modern artificial turfs (such as those used in field hockey) also require large quantities of water. Sporting activities can also compromise water quality by contributing to sewage discharge, increased sediment loads, 'storm-water' run-off, increased nutrient loads, chemical spills and discharges and so on. While it can be argued that sport tourism is a relatively minor contributor to such problems (at least in comparison to some other industries), such impacts can and do occur as a result of sport tourism development and activities.

5 *Flora*. Plants fulfil a vital role in the health and functioning of the planet and, of course, form the base of most ecological food chains. Thus they are of critical importance. Whilst plants are relatively robust and can cope with quite substantial human-induced changes, there are a number of changes that can be detrimental in the long term. Probably the most significant is the introduction of new non-native species. These 'exotic' species often proliferate, subdue and dominate local native species, and radically change the ecology of an area. Tourism does play a major role in this phenomenon, primarily because the movement of tourists (and their cars, boats, sporting equipment, etc.) can transport seeds and plants to new areas. A further impact from tourism is the direct trampling that can occur when sporting enthusiasts walk, run, bike and drive over vegetation. In some cases such trampling can reduce plant cover, decrease stability and contribute to erosion – particularly in sensitive areas such as deserts, alpine meadows and coastal dunes.

6 *Fauna*. Animals can be impacted by sport tourism in a number of ways. First, direct removal of animals for sport – fishing, hunting and gathering of organisms for sport – has, without doubt, significantly altered and compromised natural ecosystems. Second, the disturbance of animals by human-created noise, the feeding of wildlife and even the simple physical presence of people is common. Third, the introduction of non-native species to natural areas for sporting purposes has had widespread and sometimes devastating consequences for nature. Finally, the domestication, training and use of animals as a basis for sport (for example, for rodeos, equestrian events, sheepdog trials, duck shooting and so on) has in some cases impacted certain species so that they today bear little resemblance to their original natural forms, habitats or behaviours.

7 *Scenery/amenities*. The amenity value of natural ecosystems is widely understood. The importance of wilderness, natural scenic vistas and the visual appeal of nature are valued by humans, and may well also be important for some animals. As a consequence, the development and/or use of natural areas for sport can compromise these values. This issue is particularly relevant to those sports that tend to be based on wild natural areas (for example, cross-country skiing, snowmobiling, white-water rafting and mountaineering). The presence of such sports people and their equipment reduces the 'naturalness' of an area.

8 *Cultural and historic resources*. While not always explicitly part of the natural environment, many resources impacted by sport tourism are important from a cultural and/or historic perspective. Indigenous people can find the pursuit of

a sporting objective offensive. For example, Ngai Tahu Maori of New Zealand's South Island have objected to mountaineers summiting on Aorangi – Mt Cook (New Zealand's highest peak) – because it is of spiritual significance for them. Caving activities have resulted in the deterioration of historic cave paintings, hunting of some animal species has caused offence to cultures that regard them as sacred, and the use of animal or traditional symbols as 'mascots' or 'brands' for sporting teams and events has been seen as sacrilegious by some native peoples (e.g. opposition to use of the name 'Redskins' by the Washington NFL and 'Seminoles' by the Florida State American Football teams).

Factors that particularly impact on the natural environment include the following:

1 *Noise*. The audiological environment is being increasingly recognized as an important component of nature. While most research on noise pollution has focused on its impact on human enjoyment and hearing quality, there is an increasing recognition that sound is a critical component of some ecosystems and for some animal species. For example, sound is fundamentally important for most marine creatures, particularly marine mammals, and there is growing concern that human activities – such as sporting activities and events like powerboat racing, personal water craft usage and water skiing could detrimentally impact whales and dolphins.
2 *Litter*. Human-made waste products, particularly those that are non-biodegradable, have major impacts on nature. Most people are now aware that plastics are a growing problem for a variety of animals – entanglement and ingestion cause injury and, in some cases, a slow and painful death. Unfortunately, sporting participants and spectators are extremely careless in terms of their rubbish or trash (witness the aftermath of any major sporting event), and while most major events now have major after-event clean-up operations, much is left behind and washed or blown into natural areas to cause problems for wildlife.

The impacts of sport tourism are widespread and growing in proportion to the growth of the industry. Impacts are not always direct or obvious; some negative environmental impacts only manifest many decades after the sport tourism activity has begun. It is also important to recognize that, as in all things with nature, an impact on one aspect of an ecosystem inevitably has 'downstream' impacts on other aspects of that ecosystem. Thus sport tourism can, has and will continue to result in negative outcomes for the natural environment.

Positive impacts of sport tourism for nature

It's not all 'doom and gloom' with regard to sport tourism and nature. While there is a tendency for self-flagellation with regard to examinations of human impacts on nature, sport tourism has in some cases resulted in improved natural ecosystems. It should be noted, however, that this has seldom (if ever) happened by accident – improvements occur when management strategies are designed to do just that. Certainly some host communities appear to recognize the impetus that sport tourism has had in terms of promoting an improved local environment. For example, residents of Chamsil in South Korea identified that the local water supply, roads and sanitation system had all been improved as a result of hosting the 1988 Seoul Olympic Games. They also agreed that local natural environments had been preserved as a result (Jeong, 1999). Similarly, hunting and fishing clubs (and others) have often become the most vigorous advocates for change to management systems in order to ensure sustained populations of the wildlife that are the basis for their sports (Shackley, 1996). In some cases, the value of natural resources as a tourism attraction has provided a justification for their continued protection and/or their maintenance as an alternative to their exploitation for a consumptive and more environmentally damaging use. For example, the value of forests surrounding Rotorua (New Zealand) as a location for mountain biking has provided an impetus for their continued protection and lessened the likelihood of their use as simply a commercial forestry resource (personal observation).

The lessons here for sport tourism managers and those who are involved in the planning for sport tourism are clear. If the natural environment is included as a priority in that planning and management, then positive outcomes can be achieved.

Case study 18.1 The impact of the America's Cup, Auckland, New Zealand

The America's Cup is reputed to be the world's oldest international sporting competition. It has been contested between yachts representing sailing clubs of foreign nations since 1851. Team New Zealand, representing the Royal New Zealand Yacht Squadron, successfully challenged for the Cup off San Diego, California in 1995. In March 2000, on the waters of the Hauraki Gulf off New Zealand's largest city Auckland, the America's Cup was successfully defended by Team New Zealand; however, the team was unsuccessful in the next defence in February 2003, losing to the Alinghi team from Switzerland.

The hosting of the America's Cup presented a challenge for a small, isolated nation like New Zealand. The requirements of America's Cup class yachts are significant – they are over 20 metres long and need a minimum depth of 7 metres. In addition, these yachts do not carry their own engines and therefore are towed to and from the sailing area (as a result they require a large 'turning' area). Furthermore, they must be removed from the water each day and stored on land where maintenance and development activities are carried out. As a consequence, the water space, docking areas and 'hardstand–compound' areas needed to host an America's Cup syndicate are large, deep, and require sheltered waters and all tide access. In 1995 when Team New Zealand first won the Cup there was nowhere in New Zealand where all these requirements could be met. As a consequence, a large-scale $NZ 60 million re-development of the downtown waterfront 'viaduct basin' was undertaken, transforming this underutilized and polluted harbour into an 'America's Cup Village' – an attractive recreational, residential and commercial centre for tourists and residents alike. The America's Cup Village not only hosts America's Cup competitors' bases but also restaurants, cafes, retail outlets, 'up-market' apartments, a small stadium used for concerts and special events, and is also a venue for marine tourism operators such as water taxis, charter yachts and hospitality boats.

The hosting of the 30th and 31st America's Cups involved the securing of international commercial sponsors and large numbers of local volunteers to help with the funding and running of the event. Central, regional and local government were involved in planning and initiatives to cope with the estimated additional 400 000 visitors to the city of Auckland during each competition. Over 1500 media representatives from over 40 countries, three cruise ships and 80 'super-yachts' (45–120 metres in length) were hosted over the 5-month duration of each event. A significant challenge in hosting this event was the management of the large numbers of on-water spectators. On peak days, in excess of 500 spectator craft transited the inner harbour via the main shipping harbour out to the yacht racecourse area in the Hauraki Gulf.

The Hauraki Gulf is widely recognized as an important and diverse marine ecosystem – so much so that it was designated a marine park in 1999. A number of important and endangered animal species are found in the Hauraki Gulf; these include the Brydes, Sei, Minke, Orca and Pilot whales; rare beaked whales; common and bottlenose dolphins; the Australasian Gannet; Takapu, a variety of Shearwater species (Bullers, fluttering and flesh-footed); petrel species (including the black, Cooks, diving, grey-faced and Pycofts petrels); and the little blue penguin. A wide variety of fish species and invertebrates are also resident in the area.

The sheer number of spectator craft on weekend race days (over 500) and the potential for disturbance of wildlife was of concern during this sporting event. On a number of occasions 'flight' responses were observed from dolphin species, Orca and a Brydes whale in the vicinity of spectator craft, and several incidents of boat strike on little blue penguins occurred (personal observation). In addition, increased marine litter and discharge of sewage from vessels were apparent during the summers (1999/2000 and 2002/2003) when the Cup was held.

Thus, while hosting the Cup was worth many hundreds of millions of dollars to the local and national economy, there were also, potentially, a number of negative environmental impacts that resulted. At the same time, it is important to recognize that the re-development of the 'Viaduct Harbour' into the 'America's Cup Village' was a significant improvement in that local environment. Water quality was significantly improved, as was the aesthetics and amenity value of the surrounding area.

Sport tourism and sustainability

The issue of environmental sustainability has become widely debated and discussed over the past decade. Tourism and sustainability has been at the forefront of this debate (Coccossis and Nijkamp, 1995), and issues of sustainability are now becoming mainstream agenda items for sport tourism. For example, United States ski resorts have recently developed a 'Sustainable Slopes' charter – a voluntary set of guidelines that commits ski resorts to environmental protection and 'environmentally friendly' practices (Hudson, 2003). Planning for the Sydney 2000 Olympic Games included an explicit commitment to create the 'Green Games', where environmental sustainability principles provided the impetus for a number of environmental conservation-based initiatives in the planning and management of the Games (Keller, 2001). Similarly, the United States Golf Association has formed a partnership with the conservation organization 'Audubon International' to promote environmentally sound planning and management in golf courses in the USA, including certification for those courses that conform to environmental guidelines (Readman, 2003).

The environment and its sustainability are therefore important considerations in the planning and management of sport tourism – at least in a number of relatively wealthy and high-profile sports. This is a good thing, because much of the attention that sport tourism has received has painted a very positive picture and many governments and locations are actively pursuing sport tourism as a potential mechanism by which they hope to facilitate economic growth, improve infrastructure and benefit from the enhanced image their area will receive. However, the lessons from other types of tourism development are clear — tourism is not a panacea, no matter what form it takes. For example, Ashworth (1995: 49) points out that the development of heritage-based tourism comes at a cost to the environment. He states that:

> it is undeniable that tourism based upon historic resources is an activity that has conveyed demonstrable economic and social benefits: its very success, however, has generated costs that can no longer be dismissed as a marginal and acceptable inconvenience.

The same argument can certainly be made with regard to sport tourism.

Conclusions

Sport tourism has been lauded as a significant contributor to regional and national economies. Many governments are not only embracing sport tourism but are also actively seeking opportunities to host sport tourism events. What is not as widely recognized is that sport tourism (or indeed any tourism development) is not a panacea; there are negative impacts that need to be considered and planned for. There is a multitude of examples of the negative consequences for the natural environment that can arise from tourism. There is also a growing number of examples of such consequences arising from sport tourism specifically (for example, see Ciminade, 1997 and Pigeassou et al., 1999). Thus the environment must become a pivotal consideration in the planning and management of sport tourism if sport tourism is not to be added to the long list of human activities which are short sighted and exploitive of nature.

References

Ashworth, G. J. (1995). Environmental quality and tourism and the environment. In H. Coccossis and P. Nijkamp (eds), *Sustainable Tourism Development*. Avebury: Ashgate Publishing, pp. 49–63.

Ciminade, D. (1997). Sport, tourism and the environment: for a concerted development. *Cahiers Espaces*, 52, 34–47.

Coccossis, H. and Nijkamp, P. (eds) (1995). *Sustainable Tourism Development*. Avebury: Ashgate Publishing.

Delpy Neirotti, L. (2003). An introduction to sport and adventure tourism. In S. Hudson (ed.), *Sport and Adventure Tourism*. Binghampton, NY: Haworth Hospitality Press, pp. 1–25.

Findlay, K. (2001). Can we watch whales and not disturb them? *Abstracts of the Southern Hemisphere Marine Mammal Conference 2001, 29 May–1 June, Philip Island Conference Centre, Cowes, Philip Island, Victoria, Australia*. Philip Island: Philip Island Nature Park.

Giard, D. (1997). The situation regarding nature sport tourism in mountain areas. *Cahiers Espaces*, 52, 48–57.

Gibson, H., Attle, S. and Yiannakis, A. (1997). Segmenting the active sport tourist market: a life span perspective. *Journal of Vacation Marketing*, 4(1), 52–64.

Hudson, S. (ed.) (2003). *Sport and Adventure Tourism*. Binghampton, NY: Haworth Hospitality Press.

Hudson, S. (2003). Winter sport tourism. In S. Hudson (ed.), *Sport and Adventure Tourism*. Binghampton, NY: Haworth Hospitality Press, pp. 89–123.

Inskeep, E. (1991). *Tourism Planning. An Integrated and Sustainable Development Approach*. New York: Van Nostrand Reinhold.

Jeong, G. H. (1999). Residents' perceptions on the long-term impacts of the Seoul Olympics to the Chamsil area development in a tourism perspective. In T. D. Anderson, C. Persson, B. Sahlberg and L. Strom (eds), *The Impact of Mega Events*. Ostersund: European Tourism Research Institute, pp. 169–178.

Keller, P. (2001). Tourism, sport and the environment. In *Sport and Tourism* (1st World Conference Proceedings). Madrid: World Tourism Organization and the International Olympic Committee, pp. 111–116.

Manning, R. E. (1999). Carry capacity: an organizational framework. In *Studies in Outdoor Recreation*. Corvallis, OR: Oregon University Press, pp. 49–66.

Pigeassou, C., Vanreusel, B., Miranda, J. and Monserrat, S. (1999). Conflicts between sport tourism and the environment in several European countries: a worrying situation. *Cahiers Espaces*, 62, 12–20.

Prosser, G. (1986). The limits of acceptable change: an introduction to a framework for natural area planning. *Australian Parks and Recreation*, 22(2), 5–10.

Readman, M. (2003). Golf tourism. In S. Hudson (ed.), *Sport and Adventure Tourism*. Binghampton, NY: Haworth Hospitality Press, pp. 165–203.

Saunders, A. (2003). Moves to put boaties in poo. *Shore News*, Wednesday 7 May, p. 10.

Shackley, M. (1996). *Wildlife Tourism*. London: International Thompson Business Press.

Ward, J. C. and Beanland, R. A. (1996). *Biophysical Impacts of Tourism*. Information Paper No. 6. Lincoln, NZ: Lincoln Environmental.

19

Culture, sport and tourism: the case of the Arctic Winter Games

Tom Hinch and Suzanne de la Barre

Introduction

Successful sport tourism destinations require successful sport tourism attractions. While the physical attractions in a destination are tangible, the cultural attractions of a destination are not. Sport includes both of these dimensions. Built and natural features that provide exceptional sporting environments can be readily positioned as sport attractions. It is much more challenging, however, to position the cultural dimension of sport as a tourist attraction. Not only is this cultural dimension less concrete, it is also more sensitive to issues associated with commodification, globalization and control. Despite these challenges, the cultural dimensions of sport make it one of the most powerful types of attractions in terms of facilitating an authentic experience of place. It has been suggested that sport is a 'cultural experience of physical activity' while tourism is a 'cultural experience of place' (Standeven and De Knop, 1999: 58). The combination of these relationships as found in sport tourism represents a unique opportunity and challenge for destinations. These ties between culture, sport and tourism form the underlying themes of the following discussion.

More specifically, this chapter explores the potential for sporting events to serve as cultural tourist attractions that facilitate authentic experiences in northern Canada. It does this by describing how culturally based sporting events can be positioned as tourist attractions and by highlighting the fundamental issues that exist in relation to this strategy. The latter half of the chapter examines the potential of the Arctic Winter Games to function as a tourist attraction.

Sport attractions and the cultural dimensions of sport

The argument presented in this chapter is premised on the idea that sport can function as a culturally based tourist attraction. While this may seem to be obvious in terms of observable tourist behaviour, it is worth articulating in the context of attraction theory. It is also necessary to expand on the connection between sport and culture, as this relationship is critical to the way that sport events function as tourist attractions.

Attraction framework

Leiper (1990: 371) defines a tourist attraction as 'a system comprising three elements: a tourist or human element, a nucleus or central element, and a marker or informative element. A tourist attraction comes into existence when the three elements are connected'. In the case of sport tourism attractions, the tourist or human element consists of persons who are travelling away from home to the extent that their behaviour is motivated by sport-related factors. Sport may be a primary, secondary or even tertiary motivation. This dimension of sport attractions is unique given the extent and breadth of sport participants (event, active and nostalgia) (Gibson, 1998). A second element of the attraction system consists of 'markers', which are items of information about the attraction (Leiper, 1990). Examples of conscious attraction markers featuring sport include travel advertisements showing visitors involved in destination-specific sport activities and events. Perhaps even more pervasive are the unconscious markers. At the forefront of these are televised broadcasts of elite sport competitions and advertisements for an assortment of non-travel related products featuring sports in recognizable destinations. The audience exposed to these broadcasts and advertisements have the location marked for them as a tourist attraction, which may influence future travel decisions (Hinch and Higham, 2004).

The central element of the tourist attraction system is, however, the nucleus, which is where the tourist experience is produced and consumed. In the context of sport, it consists of the attributes of the sporting activity. A sociological perspective of sport highlights the unique characteristics of sport as an attraction nucleus. First, each sport has its own set of rules that articulate spatial and temporal structures such as the dimensions of a playing surface or the duration of a match (Bale, 1989). Second, competition relating to physical prowess encompasses the goal orientation, competition and contest-based aspects of sport (McPherson

261

et al., 1989). Goal orientation ranges from elite competition to recreational sport or 'sport for all'. It also suggests that unique types of skills and strategies are associated with different sports. Third, sport is characterized by its playful nature. This element includes the notions of uncertainty of outcome and sanctioned display. In more competitive versions of sport one of the basic objectives is that the competitors should be evenly matched, thereby making the outcome uncertain. Unpredictable outcomes help to ensure authenticity and renewability, which are central to the sustainability of a tourist attraction (Hall and Page, 1999). Sanctioned display is also characteristic of sport inasmuch as sport is not limited to acts of physical prowess but is also inclusive of their demonstration or display. Many different types of sports involvement are therefore possible for sport tourists, including spectatorship (Gibson, 1998; Standeven and De Knop, 1999).

The sport and culture dynamic

Sport relates to culture in a number of ways, but two of the most common are sport as a complement to culture, and sport as a form of culture (Hinch and Higham, 2004). In the first instance, culture implies refinement and civilization. Its meaning is consistent with Veblen's (1934) theory of the 'leisure class' in terms of the cultivation of skill and knowledge in a range of non-productive pursuits such as music and painting (Hall *et al.*, 1991). Such practices are often used to delineate social status, and have been referred to as 'high culture'. They are also commonly referred to as the visual and performing arts. In some ways this form of culture is the antithesis of sport in that it is seen as an intellectual activity in contrast to the physical nature of sport. Nevertheless, it is often positioned as a complementary activity at major sporting events. The opening and closing ceremonies of the Olympic Games provide a good example of this conscious mix (Purijk, 1999), as do the separate Olympic cultural programmes organized by host cities (Voumard, 1995).

Culture may also be thought of in terms of mass or popular culture. Rather than focusing on the activities of the elite, popular culture involves the activities and interest of the masses. It generally refers to: '... all those spectator entertainments, including sport, whose appeal is primarily an emotional or sensual one and whose 'fans' are seeking excitement or entertainment rather than intellectual development in their leisure time' (Hall *et al.*, 1991: 29). A variation of this view is culture as a way of life. From this perspective, culture is:

> ... what we are all about. It is a crystallization of what we feel, what we want, what we fear, what we live for. We shape it, it shapes us, it both reflects and determines our being, it is the way we try to understand and give meaning to our lives. Our culture is us. (McGregor, 1983: 99)

The sports played in a destination not only reflect the behaviours of the host population, but also represent manifestations of the values and character of the hosts. From this perspective, sport is culture; it is an authentic dimension of place, and it is often accessible to visitors.

Development issues

Sport tourism development is characterized by an assortment of issues that need to be recognized and addressed if initiatives in this area are to be sustainable. Three of the most fundamental issues are commodification, globalization and control.

Commodification and authenticity

Commodification 'is a process by which things (and activities) come to be evaluated primarily in terms of their exchange value, in a context of trade, thereby becoming goods (and services)' (Cohen, 1988: 380). In market systems, the value of these things and activities is measured in terms of price.

Critics of cultural tourism argue that commodification introduces economic relations into an area where previously they played no part. In the process of commercialization, real authenticity is destroyed and a covert 'staged authenticity' emerges (Boorstin, 1975; Greenwood, 1989; MacCannell, 1999). It is contended that as the fact that this staged authenticity is not real dawns on tourists, their search for authenticity will be thwarted. Similar arguments have been made in the case of the commodification of sport (McKay and Kirk, 1992). Counter-arguments suggest that while commodification may change cultural meanings, it does not necessarily destroy them (Cohen, 1988). This argument is strengthened when culture is seen as a dynamic rather than a static phenomenon. It has also been pointed out that there are different types of authenticity, with a major distinction being made between objective and experiential authenticity (McIntosh and Prentice, 1999; Wang, 1999). Objective authenticity involves the assessment of whether an object is real (e.g. a museum curator's assessment of an historic work of art), while experiential authenticity is the assessment of whether a travel experience was real from the perspective of the traveller. Typically, major breaks from tradition in sport are seen as undermining objective authenticity. In contrast, the authenticity of sport is much more resilient from an experiential perspective since sport tends to engage participants physically, cognitively and emotionally. Sport offers the same advantages for spectators, with the exception of the physical involvement. Authentic experience is, however, fostered by spectator sport's emphasis on performance, competition and the uncertainty of outcomes. It is also consistent with Getz's (1998) argument that community-based festivals provide a window on the living or authentic community. He argues that 'an "authentic cultural experience" is not a commodity negotiated between visitor and community, but a realization of the visitor that the experience truly reflects local values' (Getz, 1998: 426). Attendance at genuine community-based celebrations of sport can provide this insight into local values.

Globalization

Globalization is a second major issue facing sport tourism development. In general terms, globalization is the process that leads to an ever-tightening network of connections that cut across national boundaries. It is characterized by the worldwide compression of time and space (Mowforth and Munt, 1999). For sport tourism development, the heart of the issue is whether globalization leads to homogenization or heterogenization. If the landscape were to evolve into a homogeneous culture throughout the world, much of the existing incentive to travel for sport would be lost. The issue is therefore an important one for sport tourism destinations.

The essence of the homogenization/heterogenization debate in sport is nicely summarized in the words of Silk and Jackson (2000: 102):

> Homogenization heralds the advent of an era dominated by creeping global standardization. Heterogenization, however, rejects the influence of global technologies and products in favour of stressing the inherent uniqueness of localities. The former category suggests that we are becoming more alike and heading towards a uniform global culture. The latter emphasizes cultural differences and the power of the particular.

Rowe and Lawrence (1996) have argued that there is considerable evidence that sport is becoming more homogenized (e.g. the growth of global media spectacles like the Olympics, the increase in geographically mobile sports such as golf, and the prevalence of US-style commercialization of sport). Maguire (1999) counters that these homogenizing trends are balanced by an increasing diversification of sport cultures as local negotiation and resistance ensure that a heterogeneous sport landscape flourishes.

Control/partnership

The sport tourism industry is complex, and includes multiple stakeholders. Not only does the provision of a sport tourism experience require input from both the sport and the tourism sector, it also requires inputs from a multitude of parties within each of these sectors. To maximize the potential benefits of sport tourism, these stakeholders must be willing and able to work together in pursuit of their common interests. To this point, sport tourism has been plagued by a lack of coordination between sport and tourism agencies – especially within the public sector (Weed and Bull, 1997).

The need for partnerships and strategic alliances in tourism and in sport has been increasingly recognized over the past 10 years, especially as government resources that were traditionally directed toward these areas have been reduced (Jamal and Getz, 1994). While a broad range of models for partnership has emerged, it can generally be described as '... a voluntary pooling of resources (labour, money, information, etc.) between two or more parties to accomplish collaborative goals' (Selin and Chavez, 1995: 845).

Despite their advantages, these partnerships represent a 'double-edged sword'. On the one hand, they provide the potential to capture the synergies of multiple stakeholders working together in their common interest. On the other hand, they can redistribute control and power in a way that is not always attractive to individual stakeholders. Partnership models mean that destination communities must share decision-making power with outside agencies. This redistribution of control is especially sensitive in the case of culturally based tourism, where the destination hosts are part of the tourist attraction.

Tourism in northern Canada

'The North' is a central icon in Canada's image as a tourist destination. This image reflects both the reality and the mythology of the North as one of the world's last wilderness frontiers. With the development of a market-based northern economy, tourism has become increasingly important as a way for local communities to generate income for their residents. Territorial governments have recognized this, and have actively positioned their regions in international and domestic tourism markets. One of the ways that they have positioned themselves is as adventure sport destinations.

The tourism economy

Northern destinations report growing tourism economies, with positive implications for local employment and community development (Haider and Johnston, 1993). Non-renewable resource-dependent regions have increasingly turned to tourism as a feasible development alternative, and their governments are planning accordingly (Tourism Yukon, 2000).

Data from the NWT and the Yukon reflect a dramatic growth in the number of visitors to these territories (Hinch, 2001). In 1959, only 600 visitors to the NWT (inclusive of Nunavut) were recorded. By 1998, over 45 000 visitors were counted, with a total of $CAN 30 million in expenditures. The Yukon, with its better road access and positioning relative to Alaska, had 299 267 visitors in 1998, with total visitor expenditures of over $CAN 124 million. This compares to just over 100 000 visitors in 1969, the first year for which comparable data are available.

In addition to the high cost of transportation and infrastructure limitations in Canada's northern tourism periphery, one of the key constraints that it faces as a tourism destination is seasonality. Rogers' (1997) analysis of northern tourism concluded that it was a 'fair weather' destination for the non-domestic market. Fifty-eight per cent of all trips to the Yukon by Americans and 57 per cent of those by overseas visitors occur during July, August and September, while a more moderate 37 per cent of Canadian visits occur during this period. This seasonal pattern is consistent with a market that sees the North as a pleasure trip destination. Tourism Yukon (2000) has recently initiated a strategy to increase the winter tourism market. This strategy focuses on adventure sports, including dog sled races, ski jooring (a blend of Nordic skiing and dog sledding), reindeer racing and winter 'ironman' races.

The lure of the North

The North is a land of contrasts and extremes, of light and dark, of long winters and short summers, of a barren landscape and an exotic wildlife, and of traditional and contemporary cultures. These images have been created and perpetuated through southern-based media, tourism promoters, and northerners themselves (Milne et al., 1998). As is the nature of the tourism industry, various stakeholders have actively tried to mould the image of the North to attract tourists. One has only to scan northern Canada's tourism websites to capture the essence of its tourism positioning – for example, 'Canada's True North' (Yukon Territorial Government, 2003); 'Within reach, yet beyond belief' (Department of Economic Development and Tourism, undated); and 'Canada's Arctic...for Real Travellers' (*Nunavut Tourism*, 2003).

These slogans are designed to lure tourists to a northern adventure with wilderness and culture as central elements. Featured tourist activities include hiking, canoeing and fishing in the summer, and snowmobiling, dog sledding and snow-shoeing in the winter. Participants in these activities are immersed in the region's physical culture and frontier landscape.

Visitors are also invited to experience aboriginal tradition 'where it's still lived' (*Nunavut Handbook*, 2003). However, to a large extent the featured sports focus on wilderness adventure rather than cultural experience. A noteworthy exception includes the annual Alaska–Yukon Quest dog sled race, which is actively presented as a tourist attraction. Yet even these sport activities do not emphasize the indigenous cultures that dominate much of the North. The Arctic Winter Games (AWG) include very significant indigenous cultural components. While they have not been aggressively positioned as tourist attractions to date, they represent intriguing possibilities for sport tourism development in the future (see Case study 19.1).

Case study 19.1 The Arctic Winter Games

Initiated in 1970, the Arctic Winter Games were developed to provide northerners with an opportunity to compete in athletic competitions against other northerners (Arctic Winter Games, 2003). The mission of the AWG is to facilitate athletic competition, cultural exhibition and social interchange between northerners. The stated values underlying the competition include cultural awareness and understanding, fair play, access and equity, integrity, respect for self and others, partnerships, personal development, and community development (Szabo, 2003). Competitions are held on a biennial basis, with the most recent being the XVII Arctic Winter Games co-hosted in 2002 by Nuuk, Greenland and Iqualuit, Nunavut. The Games have grown from a modest beginning of 500 athletes, coaches, mission staff, officials and cultural performers in the inaugural 1970 Games in Yellowknife to over 1600 participants in 2002. Participating regions have included the Northwest Territories, Yukon, Northern Alberta and Quebec, Alaska, Greenland and Russia.

The Arctic Winter Games' success has been at least partially due to its capacity to make the compromises necessary to represent natives and non-natives, to engage large and small communities, and to encourage widespread participation. The Games are intended to foster the development of sport in the North and to prepare northern athletes for southern-based competition. In so doing, the AWG are meant to complement north–south competitions rather than replace them (AWG Corporation, 1982).

Notwithstanding this complementary relationship with southern sporting competitions, there is a recognized need to retain the 'uniqueness of North' (AWG

Corporation, 1982). Given the distinctive communities of the North, it is only reasonable for the sport development system to have significant variations from southern-based systems. For example, the AWG fosters broad-based participation, exhibiting more flexibility in the selection process for athletes than is found in southern Canada (AWG Corporation, 1982: 73). Similarly, traditional indigenous Arctic sports were added as an official component in 1974, and were expanded in 1990 (Paraschak, 1997).

Positioning the AWG as a tourist attraction

At present there is no formal commitment to tourism in the mission of the AWG. However, the fact that the vast majority of participants travel more than 80 kilometres to compete means that it is already technically functioning as a tourist attraction. The AWG fit nicely into the tourist attraction framework previously described. The human or tourist element consists of athletes, coaches, officials, cultural performers and an assortment of other friends and associates. In terms of the nucleus, the AWG includes an intriguing mix of contemporary (e.g. cross-country skiing, snowboarding, and alpine skiing), emerging (dog mushing, snow-shoeing, and snowshoe biathlon) and Arctic (traditional Inuit and Dene Games) sports. Finally, the AWG are clearly marked as a tourist attraction through the promotional materials provided to potential participants, and through the media coverage of the event.

At one level the AWG separates culture from sport, as highlighted by the formal distinction made between the athletic competition and cultural exhibition. The latter includes visual arts and performing artists representing the various regions of the North. At a deeper level, the athletic events themselves reflect the unique range of contemporary and traditional cultures found in the North. Contemporary sports reflect global influences; emerging sports are hybrids of southern and northern culture; while Arctic sports draw on the traditional cultures of the indigenous people of the North. Sports in these latter two categories would be particularly appealing to southern tourists wanting insight into the northern way of life, although Paraschak (1997) suggests that the AWG have significant limitations in terms of their relevance for indigenous peoples.

While there is evidence that the AWG are currently functioning as a domestic tourist attraction, there is much less support to suggest that they are being consciously positioned as an attraction for tourists from the south. There is, however, some indication that this event may be positioned more actively to attract these tourists in the future. For example, in 1988 a northern politician emphasized the need for the AWG to strengthen their 'unique Northern identity' (Paraschak, 1997). While this call was partly based on a desire to protect the cultural interests of indigenous people in the North, it was also presented as a way to garner the support from southern-based media. Such support not only helps to secure funding from southern-based governments and corporate sponsors, but also it is conducive to increased tourism.

Host communities are placing more and more emphasis on the economic impacts of the AWG. An economic impact study of the 2000 Whitehorse AWG states that:

... although the focus of the AWG is to provide competitive and artistic opportunities for athletes and cultural performers who reside in the North, it is becoming increasingly imperative for event organizers and promoters to estimate the impact that the Games have on the economies of the host jurisdictions. (Berrett, 1998: 4)

In the **Nuuk Press Catalogue** for the 2002 AWG, the promoters highlighted the fact that the AWG is 'a unique event that gives equal focus to both sports and culture'therefore making it attractive for tourism (AWG Corporation, 2002: 4). Similarly, in assessing a bid for the 2006 AWG, the Kenai Peninsula Economic Development District (2002: 15) openly state their interest in tourism by arguing that 'the 2006 AWG if held on the Peninsula, would put the winter tourism potential in the national and international spotlight'.

Issue analysis

While there seems to be increasing interest and considerable potential in positioning the AWG as an attraction for southern-based tourists, there are several issues that merit further consideration prior to committing to a tourism-based strategy. In particular, issues associated with commodification, globalization and control all need to be addressed.

Commodification/authenticity

Positioning the AWG as a tourist attraction for southern visitors represents an explicit form of commodification. AWG organizers need to decide whether the Games' long-standing mission would be compromised by the change in meaning of the Games that would necessarily occur under a more commercialized approach. The cultural exhibition portion of the event would face the challenge of 'staged authenticity'. This challenge is not that dissimilar to what this aspect of the Games currently faces. They will remain performances, with the main difference being a change in audience. Rather than cultural performances aimed at other northerners (many of whom have significantly different cultures), the performers will have to aim their performances at audiences that are even more distant in cultural terms. Care will need to be taken not to modify the performance so much that it loses its relevance to northern audiences and, more importantly, to the performers themselves.

Commodification of the sporting competition does not pose as much of a risk, given the athletes' focus on competition, and the uncertainty of outcomes. However, the authenticity of the 'Arctic' sports very much depends on the retention of the playful dimension of these Games.

In the cases of both the athletic competition and the cultural exhibition, experiential authenticity is likely to be more resilient than the authenticity of the toured object. Tourists, athletes and to a lesser extent cultural performers are probably going to continue having authentic experiences, but the introduction of a new audience may cause concern in terms of objective authenticity as the cultural exhibits are packaged as products. For example, the scheduling of events and performances will have to cater to the needs of the southern visitors rather than the less-structured practical consciousness of indigenous northerners (Paraschak, 1997; Notkze, 1998). This means that events will have to begin at a pre-arranged time rather than the more flexible scheduling of traditional indigenous sporting activities.

The fact that the AWG have already been consciously positioned in relation to southern-based sport events creates a favourable situation for tourism development. While the structure of the AWG, as well as the nature of its sport–culture relationship, is primarily a consequence of its three-part mandate (sport competition, cultural exhibition and social exchange), the southern-influenced institutional framework of the event is compatible with that required for tourism development.

Care must be taken not to spectacularize the event too much. To do so runs the risk of changing the extraordinary into the ordinary (Whitson and Macintosh, 1996). The challenge for the AWG is to remain a community-based celebration so that it retains its appeal to locals and visitors.

Globalization

In positioning the AWG as an attraction for southern-based tourists, the issue of globalization must be considered. Two dimensions of this issue are particularly relevant: the first is how the globalization of sport may affect the attractiveness of the AWG to southern-based tourists, while the second is the role of tourism as an agent for globalization in the North. In both cases, the essence of the issue is whether globalization will lead to a homogenization and/or a heterogenization of culture in the North.

The sporting events offered at the AWG are already affected by globalization. This is especially evident in the grouping that was previously labelled as contemporary. Sports like cross-country skiing, snowboarding and alpine skiing are found throughout the world under appropriate climatic conditions. Their popularity is part of a global phenomenon, and is an accurate reflection of contemporary sporting culture in the North. The adoption of 'meritocracy' as an underlying principle of the AWG (Paraschak, 1997) is also consistent with the global sport culture. These manifestations of the global sport structure contribute to a global homogeneity which, if carried to the extreme, would undercut the distinctiveness of the AWG as an attraction for southern tourists.

It is, however, unlikely that the AWG will ever succumb totally to these pressures. Richards and Hall's (2000) concept of 'neotribalism' seems applicable in this case. They suggest that neotribalism can strengthen 'a sense of identity that can create both the potential for tourism development as well as increase the potential for resistance to modernization and the effects of globalization' (Richards and Hall, 2000: 4). Three forms of neotribalism are readily apparent in the AWG. The first is the inclusion of a cultural exhibition designed to celebrate the diverse cultures of the North. The second is the presence of hybrid sports, like the snow-shoe biathlon, that mix contemporary global sport with local interests and conditions. The third is the inclusion of Arctic sports in the form of traditional

Inuit and Dene games into the athletic competition. The inclusion of these events into the AWG reflects the strongly voiced views of the indigenous peoples of the North (Paraschak, 1997). It epitomizes a neotribalism that promotes the local over the global. In combination, all three expressions of neotribalism result in a distinctive sporting event tied to place, thereby providing a competitive advantage for the AWG to act as a tourist attraction.

The extent to which tourism itself would act as a force for homogenization or heterogenization is difficult to predict at this point. To a considerable degree, it depends on the retention of authenticity. The presence of spectators from the south will change the nature of the event, but it is in the interests of tourism promoters as well as northern sport enthusiasts to protect the integrity of the event. Its sustainability as a tourist attraction will require that it remains distinct in character from southern-based sport festivals.

Control versus partnership

In his opening ceremony address to the athletes of the 1978 AWG, the then Commissioner of the NWT closed his remarks by exclaiming 'These are your Games. Do with them what you will' (Government of the Northwest Territories, 1978). The broader context of his remarks expressed the view that the AWG were a product of the North in that they are organized by northerners for northerners. This idea of northern focus and control underlies the essence of the Games, but it is increasingly being confronted with the need for partnership.

Despite its relatively low population, the North features a number of different interest groups, whether divided by territorial jurisdiction or cultural affiliation. For example, annual funding is provided by jurisdictions represented on the Board of Directors of the AWG International Committee including the NWT, Yukon, Alaska, Alberta and Greenland. The Government of Canada and host municipalities also actively support the AWG through cash grants and substantial donations in kind (AWG, 2003). Increasingly, private sector sponsors have joined the AWG partnership to provide the resources required to operate the Games. While the principle of northern control is recognized in this structure, the need for partnership is explicitly identified in the stated values of the AWG (Szabo, 2003).

If the AWG were to be positioned as an attraction for southern tourists, these partnerships would have to be expanded in the North to include tourism as well as sport interests. It would also require operational partnerships with travel operators in the south.

An inevitable trade-off exists between partnership and control. The nature and extent of the partnerships need to be more fully articulated so that the implications for northern control can be assessed. A decision needs to be made in terms of the level of control that the North wants to retain, so that these partnerships can be negotiated on favourable terms. As with the previous issues discussed, control is directly related to authenticity. If northerners fail to retain the balance of control of the AWG, the authenticity of these Games from the perspective of both the residents and tourists will be compromised. Such a compromise would not only detract from the local celebration of sport but also reduce the attractiveness of the AWG for southern tourists interested in a true northern experience.

Conclusion

Sport event tourism faces many of the same challenges that other forms of tourism do in northern Canadian destinations. It is subject to transportation, infrastructure and seasonality constraints tied to its relative isolation, northern location and low population. Development in the realm of sport event tourism in the North is also faced with challenges related to commodification, globalization and control. These challenges are balanced, however, with the potential for community-based sport festivals to provide an authentic sense of place for visitors to northern destinations. Positioning sporting events like the Arctic Winter Games as tourist attractions has the potential to allow visitors to be active participants in the northern community and to experience local values firsthand.

The Arctic Winter Games have the potential of allowing southerners the opportunity to experience the culture of physical activity as well as the culture of place. They do this at many different levels, including cultural exhibitions to complement the sporting competitions and the sporting competitions themselves as a reflection of the way of life of the North. They also offer the opportunity to highlight contemporary culture along with traditional culture, thereby avoiding the pitfalls of many types of cultural tourism products. There will be trade-offs involved should the Games be actively positioned as an attraction. These trade-offs include the need to consider scheduling the Games in a way that packages culture so that it is consumable for southern-based visitors, the need to position the local against global sport tourism interests, and the need to find an appropriate balance of development control in the face of partnerships that may redistribute power. From a tourism perspective, the success of this sport tourism attraction in the destination depends on its ability to remain a community celebration of sport. While tourism interests can provide valuable input, the decision actively to position the Arctic Winter Games as a tourist attraction needs to be made by the sport organizations and communities that are the essence of this celebration.

References

Arctic Winter Games (2003). *Homepage* (available at http://www.arcticwintergames.org/, accessed 10 July 2003).

Arctic Winter Games Corporation (1982). *The Arctic Winter Games 1972–1982: An Analysis.* Calgary: Makale & Kyllo Planning Associates Ltd.

Arctic Winter Games Corporation (2002). *Press Catalogue.* Nuuk: AWG.

Bale, J. (1989). *Sports Geography.* London: E & FN Spon.

Berrett, T. (1998). *1998 Arctic Winter Games: Economic Impact.* Final Report submitted to the Arctic Winter Games International Committee, Whitehorse, Yukon. Available at: http://www.lin.ca/lin/resource/html/arctic.htm.

Boorstin, D. J. (1975). *The Image: A Guide to Pseudo-Events in America.* New York: Atheneum.

Cohen, E. (1988). Authenticity and commoditization in tourism. *Journal of Tourism Research*, 15, 371–386.

Department of Economic Development and Tourism (undated). *Canada's Northwest Territories, 1993 Explorers' Guide.* Yellowknife: Government of the Northwest Territories.

Getz, D. (1998). Event tourism and the authenticity dilemma. In W. F. Theobald (ed.), *Global Tourism* (2nd edn). Oxford: Butterworth-Heinemann, pp. 410–427.

Gibson, H. (1998). Sport tourism: a critical analysis of research. *Sport Management Review*, 1, 45–76.

Government of the Northwest Territories (1978). *For Those Who Were There*. Yellowknife: Department of Information.

Government of the Northwest Territories (2003). *Canada's Northwest Territories* (available at http://www.nwttravel.nt.ca/04_activities/CultureHistory/Experiences.asp, accessed 18 March 2003).

Greenwood, D. J. (1989). Culture by the pound: an anthropological perspective on tourism as cultural commodification. In V. L. Smith (ed.), *Hosts and Guests: The Anthropology of Tourism*. Philadelphia, PA: University of Pennsylvania Press, pp. 17–31.

Haider, W. and Johnston, M. E. (1993). Introduction: communities, resources and tourism in the North. In W. Haider and M. Johnston (eds), *Communities, Resources and Tourism in the North, Northern and Regional Studies Series, Volume 2*. Thunder Bay: Lakehead University, Centre for Northern Studies, pp. v–xviii.

Hall, C. M., and Page, S. J. (1999). *Geography of Tourism and Recreation: Environment, Place, and Space*. London: Routledge.

Hall, A., Slack, T., Smith, G. and Whitson, D. (1991). *Sport in Canadian Society*. Toronto: McClelland & Stewart Inc.

Hinch, T. (2001). Tourism in Canada's Northwest Territories. In B. Sahlberg (ed.), *Going North: Peripheral Tourism in Canada and Sweden*. Ostersund: European Tourism Research Institute (ETOUR), pp. 105–122.

Hinch, T. and Higham, J. (2004). *Sport Tourism Development*. Clevedon, OH: Channel View.

Jamal, T. and Getz, D. (1995). Collaboration theory and community tourism planning. *Annals of Tourism Research*, 22(1), 186–204.

Kenai Peninsula Economic Development District, Inc. (2002). *Comprehensive Economic Development Strategy Kenai Peninsula Borough, Alaska*. 15 June.

Leiper, N. (1990). Tourist attraction systems. *Annals of Tourism Research*, 17(3), 367–384.

MacCannell, D. (1999). *The Tourist: A New Theory of the Leisure Class*. Los Angeles, CA: University of California Press.

Maguire, J. (1999). *Global Sport: Identities, Societies and Civilisations*. Cambridge: Polity Press.

McGregor, C. (1983). *Pop Goes the Culture*. London: Pluto Press.

McIntosh, A. J. and Prentice, R. C. (1999). Affirming authenticity: consuming cultural heritage. *Annals of Tourism Research*, 26, 589–612.

McKay, J. and Kirk, D. (1992). Ronald McDonald meets Baron De Coubertin: prime time sport and commodification. *Sport and the Media*, Winter, 10–13.

McPherson, B. D., Curtis, J. E. and Loy, J. W. (1989). *The Social Significance of Sport: An Introduction to the Sociology of Sport*. Champaign, IL: Human Kinetics.

Milne, S., Grekin, J. and Woodley, S. (1998). Tourism and the construction of place in Canada's Eastern Arctic. In G. Ringer (ed.), *Destinations: Cultural Landscapes of Tourism*. London: Routledge, pp. 101–120.

Mowforth, M. and Munt, I. (1998). *Tourism and Sustainability: New Tourism in the Third World*. London: Routledge.

Notze, C. (1998). Indigenous tourism development in the Arctic. *Annals of Tourism Research*, 26(1), 55–76.

Nunavut Handbook (2003). Available at http://www.arctictravel.com/, accessed 18 March 2003.

Nunavut Tourism (2003). Available at http://www.nunavuttourism.com/ADV/ADV2.htm, accessed 18 March 2003.

Paraschak, V. (1997). Variations in race relations: sporting events for native peoples in Canada. *Sociology of Sport Journal*, 14, 1–21.

Purijk, R. (1999). Producing Norwegian culture for domestic and foreign gazes: the Lillehammer Olympic Opening Ceremony. In A. M. Klausen (ed.), *Olympic Games as Performance and Public Event*. New York: Berghahn Books.

Richards, G. and Hall, D. (2000). *Tourism and Sustainable Community Development*. New York: Routledge.

Rogers, J. (1997). *The Northern Tourism Experience: Challenges & Opportunities*. Ottawa: The Canadian Tourism Commission.

Rowe, D. and Lawrence, G. (1996). Beyond national sport: sociology, history and postmodernity. *Sporting Traditions*, 12(2), 3–16.

Selin, S. and Chavez, D. (1995). Developing an evolutionary tourism partnership model. *Annals of Tourism Research*, 22(4), 844–856.

Silk, M. and Jackson, S. J. (2000). Globalisation and sport in New Zealand. In C. Collins (ed.), *Sport in New Zealand Society*. Palmerston North: Dunmore Press, pp. 99–113.

Standeven, J. and De Knop, P. (1999). *Sport Tourism*. Champaign, IL: Human Kinetics.

Szabo, C. (2003). The Arctic Winter Games are hot. *Parks & Recreation Canada*, 60(5), 38–44.

Tourism Yukon (2000). *Tourism Yukon Winter Tourism Development Study: An Initial Review*. Prepared by Western Management Consultants in association with Peter Williams.

Veblen, T. (1934). *The Theory of the Leisure Class: An Economic Study of Institutions*. New York: The Modern Library.

Voumard, S. (1995). Jonah's big date. *The Sydney Morning Herald*, 25 November, p. 14.

Wang, N. (1999). Rethinking authenticity in tourism experience. *Annals of Tourism Research*, 26(2), 349–370.

Weed, M. and Bull, C. (1997). Influences on sport tourism relations in Britain: the effects of government policy. *Tourism Recreation Research*, 22(2), 5–12.

Whitson, D. and Macintosh, D. (1996). The global circus: international sport, tourism and the marketing of cities. *Journal of Sport and Social Issues*, 3, 278–295.

Yukon Territorial Government (2003). *Yukon Departure of Business Tourism and Culture* (available at http://touryukon.com/index.asp, accessed 1 April 2003).

20

The influence of sport on destination development: the example of golf at St Andrews, Scotland

Richard Butler

Introduction

In most cases tourist destinations become established because they possess one or more of a set of specific attributes or qualities. These have generally included factors such as specific environmental features (e.g. beaches, mountains, bodies of water), unique or distinctive cultural features (e.g. built heritage, or structures possessing associations with famous individuals), attractive climatic features (e.g. temperature, sunshine, snow), a high level of accessibility (e.g. by railway or airplane), or contemporary purpose-built facilities (e.g. hotels, theme parks). Once such destinations have become established and proven attractive to tourists, they tend to proceed through a general process of development (Butler, 1980), sometimes eventually declining and even going out of tourism (Baum, 2004), in other cases being rejuvenated through adding new attractions (Stansfield, 2004) or revitalizing existing ones. In a few cases, destinations become tourist attractions through uniqueness, accident, serendipity or individual entrepreneurial efforts (Russell, 2004), even though they may be lacking in what have been described as conventional resources noted above.

One of the less common cases is that of St Andrews, a small community on the east coast of Scotland, some 80 kilometres northeast of Edinburgh. While St Andrews does possess some of the attributes of a conventional tourist destination, in particular two excellent beaches (one made famous in the film *Chariots of Fire*, although transplanted to southern England in the movie), its major claim to fame as a tourist destination over the past half century or more is its sporting associations – in particular, its golf courses and related heritage. This chapter reviews the emergence of St Andrews as a tourist destination, discusses whether it can be correctly so described in terms of its physical development and morphology, and evaluates the significance of the role of golf in shaping the form and function of the town as a tourist destination.

The emergence of St Andrews as a tourist destination

St Andrews is a small town (under 20000 in population) located at the easternmost extremity of the Fife peninsula on the east coast of Scotland, and in many respects is little different to many other similar small rural communities in Scotland and Western Europe. It has a small harbour, the last remnants of a once active fishing fleet, some historical ruins, two beaches and a university, yet its name is known throughout the world and it is visited each year by many visitors intent on deriving pleasure from other of its attributes. St Andrews first came to the notice of those outside its local boundaries more than a thousand years ago because of its religious connections. Until the Reformation in the sixteenth century it was the ecclesiastical capital of Scotland. Its cathedral was a magnificent building attracting many pilgrims, its castle was the Bishop's Palace, and its harbour had trade with Europe. After the cathedral and castle were sacked by the followers of John Knox in the sixteenth century, the town's importance waned, although it still attracted visitors. As well as being the country's religious centre, St Andrews was also the site of the first of Scotland's universities, founded in 1413, and was thus a seat of learning as well as religion. The university survived the Reformation and has continued as one of Scotland's premiere education institutions; it is now one of the cornerstones of the economy of the town in the twenty-first century.

Through medieval times, the Union of the Crowns in 1603, the Union of England and Scotland in 1707 and until well into the Victorian era, St Andrews survived as a small market town with a fishing industry, a university and interesting ruins that attracted visitors. The beaches were not viewed as major tourist attractions until the middle of the nineteenth century, and there was little indication, even 50 years ago, that the town would regain its international reputation and once more become an attraction to visitors in considerable numbers. The reasons for this transformation lie in improvements in accessibility, and the growing popularity of the game of golf.

The transportation improvements came in the form of the development of a railway link to the main line from Edinburgh to Aberdeen. This main line crossed the

Firths of Forth and Tay in two impressive and famous bridges, and transected the Fife peninsula, passing close to but not serving St Andrews directly. In 1845 a survey was made for a branch line to St Andrews from the main line at Guardbridge. The line of the original route was fiercely opposed because it cut into the green on the seventeenth hole of the then only golf course (The Old Course as it is currently known), and in 1852 a line following a new route was opened (Jarrett, 1995). The then Provost (mayor) of St Andrews welcomed the line on the basis that it would bring visitors to the town for 'the bracing breezes and sea-bathing and to play the national game of golf' (cited in Jarrett 1995: 28). The railway remained the principal form of access for visitors to St Andrews until after the Second World War, by which time trains were gradually being replaced by cars as the transport mode of choice. The line was eventually closed, along with many others, in 1969, although there is still local interest and hopes of re-opening a rail service. Currently travellers by rail have to leave the main line service at Leuchars, some 10 kilometres from St Andrews, and complete their journey by road. Relatively few tourists now use this method of transportation, with the exception of the occasions when 'The Open' (golf championship) is being held in the town.

The fact that the Provost specifically referred to golf as an attraction to visitors in 1852 reflects the fact that at that time St Andrews was already known as a significant golf centre, although the number of tourists who came specifically for golf appears to have been very small. The existence of golf at St Andrews is based on the sand dunes along the West Sands, which provide the 'links' landscape in which golf first developed and which, to purists, is still the proper setting for a golf course. The hazards on such courses are not the trees or water features, so beloved of many contemporary golf course designers, but the irregular slopes and bumps of sand dunes, natural (although normally 'improved') sand outcrops, vegetation (long, rough grass and bushes) and, perhaps above all, the wind – which, as in most coastal locations, is infinitely variable in direction and strength. Many other locations in Scotland and elsewhere have such attributes, and thus the presence of these features alone does not explain the pre-eminence of St Andrews to golfers the world over. The explanation for this lies in the cultural and economic history of the town and Scotland.

The history of golf at St Andrews

There are few, if any, communities as strongly related to sport as St Andrews is to golf. It is known worldwide as 'the home of golf', and represents an excellent example of both the positive and negative effects of being the centre of global awareness for a popular sporting activity. It has become, to all intents and purposes, a site of pilgrimage for aficionados of that activity. St Andrews' reputation as the home of golf stems from two principal factors; first, that it is generally acknowledged as the oldest site of recorded golf, and second, that it is the home of the organization (the Royal and Ancient Golf Club of Scotland) that sets the rules for the sport throughout the world (except in the USA and Mexico).

The origins of golf are shrouded in antiquity, but it is recorded in Scottish legislation that King James II banned both football and golf by an act in 1457, an action repeated by his son, James III, in 1471, and in turn by his successor, James IV, in 1492. This last monarch repented and acquired his own set of golf clubs in 1502. The problem appears to have been that young men were neglecting archery and practice for war in preference for playing golf. The lands over which they were playing were granted to the Burgh of St Andrews in 1123 by King David – a significant, if not fully appreciated, act at the time in terms of the development of both golf and St Andrews. The land was seen as being much more important than the game in economic terms for many years because it was particularly rich habitat for breeding rabbits. In 1552, Archbishop Hamilton granted the community a charter guaranteeing the people the right of 'playing at golff, futball, shuteing at all gamis with iither manner of pastimes as ever thai plais' (cited in Jarrett 1995: 14), a right confirmed again in 1614. The reason behind the charter is felt to be that it strengthened the rights of the Church to farm the rabbits by establishing its control over the links. The relationship between rabbits and golf continued for many years, as the value of the land from rabbit production far exceeded that for other sources of income. Various efforts over the years by the town representatives to sell the land in order to raise money to replenish dwindling public coffers were frustrated by citizens who wished to keep the links in public ownership, and their efforts were successful for several centuries and through to the present. While several individuals were given the right to rear rabbits on the links, it was specified that the 'links are not to be spoiled where the golfing is used' (Jarrett, 1995: 14).

The arrangements for golf in St Andrews for much of the period until the nineteenth century were primitive, and it was not until 1754 that rules were laid down for playing on the links (some 8 years after similar rules had been established by the Honourable Company of Edinburgh Golfers). It was not until 1834 that the Royal and Ancient Golf Club of St Andrews was established, and it was only in 1877 that the local clubs were amalgamated and a single body emerged to manage golf at St Andrews and establish general rules. The game was originally played on the public links over what is now the Old Course, at first over 22 holes. In 1764 the number of holes was reduced to 18, the number now accepted as the standard round of golf. The conflicts between rabbit farmers, town councillors and golfers were temporarily resolved when the land was purchased privately by the Royal and Ancient Club for golf, but differences of opinion over the relative roles of golf and tourism complicated the picture. The establishment of the Open Golf Championship in 1872 began to attract more and more people to the game, both as players and spectators. St Andrews was one of three locations used for hosting the tournament (Prestwick and Edinburgh being the others) until 1919, when three English locations were added to the list of host clubs, and thus the event became a regular feature for the town. Towards the end of the nineteenth century three citizens of the town emerged as frequent Open Champions for several years – the Old and the Young Tom Morris, and Laurie Auchterlonie – bringing the town further fame.

The Town Council saw tourism based in part on golf as being a source of income for the town, and Jarrett (1995: 35) notes that 'The Town Council wanted people to come to St Andrews to boost the economy: the Royal and Ancient wanted them to stay away because their presence took up starting times, and larger numbers on the course meant bigger maintenance bills'. At this time (the late nineteenth century), no charges were made for playing on the links. The increased demand from both local players and visitors meant that additional facilities were urgently needed, and in 1895 a second course was opened (The New Course). By 1914 two more courses, the Jubilee and the Eden, had been established by the Royal and Ancient Club. During this period the first major hotel in St Andrews was built, the Grand Hotel in 1895 (now Hamilton Hall, a university residence).

Over the next four decades a series of Acts of Legislation changed the nature of the organization of golf at St Andrews, the ownership of the links and the courses, and the rights of local residents. The local residents lost many of their privileges and rights, including freedom from charges to play, while the organizing body gained the right to close the courses when major events were being played, and to remove limits on the level of charges and discounts for locals. While the ancient right of the public (really the citizens of St Andrews) to walk over the links on Sunday was maintained, the institution of limits and charges for locals was fiercely opposed but in vain. The local residents retained minor privileges in terms of a number of starting times being reserved for them on the Old Course, but little else. Control over the operation of the courses, the setting of charges for play, and the maintenance of the courses passed from the St Andrews Town Council to the St Andrews Links Trust in 1974. This transfer of control was made in an effort to retain control of the links and golf in local (St Andrews) hands in the face of local government reorganization, which threatened to replace the Council as the local authority with a unitary authority in the form of Fife County Council. This arrangement remains in force today, although disagreements between local residents and the Links Trust over the organization of golf on the courses are frequent local political issues.

Current golf facilities and use in and around St Andrews

The last round of development by the Links Trust saw a fifth course, the Strathtyrum, opened in 1993, and a nine-hole course for junior golfers, the Balgrove, reconstructed in response to increased demand generated by both locals and visitors. Today there are six public golf courses (99 holes in all) on the links, and driving and practice grounds, and this constitutes the largest golfing complex in Europe. Two clubhouses have been constructed in the last 10 years and are open to the public, standing in addition to the famous clubhouse of the Royal and Ancient Club (the latter being strictly private for members only). Up to 250 people are employed in the high season and just under 200 year-round. In addition, approximately 250 licensed caddies find employment on the Links courses, particularly The Old Course. Plans for a seventh course to be developed were presented to local residents for consideration in July 2003, although these have not been met with universal support and objections to the development have been filed with the county planning office. This new development would be to the south-east of the town on hill ground overlooking the town, close to a private development at St Andrews Bay. It would represent a significant change in terms of the type of golf course provided by the Links Trust; the proposed course is not a links course, and would be several kilometres away from the West Sands complex centred on the Old Course. The cost of land acquisition has been put at in excess of £1 million at 2003 prices.

Currently over 200 000 rounds are played annually on the six Links Trust courses, and of these approximately 60 per cent are played by 'locals' (residents of the town or of the Kingdom of Fife), reflecting the commitment of residents to golf as a pastime as well as its importance as a tourism magnet (St Andrews Links Trust).

The presence of the Royal and Ancient Golf Club and the relatively frequent holding of the Open Championship at St Andrews (currently approximately every 6 years) serve to keep the town in the international golf audience's mind. In the past decade several other developments have strengthened this association and reflected the importance of golf to tourism in the town, marking the most recent era of golf tourism at St Andrews. The two largest hotels in the town are located adjoining the Old Course, Rusaks being built in the nineteenth century and renovated and expanded in the last decade, and The Old Course Hotel being built in the 1980s and subsequently expanded over the last decade. This hotel, which stands beside the seventeenth fairway, has around 150 rooms and suites, with rates running from Euros 600–1200 a night for half of the year. It had the claim to be the largest hotel in the area until 2001, when the St Andrews Bay Resort opened some 8 kilometres south of the town, with just over 200 rooms, its own two golf courses and luxurious facilities. In 2003 the Old Course Hotel and Resort was designated as the leading golf resort in the world (*St Andrews Citizen*, 2003).

A slightly greater distance to the north of the town is the Drumoig Golf Resort. Although this has a much smaller hotel development (only 29 rooms), it is the site of not only yet another new golf course but also the National Golf Academy (the Scottish National Golf Centre). Its operators claim it to be Europe's finest purpose-built coaching facility, constructed in association with the sports equipment giant Nike. Its extensive coaching and training facilities make it a valuable addition to the range of facilities in the area. Despite the quality of the facilities the Centre has proved uneconomic in operation, and at the time of writing is facing bankruptcy and closure. The reasons for the uneconomic operation are not clear at this time, although the somewhat isolated location relative to the town and the famous courses may be a factor.

On the southern edge of the town at Craigtoun is the Duke's Course, which was opened in 1995 and is affiliated with the Old Course Hotel. This is an inland course, offering golfers an alternative to the traditional links courses of the town. In addition, a large number of the neighbouring small towns and villages in eastern Fife have their own golf courses; in many cases these are close to championship quality themselves, with long histories of public access to their facilities for very reasonable fees – especially compared to charges in other locations.

Golf and tourism in St Andrews

Today St Andrews has an economy which is surprisingly broadly based for a small town. The oldest surviving leg of the economy is the university, the third oldest in the United Kingdom and one which has been highly rated in all assessments of quality over recent decades. It remains the largest employer in the town, and since becoming the university of choice for Prince William in 2001 has seen a 44 per cent increase in student applications. Across the Eden River is Royal Air Force Leuchars, one of what is now a small number of front-line bases in the United Kingdom, and a second leg in the economy of St Andrews, since a considerable number of the personnel live in and around the town. The Church and the harbour offer little employment compared to a millennium ago, but serve as attractions to the third leg of the economy, which is tourism. While St Andrews is an attractive medieval town, its market square and old street layout surviving still, the main attractions for conventional tourism are clearly the beaches. While the attractive East Sands at the harbour attract relatively few tourists, the West Sands (the setting for the opening sequences of not only *Chariots of Fire* but also of *Macbeth*) form one of the most impressive beaches in Scotland and, being next to the golf courses and close to the university, are much more visible to visitors. The traditional tourist also finds attractions such as putting greens, a bandstand with concerts, and a commercial aquarium adjacent to the West Sands.

The beaches and related facilities still attract tourist visitors at weekends and holidays, but none of the Fife resorts now attract the once large numbers of tourists staying for a traditional 'bucket and spade' holiday.

Today the beaches provide the edge of the golf links, and golf is the major focus of tourists staying overnight at St Andrews – almost entirely so for the international tourists who visit the town. The pre-eminence of golf is seen in the location of tourist facilities, as well as the nature and number of those facilities. The current morphology of the centre of the town was predetermined by its medieval layout and street structure, and within the confines of this arrangement the tourist infrastructure is marked by its specific location and dimensions. The established links golf courses are all on the northern edge of the town, alongside the West Sands. Adjacent to the clubhouse of the Royal and Ancient Golf Club, at the first tee of the Old Course, is the new British Golf Museum. This has become a major tourist attraction in its own right, with eating facilities and a sales department, and was developed in the last decade. In the street adjoining the eighteenth fairway are two shops selling golf-related items, and several golf clubhouses, as well as Rusaks Hotel. In the adjoining street, which runs behind the clubhouse and the first tee of the Old Course, are two more shops selling golf items, a bookstore specializing in golf books, and the offices of the Open Championship. In North Street are a number of smaller hotels, three shops also selling golf attire and equipment, and a golf club manufacturer. There is also one of several companies that have opened in the last decade organizing golf package holidays. The Scores, which runs east from the Old Course, has several more hotels and guest houses, and an adjoining street (Murray Place) also has a considerable number of accommodation units.

This concentration is all the more marked by the fact that there is only one other shop exclusively selling golf-related goods, and that is on the central of the three ancient streets (Market Street). No major commercial tourist accommodation exists in the town other than that within two streets of the Old Course, although some smaller facilities including bed and breakfast establishments are located in other parts of the town. Two establishments that manufacture replica and modern golf clubs are located on the southern edge of the town in a small mall and adjacent to a supermarket. The Old Course Hotel, as its name implies, is immediately adjacent to the seventeenth fairway of the Old Course on the site of former maintenance sheds. To preserve the old image and character of the course, mesh fencing was erected adjacent to the seventeenth tee in the same dimensions and location as the since removed sheds, so the drive from the tee is as it was for many years. Restaurants and bars exist throughout the town, but a review of the names of such establishments reveals that few have golf-related names except for those in immediate proximity to the courses. There is, quite clearly, a version of a Recreational Business District (RBD) (Stansfield and Rickert 1970) in St Andrews, which is similar in many respects to the classic form of an RBD, with the Old Course replacing the traditional pier in classic seaside resorts. The retail and service functions within the RBD of St Andrews relate closely to golf, even in terms of the names of establishments (a taxi firm is titled

'Golf City Taxis'), the facilities are spatially concentrated, and access is highly pedestrianized. Considerable opportunities exist for extracting money from tourists, and conventional retail functions are generally absent. On the other hand, while there is a distinct summer peak in visitation, golfers visit St Andrews throughout the year, and all of the retail and accommodation facilities remain open year long – as do all of the restaurants and bars.

The attraction of St Andrews for golf also results in visits by many celebrities, ranging from royalty (Prince Andrew became Captain of the Royal and Ancient Club in 2003) to presidents (for example, almost all of the US presidents from Eisenhower onwards have played the Old Course) and from movie stars to sports personalities, which means that celebrity watching has become a spectator sport also. When the Open Championship is being held in St Andrews, the town becomes virtually besieged. In the year 2000, over 230 000 visitors came over the duration of the Millennium Open, for example (St Andrews Links Trust), and access to and within the town at such times is severely limited. Major temporary development takes place adjacent to the links (of grandstands, retail stalls, and administration, corporate hospitality and press facilities), severe but necessary restrictions are placed on vehicle use in the town, and residential properties are rented for close to a year's normal rental for the 2 weeks involved (the Open begins in one week and ends in the next). Ironically, some merchants experience a loss of business during the main week of the tournament, particularly those who do not cater to tourists. Many local residents cannot (or choose not to try to) access the centre of the town during this period and, as in the case of many mega-events, a proportion of locals choose to take their holidays during this time. Overall, however, given the fact that golf has been an integral part of the life of St Andrews for 600 years at least, it not unnaturally has strong support from the local residents.

Conclusions

One may conclude, therefore, that St Andrews is most certainly a tourist destination, and that golf has become the major factor in the expansion and maintenance of the tourism-related development. As noted above, the economy of the town is diverse and there is little indication that any of the elements discussed are likely to decline in the near future at least, but of all of them, tourism based on golf seems to have the greatest potential for continued growth, given the increasing global popularity of the game and St Andrews' unique position. Over the past few decades interest and participation in golf has continued to expand and, as discussed earlier, considerable development has taken place outside, but close to the town itself. These developments have not reduced pressure upon the town or its original links; if anything, they have increased pressure on the town's original courses. While the new facilities are of a high standard, the unique appeal of playing on the Old Course cannot be replaced by playing on any other course anywhere in the world, and thus a golfing holiday to the St Andrews area is rarely seen as complete without visiting and playing at the original home of golf on the 'original' course. This is not only the greatest asset of the town as far as tourism is concerned, but also, as has been the case for the past century, the greatest problem.

The Old Course in particular is at capacity for much of the summer, and cannot accommodate more rounds at that time. This pressure from visitors is a constant grievance to local players, who have experienced decreased reserved opportunities to play the Old Course during the summer over the years – in part, in their view, because of the revenues generated by non-locals, who pay approximately $US 150 a round. Given the nature of the game of golf, a maximum of four people can participate in a round together and each group needs at least 10 minutes between themselves and the preceding and following groups. (The Links Trust stamps golf balls used at the practice facilities with the numbers 3:57. This is not homage to 'Dirty Harry' but, as noted in their facilities, refers to the amount of time it is expected a foursome would take to play a round on the Old Course.) The creation of additional courses on the original links is barely possible – certainly not beyond perhaps one more course at most – and there are no plans to create another course here by the Links Trust, but rather to the south of the town as noted earlier. The natural limits on development of facilities and a market that shows no sign of reaching its peak would seem to suggest that not only is St Andrews likely to have a successful future in tourism based on golf over the long term; if carefully managed, it should also be a sustainable future.

Acknowledgements

The generous assistance of Carolyne Nurse, St Andrews Links Trust, in providing statistics and information is gratefully acknowledged.

References

Baum, T. G. Revisiting the TALC – is there an off-ramp? In R. W. Butler (ed.), *The TALC: Conceptual and Methodological Issues*. Clevedon, OH: Channel View (in press).

Butler, R. W. (1980). The concept of a tourist area cycle of evolution and implications for management. *The Canadian Geographer*, 24, 5–12.

Jarrett, T. (1995). *St Andrews Golf Links The First 600 Years*. Edinburgh: Mainstream Publishing.

Russell, R. The contribution of entrepreneurship theory to the TALC model. In R. W. Butler (ed.), *The TALC: Conceptual and Methodological Issues*. Clevedon, OH: Channel View (in press).

Stansfield, C. A. The rejuvenation of Atlantic City: the resort cycle recycles. In R. W. Butler (ed.), *The TALC: Conceptual and Methodological Issues*. Clevedon, OH: Channel View (in press).

Stansfield, C. A. and Rickert, J. E. (1970). The recreational business district. *Journal of Leisure Research*, 2(4), 213–225.

St Andrews Citizen (2003). Friday 31 October.

St Andrews Links Trust (Various) *Annual Report and Accounts*. St Andrews: Links Trust.

Part Five: Conclusion

21

The future of sport tourism

James Higham

Introduction

Few phenomena are more problematic in forecasting than trends in sport and tourism. Both sport and tourism have experienced rapid and sustained increases in participation rates in recent decades and, because of this, sport and tourism have been recognized to be generally robust industries. However, such generalizations obscure the reality that upon closer examination both sport and tourism phenomena are dynamic and fragile. Individual sports and specific tourism destinations exist within product lifecycles, which require responsiveness to ever-changing sport participant and spectator, and tourism consumer preferences. Individual sports rise and fall in popularity, existing sports evolve into hybrid forms, and new sports are constantly being innovated – often in response to emerging technologies, but also in response to changing social needs. Similarly, and perhaps more particularly, tourism destinations lie at the mercy of various influences that may pose threats and/or present opportunities to destination managers. Foremost among them, tourism destinations are subject to trends, fashions and preferences that change from one season to the next. Furthermore, and less directly managed to varying degrees, tourism destinations are influenced by economic circumstances, political influences, technological advances and, in cases such as extreme weather events and outbreaks of disease, abrupt changes in fortune.

Both sport and tourism are subject to specific niche-market demands. In instances where these demands are not being met, changing preferences and purchase patterns swiftly follow. Sports are cultural practices and social constructions, and as such they evolve as people interact (Coakley, 2004). Sport tourism is one medium of social interaction that may provide a platform for the evolution of sports (Hinch and Higham, 2004). Tourism, like sport, is a discretionary activity that is immediately influenced by economic circumstances and levels of discretionary income. While sport and tourism futures are, by the very nature of sport and tourism, problematic in forecasting, various existing trends provide insights into possible futures influencing the interests of sport tourism destinations.

In speculating on the future of sports, it is useful to differentiate between power and performance sports on one hand, and participation and pleasure sports on the other. Coakley (2004) suggests that power and performance sports will remain the most visible forms of sport, and those that generally dominate media interests in reporting and broadcasting sports. The continuation of this trend is manifest in the professionalization of sports competitions, the development of sports academies and sport development programmes, and the expansion of business travel flows associated with the administration and management of professional sports and sports events. Power and performance sports are likely to continue as the dominant forces in sport spectatorship, sports marketing, sponsorship in sport, and the development of cultural celebrities through sport.

While this is the established formula for sport, it is noteworthy that the management of power and performance sports has changed dramatically in association with the professionalization of sport and the expansion of commercial interests in sport. These changes include the development of new and negotiated structures for partnership and control relating, for example, to media broadcasting interests. The financial structures associated with power and performance sports have expanded far beyond gate receipts. Power and performance sports dominate commercial sponsorship in sports. In addition to sponsorship, the financial structures associated with these sports have expanded to include advertising, corporate hospitality and television rights. The requirements expected of modern, well-appointed sports facilities have moved beyond standing and seating areas for spectators to include such things as customized seating, closed-circuit television, replay screens, audio-connections from officials to spectators, entertainment during breaks between play, and a broad range of hospitality and merchandise options. While some supporter groups remain singular and parochial, fan loyalties have generally multiplied, diversified (regional/national/international) and become increasingly transitory. These trends have raised the need to compete within the broader entertainment industry. Promotion of sports has, by necessity, become extensive and targeted as formerly undifferentiated sports markets have become increasingly fragmented and specialized (Stewart and Smith, 2000).

Notwithstanding the dominance of power and performances sports, particularly in relation to event sport tourism, the diverse interests of tourism destinations require that changing preferences relating to participation/pleasure sports are recognized and understood. Increasing new and emerging sport-related development opportunities at tourism destinations have emerged in association with participation and pleasure sports. This presents new opportunities associated with active sport tourism. Murray and Dixon (2000) have argued that the emergence of 'instant sports' is consistent with the emphasis on consumer orientations over collective/social orientations, and unstructured over structured sports. The growing importance of participation and pleasure sports reflects two important trends: that 'there are many ways to do sports, and power and performance sports may not be consistent with personal values and experiences' (Coakley, 2004: 567–568).

These realizations have contributed to expanding demand for participation and pleasure sports that are accessible; provide opportunities for self-expression; offer participants freedom, autonomy, and opportunities to experiment; and are free of time constraints and long-term (e.g. seasonal) time commitments. Stewart and Smith (2000) highlight the points of difference between modern power and performance sports, and new generation participation and pleasure sports. They note that the former are founded on the strict application of rules, conservative notions of team leadership and respect for administrative hierarchies. The latter, by contrast, offer opportunities to experiment with rules, innovate, and enjoy complete freedom from administrative authority and commitment beyond day-to-day participation. The continued growth of participation and pleasure sports is supported by various current trends that, according to Coakley (2004), include:

1 *Increasing and sustained interest in health and fitness*. Changing healthcare policies and health insurance programmes give heightened priority to retaining good health as opposed to restoring poor health. Educational curricula are becoming less focused on playing power and performance sports, and increasingly introduce students to alternative sports, non-competitive sports, participation philosophies and cultural and environmental issues relating to sports.
2 *Increasing participation preferences in advancing age*. Demand for participation sports has increased as many populations experience increasing median ages. Elderly sports people tend to give priority to non-competitive participation sports that offer pleasure and social interaction. These include golf, swimming, walking, hiking, and disciplines that promote strength and flexibility (e.g. yoga). This trend has also seen the establishment of senior sports leagues for competitive and performance sports. Within this context, these sports are pursued within specific social settings and in locations where pleasure rather than competition is the primary goal.
3 *Values and experiences of female sport*. The growth of female sports has been associated with the preference for participation and pleasure sports over power and performance sports. The values and experiences of female sport have also heralded a new spirit of participation in power and performance sports based on inclusiveness and expressiveness. These emerging trends in female sport demand considered responses from a wide range of stakeholders, including sport administrators, sponsors, event managers and tourism destination organizations seeking to attract active female participants to sports events.

4 *The growth of groups seeking alternative sports*. Sport participants who place priority on enjoyment and the experience of participation over competition and winning have generated significant interest in alternative sports. Unique sport subcultures have emerged in association with alternative sports. The members of many sport subcultures have actively resisted attempts to commercialize their sports. Participants in sports such as skateboarding and snowboarding have actively subverted the power and performance dimensions of sports events.

Increasing participation in sports in combination with evolving trends and diversifying patterns of participation offer considerable opportunities relating to tourism. The status of sport tourism destinations can be enhanced through timely and effective responses to the emergence of new demands for sport experiences. This requires recognition of specialized niche markets and specific demands of tourists seeking sport experiences. Sport tourist experiences vary along active–passive, social–competitive, professional–amateur, and success–participation continua. This promotes the need to understand specific visitor motivations and accommodate distinct visitor preferences relating to sport experiences.

Interests in sport tourism will continue to be influenced by a wide range of social, cultural, political, economic and environmental factors. Socio-demographic trends will exert considerable influence over the future of sport tourism (Delpy, 2001). The dominant demographic trend of relevance to sport tourism relates to aging western populations, which will increasingly bear influence over preferences for participation and pleasure activities, modern equipment, and social and family activities associated with sports (Loverseed, 2000: 53). The emergence and expansion of niche markets with specific interests relating to sport tourism, such as high school/youth, disabled, gay and lesbian groups is a dominant trend in this field. This requires innovative, flexible and informed approaches to the development of sport tourism products to match the needs of specific market groups.

Globalization is arguably the dominant economic trend that has exerted, through the processes of commodification, considerable influence on interests in sport and tourism. Social trends influencing demand for sport tourism include individualism, flexibility, time fragmentation, new technologies, innovative communication networks and commercialization (Merkel *et al.*, 1998; Coalter, 1999; Steward and Smith, 2000). Sports resources that can be transported and reproduced will be developed in response to changing technologies, urbanization and demands for immediate accessibility. The development of artificial climbing walls, sports theme parks, golf driving ranges, skateboard facilities and a wide range of water sports has been a response to demand for participation and pleasure sport in urban communities. The rapid development of new technologies such as interactive television, Internet, virtual reality and new generation video games demonstrate the convergence of interests in sport, leisure, tourism and entertainment.

Spectator and participant perspectives relating to professional sport experiences at tourism destinations are also experiencing the processes of dynamic change. The presentation of professional team sports has responded to competition within the wider entertainment industry and changing spectator demands, resulting in the merging of sport and entertainment values (de Villiers, 2001; Keller, 2001). A greater understanding of the experiences of professional sports teams and athletes is also emerging, and it is in this domain that a broad range of new development opportunities exists for tourism destinations. Interests in sport tourism will continue to be subject to changing institutional arrangements and government policy initiatives relating to sport and tourism. Local, regional and central government investment in sports resources and facilities such as stadia will continue, but with increasing priority placed upon achieving an accurate and comprehensive appreciation of returns on investment. Direct or indirect public subsidization of professional sports will, in the absence of direct returns for local communities, be the subject of increasingly audible local resistance.

The media will increasingly perform important roles relating to the profile and image of tourism destinations. A long and dynamic association exists between media and sport. The television broadcasting of elite sport has transformed professional sports (McKay and Kirk, 1992). Sport tourism destination marketing initiatives require a high degree of responsiveness to changing media technologies. The Internet will grow as a medium for communicating with and influencing the demands of participants and spectators. Personal interaction with sport stars via Internet sites has already become a medium for communicating to fans the preferences and interests of sport stars (Coakley, 2004). The Internet will increase in importance as a medium for recruiting the interest of fans in sports leagues through such initiatives as fantasy leagues, simulated games and virtual sport experiences. These avenues of electronic media development are associated increasingly with unique sport experiences, often in association with images of specific places. Simulated games taking place at recognizable locations, such as specific ski runs at specific places (e.g. Aspen, Colorado), demonstrate the convergence of interests in sport and the prominence of tourism destinations.

The influential role performed by the media is no less relevant to participation and pleasure sports. Beyond the mainstream media sports that are associated with distinctive subcultures are also associated with specialized media outlets. Increasingly the Internet plays significant roles in communicating information about such things as techniques and equipment, but extended to specific locations and destinations where subcultural interests in sport are best served (Bourdeau et al., 2002).

The interests of sport tourism destination managers will be well served by understanding the motivations, expectations and behaviours associated with specific sport-related travel markets. The diverse motivations and expectation profiles of different niche markets need to be understood to attract visitors to a destination and provide sport-related experiences – be it through standards of service, safety and security, facility design, tourist attractions or activities – that provide high levels of visitor satisfaction. Understanding the behaviours commonly associated with sport tourist niche markets is important because tourist behaviour may generate positive and/or negative social impacts that are felt by members of the host community. The behaviours that typically accompany groups of sport tourists may facilitate or deflect flows of travellers to a destination, while contributing to or detracting from the desired destination image.

The development of integrated sport tourism precincts has clearly emerged as an important goal for urban sport tourism destinations. Urban centres will remain at the forefront of high-profile, mass participation spectator sports and sports events. New opportunities are emerging for urban sport tourism destinations in this regard. An important trend in professional sports is the expansion of existing professional sports leagues and the development of new league competitions.

The tendency for sports organizations to expand professional competitions has resulted in increasing numbers of travelling teams and athletes from an expanding range of participating countries. As cities have come to compete to host professional competitions, the development of venues where professional sports are contested has become locked into a competitive hierarchy.

The status of urban sport tourism destinations is determined by the existence of a modern stadium more so today than ever in the past. New stadia are being designed and constructed to function as 'sport malls', where socializing, corporate hospitality, dining, sport entertainment and activities, and sport-related tourism attractions are available in addition to live sport spectatorship. As the modern sport stadium has evolved into a total entertainment venue, the need to protect the authenticity of the sport competition has been heightened (Hinch and Higham, 2004). If in the past the stadium has been the home of homogeneous groups of 'home' fans and 'travelling' fans, this scenario no longer applies to such an extent. While continuing to provide for the spectator experiences of sports fans, the stadium must increasingly perform multiple and spatially segregated functions relating to such diverse markets as season-ticket, family and casual spectators, as well as the interests of sponsors, sports organizations, media, corporate visitors and corporate hospitality.

As destinations compete to attract sports-related travel markets, the decisions relating to sport tourism development will, by necessity, be built upon informed economic considerations. While competition to attract sports teams, revenues associated with professional sports, spectators and other sport tourism markets will intensify, so too will demand for investments in sport tourism to be directed towards specific economic outcomes. Furthermore, the sustained success of sport tourism destinations will necessitate the careful management of physical impacts and consideration of the sustainability of sport and tourism development.

The fact that tourism destinations rise and fall in popularity and tourism products evolve over time are features commonly associated with tourism (Christaller, 1963/64; Doxey, 1975; Stansfield, 1978). At the same time, there is little evidence to suggest that the expansion and diversification of sports-related travel will not continue into the future. As such, sports play an increasingly prominent role in the development of new (or rejuvenation of existing) tourism destinations. Thus sports may play a significant role in the lifecycles of many destinations. There is much evidence to indicate that sport is commonly used as a deliberate destination development strategy. Given that sports, too, are fashion driven and evolve through stages of a product lifecycle, the implementation of this strategy requires that tourism managers are informed about the dynamics of modern sports (Keller, 2001) – particularly how they differ between structured team sports and the more autonomous individual sports. This would indicate the need for sport tourism destination managers to develop specific strategies relating to specific sports, whether mainstream professional team sports or alternative participation and pleasure sports. The increasing competitiveness of the sport tourism industry demands specific insights of the unique experiences associated with niche sports markets.

The sport and tourism industries are vibrant and dynamic. Recognition of the tourism destination interests associated with the sports industry has occurred remarkably recently. The growing diversity of sports, and the range of sport-related products and experiences that are of interest to sport tourists, offers tourism destination managers rich development opportunities. Equally, tourism development goals may serve the interests of sports managers who seek to maximize the use of sports facilities, encourage participation in sports events, develop sports resources, and expand spectator and merchandise markets.

The fields of sport and tourism offer many striking parallels. Both are discretionary activities that are influenced by economic, political, socio-demographic and technological changes. These existing trends provide insights of importance to sport tourism destination managers. By understanding and responding to these trends in an effective and timely manner, destination managers may achieve a competitive advantage in the dynamic sport tourism field. As participation rates in both sport and tourism continue to grow, the opportunities relating to sport tourism that are available to destination organizations and other sport tourism industry stakeholders will continue to diversify and expand. Informed insights in the fields of sport, tourism and destination management are critical to capturing and achieving sustained success in the development of sport tourism destinations.

References

Bourdeau, P., Corneloup, J. and Mao, P. (2002). Adventure sports and tourism in the French Mountains: dynamics of change and challenges for sustainable development. *Current Issues in Tourism*, 5(1), 22–32.

Christaller, W. (1963/1964). Some considerations of tourism location in Europe: the peripheral regions – underdeveloped countries – recreation areas. *Papers, Regional Science Association*, 12, 95–105.

Coakley, J. (2004). *Sports in Society: Issues and Controversies* (8th edn). Boston: McGraw Hill Higher Education.

Coalter, F. (1999). Sport and recreation in the United Kingdom: flow with the flow or buck with the trends? *Managing Leisure*, 4(1), 24–39.

Delpy, L. (2001). *Preparing for the Rise in Sports Tourism.* Paper presented at the World Conference on Sport and Tourism, Barcelona, Spain, 22–23 February.

de Villers, D. J. (2001). Sport and tourism to stimulate development. *Olympic Review*, 27(38), 11–13.

Doxey, G. (1975). *Visitor–Resident Interaction in Tourist Destinations: Inferences from Empirical Research in Barbados, West Indies and Niagara-on-the-Lake, Ontario.* Paper presented at the Symposium on the Planning and Development of the Tourist Industry in the ECC Region, Dubrovnik, Yugoslavia, 8–11 September.

Hinch, T. D. and Higham, J. E. S. (2004). *Sport Tourism Development.* Clevedon, OH: Channel View.

Keller, P. (2001). *Sport and Tourism: Introductory Report.* Paper presented at the World Conference on Sport and Tourism, Barcelona, Spain, 22–23 February. Madrid: World Tourism Organization.

Loverseed, H. (2000). Winter sports in North America. *Travel and Tourism Analyst*, 6, 45–62.

McKay, J. and Kirk, D. (1992). Ronald McDonald meets Baron De Coubertin: Prime time sport and commodification. *Sport and the Media*, Winter, 10–13.

Merkel, U., Lines, G. and McDonald, I. (eds) (1998). *The Production and Consumption of Sport Cultures: Leisure, Culture and Commerce* (Publication No. 62). Eastbourne: Leisure Studies Association.

Murray, D. and Dixon, L. (2000). Investigating the growth of 'instant' sports: practical implications for community leisure service providers. *The ACHPER Healthy Lifestyles Journal*, 47(3/4), 27–31.

Stansfield, C. J. (1978). The development of modern seaside resorts. *Parks and Recreation*, 5(10), 14–46.

Stewart, B. and Smith, A. (2000). Australian sport in a postmodern age. *International Journal of the History of Sport*, 17(2/3), 278–304.

Index